D1382229

THE
NEWSPAPER BOOK

THE NEWSPAPER BOOK

A History of Newspapers in Ireland, 1649 * 1983

HUGH ORAM

BOOKS

First published 1983 by
MO Books, 12 Magennis Place,
Dublin 2.

Copyright © Hugh Oram, 1983. All rights reserved.

British Library Cataloguing in Publication Data
Oram, Hugh
The Newspaper Book:
A History of Newspapers in Ireland, 1649-1983.
I. Newspapers-Ireland-History
I. Title
079'.415   PN5118
ISBN 0-9509184-0-7
ISBN 0-9509184-1-5 Pbk.

Designed by Jarlath Hayes
Typeset by Photo-Set Ltd., Dublin
Printed and bound in Ireland by Mount Salus Press Ltd., Dublin

Foreword

Irish newspapers have been chronicling the passing of time for over three centuries. By contrast, they have been singularly slight in recording their own progress for posterity. The newspaper industry has had its own fair share of dramatic news stories, as well as a great abundance of splendidly talented and often eccentric characters. To record every story about newspapers in this country would need many volumes; I have tried to give an overall picture of their development and to paint fleeting portraits of some of the more memorable protagonists. In many instances, newspaper file material was non-existent. Leading newspapers have thrown out many valuable photographs; in some cases, the antiquity of original photographs means that their reproduction in this book falls far short of modern standards.

Many areas of the industry deserve books of their own. The various newspaper critics merit a book, as do certain critics in their own right. Also, an up-to-date book on the history of Irish language newspapers would be most useful. Several books could be written on the many aspects of the press and politics. Finally, many newspapers could give birth to their own history in book form.

Hugh Oram
Dublin. October, 1983

A word of thanks

Many people have helped in the preparation of this book. First of all, I should like to thank my wife Bernadette for her limitless patience and her wise counsels. Derek Garvey, my publisher deserves thanks for his endless energy during the book's preparation. Jarlath Hayes, the book's designer, is also thanked for his contribution. I should also like to express my appreciation of the help given by the staffs of the National Library, Dublin and the British Newspaper Library, Colindale, London. Thanks are also expressed to the under-named for their generous help in making ready the book:

Bob Adams, Dublin;
Anglo-Celt, Cavan: *Andy McEntee, Edward O'Hanlon, Willie O'Hanlon;*
Lady Arnott, Dublin;
T. D. Atkinson, Collon, Co Louth;
Banbridge Chronicle: *Andrew Doloughan;*
Brian Barrett, Booterstown, Co Dublin;
Tom Barrett, Dublin;
Belfast Telegraph: *Roy Lilley, Walter Macauley, Ivan Peebles;*
Alan Bestic, Surrey;
Liam Boyd, Dublin;
Wesley Boyd, Dublin;
Maureen Browne, Dublin;
Niall Brunicardi, Fermoy, Co Cork;
Vincent Caprani, Malahide, Co Dublin;
Francis X. Carty, Dublin;
John Caughey, Belfast;
Century Newspapers, Belfast: *Pat Carville;*
Clare Champion, Ennis: *Flan Galvin;*
Jimmy Clarke, Longford;
Tommy Cleary, Dublin;
Ian Collie, Dublin;
Michael Colley, Dublin;
Pan Collins, Dublin;
Connaught Telegraph, Castlebar: *Tom Courell;*
Connacht Tribune, Galway: *John Hickey, John Robinson;*
Cork Examiner: *Stephen Coughlan, Ted Crosbie, John Crichton Healy, Michael Kelly, Declan O'Connell, Jim O'Neill, Tony Ring;*
Alfred Dalton, Dun Laoghaire, Co. Dublin;
Derry Journal: *Colm McCarroll;*
Down Recorder, Downpatrick: *Colin Crichton;*
Maurice Downey, Waterford;
Drogheda Independent: *Ann Kane;*

Dundalk Democrat: *Owen McGahon;*
Dungarvan Leader: *Michael Nagle;*
Dungarvan Observer: *Paddy Lynch;*
Honor Edgar, Dublin.
Enniscorthy Echo: *Christy Courtney, Brendan Furlong, Kevin McCarthy,*
Pat McCarthy;
Joe Fahy, Dublin;
Paddy Farrell, Dublin;
Peter Finnegan, Dublin;
Pat Foley, Mount Merrion, Co Dublin;
Anne Gallagher, Dublin;
Edward Gallagher, Belfast;
Denis Garvey, Dublin;
Mrs Frank Geary, Dublin;
Peter Heaney, Galway;
George Hetherington, Dublin;
Impartial Reporter, Enniskillen: *Colin Greaves, Joan Trimble;*
Independent Newspapers, Dublin: *Mitchel Cogley, Paul Meehan, Aidan Pender,*
Bartle Pitcher, Dick Roche, Michael Rooney;
Ireland's Own, Wexford: *John McDonnell;*
Irish News, Belfast: *Terry McLaughlin, Martin O'Brien, Tom Samways;*
Irish Press Group, Dublin: *Paddy Clare, Tim Pat Coogan, Michael Cronin,*
Eileen Davis, Matt Farrell, Fintan Faulkner, Eddie Fitzgerald, Liam Flynn,
Jim Griffiths, Tommy McCann, Padraig O Criogáin, Maurice Sweeney, Sean Ward,
Alan Wilkes;
Irish Times, Dublin: *William Alford, Noel Anderson, Maeve Binchy, George Burrows,*
Bill Byrne, Jim Cooke, William Corry, Horace Denham, Dick English, Joe Fleming,
Douglas Gageby, John Grant, Ken Gray, Tony Gray, Benny Green, Dermot James,
Tony Lennon, Malachy Logan, Mary Maher, Dessie Mahon, Leslie Maybury,
Charles Mullock, Gerry Mulvey, Jack Nagle, Eileen O'Brien, Dessie O'Leary,
Paddy O'Leary, Jimmy O'Shea, Sydney Robbins, Pat Ruane, Bruce Williamson;
Paul Kavanagh, Dublin;
Brian Kelly, Bangor, Co Down;
Henry Kelly, London;
Joe Kelly, Longford;
Ruth Kelly, Dublin;
Tony Kelly, Dublin;
Brian Kenealy, Kilkenny;
Mrs Mary Kenealy, Kilkenny;
Ted Kenny, Dublin;
Ben Kiely, Dublin;
Kilkenny People: *Peter Houlihan, John Kerry Keane, Billy Sullivan;*
Billy King, Dublin;
Anne Lawler, Dublin;
Mrs Ned Lawler, Dublin;
Leader, Dromore, Co Down: *Harry McCandless;*
Hector Legge, Dublin;
Leinster Leader, Naas, Co Kildare: *Bill Britton, Seamus Morahan;*
Leitrim Observer, Carrick-on-Shannon: *Gregory Dunne, Patrick Dunne, Eugene Phelan;*

Limerick Leader: *Bernard Carey, Earl Connolly, Joe Gleeson, Willie Gleeson;*
Mrs Geraldine Logan, Blackrock, Co Dublin;
Londonderry Sentinel: *Sidney Buchanan;*
Longford Leader: *Lucius Farrell;*
Longford News: *Derek Cobbe;*
David Luke, Dublin;
Dermot Maguire, Dublin;
Brid Mahon, Dublin;
Prionsias MacAonghusa, Co Dublin;
Sean MacBride, Dublin;
Donal & Paddy MacMonagle, Killarney;
Myles MacWeeney, Dublin;
J. J. McCann, Kells, Co Meath;
Mrs Muriel McCarthy, Dublin;
Dermot McEvoy, Foxrock, Co Dublin;
Mrs Phenie MacGabhann, Sallynoggin, Co Dublin;
Jim McGuinness, Foxrock, Co Dublin;
Brendan Malin, Massachusetts, USA;
Mayo News, Westport: *Gerard Bracken, Joe Kenny;*
Meath Chronicle, Navan: *Jack Davis, Mary Flynn;*
Midland Tribune, Birr, Co Offaly: *Bud Burke, J. I. Fanning;*
Alan Montgomery, Dublin;
Mrs W. J. Moran, Dublin;
Norman Morgan, Loughrea, Co Galway;
Morton Newspapers, Lurgan, Co Armagh: *Jim Morton;*
Mourne Observer, Newcastle, Co Down: *D. J. Hawthorne;*
Dr Maurice Moynihan, Dublin;
Vincent Mulligan, London;
Munster Express, Waterford: *J. J. Walsh, Priscilla Walsh;*
Des Murphy, Dublin;
T. V. Murphy, Dublin;
National Trust, Northern Ireland;
Nationalist & Leinster Times, Carlow: *Liam D. Bergin;*
Ted Nealon, T.D.;
Nenagh Guardian: *Pat Ryan;*
Dan Nolan, Dublin;
Northern Constitution, Coleraine: *Samuel S. Troy;*
Northern Standard, Monaghan: *Patrick Smith;*
Dr Conor Cruise O'Brien, Howth, Co Dublin;
Tommy O'Brien, Clonmel, Co Tipperary;
Mrs Maureen O'Connor, Dublin;
Peadar O'Curry, Dublin;
George A. O'Gorman, Drogheda;
Marie O'Kelly, Dublin;
Brian O'Neill, Dublin;
Quentin Doran O'Reilly, Co Kildare;
Cathal O'Shannon, Limerick;
Aileen O'Toole, Dublin;
Michael O'Toole, Dollymount, Dublin;

Dr Gerald H. Owens, Dublin;
Garry Redmond, Co. Dublin.
Albert Reynolds, T.D.;
Mairead Reynolds, Dublin;
Ray Rosenfield, Belfast;
Roscommon Herald, Boyle: *Geraldine Nerney, Mrs Lillie Nerney, Micheál O'Callaghan;*
John Ross, Dublin;
Eddie Sherry, Clones;
Pat Smyllie, Dublin;
Patricia Smyllie, London;
Southern Star, Skibbereen: *Liam O'Regan;*
Sunday World, Dublin: *Kevin Marron, Colin McClelland;*
Brian Sweeny, Dublin;
Bill Sweetman, Dublin;
Tom Tobin, Limerick;
Tuam Herald: *David Burke;*
P. V. Turley, Monaghan;
Tyrone Constitution, Omagh: *Norman Armstrong;*
Waterford News & Star: *Kevin Cadogan;*
Jack Webb, Malahide, Co Dublin;
Western People, Ballina: *Peter Maguire, Terry Reilly;*
Westmeath Examiner, Mullingar: *Nicholas Nally;*
Harry White, Dublin.

For Bernadette

Contents

CHAPTER I

Smyllie and his people, 1940

McBirney's free-to-bend knickers. Special offer. O.S. 4/6d.
THE IRISH TIMES, April, 1940

*John Jameson and Son – rare liqueur whiskey over 20 years old.
21/- per bottle. John Morgan and Sons, wine and spirit
merchants, Dawson Street.*
IRISH INDEPENDENT, December, 1940

A special diplomatic messenger drove up Pembroke Park in Dublin one grey, war-time day in 1940 until he found Number 23. A couple of rings on the doorbell produced Margaret the maid; she smoothed down her apron before accepting the long brown envelope, curiously imposing in its anonymity. A pause for a moment or two, then she in turn handed on the envelope to the fat, shambling man in his pyjamas, hovering at the back of the hallway.

His pudgy fingers, the nail of one filed sharp to make a pen "nib", gouged open the letter; it was signed personally by Churchill, the British Prime Minister. He invited Robert Maire Smyllie, editor of *The Irish Times* for the past six years, to join his staff in London and help the British war effort. Smyllie gave a small yelp of joy. Until now, his active participation in the British war machine had been limited to encouraging able-bodied reporters on his paper, such as John A. Robinson, to join up and refusing to employ talented young men from England, trying to evade what he thought were their responsibilities with the armed forces of the Crown.

The Shelbourne Hotel, the Wicklow Hotel and Jammet's Restaurant were packed with strange, eccentric English people who had enough money to flee the war. The Shelbourne bar rang with the strangled accents of the Home Counties. On *The Irish Times* itself, the Anglo-Irish mentality was nearly all-pervasive; only one reporter could speak Irish

R. M. Smyllie in an
unusual outburst of
sartorial elegance; he is
seen at a race meeting
with an unnamed
friend, during the
1940s.
–The Irish Times

and one sub-editor and one advertising man had Republican sympathies.

Many of the reporters on the paper had been there for far longer than they cared to remember; one cast his mind back three times a week, to the eternal boredom of his colleagues, to his reporting of the Franco-Prussian war, seventy years previously. Pensions were so derisory that no-one could afford to retire unless they had private means, yet paradoxically, the reporters could be drunk, incompetent and indolent without risking expulsion from the surrounds of the warming coal fire in the reporters' room. It had one antique stem-like telephone; there was no constant ringing. Stories and rumours of stories were savoured at leisure.

Smyllie's joy was exceedingly short-lived. His wife, Kathlyn, was a quirky woman, besotted with the fancies of middle class rectitude. She treated Smyllie like a belittled small boy and ensured that the practical matters of the household were arranged entirely between Margaret the maid and herself. Sandwiched between the two women, Smyllie stood little chance, so that when Kathlyn tore up the letter from Churchill, Smyllie promptly caved in.

Glory in the loyalist cause had flitted across Smyllie's byzantine mind and lit up his muddled features for a brief moment or two. He thought back to his first summer vacation from Trinity College, Dublin, when he had answered an advertisement from a very wealthy German-American looking for a tutor for his son in Germany. Smyllie secured the job, but had the misfortune to be in Munich very early in August, 1914, with his young charge. When war was declared, the latter's father promptly disappeared, leaving the penniless Smyllie to suffer the indignity of being one of the first foreigners to be interned in Germany. He spent the next four years in the Ruhleben internment camp just outside Berlin, an experience which left him fluent in German and with his first craving for journalism indulged, running the camp's fortnightly magazine.

In the years immediately prior to World War II, Smyllie travelled extensively in central Europe, particularly in Czechoslovakia. He saw

The Pearl Bar in Fleet Street, Dublin, beside The Irish Times, was taken over by "Gus" Weldon in 1940. He sold the premises to Allied Irish Banks about ten years ago.
–*The Irish Times*

3

An *Evening Herald* newsboy with the tidings of war.

at first hand the welling thunderclouds. His knowledge of German and his central European contacts would have been invaluable to Churchill and the British war effort, of which he so thoroughly approved.

Churchill had omitted to consider the wily Kathlyn. When she issued her edict, peremptorily and with no further discussion allowed, all Smyllie could do was put on his smelly pullover, wrap his long raincoat around himself and still fundamentally dressed in his pyjamas, disappear in the direction of the Pearl Bar. Eventually, he would surface in the office, maybe even play a few tunes on his violin, having successfully routed the bar bores, which he divided into First and Second Elevens. Only a few months previously, Smyllie had begun to transfer his spiritual allegiance from the Palace Bar, which was in Fleet Street, next to one of Bewley's entrances, on the far side of Westmoreland Street, to the Pearl Bar, opposite the works entrance of the paper in Fleet Street. The traffic hazards of Westmoreland Street in 1940 were not the cause of the move — nothing more serious than the occasional tram or horse and cart disturbed the peace — but the death two years previously of the Palace Bar owner, Tipperary man George Ryan. 1940 saw the youthful "Gus" Weldon take over the Pearl Bar, so on this fateful day (for *The Irish Times* and for the British war effort), he dispensed the liquid solace needed on this singularly bleak occasion in Smyllie's life. Then Smyllie settled in to attend to his chores; he arranged in Harrison's café in Westmoreland Street for a sack of crusts for his ferocious dog, "Mick", and a helping of his special tobacco mixture at Kapp and Peterson at the bottom of Grafton Street.

By the time he came to write his main leader that night, phrasing his sentiments most carefully for the benefit of the censors in Dublin Castle, a little of the pain from one of the greatest indignities of his life was beginning to wear off.

Had he not gone to the Pearl Bar that day for convivial consolation, the history of Irish newspapers could have been quite different and the Allied war effort would have gained an extraordinary, but remarkably perceptive intellectual recruit. Instead, Smyllie turned his abundant energies towards thwarting the press censors and getting on famously in private with de Valera, a friendship that helped procure scarce newsprint for *The Irish Times* more than once during the war.

Yet by the time that Kathlyn had made the climactic decision for her husband, signs and effects of the distant war were already creeping in on neutral Ireland. Most of the English showgirls had left Dublin, where they formed the backbone of variety at theatres like the Royal. The crusty white loaves fenced in behind the rails of the bread shelves at Bewley's already had streaks of grey, which became darker as the war progressed. Some streets in Dublin already had vast open water tanks, as provision for the fire fighters. Up at the corner of Parliament Street and Cork Hill, Joe Anderson, pipe-smoking editor of the *Dublin Evening Mail,* and his colleagues had already made the painful decision to

Tom Kenny, founding editor of the Connacht Tribune, **Galway.**
–*Connacht Tribune*

Workmen dig air raid shelters near St Patrick's cathedral, Dublin.–*Evening Herald*

drop their Saturday night sports paper. Before the war, the *Sports Mail* had been a great favourite in the city. Touted round the city pubs by hungry-faced newsboys wearing great cloth caps, its columns of cross-channel results were pored over by football aficionados.

Newsprint supplies were being trimmed back by commercial considerations rather than by Government decree; that came in 1941. But in 1940, as the Battle of Britain raged over the skies of south-east England and Britain teetered on the brink of a Nazi invasion, clothes, food, all the necessities of life were being edged back into austerity and "make-do". Just before the *Sunday Independent* went down to a single sheet, it received the infusion of a new editor. Golf-mad Hector Legge, who had joined Independent Newspapers in 1922 to serve his journalistic apprenticeship, took over what was Ireland's only Sunday paper in 1940. Nine years were to elapse before it had a rival, the *Sunday Press.*

Another editor in the house was being forced to let slip the reins. Michael Brunicardi, a barrister by profession and a newspaper editor by vocation, had been editor of the *Evening Herald* since 1922, the year that Hector Legge joined the *Irish Independent* organisation. Brunicardi was an able but cautious editor, very much in the keeping of that

J. J. Walsh of the Munster Express, **Waterford, pictured on the quays outside his office.**

newspaper era. His reputation with women caused far more casual interest among his colleagues than his considerable editorial skills, just as the comedian, Jimmy O'Dea, created excitement among the prurient by his womanising. On at least one occasion, an over-zealous woman in pursuit of the unobtainable Brunicardi, had to be prevented by the courts from picketing Independent House.

By 1940, Brunicardi was a weary, disillusioned man. His eyesight was fading so fast that at the age of 51, he was forced into giving up his editorship. For the rest of his life, he lived mainly on the modest returns from lower middle class terraced property he owned on the northside of Dublin.

In Galway, another great newspaperman died suddenly. Tom Kenny, founding editor of the *Connacht Tribune,* had guided the paper through its early vicissitudes. Until a short while before his death in 1940, he had been in his customary good form, so that his sudden collapse came as a profound shock to his friends. "Tom Cork" was his pen name, because he came from Cork, and as such was known to his readers. Many were the "firsts" he had to his name, such as that on May 11, 1919, when he was the first journalist to greet Alcock and Brown when they landed near Clifden after their pioneering trans-Atlantic flight. In succession to Kenny, a Dublin journalist, J. A. Power, known universally as "Jap", came to Galway, causing almost as much surprise to his Dublin colleagues, who never expected him to move from the capital, as the news of Kenny's early death. "Jap" was to spend five improvising years at the *Connacht Tribune,* before heading back to Dublin, his true home, and a final stint at his "Argus" column in the

Evening Herald before his own untimely death. Still, in Galway in 1940 and for the duration of the war, the privations of the Emergency were less severe than those of Dublin. Great blocks of butter, fresh from the farm, patted into shape, and tender steaks, were as commonplace in Galway as they were rare in Dublin.

J. J. Walsh of Waterford was an energetic young man, good-looking too, gazing out over the coasters tied up at the quays just outside his office, bringing dwindling supplies into the country. He quickly

Citizens of Cork are fitted with gas masks at Fitzgerald Park.–*Cork Examiner*

Vincent Gill in Longford.

Vincent Gill seen
signing his last issue
of the Longford News,
with incoming editor,
Derek Cobbe (left).

8

summed up their commercial possibilities for Waterford, if not for himself. With the declining health of his father, Edward Walsh, J. J. had taken on much of the responsibility for running the family-owned paper, the *Munster Express,* while not far away, the dreamy Alan Downey ran the *Waterford News,* in between writing books and plays for the fledgling Radio Eireann, only just escaped from the crystal set era.

In May, 1940, France fell. Churchill made his famous Dunkirk declaration: "We shall go on to the end, whatever the cost may be." Sean Lemass, Minister for Industry and Commerce, urged Irish businessmen to lay in stocks to the limit of their financial resources. Waterford's J. J. Walsh was not slow to build up stocks of newsprint, so much so that until the size of newspapers was limited by Government decree, the *Munster Express* was able to continue with its usual number of pages.

The cute, foxy Vincent Gill, founder of the *Longford News,* resorted to the most devious means of keeping his paper published in 1940 as newsprint ran scarce. Sometimes, the paper was printed on sugar bags, while on other occasions, the rival *Longford Leader,* run by the venerable Lucius Farrell, son of the founder, unwittingly helped Gill produce *his* paper. If the works gate was left open by mistake after hours, chances were that Gill would sneak into the deserted printing works, tuck a ream of paper under his arm and walk back, quite nonchalantly, to the nearby cottage in Harbour Row to finish production of his own paper.

By 1940, the *Longford News* had been appearing for four fitful years; it started because Gill had had a falling out with the Garda authorities. The most unlikely guard ever recruited to the force, Gill was taking a prisoner to Limerick Jail when he lost his man.

The two, guard and prisoner, had been having a few friendly "jars" on the train down to Limerick Junction. When they arrived at that desolate spot in the middle of nowhere, Gill's prisoner decided he could do with some cigarettes. Gill lent him his last two shillings; the happy prisoner strolled off into the sunset, never to be seen again. Gill spent the next nine months cooking for the unfortunate denizens of Limerick garda barracks. After his transfer to remote Cloghan in the far west of the Dingle peninsula in Co. Kerry, Gill refused to take part in an eviction. He wandered off to found the *Longford News,* in 1936. After his many adventures and privations, printing on sugar bags in 1940 was small hardship indeed.

A young lad growing up with the poverty in and around war-time Waterford heard vague rumblings about the great newspaper burgeoning of Dungarvan, just down the road from his native Gaeltacht village of Ring. A bluff-faced Kerryman called John B. Nagle, renowned for his prominent nose, had moved to Dungarvan in 1931 to work for the *Dungarvan Observer.* An evident falling-out with that paper, or simply a desire to put what he had learned about newspapers into practice, led him to leave in 1938 and set up on his own, with the

Myles na gCopaleen, described by one source on The Irish Times as a brilliant writer, but not a nice person to know. "Everyone used to scarper when he arrived."

Dungarvan Leader. By 1940, his fledgling newspaper was headed into the emergency; the young Donal Foley, then a teenager, must have been inspired himself to trudge out along the long, wearing road that brought him eventually to *The Irish Times,* where men bit dogs.

Some Dublin journalists bemoaned the loss of another newspaper venture, the *East Coast Express,* in this year of grace, 1940. Set up in 1936, it ran for four pioneering years, but with its classy broadsheet layout contrasting starkly with the poor newspaper layout then common in Ireland, it may have been too good for its times. Its publisher was John Flynn, a blind and very mean printer who exercised quite remarkable control of his enterprises through his secretary. From Booterstown to Bray, the paper covered the doings of the day, although the Bray edition staggered on like a drunk, rapidly running out of sense and money, until after the end of the war. J. J. McCann, who later founded the *Radio Review* and became closely involved at *The Irish Times* for two turbulent years, was one corespondent; another was Denis Garvey, the advertising man, who covered everything from funerals to football matches between Booterstown and Dalkey.

The *East Coast Express* may have closed down, but in 1940, the *Irish Press* was showing reasonable signs of stability, having survived for nine years. Frank Gallagher had left the editorship in 1935 to become deputy director of Radio Eireann, moving on further in 1939 to head the Government Information Bureau. As Roibéard Ó Farachain was to say later: "I never learned why Gallagher ceased to be editor of the *Irish Press.* It was not even because of the slightest shade of disloyalty to de Valera, but Gallagher was translated from one job to the other like Bottom in a Midsummer Night's Dream."

Two years of uncertainty followed on Burgh Quay; one Irish-American journalist brought in to edit the paper lasted precisely half a night: as long as it took one of de Valera's cronies to find out that the man had allegedly Communist sympathies. Then followed a London-Irish journalist, able to dodge the flying writs and well trained in the wiles of the Westminster lobby, but not in the mystical, floating rivalries of Burgh Quay. He fared off slightly better than the Irish-American gentleman, but it was not until Bill Sweetman took over as editor in 1937 (he stayed until 1951 when he too was translated upwards and outwards, becoming a District Justice) that the place began to calm down. Sweetman even coped with the tantrums of the strong-willed Anna Kelly, who was not above the occasional mistake

A Dublin newspaper group photographed making a presentation to J. J. Simington, manager, The Irish Times, in that newspaper's old boardroom. From left: J. C. Dann (Dublin Evening Mail and secretary, Dublin Newspaper Managers' Committee), J. C. Dempsey (advertisement manager, Irish Press), J. J. Simington, J. Beggs (manager, Dublin Evening Mail) and J. Donohoe (manager, Independent Newspapers). –Irish Times

herself, like the time when she typed out an *Irish Press* Christmas cake recipe and left out the flour.

The "japes" period at the *Irish Press* had come to an end by 1940. The middle of the previous decade had seen uproarious behaviour by some of the freer spirits at Burgh Quay, such as the occasion when Paddy Fennessy (a reporter long dead who was constantly fired from the *Irish Press* for drunkenness) and another reporter (still alive), who for a lark one night took the light bulb out of the men's lavatory. They decided to "rumble" the first person in, who happened to be Bob Brennan, the general manager. Exit rapidly two fast-sobering journalists. Dear, departed days.

Meanwhile, another talent, of peculiar literary inclination, was emerging. Brian O'Nolan, a strange class of man who on one occasion borrowed samples of ladies' corsets from a traveller in underwear to try on in the snug of Ryan's pub on the way to Sandymount, was quietly despairing in the doldrums of the Civil Service. He had had a brilliant student career at University College, Dublin, where his contemporaries included Vivion de Valera (later to become the quirky, querulous managing director of the *Irish Press* group), Cyril Cusack, the actor, Donagh MacDonagh, writer and DJ, Cearbhall Ó Dálaigh, later President, and Seán Ó Faoláin, the writer.

Myles na gCopaleen at his purest appeared in the *Irish Press* in six occasions in 1932; Gallagher let the opportunity slip past and for another seven years, O'Nolan did no more newspaper work. Then in January, 1939, just before the publication in London of *At Swim Two-Birds,* O'Nolan and Dublin architect and writer Niall Sheridan, with a little help from Frank O'Connor and Seán Ó Faoláin, started a great correspondence in *The Irish Times* about pretensions to high art. For weeks and weeks, the arguments raged backwards and forwards under Letters to the Editor, the kind of high-flown, ethereal correspondence that can keep *Irish Times'* readers going for ages, just as the Liberal Ethic controversy did in 1950 — one of the very few occasions when Letters to the Editor coalesced into book form.

O'Nolan and Sheridan branched out, writing all kinds of letters under a veritable barrage of pseudonyms. The letters proved yeast to *The Irish Times'* circulation, so much so that Smyllie wanted to meet O'Nolan, who had been taking some of the correspondents' names from Thom's directory. The protests began to roll in; Smyllie was concerned about the possibility of libel. The two met in the Palace Bar and during the course of the evening, Smyllie asked O'Nolan to write a regular column.

So it was that "Cruiskeen Lawn" first appeared, after a lengthy gestation, on October 4, 1940. It was written turn and turn about, in English and Irish: not until March, 1943, did English gain almost permanent exclusivity.

By day, O'Nolan laboured in the Custom House; he was to spend

Frank Geary, editor of the Irish Independent, **at his desk.**

eighteen years in the Civil Service, in the Department of Local Government, as private secretary to four successive ministers, eventually taking the unlikely rôle of principal officer for town planning. Even there, his notoriety preceded him. On one occasion, he took a sheaf of reports to a senior civil servant to be signed. The other man retorted: "Come back with these when there is the smell of *fresh* drink off you."

That day, October 4, 1940, marked one of the epochal anniversaries in the twentieth century calendar of Irish newspapers. Brian O'Nolan, alias Myles na gCopaleen, despite increasing bitterness, frustration and illness, was to write for *The Irish Times* (and occasionally other newspapers like the Carlow *Nationalist*) until shortly before he died in 1966. At the height of his powers (how he would have approved of that pun), he was writing up to six columns a week after gaining an unfriendly remission from the civil service.

Myles na gCopaleen engendered disputes with many noted people; in one early quarrel, he fell out with Andy Clarkin, the Lord Mayor of Dublin. Clarkin had a coal importers' office in Pearse Street; the clock above the office had two faces, neither of which told the correct time. One day, Myles caused great consternation by putting the initials "ACC ISS" at the top of his column: the translation read "Andy Clarkin's clock is stopped (again)."

Smyllie, the loyal Protestant and Frank Geary, the upstanding Catholic editor of the *Irish Independent,* were on the best of terms. Quite

**Paddy Campbell —
hilarious naval
encounters at** The Irish
Times.
–Penguin Books

often, Smyllie would go over to Geary's house in Sandymount for a game of cards. Similarly, in *The Irish Times* itself, then an utterly ramshackle collection of three houses, each facing in different directions in the triangle of land bounded by Westmoreland Street, Fleet Street and D'Olier Street, and connected by a straggling mass of passageways and staircases, a harmony existed among staff that pre-dated that of society in the larger sense.

According to Brian Inglis (one of some fifteen members of *The Irish Times'* staff who have graduated to write books) Smyllie was incapable of organisation. He believed that if an urgent, insoluble problem was ignored long enough, it would eventually cease to become either urgent or insoluble. Similarly, on the way to his dark, windowless office, the roof of which was formed by a dome of opaque glass, he developed a great skill for dodging the flock of suitors that emerged from behind counters, out of passageways and doorways.

He even managed to ingore the detective sitting guard by his office. That guard was placed there in 1940, following IRA threats to the paper and its already venerable editor. In one form or other, the guard on Smyllie was to remain for most of the war. Smyllie disregarded the whole performance and seemed blithely ignorant of the fact that the Cork offices of the paper had just been damaged by a bomb.

Repeating an episode of 1914, when a *Midland Tribune* compositor joined the forces of the Crown to fight for the rights of small nations (excluding Ireland), a compositor, Dermot Hayden, left the same paper in 1940 to join up. This historic year, he went North to sign up at RAF, Ballykelly, in Co Derry. Hayden survived the war in North Africa and Palestine and like his predecessor, returned home untouched after the war was over to don his printer's apron once again.

While some newspaper people joined the British forces, others joined the Irish defence forces, apart from those in the LDF newspaper unit in Dublin. Patrick Campbell, who had left *The Irish Times* for London, decided to come home to a Dublin packed with exotic and interesting refugees. Paul MacWeeney, the sports editor of *The Irish Times,* interceded with Smyllie as Campbell attempted to get his job back. Campbell had also joined the new Marine Service and went in to see Smyllie one night dressed in his naval uniform.

"Lavatory attendants and commissionaires are not required in the editorial sanctum," thundered Smyllie, still smarting from Campbell's abrupt departure for the *Daily Express* in London. He set Campbell to work improving the "Irishman's Diary", telling him that it consisted of a "shower of lapidary crap".

This momentous year, Patrick Campbell had got very drunk one afternoon with Pat Dunne of the *Leitrim Observer*. Campbell had returned from London to sail alone up and down the Shannon. At Carrick-on-Shannon, he met up with Dunne, who during the course of much imbibing tried unsuccessfully to persuade Campbell to write for the *Leitrim Observer*. The liaison was too bizarre for even Campbell to contemplate; he had been writing extensively for *The Irish Times*. No doubt Dunne pressed upon Campbell his views of the war: he was said to have been the most pro-German of any Irish newspaper editor.

Although an active Freemason, absentmindedly wearing his regalia on one occasion he met de Valera, Smyllie had little interest in the religion of editorial recruits, although most were Protestant, by founding faith if not active persuasion. One sub-editor was pointed out, during and after his departure from the paper, with almost anthropological interest. He was Larry de Lacy, an old-style newspaper man with strong Republican connections who had played an important propaganda role for de Valera in the United States of America after 1916. De Lacy was virtually the sole representative of this exotic species on *The Irish Times'* staff in 1940. Curiously, the pro-Fine Gael *Irish Independent* employed many more men who had been active in the IRA. After all, 1940 only post-dated the War of Independence by some twenty years.

Into this maelstrom of filthy songs and late-night drinking in *The Irish Times'* club after cut-line time, when the newspaper went to press, came an innocent young boy in 1940: Alan Bestic. He spent four years there, before going on to the *Irish Press* and eventually, Fleet Street.

He remembers those far-off newspaper days — delightfully slow and the very essence of easy-going formality. Around this time, too,

**Dan Nolan with his
Kerryman logo.**

Donal Foley — as a
youngster watched the
Dungarvan newspaper
battle with curiosity.

another recruit found his way to *The Irish Times* — Garry Redmond, whose father Christopher had worked for the paper since the early 1920s, doing all kinds of editorial jobs, including that of music critic when the occasion arose. Full-time, professional critics, like Charles Acton, were further into the future.

Redmond still has remarkable memories of the manager of *The Irish Times* in 1940: J. J. Simington, an elderly man with a goatee beard that made him look like Jan Smuts, the South African leader. Simington was a venerable elder statesman of the Dublin newspaper world; he had a wise habit of writing notes to himself, which he filed away inside an old-fashioned roll-top desk. When one desk was full, he sent for a second. After his death, these two desks were found to be crammed to explosion point with thousands of notes written in an almost indecipherable hand. Simington's age and august appearance were in marked contrast to that of lean, hungry-looking Jack Dempsey, then advertisement manager of the *Irish Press,* which tightened up its pages as the war advanced across Europe.

On the *Northern Constitution* in Coleraine, life was unhurried, as it was on all Irish country newspapers, especially in the sub-editor's room.

The paper had one, elderly sub-editor, a man called James Henderson, who in the 1930s was one of only two National Union of Journalists' members in Northern Ireland. He loved to tell the story of how one day he heard a splintering of glass in the distance, turned round and saw a bottle of whiskey on a rope being pulled up to the floor above for the refreshment of the printers. But reporting then was far more arduous: Bob Acheson, one of the reporters on the *Constitution*, came back late one Thursday night from covering an all-day Orange banner unveiling. He had sat on a flat tombstone in the pouring rain until his notebook was sodden, waiting for the bus, which eventually arrived.

Another journalist on the paper, Ernie Sandford, later with the Northern Ireland Tourist Board, suggested that since all Orange speeches since 1785 were identical, standing matter would fit the bill admirably, since Acheson was clearly unable to unravel his notes. The editor insisted and Acheson had to write his copy from memory and the odd piece of Pitman shorthand that had escaped the rain. Dan Duffy, the other reporter on the *Northern Constitution* at the time, relished many battles over work rates. He inevitably won, good training for when he came to *The Irish Times* in Dublin in 1945 and the NUJ's inaugural campaign in the city, resulting in the first-ever wages and conditions' agreement between Dublin journalists and newspaper managements.

Already, in 1940, many of the old ways of people and newspapers were starting to slip away. "Songs of the People" had just ended in the *Northern Constitution*, a feature straight out of many a nineteenth century Irish newspaper. Years before, Sam Henry started publishing the words and music of old folk songs; over sixteen years, he had put into print 836, many previously unrecorded. "It's in my native country, old Ireland, I do dwell" went the very first line of Sam Henry's very first song to be printed in the *Northern Constitution*. He was recording the fading away of an era, replaced in 1940 by the frantic, ceaseless hammering of rivets at Harland and Wolff, the Belfast shipyard. Many in the North earned tremendous money that year building for the British war effort; at weekends, they slipped away on the steam train excursions to Dublin, to sample the insouciant gaiety that still seeped through the black-out curtains from the 1930s.

On the *Belfast Telegraph*, a dour, disapproving Presbyterian spirit hung in the editorial air, as indeed as it did at Belfast's other two Protestant papers, the *Northern Whig* and the Belfast *News Letter*. Catholic counter-balance was provided by the *Irish News*. At the *Belfast Telegraph*, the editor was Robert McMaster Sayers (the second of the three Sayers to occupy the editorial chair at the paper); he had been with the paper thirty-eight years. A prominent Mason, he brought a dry, Northern didacticism to the running of the paper. His fellow-Mason, Smyllie of *The Irish Times*, was in a very foreign country, whooping it up with the Free Staters. None of Smyllie's venerable drinking songs were ever

Liam D. Bergin of the Nationalist and Leinster Times, **Carlow, pictured as a young man.**

heard emanating from the dull, august portals of the editor's sanctum in Royal Avenue, Belfast. Sayers had only just taken over the editor's seat from his brother John, who had died in 1939 after just two years in the position. John Sayers' chief claim to fame was the utter discretion with which he wrote the *Belfast Telegraph* leaders on the subject of the Duke of Windsor and Mrs Simpson in 1936. Very respectable, very dull and long since confined to the footnotes of history.

Back in Dublin, even though the Emergency was putting the pincers on everyday supplies and people were prevented from enjoying much physical comfort, at least they could bear the misfortunes of distant war with some humour.

Ernie Murray was prepared to play his part; years before, he had started his climb from the lowest of low newspaper positions, copyholder at the *Irish Independent*. By 1940, he had a good sideline going, writing gags and sketches for the Crazy Gang at the Queen's Theatre. Life in the subs' room of the *Independent* must have been something of a rehearsal for the rôle he enjoyed most, that of theatrical scriptwriter in the best comic tradition. Yet poor Ernie Murray's personal life was tragic; around this period, his marriage broke up and he transferred to the *Dublin Evening Mail*. He is remembered, even to this day, as an old-fashioned figure there, like someone out of Strumpet City. His chief claim to fame was the disability he is said to have suffered, similar to that suffered by Hitler. Ernie was reckoned to have been partially robbed of his manhood by a British bullet fired in anger during the War of Independence, in which he took an active part. For years and years, Ernie Murray was surrounded by an aura of legend in the Dublin newsrooms, principally activated by his alleged physical disability. This did not prevent him, however, from carrying out his patriotic duty in 1940, just as he had done twenty years previously. A special Local Defence Force battalion was formed from the ranks of newspaper workers. Nicknamed the "Owls" because of their night-time proclivities, Ernie was the Chief Owl and in that position, did his patriotic best in between shifts on the subs' desk at the *Mail*.

One young journalist who was going strong in 1940 is happily still going strong today: Liam D. Bergin, editor of the *Nationalist and Leinster Times*, Carlow. He had joined the paper in the 1920s, when many children still went to school in bare feet. Bergin was one of the few Irish journalists to see at first hand the relentless build-up of war in the second half of the 1930s. He travelled in France, Germany and Italy; he was in Barcelona in 1936 when the Spanish Civil War broke out. He was unable to pawn his typewriter for the fare out of the country; an American woman befriended him and gave him the price of his fare on one of the last ships out. In April, 1939, Bergin returned from a trip to Germany and told James Reddy, the general manager: "You had better get some paper in, there is going to be a war." Reddy was totally disbelieving.

In 1940, two of the towering personalities of early twentieth century provincial journalism were still at their typewriters, thunder rolling off the keys. E. T. Keane, who had come from Kerry to found the *Kilkenny People* in 1892, was still going strong in 1940, showing a rock-like durability as editor and owner. Described by Bergin as something of a Tully-like figure (after the irascible and eccentric Jasper Tully of the *Roscommon Herald* in Boyle, who died in 1938 after wreaking a lifetime of editorial vengeance), Keane saw out not only the Golden Jubilee of his paper, but the end of World War II.

An even more durable permanence was anchored behind the black, high-sided typewriter in the editor's office at the *Westmeath Examiner*, Mullingar. John P. Hayden was seventy-seven years old in 1940 and still had another fourteen years of editorial life in him. A coal fire burned in the grate as he pondered his leader. He had worked for the *Roscommon Messenger*, owned and edited by his brother, Luke P. Hayden, before founding the *Westmeath Examiner* in September, 1882.

Pat Layde, the Mullingar-born actor who died in 1983, recalled that as a small boy going into the *Examiner* offices during the war to sell the waste paper he had assiduously collected, he caught glimpses of the remote, mountainy editor tucked away in his office, beard straggling into the typewriter. In 1940, another great figure of the provincial press, Dan Nolan, was settling into his father's footsteps at the *Kerryman* in Tralee. He was as perspicacious as Liam Bergin of Carlow in laying in paper stocks to see out the war. He had become managing director of the *Kerryman* the day before war broke out in September, 1939, and promptly bought as much paper as he could for stacking in every odd nook of Tralee, even though the price per tonne rocketed from around £15 to as much as £25 in a matter of days.

Others in the Irish newspaper business contributed to the war effort in more direct ways. While the 26 counties remained steadfastly neutral (the *Kerryman* was sometimes reproved by the censor for not being sufficiently pro-British), the Unionist newspapers in Northern Ireland did their more direct bit for their war. James Lyttle, who became manager of the *Londonderry Sentinel* in 1928, was a fervent member of the Ulster Special Constabulary, the greatly-feared "B Specials". A publicity brochure of the time described his hobby as gardening. John Morton of the *Lurgan Mail* was a Lieutenant-Colonel in the Home Guard.

In Clare, Andy McEvoy, father of Dermot (latterly *Hibernia* and *Sunday Independent* columnist) was still going well as editor of the *Clare Champion*. He had learned his trade under the extraordinarily belligerent Jasper Tully; one of his many stories about Tully concerned his decision to pay his reporters by weight of copy. McEvoy and his colleagues developed a remarkable ability to write in 24pt sized handwriting, a move which quickly killed off this particular mad idea of Tully. McEvoy senior had been around so long by 1940 that he had

Andy McEvoy of the Clare Champion, **father of Dermot.**

vivid memories of the relaunch by William Martin Murphy of the *Irish Independent* as Ireland's first popular ¹/₂d newspaper along the lines of *Daily Mail* and *Daily Mirror,* back in January, 1905. In 1940, apart from an interlude at the *Irish Press,* McEvoy had worked for the best part of 30 years at the *Clare Champion.* By 1940, McEvoy junior was still recounting the levity he had brought to the Republican solemnity of the *Irish Press.* On one occasion, Frank Gallagher, *Irish Press* editor, had sent McEvoy off to Mount Mellerary Abbey in Co Waterford to do a little recovery from alcoholic refreshment. Two days later, McEvoy, a perfect mimic, telephoned from the fastness of Rathmines and in a marvellous impersonation of the Abbot, informed Mr Gallagher that his young protégé was making really excellent progress.

There were personal tragedies, too, in the press world. At the *Drogheda Independent* young Joachim Casey had spent less than a year as editor before dropping dead. The brevity of his tenure of office contrasted sharply with that of his father, Michael A. Casey, who had been editor from 1887 until the early part of 1939. After the tragic death of his brother, Joachim, Peter Casey took over as editor at the age of thirty-one, remarkably young for the job in 1940. Young Peter Casey went on to enjoy a total of fifty-six years in journalism.

So, as the peace ran out, the newspapers prepared for their own greatest emergency. The Cork *Evening Echo* carried a striking photograph some of the Cork citizenry trying on gas masks in Fitzgerald Park, while R. M. Smyllie prepared to do battle with the censors of Dublin Castle, led by Michael Knightly, himself a poacher turned gamekeeper, since he had once worked on the reporting staff of the *Irish Independent.*

Ahead lay all the restrictions; in the southern part of the country, newspapers would have five years of shortages and unbending control by the Government. In the North, the Belfast papers were soon to be bombed out by the Luftwaffe, but that did not put a halt to production. The tales of the emergency years would live on heroic stories of the years when the newspaper presses kept rolling. In the war years that followed 1940, some of the greatest characters and legends to emerge from Irish newspapers in the twentieth century took seed and flowered. And in those years, apparently bleak and lean, some of the names best-known in today's newspapers, like Douglas Gageby, editor of *The Irish Times,* were starting the very first steps of their careers. Sons and daughters, too, of the great men and women of that era of blitz and blackout were growing up to become bold by-lines themselves.

CHAPTER II

Cromwell's heritage, 1649-1800

A neat, beautiful, black negro girl, just brought from Carolina, aged 11 or 12 years, to be disposed of. Applications to James Carolan, Carrickmacross.

DUBLIN MERCURY, 1768

The moſt Excellent WORM-deſtroying Sugar-Cakes. Price 1s 1d. D. Chamberlaine's, Book Feller, Dame St.

FREEMAN'S JOURNAL, 1773

IN the ultimate beginning of Irish newspapers, Oliver Cromwell, puritan and dictatorial butcher, pressed the button.

His armies in Cork published the *Irish Monthly Mercury* on two occasions in 1649 and 1650. Ireland's first faltering newspaper, it depicted simply the Cromwellian victories, the chronicle of his gory progress across Ireland, "brave Cromwell and his valiant blades", as he was described by a contemporary English source. The florid and bloody deeds of Cromwellian forces in Ireland cut little ice with the inhabitants of Cork, for although there were no mass communications of any kind in the country in 1649, whispered stories of the dreadful atrocities in Drogheda and Wexford must have seeped as far south as Cork.

Ireland was very slow in developing a newspaper industry, surprisingly so, since the printing press had arrived in the country a full century before that first publication in Cork. Elsewhere in the world, the idea of newspapers had already taken firm root. The Chinese were first, publishing official newspapers as far back as the Tang dynasty (618-907). In Hungary in 1485, *Dracola Waida* or the "Devil Prince" was initiated as a summary of events; the Hungarians sometimes claim this as the oldest news publication in the world. Before 1626, there were 140 separate news publications in Dutch and the very year that the second and last issue of the Cromwellian news-

Oliver Cromwell, whose army in Cork established Ireland's first faltering newspaper in 1649.
–Film & Illustrations Library RTE

Christ Church cathedral, Dublin. Just opposite, at Skinner's Row (now Christchurch Place), many of Dublin's first newspapers were printed and published.

sheet appeared in Cork, what is now the oldest surviving daily publication in the world, *Einkommende Zeitung* or "Incoming News", was first published in Leipzig, Germany.

Before that publication of the *Irish Monthly Mercury,* several periodicals about Ireland had been printed and published — in London. Despite this initial interest, the troubled state of the country meant that no further developments took place until 1659 (1660 by the modern calendar), when the first issue of *An Account of the Chief Occurrences of Ireland together with Some Particulars from England* was published by Sir Charles Coote. He wanted to support the restoration of Charles II, but his political ambitions were more successful than his aim for the news-sheets, which last for just five issues.

The new king, Charles II, ensured that strict control was kept over the publication of newspapers. Already, journalists had a bad name; one London editor was described as a "bald-headed buzzard, constant in nothing but wenching, lying and drinking."

Printers of the new-fangled news-sheets needed tremendous muscle power to ensure that the primitive presses produced clear impressions on the paper. A strong printer could turn out up to 150 sheets an hour. Typesetting, too, was a laborious hand-craft; a good man could set one page of the Gutenberg Bible in a day's work.

Despite the political and mechanical limitations, the pace of the newspaper industry in Ireland began to quicken. In 1663, a Dublin bookseller called Samuel Dancer brought out the *Mercurius Hibernicus* or the *Irish Intelligencer;* it did rather better than its predecessor by surviving for all of fifteen issues.

Dancer's newspaper efforts did not set the Liffey alight and there was no great rush to emulate his example. In 1685, the *Dublin News-Letter* appeared for the first time and set precedents for the newspaper industry, unlike its two predecessors. The *Dublin News-Letter* was published by one Robert Thornton at the Leather Bottle tavern in Skinner's Row, directly opposite Christ Church cathedral and just a few steps from Dublin Castle, seat of political power in Ireland. The

Dublin Castle, from where the British administration tried to exercise control over Irish newspapers almost as soon as the first publications rolled off the presses. The Castle influence on Irish newspapers (through subsidies in the shape of pensions for owners, cash grants to newspapers and advertising support, as well as by means of seditious libel charges against offending journalists) lasted until the nineteenth century.
–The Irish Times

An early wooden newspaper printing press.

An early newspaper seller.

intimate entanglement between the newspaper industry and the vintners' trade that continues unabashed to the present day, was established in Ireland by Thornton. By setting up for business so near the Castle, he also highlighted the relationship between newspapers and political authority, alternately subservient and symbiotic. The third precedent set by Thornton (he was responsible for far more than he ever imagined) was in page size.

His *Dublin News-Letter* was printed on both sides of a single sheet of paper measuring 11½″ long by 6½″ wide; part of the second side was left blank to take the seal and address for sending to the country by post. In technical terms, it was a half-folio sheet; in time to come, this evolved into the folio size, then into the broadsheet dimension still used by most Irish newspapers. Thornton brought out his newspaper on a fairly regular basis, every three or four days; he managed to keep it going for seven months, but during that short lifespan, Robert Thornton had managed to give the embryonic newspaper industry a significant nudge forward.

Five years later and even more directly under the shadow of Dublin Castle, Dublin (and Ireland's) next newspaper emerged, printed by Andrew Crook (a superbly apposite name for an early newspaper publisher) at Their Majesties' Printing Office, Ormond Quay. The *Dublin Intelligence* lasted from 1690 until 1694 and it too set a "first" for the newspaper industry.

The publication appeared on fixed days and kept to its self-ordained publishing schedule, even if some of its news was lamentably out of date. One of its first issues in 1690 carried "a full an' particular account of the routing of the Irish army at the Battle of Aughrim on July 12, 1671". The thoughts of its Protestant readers on being served up with news that was nineteen years old were sadly not recorded in any Letters to the Editor.

A gentleman called Dick ran an eponymous Coffee House in Skinner's Row, just a couple of doors up from the Leather Bottle used by Robert Thornton. In the ancient version of the shed in the garden, so beloved of the printing trade, the *Flying Post* or the *Post Master* was printed in a hideout at the rear of Dick's Coffee House. The first issue came out in 1699; this newspaper ran and ran, compared with its predecessors, for all of ten years in fact. Its very first issue showed many signs of intimate liaison with the nearby Dublin Castle: plenty of proclamations and one Royal speech. The *Flying Post* also carried an advertisement, probably the first ever published in an Irish newspaper.

It also set a regrettable trend that lasted for the best part of 200 years in Irish newspapers — little local news, mostly foreign dispatches lifted wholesale from newspapers published in London weeks before.

As the seventeenth century swung into the eighteenth, marked by

Dublin's first newspapers were read avidly in the city's numerous coffee houses.

The old Irish
Parliament House, now
the Bank of Ireland at
College Green, Dublin.
The construction of the
building meant news
copy for Faulkner's
Dublin Journal not long
after it was founded in
1725 and on several
occasions, George
Faulkner, owner of the
newspaper, had to
beseech the forgiveness
of the House for
certain political
comments.
–The Irish Times

the bells of Christ Church cathedral, just across the road from Skinner's Row, home of the Dublin newspaper trade, the pace began to accelerate. Abroad, too, important developments were taking place. London saw its first daily newspaper, the *Daily Courant,* in 1702, while America's first major newspaper, the *Boston News-Letter,* was founded in 1704.

In Dublin, Thomas Hume began to publish the *Dublin Gazette* or *Weekly Courant* in Essex Street in 1703; it survived for twenty-five years, while the rival *Dublin Mercury,* launched the year after the *Gazette,* stayed the course until 1760. A second *Dublin Gazette* (there was no copyright on titles then) was born in 1705 as the official Dublin Castle publication and the forerunner of the present twice weekly official Government publication, *Iris Oifigiúil.* The Dublin printing presses clanked ever faster; the *Protestant Post Boy* of 1712 recognised by its title that its readership, as well as that of all other newspapers, was entirely Protestant, although the Protestant ruling caste represented a numerically small section of the population.

Dean Swift of St
Patrick's cathedral. His
printer, George
Faulkner, started
Faulkner's Dublin
Journal in 1725. Today's
Irish Times can trace its
antecedents back to this
newspaper.
–The Irish Times

Although stamp duties were not imposed on Irish newspapers until
1774, other limitations were quickly put on the infant press. In law, the
printer became responsible for checking the contents of a newspaper.
However, even though printers automatically escaped liability in court
if they named the reporter responsible for an offending story, printers
considered it their duty to keep such names secret. Printers today still
have a legal responsibility for the contents of a publication.

Book selling, the stationery trade and the new-fangled newspapers
were closely intertwined. The publishing of newspapers in Dublin
became so much of a family affair that out of the 160 titles published in
the city by 1760, no fewer than 120 were produced by just twenty-two
stationers and their families. Today, the newspaper business still
breeds the family dynasties, such as the Byrnes, the Fallons, the Flynns
and the Smyllies. As more and more newspapers were turned out in
Dublin as the eighteenth century wore on, another regular pattern
was established; many newspapers came out on Tuesdays and
Saturdays, to catch the post for the country, although country
readerships for the Dublin papers were built up exceedingly slowly.

1725 saw the publication of the most remarkable newspaper of the century — the *Dublin Journal,* published by George Faulkner. Today's *Irish Times,* with certain breaks, can trace its antecedents back to Faulkner's publication.

Faulkner was printer to Dean Swift of St. Patrick's cathedral, who also founded St. Patrick's hospital in an attempt to give shelter to some of the lunatics who roamed the streets of the city uncontrolled and unloved. Swift was not a financially successful writer, since he was only paid for one of his books, *Gulliver's Travels.* Faulkner, on the other hand, became so powerful with his newspaper that fourteen years after it was started, he was said to have monopolised the listings of sales and rentals of Dublin lodgings. Social life in Dublin was so vibrant that at most parties, the company was described as being "too numerous for the apartments".

Faulkner's newspaper started life in Pembroke Court, off Castle Street. By the time it died, exactly a century later, in 1825, it was located at Parliament Street, which was also home of the then-newly founded *Dublin Evening Mail.* To start, George Faulkner brought out his paper in four pages, each with twelve columns of type, twice a week. It sold for a penny a copy, or around £3 in today's currency. With no reporting staff, he managed to carry a fair amount of the type of news that is still exceedingly popular today-accidents, births, deaths, marriages and robberies. His editorial "mix" was so well received that the frequency of publication was soon stepped up to three times a week.

He also published what was said to have been the first illustration ever used in an Irish newspaper, a crude but effective woodcut showing a dentist pulling a patient's tooth. Soon, other Dublin newspapers started using woodcuts.

Much of Faulkner's social life centred around the upper class social round that fluttered in the limelight of Dublin Castle. He was a friend of many of the leading figures of the day, ranging from the abrasive Swift, hurling literary and political arrows with deadly accuracy, to the unctuous and smoothly scheming Lord Chesterfield, at the centre of Castle politics. The contrast between Dublin life enjoyed by Faulkner and his cronies could not have been in greater contrast with that endured by the great bulk of the Irish population.

Hearth tax was imposed on all homes, but houses with just one hearth, or exempted on the grounds of poverty, totalled eighty-five per cent of all homes in the country. The cabins of the labouring classes were described as "warm but dirty". Potatoes, meal, milk and eggs formed the staple diet of most people, but there were "great feastings of beef, mutton and pork at Christmas and Easter". One condescending English writer noted that the labouring people of Ireland "for all their idleness, dirt and nakedness, looked much happier than those in England and Scotland."

Children in Monaghan were sent to bed at this period in the

June. GEORGE · FAULKNER. NUMB. 2218

The Dublin Journal.

From TUESDAY June the 14th, to SATURDAY June the 18th, 1748.

...nce my laft arrived Two Britifh Packets, which brought the foreign Mails due, viz.

From the LONDON GAZETTE, June 11.

Whitehall, June 11.

THESE are to give Notice to all Mafters of Ships, that they may be furnifhed with proper Paffes, upon Application to the Office of one of his Majefty's Principal Secretaries of State.

Whitehall, June 11. Laft Thurfday Morning his Grace the Duke of Newcaftle, one of his Majefty's Principal Secretaries of State, fet out for Harwich, where his Grace embarked between Four and Five o'Clock that Afternoon for Holland, in his Way to Hanover.

Dresden, June 12. The King and Queen of Poland arrived in good Health at Warfaw on the 1ft Inftant.

Hague, June 14. N. S. The Succefs which the Peafants had in the Province of Friefland, in obtaining of the States the Abolition of feveral Taxes, has encouraged the Inhabitants of fome of the other Provinces to expect the fame of their Superiors, and there have been fome Diforders at Rotterdam and other Towns of Holland. In order to prevent the bad Confequences of thefe Commotions, the Prince of Orange and the Deputies of the Court have iffued a Proclamation, in which they fet forth the many Inconveniencies that would infallibly attend the Abolition of the Taxes demanded, and reprefent the Impoffibility the States are in, of fupporting the Expences that are incumbent on them, without thofe Taxes, or others which would fall heavier on the Inhabitants of the Province. For which Reafon, they exhort every one not to oppofe or refift the Patchers or their Subftitutes in the Collection of the Revenues which they farm, but to remain quiet till the Government can conveniently examine into the Grievances of which they complain; declaring, at the fame Time, that the Refractory fhall be feverely punifhed as Difturbers of the publick Peace.

Rotterdam, June 18. The Rabble committed fome Diforders Yefterday at Leyden, and laft Night pulled down fome Houfes, but no great Mifchief was done. The People of Am-

Encouragement he gives to Foreigners, who are under Hardfhips either on a Civil or Religious Account, to come and fettle in them. Fifty-two Perfons are very lately arrived on this Account from the Dutchy of Deux-Ponts. What can a Prince think of more than our Sovereign has done during the Eight Years he has reigned over us. He has reformed our Laws, and abridged the Proceedings in the Courts of Juftice: He has raifed the Character of his Houfe amongft the moft powerful Princes of Europe: He has greatly augmented the Dominions that were left him: He has laid a Plan for making his Subjects a commercial People, and already obtained confiderable Honours to his Flag: He has increafed the Numbers of thofe Subjects, in almoft every State he poffeffes; and now his Cares are extended to the Cultivation of the Soil in the moft advantageous Manner.

FRANCE.

Paris, May 31. O.S. The King has conferr'd the Title of Duke upon the Marquis de Puyfieux Minifter of State for foreign Affairs; the Count de St. Severin d'Arragon; and the Marquis de Mirepoix, who commands in Italy; as a Reward for the Satisfaction they have given him in their feveral Stations.

Paris, June 3, O.S. All the Officers of the Army, who had obtained Leave to remain here upon Account of the Truce, have received Orders to repair immediately to their refpective Corps; and all the young Fellows who are willing to ferve his Majefty continue to be enlifted. The Dauphin got a Fever, which lafted him three Days, by bathing in too cold Water; but is recovered again.

Paris, June 11. The 11th Article of the Preliminaries not allowing the Chevalier's eldeft Son to refide any longer in this Kingdom, he is preparing to depart, but it is not likely he will return to Rome, becaufe he has declared, that when he left that City it was with a firm Refolution never to fee it more. It is confirmed that fome Meafures are actually concerted to enable the Steuart Family to fubfift without any Affiftance from the Pope; and it is given out, that Prince Edward will have the Country of Commercy...

...cable Expedient which could be found to engage the Emprefs-Queen to confent to the faid Eftablifhment; and that it was eafy to forefee, that much greater and more infurmountable Difficulties would inevitably refult from the leaft Change in the prefent Difpofition of that Point.——The Return of the Courier which has been difpatched by the above Minifter to his Court, 'tis expected, will remove this Difficulty, which has hitherto retarded the Acceffion of his Catholick Majefty to the Preliminary Articles of Peace.

Extract of a Letter from Hamburgh, June 5.

"The fame Poft that acquainted us with the Efcape of Col. La Salle from the Fort of Weixelmunde, brought us likewife the News of his having been retaken after feventeen Hours only of Liberty. This Misfortune, it feems, is entirely owing to his own want of prefence of Mind, by which he difcovered himfelf at the Place where he was retaken, and where he had unadvifedly ftop'd to take a little Refrefhment. His Elopement has however brought to Mind fome Circumftances relating to the unfortunate Patkull, who was arrefted by the late King of Poland, at the Inftance of Charles XII. 'Tis well known that Orders were given to connive at an Efcape which he was advifed to attempt before the Arrival of the Swedifh Detachment, that was on the March to conduct him to his offended Sovereign; but depending too much on his Character of Minifter from the Czar, he made fome Difficulty to comply with the Advice, and the Demand of a Sum of Money which he expected, expected, and thereby gave time to the Swedifh Detachment to arrive to carry him off: Something of this Kind is thought to have happened in the prefent Cafe, which has occafioned the arrefting of the Officer that was upon Duty when the Prifoner gave him the Slip. The Colonel, however, continues in his Spirits, and feems not at all dejected at his Return to his former Confinement."

(11) By Letters from Mofcow we have Advice of a dreadful Fire in that City, which was yet burning when the Poft fet out and had already confumed 4000 Houfes. The fame Letter...

eighteenth century with warnings of Parra Glass, whose real name was Patrick O'Connolly, the county's most famous Raparee. He boasted long hair and an equally unkempt beard, both in a greenish-grey colour.

Faulkner suffered a serious accident at the height of his newspaper career. Travelling from Dublin to London in the early eighteenth century meant an unsteady boat journey across the Irish Sea, followed by a prolonged coach expedition across Wales and through England, rather more tedious than the same journey today over sea and land. Just before he climbed aboard the boat at Dublin, Faulkner slipped and fell, hurting his shin. Once on the boat, he put on his boots and strapped them tightly. He did not remove them until he arrived in London well over a day later. The tightness of the leather impeded the circulation of blood in his leg, so much so that by the time he reached London, it was noticeably sore. He was not deterred from enjoying the many frivolous pleasures that lay before him in London, despite the increasing pain. Gangrene was developing and after he returned to Dublin, the leg had to be amputated; the surgeon's skills were those of the butcher and the operation was performed without anaesthetic, the pain moderately deadened by plentiful alcohol.

The accident did not deter Faulkner; he continued to hop around Dublin and over to London, a noted figure of the day, foreshadowing a twentieth century Dublin newspaper "character", "Pussy" O'Mahony,

Masthead of Faulkner's Dublin Journal, **June, 1748.**

Primitive printing
equipment preserved at
Gray's Printing House,
Strabane, Co Tyrone.
John Dunlop, who
served his time here,
printed the first copies
of the American
Declaration of
Independence in 1776.
–National Trust, Northern
Ireland

one time manager of *The Irish Times* and father of comedian Dave Allen;
"Pussy" also lost a leg in an accident and had to be fitted with a wooden
one, which gave advance warning of his arrival.

Faulkner reported the great happenings of Dublin, the start of work
in 1729 on the Irish Parliament building at College Green (now the
Bank of Ireland) and the founding of the Royal Dublin Society in 1731.
Little did he imagine that in years to come, he would be arraigned
before the Bar of both Houses to sue, on his one good knee, for pardon
of his grievous offences against the honour and privilege of
Parliament. He was not always successful in seeking mercy; on more
than one occasion, he was thrown into prison for contempt and to add
injury to existing indignation, had to pay heavy fines before he was
considered safe for release.

There were great social occasions to report, too. In November, 1741,
Handel arrived in Dublin to great trumpeting from the Dublin press.
By April the following year, he had his "Messiah" ready for
performance at the newly-built music hall in Fishamble Street.
Hundreds of people were turned away from the first performance and
Faulkner's *Dublin Journal* reported: "Words are wanting to express the
exquisite Delight it afforded to the admiring crowded Audience."

Faulkner also had to contend with another challenger: the *Dublin
Evening Post*, which first saw the light of day in 1732 in Crane Lane. An

early issue reported that burying of corpses in wool had been banned in order to stimulate consumption of wool in Ireland. The *Evening Post* ran for two years, died for three years and was revived by a man called McCulloch, who reverted to the traditional Dublin newspaper publishing territory, at Skinner's Row. He fell foul of the same pressures that dogged Faulkner; a prosection was brought against him for "many vehement suspicions of sundry treasons". It killed the paper.

Dublin also had its first, brief attempt at a daily paper when *Hamilton's Advertiser* was brought out in 1736. Dublin's newspaper world was exciting, both for its owners and printers and for its exclusively Protestant readers, who pored over their papers in the many coffee houses that graced the city. Much of the news percolated through from the London papers; one Dublin newspaper owner had the effrontery to state in print that his paper had the services of the best London journalists — for nothing. Yet it would be wrong to see eighteenth century newspaper development entirely in terms of Dublin; towns outside the Pale were quick to start their own newspapers.

Cork was the first town in Ireland outside Dublin to produce its own newspaper, generally believed to have been the *Cork Idler* of 1715. Cork was described by one contemporary writer as being a small place, splendidly set on hills, so that it had the same tempting vistas as Oporto, the second city of Portugal. However, Cork's canals were damned for being effusively smelly.

The *Cork Idler* was swiftly followed, the year after its launch, by the single sheet *Freeholder*. For the remainder of the century, small, obscure titles came and went in amoebic-like profusion in the town: the *Cork Newsletter*, the *Medley*, the *Cork Evening Post*, the *Cork Journal*, even the *Hibernian Chronicle*, which dared fate by leaving "Cork" out of its title. In mid-century, the Cork papers had a great "scoop" when the shock waves from the earthquake that destroyed Lisbon in Portugal in 1755 were felt with force across much of Munster, causing church bells to ring and slates to fall off houses.

Limerick was an early contender in the newspaper stakes, with its first newspaper, the *Limerick Newsletter*, founded in 1716 by a "blow-in" from Dublin called Brangan. Printed on both sides of a half-sheet, the yearly subscription was announced as one shilling, but Brangan's enthusiasm seems to have outrun his expertise. Only a copy of the first issue still exists, so the city's first newspaper may not have lasted long.

There was some evidence, however, that Brangan was pipped to the Limerick publishing post. During the siege of Limerick in 1691, a mobile press was used to produce news sheets of proclamations and bulletins about the Williamite wars. None of these perambulating publications now exists. Shades of 230 years later, when the IRA GHQ ran a mobile printing press on the Cork-Kerry borders to turn out 20,000 copies weekly of *An Poblacht*. Riobard O Longphuirt of the Lee

Press, with the help of Erskine Childers, who was later executed, repeated the publishing feat of the Williamite wars, but on a much grander scale.

Brangan's first issue had but one local news item: the Hon Capt Brown of the Royal Scotch Battalion left Limerick for Rose-Gray (Roscrea) "to the great regret of the ladies of this city". The departure from Mallow, Co Cork, of the Mexican pilot of a jet that made an emergency landing on the town racecourse in 1983, was reported in similar terms by the newspapers of the area. Limerick soon reported less pleasant news; in 1727, a Catholic priest was executed there for marrying a Protestant couple.

During the course of the eighteenth century, Limerick, a city of cabins, hovels and Georgian mansions, became a substantial printing and book publishing centre. One of its best-known book printers, Andrew Welsh, followed the example of George Faulkner in Dublin and diversified into newspaper printing and publishing. His *Limerick Journal,* unusually for the times, carried mainly news about the city, but this editorial policy only lasted for five years after the setting up of the newspaper in 1739. It then changed its name to the *Munster Journal* and carried news from all over the province, with as much emphasis on news and advertisements from Cork as on those from Limerick, where the newspaper continued to be printed and published until about 1784.

Waterford had its first newspaper, the *Waterford Flying Post,* in 1729. One issue, dated Thursday, August 21, 1729, printed on a sheet of common writing paper, is still in existence, otherwise nothing is known about the paper, not even how long it survived. However, in contrast to the prolific newspaper presses of Dublin, Waterford remained without a newspaper for a further thirty-six years, until 1765, when the *Waterford Journal* and *Ramsey's Waterford Chronicle,* later the *Waterford Chronicle,* were started.

Belfast saw the founding a newspaper which survives to this day, making it the oldest newspaper in continuous publication in Ireland — the Belfast *News Letter.* Francis Joy brought out his first issue on September 1, 1737. It was a twice weekly, at one penny an issue. In the 1740s Joy handed it over to his two sons, Henry and Robert. His daughter, Ann, was mother of Henry Joy McCracken, the United Irishman.

Francis Joy then went into the paper-making business, opening the first paper mill in the North of Ireland, at Randalstown in Co. Antrim in 1748. Before this momentous step, nearly all Irish newspapers were printed on paper imported from France, Genoa, the Netherlands and even Venice. Irish-made paper was considered inferior. After Joy started making paper in Randalstown, other manufacturers throughout Ireland soon followed suit, so much so that paper-making reached its peak in 1838, with sixty mills in operation. By the time Joy brought his mill into operation, the broadsheet standard still adhered

Limerick Chronicle

1766—THE OLDEST NEWSPAPER IN THE REPUBLIC—1966

200th YEAR   **SATURDAY, NOVEMBER 12, 1966**   *Price 3d.*

Masthead of the *Limerick Chronicle,* **founded 1766.**

to by most Irish newspapers was firmly established.

Despite the tremendous developments that took place in Belfast, Cork and Limerick newspapers in the period up to 1750, Dublin still remained the real centre of innovation. In the city, the Georgian building boom was well under way. One journalist of the time said that the "Irish metropolis had splendid piles springing up every year." Ireland was described as having become the "seat of arts which improve and embellish society". One fashionable young woman talked about the "constant rat-tat on her door".

One Irish writer remarked, not entirely without exaggeration, that "Dublin is the completest city in Europe, if not the world". An English barrister was unable to convince a Dublin University professor that London was the finer city. Another contemporary source observed that almost every man in Ireland was living beyond his income. A Cork Member of Parliament, who was living most graciously on £300 a year (upwards of £40,000 in today's money), was spending £6 of his income on tailor's bills. By contrast, a farm labourer in Co Derry was lucky to earn about five pence a day for his back-breaking toils. In King's County (now Offaly), women were condemned for only working at harvest time, when they regarded the money they earned as their

33

THE PRESS.

PRICE 2D.]   DUBLIN, TUESDAY, OCTOBER 3, 1797.   [No. 3.

Masthead of the short-lived Volunteer newspaper, The Press, which ran for just a few months from 1797 until early the following year.
–Mrs. W. J. Moran

exclusive right for "dress and finery". No wonder the Huguenot silk looms of Dublin were humming.

Newspapers in Dublin were as prolific as their circulations were meagre. Average circulation ranged from 400 to 800 copies; hand-setting and printing precluded bigger sales. 1755 saw the establishment of *Saunder's Newsletter* in Dublin, reporting the growing popularity of a new beverage, tea. That same year also saw the demise of George Faulkner, but his paper carried on under the auspices of his nephew, Thomas Todd Faulkner. *Saunder's Newsletter* survived until 1879, but even though it was commercially successfully, it failed to make more than an ephemeral impression. The astringent Terence de Vere White, one-time literary editor of *The Irish Times* (he still contributes book reviews), remarked of Saunder's newspaper: "Discretion is the better part of valour, but it is paid for in obscurity. Saunders' is a perfect example of a success that created no legend. "It did, however, become Ireland's first commercially successful daily paper, in 1777.

Saunder's Newsletter was also damned by that great nineteenth century newspaper historian, Dr R R Madden, who said that it could not have been more destitute of Irish news if it had been published in Iceland. Still, it provided an extremely comfortable living for its owner, Henry Saunders, who had a fine house and printing works at Christchurch Place, the Skinner's Row of old.

After Saunder's, the next major newspaper in Dublin was the *Public Register* or the *Freeman's Journal,* which made its first timid appearance in 1763; it was to become one of the most powerful newspapers in Ireland towards the end of the following century, yet collapsed in 1924. Its first editor was a man called Henry Brooke and its chief scribe, equivalent of a chief reporter, was a schoolmaster from Mary's Abbey, Bernard Clarke, who was described as having suffered considerably in 1753 from having written pamphlets in favour of the patriots.

The year that the *Freeman's Journal* was first published, the countryside was far from peaceful. The Clones "Hearts of Steel" gang attacked Belturbet barracks; seven of the attackers were killed. A Presbyterian curate in Monaghan came under fire from a churchwarden for shaving on a Sunday.

Two years after the *Freeman's Journal* came into being, it carried just half a column of local news. Of that space, more than a third was devoted to accounts of highway and house robberies. Much of the crime in the city, suggested a rival Dublin newspaper, was caused by prostitutes and street walkers.

In 1766, Limerick poet and historial John Ferrar founded the *Limerick Chronicle,* still published today by the *Limerick Leader.* The *Chronicle* is the oldest newspaper in the Republic. An actor and dramatist called John O'Keeffe gave a vivid description of Ferrar's little shop in the town centre, yards from where the city's first newspaper, the *Limerick Newsletter,* was founded fifty years previously.

In his shop, Ferrar wrote most of the editorial copy, collected the advertisements over the counter and filled in any gaps with month-old news from the London newspapers. Then, Ferrar set the type by hand, locked up the frames and laboriously hand-printed a couple of hundred copies. O'Keeffe described Ferrar as being "very deaf, yet with a cheerful, animated countenance, thin and of the middle size."

Six years later, the *Derry Journal* was set up under the full title of *The London-Derry Journal and General Advertiser.* June 3, 1772 saw the founding issue of the paper, today the third oldest in Ireland. George Douglas, a Scotsman, printed and published the newspaper at a stationery shop in the Diamond, that dull and unremarkable square at the top of the steep incline of Shipquay Street. True to his own origins, Douglas advertised in the first issue for an apprentice for his firm, someone who "must be a Protestant and well recommended. "Not until over a century later did the *Derry Journal* suffer a sea-change into a rich and strange Nationalistic hue.

The *Derry Journal* was published twice weekly, as now. The cost of subscriptions depended on distance from Derry; readers in the city could enjoy the new paper for 6s 6d a year, while those within forty miles of the city had to pay a third more. Advertisements cost 2d a line, with 1d a line "for every continuance".

Some of those very first advertisements gave a sparkling insight into the social and cultural life of Derry. James Galbraith, a self-professed mathematician, gave notice that he had a genteel apartment where he taught "young gentlemen who are grown and would not chuse (sic) to be taught in a common school". A Dancing Master called Morriss, newly arrived from Dublin, announced that he had opened his

Dancing School in the Town-hall of London-Derry where "the newest and best methods of teaching young ladies and gentlemen would be employed at half a guinea per quarter and one crown entrance fee".

Like most newspapers of the time, the *Derry Journal* was printed on locally-produced paper. Quite probably, the paper used was made at McClintock's paper mill near Clady, in the county of Derry.

Far removed from the suffocating Presbyterian atmosphere of eighteenth century Derry, John Dunlop printed the first copies of the American Declaration of Independence in 1776. He had served his time at a printing house in the Main Street of Strabane, Co. Tyrone, before emigrating to America. Today, Gray's premises in the small, scarred town contain some priceless examples of early printing equipment. In Dublin, the American revolution had some effect on public thinking, although only one newspaper, the *Freeman's Journal,* upheld liberal principles. No other publication in the country dared follow suit.

That spirit did not last long; once Francis Higgins, known as the "Sham Squire" gained control of the *Freeman's Journal,* all pretension to liberalism vanished despite his claims of impartiality. Higgins started writing for the paper in 1779, the same year that a hapless bookseller called Collins bought it over. So successfully did Higgins worm his way into the newspaper that within four years, he had absolute control of its destinies. He was also in the pay of Dublin Castle, which filled several columns of each issue with proclamations, the press subsidy of the time.

Despite his dubious origins in life, Higgins went on to become one of Dublin's most respected and influential citizens, a Justice and a coroner, no less. As Higgins scaled the heights of social prominence, so did the *Freeman's Journal* start tipping down into relative obscurity. Higgins had a sworn enemy in John Magee, who founded the *Dublin Evening Post* in 1778. The battle royal between the two was on a scale not seen among Irish newspapermen during this present century.

Magee was out to smash the influence of the *Freeman's Journal;* within three years of starting, he claimed to be selling 4,000 copies an issue, making it the biggest selling newspaper in the country. Higgins and Magee slogged it out in the public prints: Magee investigated Higgins' background and ran a series of stories claiming that he had started his working life as a pot boy in a Dublin public house, that he had seduced a merchant's daughter before being arrested and that he was being funded by the Castle, all good wholesome stuff that had the reading public of Dublin agog with excitement.

At Hyde's coffee house in Dublin, where subscribers paid a guinea's subscription a year to retire to a specially reserved apartment to read the newspapers, the arguments raged backwards and forwards. Magee not only provoked Higgins, but the Government. He exposed corruption and incompetence within the ranks of the Government to such deadly effect that the Dublin newspapers carried an

advertisement from Magee of January 28, 1785, giving his address as "New Jail". Magee might have been brought to a halt, but the affairs of the *Freeman's Journal* did not improve. Even after Higgin's death in 1802, the new owner of the paper, Philip Harvey Whitfield, received a Government pension of £200 a year. He kept his silence and the *Freeman's Journal* did not regain its much-vaunted independence until Sir John Gray, MP, became sole owner in 1853 and the paper became the champion of Catholic and Nationalist rights.

After the Irish Parliament was granted a measure of legislative independence in 1782, the old style advertising sheets (three out of four sheets in *Saunder's Newsletter* were advertisements) gave way to more politically contentious editorial material. This freedom was particularly short-lived; incensed at one particularly abusive attack on its competence, the Government start harrassing the press with a

The building of Dublin's Georgian houses and squares turned the city into one of Europe's most elegant capitals in the eighteenth century. Now, particularly on the northside, much of the Georgian-style property is dilapidated. Sean O'Casey's last Dublin home, pictured here, was at 422 North Circular Road. From here, he left in disgust for London in 1926.

series of actions for seditious libel and increased duties. Within a year, the press was reigned in. Its difficulties coincided with general economic problems. In 1783, there was a clamour to protect Irish industry and workers from English imports. Dublin coachmakers banned repair work on coaches made in Britain.

The next year, the noise against imports grew louder and violent riots took place outside the Dublin premises of importers. Workers in the city were gravely concerned at losing what little privileges they had; a typical city tailor had to work from six in the morning until eight at night, six days a week, for a maximum daily wage of 1s 8d. No wonder the *Volunteer Journal* felt encouraged to thunder about abolishing the English connection. While riots took place in Dublin, Limerick's newspaper industry was consolidating its position.

When the *Limerick Journal*, owned by Edward Flin, was first published in 1779, it was not the reappearance of the title launched in 1739 and which later became the *Munster Journal*, but a brand new newspaper. Demonstrating the greater stability of the newspaper business towards the end of the eighteenth century, the *Limerick Journal* (second version) lasted until 1819. Other Limerick newspapers were however remarkably short-lived. In 1788, a Robert Law of Mill Lane advertised in the *Limerick Chronicle* that on May 28, he would publish the *Limerick Herald and Munster Advertiser*. In July the following year, although his name was still attached to the paper as its printer, he advertised that he had severed all connection with the publication. After 1795, nothing more was heard of this twice-weekly paper, but the *Limerick Chronicle*, Protestant and with a similar frequency of circulation, continued to strengthen its editorial and financial position. The *Chronicle* remained a bi-weekly until nearly a century after its foundation.

While Limerick's newspapers were gathering steam, a quite extraordinary saga was unfolding in Kilkenny. Catherine Finn was running *Finn's Leinster Journal* after the death of her husband. During the eighteenth and nineteenth centuries, no other woman played such a major rôle in the Irish newspaper industry.

Finn could not however claim sole honours; in Waterford from 1765 to 1771, Mrs Esther Crawley produced the weekly *Waterford Journal* at the Euclid's Head tavern, Peter Street. She was helped by her son, in between dispensing refreshments to sailors from the sailing ships tied up at the nearby quays.

Fame was thrust on Catherine Finn by the death of her husband, Edmund, who had founded *Finn's Leinster Journal* (Kilkenny's first newspaper) in January, 1767. Published on Wednesdays and Saturdays, it cost 4d and was brought to such places as Carlow and Castledermot by messengers on horseback.

If there were any delays in the newspaper reaching these far-flung outposts of its circulation area, Edmund Finn was in the habit of printing apologies to his subscribers in the next issue:

"the delays were due to the villainy of the messengers (who had to supply their own horses). I intend no reflection on the honourable services of Kilkenny Post Office."

Despite the delays, Finn's paper, said to have been partially financed by his brother William, a Carlow merchant, soon prospered and at the end of 1767, he was able to move from his first unprepossessing address at St Mary's Graveyard to more imposing premises at High Street. The L & N supermarket now stands on the site. For ten years, the Finn familiy enjoyed the prosperity brought by their paper, but in 1777, Finn dropped dead.

His widow, Catherine, left with seven young children, the eldest of whom was only eight, had the unenviable choice of letting the paper go or taking over herself. Happily for posterity, she decided to meet the challenge and a month after her husband's death, announced in the columns of the paper that she intended carrying on herself. She solicited the continued custom of the gentry. The Catholic majority of Kilkenny, the lower classes, were of little interest to her.

Catherine organised the editorial content, sold the advertisements and oversaw the printing and distribution. She was suitably scavenging in her editorial approach: copyright did not exist, so she unhesitatingly filched all kinds of foreign news, rumour, gossip and war dispatches, without acknowledgement, from the Dublin and London papers. Only a fraction of the copy directly concerned Kilkenny city and county and since it was mostly "borrowed" from the Dublin papers anyway, it was either late or inaccurate and frequently both.

But the *Journal* prospered mightily on a harmless diet of births, marriages and deaths; the more absurd the circumstances, the better it suited the readers of *Finn's Leinster Journal*. Stories about old age marrying sprightly youth, about a Leixlip woman having twins after thirty years of marriage and about an Eskar woman having quads all did wonders for the paper's subscriptions' list.

Criticism was mild and infrequent; occasionally, Catherine Finn might attack the rowdyism at the Kilkenny May Day celebrations or complain about the press-gang raids on local hurling and football team in search of involuntary recruits for the Royal Navy.

A man who was the equal of Francis Higgins, the "Sham Squire", in ostentatious vulgarity, came to the fore in the Dublin newspaper world. His early career was said to have been like a parody of Higgins'. John Giffard styled himself a surgeon, but his apprenticeship to an apothecary was the nearest he ever came to this exalted professional position. He did take the eminently sensible step of marrying an heiress and once he had secured his wealth lines, his ambitions knew no bounds.

In 1788, he bought the *Dublin Journal* founded by George Faulkner and turned what had been a Conservative newspaper with a high

Reading newspapers is
as an important
pastime in Vienna's
coffee houses today as
it was in the scores of
coffee houses in
eighteenth century
Dublin.
–Österreichische
Fremdenverkehrswerbung

proportion of advertising into an outright Orange news-sheet. Giffard, like Higgins, was in the pay of Dublin Castle; a coarse, vulgar and insolent man, Giffard was regarded as the Protestant ascendancy's most vocal advocate. He survived the ignominy of a jail sentence for assaulting James Potts, who had bought *Saunder's Newsletter* and to whom he had taken a virulent dislike. He was sentenced to six months, but after he had served a month, the balance of the term was commuted to a heavy fine. As for Giffard himself, he lingered on until 1820, his paper until 1825, when it was merged with *The Irish Times*. That title was only short-lived, but was resurrected in 1859 to form the present day title.

Francis Higgins, owner of the *Freeman's Journal*, was meanwhile settling into the new offices of the paper at Trinity Street, off Dame Street. Over a century later, the *Irish Daily Independent* was established almost next door; out of this title emerged the *Irish Independent*, which took over the titles of the *Freeman's Journal* when it closed down in 1924.

Newspaper owners and editors lived in constant fear of fines and periods in jail; paradoxically, mechanical improvements were helping to make newspapers more prolific. Towards the end of the eighteenth century, the wooden press used until then for newspaper printing, started to be replaced by a cast iron press, the Stanhope, which meant a considerable reduction in the amount of muscle power needed to print the pages. In America, in 1792, all newspapers were given the benefit of cheap postal rates, while in Germany, some 1,200 newspapers were in existence by this time. After the first flush of press freedom following the French Revolution in 1789, several journalists were assassinated in France and the entire press there was put under police control. Despite the many fiscal and political controls put upon the press in Ireland, the most remarkable newspaper of the closing years of the eighteenth century flourished in Belfast, the *Northern Star*.

Set up in 1792 as the newspaper of the United Irishmen, it reflected the radicalism of Belfast. Run on very business-like lines, nevertheless, a committee of ten investors (virtually the first time an Irish newspaper was controlled by the equivalent of a board of directors) ran the publication. A sub-committee of management was elected in turn; this had three members, one of whom, Samuel Neilson, acted as editor. All over the North of Ireland, subscriptions poured in. Some Donaghadee people were pointed out as being likely subscribers to the new newspaper, until it was revealed that they were already in arrears with their subscriptions to the Belfast *News Letter*.

The circulation of the *Northern Star* extended as far as Dublin, Edinburgh and London, although its news was almost exclusively North of Ireland. It carried radical political articles and literary articles. In 1795, its presses printed *Bolg an Tsolair* (the *Gaelic Magazine*). For a few glorious years, Belfast was the centre of Irish radicalism; Henry Joy, a grandson of the founder, controlled the *News Letter*. He was also a member of the volunteers. In Dublin, a similarly minded newspaper, the *National Journal*, came and went the year that the *Northern Star* was founded. The *Harp of Erin*, which later expressed similar views in Cork, only survived a few issues. The authorities suppressed the *Northern Star* in 1797 and after the 1798 Rising had been put down with the utmost brutality, there was not a major newspaper in the country that had not been frightened or seduced into supporting the side of the administration agains the rebels.

With the suppression of the Rising, chaos reigned. After the battle of Enniscorthy, the dead bodies of men, horses and pigs lay around the streets. Most people in the countryside were more concerned about the harvest than about the fate of the newspapers. To the relief of many, the drought of the earlier months of 1798 had delayed sowing and harvesting, so that the crops that year did not suffer because of the Rising. After the rebellion had been put down that summer, the Belfast *News Letter*, by this time sold by Joy to an Edinburgh company, crowed about the different character maintained by the Catholic of the north and the Catholic of the south. "The difference is well understood by everyone acquainted with Ireland." The *News Letter* went on to point out that the insurgents made up only one per cent of the Irish population.

Few of the Catholic majority population in Ireland could read newspapers; the difference between the Protestant ruling minority and the Catholic majority was well illustrated by the difference between clergymen's salaries.

Silhouette of Alexander Mackay senior, who became part owner of the Belfast News Letter **in 1795. He was one of the Edinburgh-based consortium which took over the paper that year from the Joy family.**

Church of Ireland clergy were paid twice as much as Catholic priests. As recently as 1773, Noble Art O'Leary, a Catholic, had been killed for refusing to sell his mare to a Protestant for £5. Those newspapers in existence at the end of the eighteenth century still had an almost exclusively Protestant readership. Even the harsh way in which the 1798 Rebellion was put down excited no comment from Catherine Finn's *Leinster Journal*. Dr Madden may have derided her efforts, saying that he had not been able to discover any evidence of acquaintance with literature or political taste, but she did survive until the grand old age of eighty-three, remarkable longevity then. She even survived the antics of her eldest son, Michael, who became much involved in the spectacular collapse of a bank which operated in Dublin and Kilkenny. She also survived the merging of her paper into another *Leinster Journal*, just after the turn of the century. Catherine Finn was the only major woman newspaper owner and editor during two centuries, eighteenth and nineteenth, and she proved every bit as adept in trimming to the whims of Dublin Castle as her male counterparts. Heavily taxed and politically muzzled, the Irish newspaper industry, although it had developed well during the century, was all set to acquiesce without a murmur in the passing of the Act of Union in 1800.

CHAPTER III

With the Bishops' approval, 1801-1899

Thwaites' Soda water in pints. 13s per dozen.
FAULKNER'S DUBLIN JOURNAL, 1801

Decayed teeth stopped, 2/6d. Warranted for articulation and mastication. Mr Cumming, 45 Patrick-Street, Cork.
CORK CONSTITUTION, 1875

The nineteenth century began with nearly all Irish newspapers in firmly Protestant hands, often with the help of financial hand-outs from Dublin Castle, and ended with a vigorous new press, espousing the Nationalist cause and often enjoying the open support of the Catholic clergy.

The dullness of the early nineteenth century press in Ireland mirrored the extinction of much of the Continental press. With the advance of Napoleon across Europe, journalism was stifled to the point of virtual annihilation, not only in France, but in all the countries conquered by the French. In the German provinces captured by Napoleon, only one newspaper was permitted in each region and it had to take political articles written by Napoleon himself. Irish newspapers that supported the Dublin Castle line after the 1800 Act of Union enjoyed some juicy carrots in the form of early access to dispatches and monopolies of Government advertising and proclamations. Even the *Freeman's Journal* was a Castle paper, yet when the Government failed to deliver on its promise of Catholic Emancipation as an immediate benefit of the Act of Union, one or two brave newspaper owners went against the official line. The *Evening Herald,* which lasted from 1804 until 1814, supported the principle of Catholic Emancipation. Press support for the Castle started to fall away, so much so that by 1810, most Dublin newspapers favoured the Emancipation cause. An additional

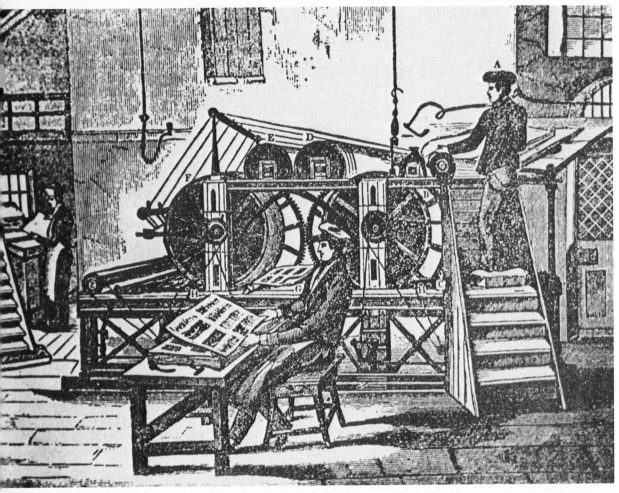

A typical Dublin newspaper printing press of the 1850s.

duty on advertisements that year only compounded the bad feelings between the two parties.

Alexander Mackay, from Edinburgh, became the sole owner of the Belfast *News Letter*; the Henderson family, the present owners, are his direct descendants by marriage. They have controlled the fortunes of their newspaper longer than any other Irish newspaper proprietors of the present day. James Henderson, owner of the *Newry Commercial Telegraph*, founded in 1812, was a close friend of Mackay and indeed worked on the *News Letter* staff at one time. Henderson's son, James Alexander Henderson, became the first Henderson to own the *News Letter*. A contrast in communications is provided by father and son; the father used to commute from Newry to Belfast on horseback, while his son graduated to a stage coach.

By today's standards, the moral climate was harsh: small children

44

were hung for stealing calico. Of one Dublin tragedy, the *Freeman's Journal* reported quite nonchalantly: "Yesterday, a boat capsized on the Grand Canal at Portobello. Five men, four women and two children were drowned, but no person of any note has suffered."

The cut and thrust of newspaper life, the hidden innuendo, the smiling sword, were even more pointed 165 years ago than today. One Saturday night in 1818, a harmless newspaper editor called Comerford was staggering home from a function he had attended in the centre of Dublin on behalf of his paper, the *Patriot*. Comerford had enjoyed himself enormously, in the best tradition of journalism, so much so that he took a carefree short cut home along the banks of the Royal Canal in Drumcondra.

Thoroughly inebriated, the unfortunate editor fell into the canal and was drowned. Dublin being Dublin, the news of the man's death, even though it had happened very late on the Saturday night, galloped with the speed of an uncontrollable bush fire through the ranks of Dublin journalists. Other ambitious journalists achieved remarkably quick recoveries from their own hangovers as Sunday dawned and sat down, quill pens at the ready, to write fawning and toadying letters of application for Comerford's job, before the man was hardly cold, let alone buried. One cleric with journalistic qualifications stood by his high moral principles: since it was the Sabbath, his application waited until nine o'clock on the Monday morning. Virtue went unrewarded.

But often, the instinct was to lie low, especially in the great depression that followed the end of the Napoleonic wars. The pro-Catholic *Dublin Chronicle* was being mooted in 1815 (it did appear, but only fleetingly) and was looking for an editor. The person required had to be "perfectly competent to be the ostensible proprietor of a patriotic religious newspaper. He must be in circumstances to enable him to say that he has no preferences for the streets of Dublin to the call of Newgate. "Unpromising as the future must have looked to anyone working on an Irish newspaper in 1820, the coming decade turned out to represent one of the most exciting periods in the history of newspaper publishing in Ireland, spurred on by technical improvements. Many of the foundations of the present day press were laid. Two French brothers, called Fourdrinier, invented a new paper-making process that year; it was so effective that it swept Europe, cutting the price of newsprint by a quarter. Within the space of forty years, it became common practice, including here in Ireland, for newspapers to be printed from rolls of paper, rather than on single sheets. 1820 also saw the invention of the Koenig press, which was able to turn out 1,000 copies an hour. The London *Times* installed this new machine, which replaced rows of Stanhope presses; these had been little more than metal equivalents of the hand-operated wooden presses in use since newspaper printing started in the seventeenth century. Soon, a less elaborate, but mechanically advanced press, the

Columbian, topped by a giant eagle, became a common sight in Irish newspaper offices. In 1809, the Dublin printers had started to organise themselves into an embryonic union.

Then in 1824, a new paper called the *Morning Register* employed Dublin's first corps of reporters. Out went all the foreign dispatches, culled at no cost from the London newspapers and in for tedious hand-setting went local news copy written by these reporters. The *Morning Register* changed the journalistic world of Dublin and later the rest of the country so much that its founding editor, a man called Staunton, was presented with an illuminated address when he became Lord Mayor of Dublin.

He was referred to as the "Creator of the Irish press". He also supported Catholic Emancipation.

Just as Staunton of the *Morning Register* was known as the father of the Irish press, so too was another remarkable character, for an entirely different and much more literal reason. William Trimble, who set up the *Impartial Reporter* in Enniskillen in 1825, just four years before the "split" on the *Derry Journal* helped set up the *Londonderry Sentinel*, was married twice. By his two wives, he produced the grand total of twenty-six children. He was a strong, wily man; his physical strength, as well as that of his first wife, Jane, was proved the very month that the paper was launched.

The pair had travelled up from Dublin to start up the new enterprise, leaving the city one evening by mail coach and bumping through the night to arrive in Enniskillen late the following afternoon.

Emigrants bound for America in the 1850s, waiting on the quayside at Queenstown, Co Cork (now Cobh).

(opposite page) Front page of the first issue of the Cork Examiner, **1841.**
–Cork Examiner

The Cork Examiner.

No. 1.]   MONDAY EVENING, AUGUST 30, 1841.   [Price—Four Pence.

TO THE PUBLIC.

[column of introductory address, largely illegible]

THE HIGH SHERIFF OF FERMANAGH.

(From the Morning Chronicle.)

THE LIBERATION OF FEARGUS O'CONNOR.

(From the Star of Monday.)

"TO MR. JOHN CLEAVE.

—— York Castle, Sunday.

"MY DEAR CLEAVE.—An order has just arrived for my immediate liberation, in consequence of a medical application ...

"Yours very sincerely,
"F. O'CONNOR."

BIRTHDAY OF PRINCE ALBERT.

CONTINENTAL AND BRITISH WAREHOUSE, 73, GRAND PARADE.

VANCE AND COMPANY RESPECTFULLY announce the return of C. VANCE from London, Dublin, &c. &c. with an Assortment of FANCY GOODS in the newest Fashions ...

N.B.—V. and CO. return their warmest thanks to their Country Friends, for their confidence and liberal favours ...

August, 30, 1841.

ST. PATRICK'S SCHOOLS.

MASTER AND MISTRESS WANTED.

Cork, August 30, 1841.

COUNTIES OF WATERFORD AND TIPPERARY.

Most Important Auction of Highly Bred Dairy Stock, Bullocks, Sheep, Lambs, Horses ...

MR. MARSH has the honour to announce to the Nobility and Gentry of the Counties of Cork Waterford and Tipperary ...

[detailed auction listings of cattle, horses, farming implements]

GARRYDUFF is situate Three Miles from Youghal on the Tallow side; Seven and a Half from Dungarvan, and is placed twice a day by the Waterford Mail.

On the following MONDAY, the 13th September, the Entire of the Highly Bred Stock, &c. of the Farm of BALLY-GAGGIN, near Dungarvan, including ...

IRISH MANUFACTURE.

LOWER GLASHEEN CARDING & SPINNING MILLS.

JOHN BRANSFIELD, begs leave to inform the Public ...

BRUSHES.

THE SUBSCRIBERS beg the inspection of an extensive Assortment of HAIR BRUSHES, which they have just had from their Workshops ...

THE STABLE BRUSHES have long had a preference from the best Grooms both in the City and County ...

CARRIAGE RUGS and DOOR MATS, and also of Coloured MOROCCO LEATHERS ...

T. K. & L. WALSH,
45, Patrick Street.

Aug. 30.

GENUINE IRISH MANUFACTURE.

MRS. COGHLAN, 72, South Main Street, takes this opportunity of returning her grateful thanks to her friends and the public ...

MRS. COGHLAN has now an extensive variety of the best Hats, of a high quality, and perfectly durable colour ...

Cork, 8th Month, 30th, 1841.

IRISH MANUFACTURED BEAVER HATS,
No. 39, Brown-Street, Cork.

THOMAS DAVIS RESPECTFULLY informs the Public that ... BEAVER HATS ...

August, 30th, 1841.

IRISH MANUFACTURE.

RICE & LAWLOR (LATE C. LYONS), COMMISSION AGENTS, 22 and 23, South Main Street, have received a consignment of CLAFFIS, Manufactured at the HIBERNIA MILLS, DUBLIN.

SHERWIN, COPE & CO., ENGINEERS AND MILL-WRIGHTS, *Cumberland Street, Cork*.

BEG to return their thanks to the Trade ... IMPERIAL PRINTING AND INKING PRESSES ...

GEORGE S. BEALE RESPECTFULLY announce the return of the Patronize Coffee, that he has a VARIETY of Families at present, amounting to SIX DIFFERENT PRICES; all of which are Good Value, particularly the CELEBRATED MALABAR COFFEE, now so much liked.

EIGHTH MONTH, 1841.

SICKLES. SICKLES. SICKLES.

General Grocery, Tea, Spice, Cheese, and Pig-Stuff Warehouse,
110, SHANDON-STREET.

D. O'FLYN has just landed, ex Favourite and Venus, from London, 800 Doz. PRIME SICKLES ...

Cork, August 30, 1841.

NOTICE.

ROGERS & CO., respectfully inform the Nobility and Gentry of the City and County, that they are making an alteration in their Establishment ...

No. 18, OLD GEORGE'S STREET, CORNER OF PRINCE'S-STREET.

123, Old George's Street, and 29, Grand Parade, Cork,
August 30, 1841.

TO BE LET.

A GOOD HOUSE in Douglas Street. Good for a general Trade.

Apply to MR. JOHN BLACKLOCK, South Main Street.
August 30.

BRILLIANT WINDOW GLASS.

THE superiority of DUMBARTON WINDOW GLASS ...

D. KENNELLY,
General Commercial Agent, 3 & 4, Maylor Street.

TEAS.

TEAS supplied at the Stores here, or shipped to order from the Ports of London and Liverpool, by
D. KENNELLY,
General Commercial Agent, 3 & 4, Maylor Street.

Cork, August 30.

ROMAN CEMENT.

D. KENNELLY has now in Stock 500 BARRELS of a ROMAN CEMENT, of the best quality ...

August 30, 1841.

WINE AND SPIRIT VAULTS, BOTTLED LIQUOR AND TEA STORES,
120, George's Street, and 32, Prince's Street.

MICHAEL O'CONNOR

TAKES leave to inform his Friends and the Public that he has a nicely selected Stock of Fine SHERRY WINES ...

Aug. 30, 1841.

LODGINGS.

TO BE LET, Unfurnished, from the 1st September next, the UPPER PART of the HOUSE No. 8, PATRICK STREET ...

WHOLESALE TOBACCO AND SNUFF MANUFACTORY,
82, SOUTH MAIN STREET.

J. BLACKLEDGE begs to inform Country Dealers ...

August 30.

ABOUT FIVE HUNDRED TONS of Prime HOUSE COALS are now on Sale at
GEORGE S. BEALE'S,
EIGHTH MONTH, 1841.   Fish Street.

IRON AND METAL STORE,
No. 3, COBURG STREET, LEITRIM,
(Opposite Timm's Hotel.)

JOHN T. WHITE, having opened the above Establishment ...

Cork, 8th Month, 30th, 1841.

TO THE LADIES

DAVIS & CO.

LADIES' FASHIONABLE BOOT AND SHOE MANUFACTURERS, 17, GRAND PARADE, (Corner of Tuckey-Street), beg leave to inform the Ladies of Cork ...

DECLARATION OF BONUS,
BY THE
PROVIDENT LIFE COMPANY.

REGENT STREET, PICCADILLY, LONDON, AND 32, PATRICK STREET, CORK.

CAPITAL—ONE MILLION.—ESTABLISHED 1806.
President—The Right Hon. Earl Grey.

Cork, Aug. 30, 1841.

ESTABLISHED—1782.

PHOENIX FIRE INSURANCE COMPANY,
LONDON,
50, PATRICK STREET, CORK.

CAPITAL—ONE MILLION.

Sir John Arnott, First Baronet and owner of The Irish Times, **1873-1898.**

The journey took exactly twenty-one hours. A Presbyterian, he had served his time with a printer in Dungannon; his apprenticeship was completed in Dublin, where he was accustomed to getting up at five every morning so that he could read six chapters of the Bible before setting out for work. The Bible played an important part in his life, as it did for most of the population. Within the memory of older readers in the early nineteenth century, Bible serialisations were very popular items in many Irish newspapers.

Unemployment was a big problem among printers; in the 1820s, journeymen printers met in a public house on a Saturday night after work had finished for the week at 8 p.m., to decide on emigration grants to their fellow out-of-work printers. If these men went to England to seek work, they were given £4, the equivalent of a year's benefit from the prototype union. On the other hand, if they decided upon America, the grant doubled. After the meeting was over, many of the men went to help their wives with the week's shopping, which in those days, was done late on a Saturday night.

The early 1820s had a spectacular newspaper launch, that of the *Dublin Evening Mail*. It was a venerable and much-loved institution in the city from 1823 until its ultimate death in July, 1962, yet in the years after its inception it had much of the Protestant bigotry so prevalent in the eighteenth century press.

Joseph Timothy Haydn was the *Mail's* first editor; he had been enticed away from the *Patriot*, for it was he who succeeded to the editorial chair in that paper after the death by drowning of Comerford in 1818. When Haydn took over the *Patriot*, it had just a few hundred subscribers; after five years, he had built it up to become the largest selling paper in the country, helped by the frequent controversies he engendered. On one occasion, he was horsewhipped by the ADC to the Lord Lieutenant of Ireland for an insulting remark he had passed on the ADC's antecedents. Haydn took his punishment in good part, in the best tradition of a circulation-building editor.

However successful he was at the *Patriot*, the idea of the new *Dublin Evening Mail* was too much of a temptation. The paper was an immediate success and within a year of its launch in February, 1823, it had a circulation of some 2,500, nearly three times bigger than that of any other newspaper in Dublin. Much of this circulation was at the expense of those papers kept by the Castle.

The *Dublin Evening Mail* killed off what was then Ireland's oldest surviving newspaper, the *Dublin Journal*, founded by George Faulkner in 1725. Its circulation had collapsed from about 650 copies per issue in 1821 to half that number of 1824, the year after the *Mail* was launched. The *Journal* folded in 1825 and its interest was bought by the owners of *The Irish Times*, which had been founded two years previously. It was announced for a period of weeks in 1825 that the name of the *Dublin Journal* would be added to that of *The Irish Times*. The marriage of titles

never took place; instead, the paper became the *Morning Courier and Dublin Journal* in July 1825, swiftly ran into labour problems with recalitrant printers and closed down. Thirty-four years later, *The Irish Times* title was infused with life by the young Major Lawrence Knox. The second version of *The Irish Times* is fortunately still with us today.

Meanwhile, Haydn turned the *Dublin Evening Mail* into a roaring success, the *Sunday World* of its day, but nastily built on a diet of virulent anti-Catholic bigotry designed to appeal to Dublin's still largely Protestant newspaper audience. In a typical jibe, the *Mail* on one occasion ran a parody of an announcement from the Vice-Regal Lodge about a levee: "Private Chaplain's Office, Phoenix Park, Feb 17, 1826. There will be a Rosary at the Lodge on the evening of Monday the 20th inst. The ladies and gentlemen who attend are requested to bring their own beads."

The *Mail's* anti-Catholicism did for that paper's sales in the years immediately after 1823 what the bikini-clad models did for the *Sunday World* in the 1970s. Yet although Haydn was immensely successful as the founding editor, the newspaper's owners were so concerned that the substantial profits would be eroded by libel actions brought on by Haydn's impetuosity that he was bought out for a substantial sum of money, enough to enable him to live out his early retirement (he was only just over forty) in considerable comfort. The *Mail,* too, settled down to a prosperous and uneventful respectability.

The new *Clonmel Free Press* (1826) was also outspoken, in the cause of Catholic Emancipation. Its founder, John Hackett, wrote in its first

The Shelbourne Hotel, Dublin, in 1859, when it consisted of five separate houses; not until some years later were they converted into the present building.

The Bianconi "Long Car", which helped revolutionise public transport in the early nineteenth century.

issue: "We consider it almost unnecessary to call the attention of the public to the typographical appearance of the paper. It is printed with a new and beautiful type from the celebrated foundry of Caslon and Livermore of London and worked with the Columbian press which has for the first time been seen in this part of the country." Hackett added: "This journal will be the advocate of the unconditional emancipation of seven millions of British subjects." Later, he took on board the *Clonmel Advertiser* (1837); after his death, the paper was run by his son. It lasted until 1880.

Just at the time that Haydn was being eased out of the editorial chair at the *Dublin Evening Mail,* a major 'split' at the *Derry Journal* resulted in another paper being founded in the city. Strange as it may seem today, the *Derry Journal* was a staunchly Protestant and Conservative paper. It was doing so splendidly flying the Protestant banner in the city that in 1815, despite the trade slump of the time, the printing works and offices were transferred from the Diamond just a short distance to much more spacious premises in Shipquay Street, where it remained until the early 1970s.

Change was in the air and by 1829, the *Derry Journal* had changed both owners and policy; it came out in favour of Catholic Emancipation, a policy that meant so much to the oppressed Catholic peasantry of Ireland. One man did not approve, William Wallen, the editor of the *Derry Journal,* who promptly left to help in starting up the *Londonderry Sentinel,* which had no such sentiments in favour of Emancipation.

The first issue of the *Londonderry Sentinel and North-West Advertiser* appeared in September 19, 1829. Its front page carried just five news stories (all from England or further afield) and the first issue was reported by one contemporary source as being entirely free of literals.

That same year, the new County Goal in Bishop Street was reported as being "too capacious for a district in which crime is comparatively rare".

The newspaper's first press was a hand-driven Columbian model, which produced 150 copies an hour. Despite the fact that most of the city's 12,000 inhabitants could neither read nor write, the *Sentinel* sold well, so much so that soon after its launch, a single cylinder steam powered press was installed, capable of printing 1,000 copies an hour. The *Sentinel* developed into one of the most enterprising newspapers in Ireland.

John Francis Maguire, who founded the Cork Examiner **in 1841.**
–Cork Examiner

The delays in arrival of mails from Britain meant that news despatches came to Derry a week late. On one occasion in its early years, the *Sentinel* decided to report an important Royal speech made in London well ahead of its rivals. A compositor was sent by ship from Derry to Glasgow, where he picked up a copy of the Royal speech. On the ship back to Derry, he set the copy, using the cases of hand type he had brought with him. As soon as the ship docked he rushed the type from the quays to the *Sentinel's* office in Pump Street. A short time later, a special edition rolled off the presses, two days ahead of other Irish newspapers with the Royal speech.

James Colhoun was the junior partner in setting up the *Sentinel* in 1829 and descendants of his owned the paper until 1958, when it was bought over by Morton Newspapers of Lurgan, run by John Morton and his son, Jim. In 1849, after the death of the widow of William Wallen, the first editor, Colhoun entered into partnership with a Derry solicitor called Thomas Chambers. A further twenty years later, Colhoun became the sole proprietor.

Change was in the air throughout Ireland; Bianconi started his horse-drawn car service in Clonmel, Co Tipperary, in 1815, giving Ireland its first proper public transport service. A tremendous advance was noted in Monaghan eight years later, when the first street lights, using gas, were turned on. Vast multitudes of townspeople came to see this historic event. From Monaghan, people could send cargo to Belfast, Belturbet and Clones by canal boat along the newly-opened Ulster Canal.

A farmer could buy a spade for 4/- or a pitchfork for 1/7$\frac{1}{2}$d. For amusement in the little leisure time available, people played hurling, football, foot racing and throwing the sledge. Horse racing and betting

William Trimble (left), founder of the Impartial Reporter, Enniskillen and his son, William Copeland Trimble.

were the privilege of the gentry, while the labouring classes amused themselves with cock-fights.

All the while, the advance of newspapers continued. In the West of Ireland, backward in newspaper production until now, the *Connaught Telegraph* was founded in 1828 by Lord Edward Cavendish, uncle of the Lord Frederick Cavendish murdered in the Phoenix Park in 1882. The *Connaught Telegraph* was not an entirely new newspaper, since Cavendish had bought up several other newspapers in the locality, enabling the *Telegraph* to trace its antecedents back to 1808. Despite his lordly background, Lord Cavendish openly criticised the landed gentry of Co Mayo, earning him their hostility and the approval of readers further down the social scale. The *Down Recorder* was launched in 1836. One of its technical innovations was its team of "news horses"; these beasts travelled daily to Newry, thirty miles from Downpatrick, to meet the cross-channel ferry boats. Very often, Thursday's news from Westminster was published in Saturday's *Down Recorder*, thanks to the horses in its employment.

The first issue of the *Sligo Champion* in June, 1836, announced that the paper intended to put down Grand Jury jobbing. The next issue of the paper reported great enthusiasm for the planned formation of a company to be called "The Great Central Irish Railway". Almost simultaneously with the launch of the *Champion* came news of a third Derry paper, the *Derry Standard*, set up by two liberals called McCarter and Walker.

Then came Daniel O'Connell's arrival in Sligo, in January, 1837, for a dinner presided over by Daniel Jones, the first Catholic High Sheriff of Co Sligo in over two centuries. Three months later, the *Champion* took great delight in reporting the discomfiture of Cavendish in Castlebar. Most Rev. Dr Finan, Bishop of Killala was awarded £400 damages and costs in an action for libel against the *Telegraph* over a series of letters in the paper. Cavendish was unable or unwilling to pay the award and the costs and was held prisoner in his own house for twelve months, until he sent a letter of apology to the Bishop and paid the damages.

The legal hazards of newspaper editing and publishing were many in those days. A bold and fearless journalist called Richard Price ran a newspaper called the *Carlow Morning Post;* he had planned to publish it in Dublin, but against his better judgment was persuaded to opt for Carlow. Despite its location, the paper exerted much influence. Just when Price decided to move himself and his newspaper back to Dublin,

A Corpus Christi procession in Drogheda passes the Drogheda Argus **office (next to Lyons' fancy bakery). John Boyle O'Reilly, the great Irish patriot, served his time with the** Argus.
–Peter J. Lyons

The elaborate masthead
of the Skibbereen Eagle.

he dropped dead. Ownership passed to his wife.

A new editor called Thomas H. Carroll took over briefly, showing a
little of Price's journalistic daring. Indeed, there was even a
contemporary suggestion that Carroll went to prison at least once and
was also fined for daring to publish his opinion on tithes. Despite
Carroll's willingness to run this fairly normal journalistic risk, the
paper was on the road to extinction. With a sense of desperation, the
title was changed to the *Leinster Independent,* but its existence became ever
more precarious. It collapsed, only to be revived after a lapse of some
twenty years as the *Carlow Post* by Thomas, a younger brother of
Richard Price. He published the paper in its original premises at Dublin
Street, Carlow; how the ghost of Richard Price must have hovered
over the editor's desk as the leaders were being written, a faint replica
of original fire. When Thomas Price passed on, so too did the remains
of the *Carlow Morning Post,* one of the more noted newspapers of the
early nineteenth century.

Kinsale, Co Cork, had its own newspaper, but like the *Carlow Morning
Post,* it too slid into extinction, but not oblivion. About 1832, a printer
called John William Potter, who had previously worked in Wales,
started his own printing works in Kinsale and published a short-lived
newspaper called the *Bee.* Five years later, Potter moved to Skibbereen,
where he helped his son, Eldon, found the *Skibbereen Eagle.*

Flight prompted the birth of the *Nenagh Guardian.* John Kempston
had run the *Clonmel Advertiser,* a Conservative organ, but he was so
harrassed by the Whig Government of the day that he decided to move
to Nenagh. Kempston reckoned tha he was safer in Nenagh than
Clonmel; in the three months after the *Nenagh Guardian* was first
published, in 1838, fifteen murders were committed in the Nenagh
area, but Kempston seemed to show less concern over this state of
lawlessness than with the attentions paid to him by the Whigs. His
paper survived and prospered, changing its policy, in line with so many

other newspapers, from pro-Conservative to pro-Sinn Fein after the 1916 Easter Rising, a quantum leap of the political imagination that seemed to pose less of a problem than might be imagined.

Also new that same year was another western paper, the *Tuam Herald.* Its founding editor was Jasper Kelly, whose son, Richard Jasper Kelly, was the next editor and cousin of Jasper Tully, the irascible owner and editor of the *Roscommon Herald.* Tuam's first newspaper had been founded in 1774, but the *Tuam Herald* proved much more durable — to the present day.

When the first issue of the *Northern Standard,* Monaghan, was rolling off the press in March, 1839, the list of prisoners awaiting trial in the town's jail at the Spring Assizes read as follows:

Murder, 13; Rape, 5; Lifting arms by might, 5; Robbery, 16; Base coin, 6; Forgery, 2; Assault, 2; Exposing child, 3; Picking Pockets, 3; Stealing Rosin, 2; Possession of stolen goods, 1; Vagrant, 1; Wounding, 1; Misdemeanour, 1; Pig Stealing, 1.

For a fleeting moment, just after the paper was founded, Charles Gavan Duffy was its editor, on the way to great editorial achievement with the *Nation.* Gavan Duffy, a native of Monaghan, already had much newspaper experience behind him. He arrived in Dublin as an

Irish News, **Belfast, editorial staff in 1895.**

Westmoreland Street, Dublin, in the days of electric trams and horse-drawn carts. On the right-hand side of the street can be seen The Irish Times' **clock.**
–Lawrence Collection

eighteen year old and promptly secured a job as a reporter on the *Morning Register,* the Catholic newspaper founded in 1824. His starting pay was £1 a week.

Gavan Duffy soon became his rapid climb upwards, moving from the reporters' desk to the sub-editors' desk. He survived a monumental row with Daniel O'Connell, who had accused him of attributing a speech to him that he had not made. Gavan Duffy stuck to his guns and insisted that his report was entirely accurate. At the next meeting of the Precursor Society in Dublin, O'Connell attacked both the *Morning Register* and its reporters. Gavan Duffy was in high dudgeon; he swept up his papers, grabbed the top hat customarily worn by reporters in those days and stalked out of the room. Three other reporters followed Duffy's example. Later, O'Connell became reconciled to the *Morning Register* and as his autobiography so delicately phrased it, "ceased abusing reporters".

Just after the launch of the *Northern Standard,* the editor, Arthur Wellington Holmes, was struck down by a fever. He was tortured by the impossibility of bringing out the paper, but Gavan Duffy arrived, had all the proofs revised and selected the current news. His arrival mitigated the local bitterness against the new Conservative newspaper and later when Gavan Duffy and the *Nation* were in the dock charged with sedition, the *Northern Standard* remained silent amid the general uproar of the Tory press. Fifty years later, by which time Sir Charles Gavan Duffy was Premier of Australia, on a visit home to Monaghan, he was reminded cordially of his brief editorship all those years before.

Gavan Duffy went on from the *Northern Standard* to become editor of the *Belfast Vindicator*. He recalled the day in 1841 when O'Connell came to Belfast, managing to evade the mobs who were roaming the city in search of him. The Orange gangs did not find O'Connell; as a substitute, they broke every pane of glass in the *Vindicator* office.

An incident shortly afterwards was to lead eventually to Gavan Duffy's part in founding the *Nation,* that seminal influence on nineteenth century journalism and politics. A man called Hughes was sentenced to death at Armagh Assizes, despite the fact that vital evidence was invalidated by several witnesses greatly respected for their integrity. During the period of Hughes' appeal, it was assumed that he would be merely confined to prison. Instead, he was hung.

In the *Belfast Vindicator,* Gavan Duffy assailed the judges for this legal assassination; in turn, the Attorney-General prosecuted the paper. The case was tried at the Four Courts, Dublin, and to answer his case, Gavan Duffy came to Dublin. One day that summer of 1842, he was walking through the Phoenix Park with Thomas Davis and John Dillon when the three men had a sudden notion to bring out a new national paper.

The new *Cork Examiner* was already enjoying growing success in Munster. It was first published in August, 1841, by John Francis Maguire, a supporter of O'Connell and for many years, an MP at Westminster. So caught up in politics did Maguire become that he soon handed over the running of the paper to Thomas Crosbie, who joined its staff in 1842 at the age of fifteen. Crosbie, a native of Ardfert, Co Kerry, had the great ability to make at any time "an off-hand speech which delighted and captivated his audience". Crosbie ran the paper while Maguire was the absent partner, away on political business. So proficient did Crosbie become that at one stage in his career, the London *Times* offered him 700 golden guineas a year as leader writer. When it was discovered that Crosbie was a Catholic, the offer was withdrawn. After the death of Maguire in 1872, Thomas Crosbie

Charles Gavan Duffy, one of the founders of the Nation **in 1842.**
–Film and Illustrations Library RTE

The last photograph taken of Charles Stewart Parnell, who died on October 6, 1891. Two modern Irish newspapers owe their origins to the great Parnell "split", the Irish Independent, **Dublin** and the Irish News, **Belfast, while he was a founding shareholder in the** Drogheda Independent.
–*Irish Independent*

emerged as the sole owner of the *Cork Examiner,* which remains to this day in the control of the Crosbie family. Later, they founded the *Evening Echo* (1894) and the *Cork Weekly Examiner* (1896).

A few short months after Gavan Duffy's historic walk through the Phoenix Park with Davis and Dillon, the *Nation* was born; Gavan Duffy was the "father" of this immensely influential newspaper at the age of twenty-six. Just as O'Connell had scoffed at Gavan Duffy nearly ten years previously over the latter's reporting in the *Morning Register,* so too did O'Connell pour lukewarm water on the first issue of the *Nation.* He smiled benignly at its enthusiasm, but believed it would soon burn itself out. The heady mixture of news, literary criticism, poetry, political and social comment appealed greatly to the reading public; soon, it was selling 10,000 copies an issue, even though it cost sixpence a copy, making it so expensive that most readers had to borrow it from newsvendors at a penny an hour.

For the next three years the *Nation* enjoyed unparalelled success; no newspaper had been launched so favourably since the *Dublin Evening Mail* twenty years previously. The editorial planning meeting on Saturday nights was a ferment of journalistic ideas; the inner sanctum of the five men at the core of the paper's success took turns to meet in each other's houses on Saturday nights and prepare the following week's issue. Charles Gavan Duffy, whose dyspetic look was evidence enough of his physical frailty, had great bursts of mental energy; he was a positive fountain of editorial inspiration. Not everything in the paper was accurate; sometimes, hyperbole got the better of the *Nation's* staff. When O'Connell made his entry into Mullingar in May, 1843, the *Nation* reported that the Monster Repeal meeting addressed by him was attended by 130,000 people. The *Westmeath Guardian and Longford News-Letter,* caustic as ever about the Catholic religion and Nationalist politics, provided excessive counter-balance by saying that O'Connell had "perhaps the most meagre procession that ever graced the public entry of a great man".

In 1845, two great personal tragedies afflicted the *Nation,* ensuring that never again would it scale the dominant heights it had reached in its early existence. In September, 1845, Thomas Davis, who had been so instrumental in the paper's success, died. That very same month, Gavan Duffy's first wife, a Miss McLoughlin from Belfast, also died. Duffy brought in an experienced journalist, Thomas D'Arcy McGee, but the *Nation* never recovered its initial exuberance. When Gavan Duffy sailed for Australia in 1855, partly for health reasons, he sold his interest in the paper, which, however, lingered on in emaciated form for another forty-five years. Today, all that remains of the great outpouring of patriotic energy that created the *Nation,* apart from the slumbering file copies, is a small metal plaque on the front wall of Independent House in Middle Abbey Street, Dublin, recording the fact that the site once housed the offices of the *Nation.*

Edward Walsh, who founded the Wexford People **in 1853.**

As the profoundly Nationalistic *Nation* was starting to burn out in Dublin, a new country newspaper had the same lordly start in life as Castlebar's *Connaught Telegraph.*

Gustavus George Tuite Dalton, stepson of the Marquis of Headford, was the first editor of the *Anglo-Celt,* brought into life in February, 1846 to campaign for the abolition of the Corn Laws and free trade. The owner of the newspaper was Sir James Young, MP and his wish was to talk of "the union of Saxon and Celt for political purposes, since we are not now distinct races. We are neither Saxons nor Celts — we are Anglo-Celts", he declared, hence the newspaper's strange title.

Meanwhile, in Dublin, one of the city's great journalistic characters was espousing a political line in diametrical opposition to that of Charles Gavan Duffy. Sheridan Le Fanu made no secret of his diehard High Tory views and soon after graduating from Trinity College, Dublin, and being called to the Irish Bar, he abandoned the legal profession for journalism. He bought the *Warder,* later to be subsumed into the *Sports Mail and Irish Weekly Mail,* run by the *Dublin Evening Mail,* and the *Protestant Guardian.* Later, Le Fanu bought into the *Statesman,* the *Dublin Evening Post* and the *Mail* itself; through the 1840s and 1850s, he was one of Dublin's most influential owners and editors, yet he died a

Robert Wilson, alias Barney Maglone, who was one of the most famous nineteenth century newspaper columnists, first with the Impartial Reporter, Enniskillen and then with the Belfast Morning News.

shaming and solitary death at the age of fifty-nine. In the last months of his life, he withdrew so completely that not even Charles Lever, his great friend and fellow writer, was permitted access to Le Fanu's Merrion Square house.

Also taking the opposite tack to Gavan Duffy was George Victor Robinson of Coleraine, Co Derry. He told his prospective readers: "I promise to keep aloof from angry politics."

Robinson sent out his prospectus for the *Coleraine Chronicle* from 24, Stone Row in the town. He stated that there was not a town in the United Kingdom of Great Britain and Ireland or indeed in the United States of America better situated than Coleraine for the wealth of its inhabitants. The first issue had twenty columns of type and sold for fourpence. Despite the names of surrounding towns and villages, such as Kilrush, Moneymore and Portrush incorporated into the title, there was scant local news.

The first issue of the paper in 1844 advertised the express mail coach service from Belfast to Londonderry; the journey took twelve hours, but there were suitable pauses for refreshment.

Samuel Troy, editor-in-chief of the Northern Newspaper Group, which comprises the *Coleraine Chronicle*, the *Northern Constitution* and the *Ballymena Guardian*, remembers that his grandfather was apprenticed to the young *Coleraine Chronicle*. He eventually graduated to foreman printer and then, since he had good shorthand and English, became chief reporter. Troy's great grandfather was the Town Crier in Coleraine; he too must have been a success in the communications business, because on October 1, 1831, he had been made a Freeman of Coleraine.

The 1840s also saw the emergence in print of one of the nineteenth century's richest characters, in an era when the by-line was scarcely invented. Barney Maglone was born in Dunfanaghy, Co Donegal, in 1820, son of a coastguard. His real name was Robert Andrew Wilson, but his *nom de plume* was to become known the length and breadth of Ireland.

Wilson began his working life as a schoolmaster in Co Leitrim (shades of Alec Newman of *The Irish Times*). In his spare time, he started writing and sent samples of his work to William Trimble, founder of the *Impartial Reporter* in Enniskilen. Trimble, presciently offered Wilson a job as a reporter and sub-editor. The young man quickly became known in Enniskillen, especially for his voluminous black cloak, so large that on one occasion, it was said to have sheltered five men from a fierce rain storm in Co Donegal.

The talented but unstable and eccentric journalist, Robert Wilson, soon began to lead a charmed double life on the *Impartial Reporter*. As Wilson, he reported faithfully the doings of the Town Commissioners, which he referred to as "The Boord". As Maglone, writing in the paper to his fictitious "cousin in Ammeriky", he sent up the Commissioners

in rotten fashion. He was a native Irish speaker and wrote in a strong Ulster dialect, so much so that the Barney Maglone writings today seem almost "stage Irish". But in his time, it was a good enough approximation of everyday speech.

Wilson alias Maglone left Trimble's employment on three occasions. A man called John Collum started a newspaper called the *Enniskillen Advertiser* and enticed Wilson to work for him, but some sources say that he failed to quite recapture the comic freshness he had shown on the *Impartial Reporter*.

Wilson also had an unhappy spell on the *Nation* in Dublin; Trimble found him out of work and destitute, wandering the streets of the city;

A group of cyclists from Dalkey take a break near Enniskerry, Co Wicklow in the spring of 1890.
–Guinness/Robert E. Booth

61

A Quaker soup kitchen
in Cork during the
Famine, 1846.
–*Illustrated London News*

without too much difficulty, he persuaded him to return to the scene of his earlier success, Enniskillen. Wilson's last journalistic stopover was at the *Belfast Morning News.*

Amid the mirth and merriment caused by Barney Maglone, disaster was about to strike. The most prominent newspaper headlines of 1846 carried the one word destined to strike fear into the entire population: "Famine".

With the failure of the potato crop that year, much of the peasant population of the west and south of Ireland was plunged into an endless cycle of death and despair. Although the *Cork Examiner* carried reports in 1846 and 1847 of soup kitchens being set up in the city by Quakers in an attempt to relieve some of the distress, more typical reports of the time were these from the *Impartial Reporter,* Enniskillen, in Co Fermanagh, a county which lost nearly a quarter of its population through the effects of the Famine:

"At Rossorry, within a mile of Enniskillen, a mother, unattended, carried the coffined body of her child and scraped a hole in which she covered it.

Two children named Phillips died in Enniskillen, unable to buy soup from the public soup kitchen.

Treasurer Hassard of Garden Hill devised a coffin with a false bottom which could be used an indefinite number of times.

(January 1847) . . . the workhouse at Enniskillen is besieged by hundreds of shivering poor claiming admission at the workhouse door."

Some newspapers had to suspend publication because of the economic havoc wrought by the Famine: the *Anglo-Celt* stopped publication in the summer of 1847. As the economy deteriorated in the spring of that year, subscriptions started falling off. At fivepence per issue, the paper was expensive and none but the well-to-do could afford it; with the inroads of the Famine, even they stopped paying their bills, including subscription renewals to the *Anglo-Celt*. By the time it stopped publication, it was down to four pages, but after a three month break, it was back on sale, under a new owner, editor and printer, one Zachariah Wallace.

Try as they did to cover the effects of the Famine, it was not the newspapers in Ireland that brought the enormity of the tragedy to the

Dublin has always had a taste for the elegant social life: this engraving was made in 1887 on the occasion of a ball at the Leinster Hall, during the visit to the city by Prince Albert Victor and the Prince of Wales.
–Lady of the House

Michael Davitt, founder of the Land League and a frequent visitor to the Western People office after the newspaper was founded in 1883.

world's attention. That task fell to journalists from outside the country; for the first time, Ireland was host to visiting pressmen on a large scale and their reports appeared in such publications as the *Illustrated London News* and the *Morning Chronicle*, London. A top reporter on the latter paper was William Howard Russell, born at Jobstown, Co Dublin, in 1820. At the age of twenty-six, Russell was sent back to his native country to report the Famine. It was the most nauseating reporting job he ever undertook in a long and distinguished career.

Many years later, Russell described his feelings on arriving back in Ireland in 1846: "In all my subsequent career, breakfasting, dining and supping 'full of horrors', in full tide of war, I never beheld sights so shocking as those which met my eyes on that famine tour."

He described the children he saw: "Their faces, limbs and bodies became covered with fine, long hair, their arms and legs dwindle and their bodies become enormously swollen. They were bestial to behold." The following decade, Russell put the experience gained in Ireland for the *Morning Chronicle* to good use on the London *Times*, when he covered the Crimean War. He revealed the atrocious conditions under which the British troops were fighting, without proper supplies and medical care. Whole regiments, he wrote, were being murdered slowly and in accordance with military discipline. Queen Victoria's husband, Albert, dismissed Russell as a "miserable scribbler". As a result of his reports, the coalition government of Lord Aberdeen fell, one of the few instances of a journalist bringing down a government single-handedly.

Just as foreign newsmen arrived in Ireland en masse for the first time, to cover the horrors of the Famine, so too did Irish newsmen start to make their mark abroad, again for the first time. Irish journalists, emigrating to America and American-born journalists with Irish antecedents, rose to positions of great influence in the American press.

In 1867, John Francis Maguire made an extensive American tour and reported: "There are not many journals in the United States which are not to a certain extent under the control or influence of Irishmen or the sons of Irishmen. They are edited, or part-edited, or sub-edited, or reported for by men of Irish birth or blood; and with the birth of and the blood came the sympathies for the old country and an unfriendly feeling towards its 'hereditary oppressor'."

After the abortive 1848 Rising, the most notable Irish journalist to flee to America was Thomas D'Arcy McGee, who had gone to Scotland to win recruits for the cause. The *Nation* itself was proscribed for a year after the rising failed.

A young Dublin art student, John Savage, who also took part in the rising, fled to New York, where within a week of his arrival, he joined the *New York Tribune* as a proof-reader. The paper's European correspondent was another revolutionary, Karl Marx.

McGee and Savage settled into Irish-American journalism, whose father-figure was Matthew Carey. By the age of nineteen, Carey had won fame in Dublin as a pamphleteer, editor and bookseller; he then left for America, started the *Pennsylvania Herald* and became the first journalist in America to report in full the proceedings of the new House of Assembly.

Perhaps the most famous of all Irish-American newspapers, the *Boston Pilot*, was established in 1836, the same year as the *Down Recorder* and the *Sligo Champion*. Just the year before the *Boston Pilot* was set up, the *Drogheda Argus* was born. In 1855, John Boyle O'Reilly, the great patriot and most notable of the Fenian journalists, started to serve his time in the printing office of the *Drogheda Argus*. He was eleven. Later, he joined the *Boston Pilot* as war correspondent and in 1876, ended up as its owner.

Not all the Irish-American journalists ended their careers in glory. James P. Casey founded the *San Francisco Sunday Times;* the editor of the rival *San Francisco Bulletin,* James King, made the fatal mistake in 1856 of running a story on how Casey had served a prison sentence in Sing-Sing for larceny. Casey shot King dead and for his troubles, was hung by vigilantes. He was, however, given a tremendous funeral by his Irish followers.

Ireland subsided into an exhausted uneasiness after the Famine; the population of the country had been virtually halved, from eight million to four million, through death and emigration in the aptly named "coffin" ships. Dublin continued its life of gaiety and watched with interest as building work progressed on the Dublin, Wicklow and Wexford railway line through the southern suburbs of the city, culminating in the gala opening of Harcourt Street railway station in 1854. The year previous saw a great change in the *Freeman's Journal;* Sir John Gray became its new owner. Although very much the Catholic establishment figure of his day, friend and political ally of Daniel O'Connell, variously Member of Parliament for Kilkenny and Lord Mayor of Dublin, he set the *Freeman* on a new path of constitutional nationalism and catholicity that took the newspaper to the heights of influence and prestige as the nineteenth century wore on. No sooner did the twentieth century dawn then the power of the *Freeman's Journal* began to flake away, until nothing remained of the once-monolithic structure.

The industrialised areas of the North of Ireland largely escaped the worst famine terrors endured by rural Ireland. As the newly-enriched magnates of the industrial revolution in Belfast read of the famine in their newspapers, they could have been dining on catastrophe in some far distant, foreign territory that had the grace and wisdom, nevertheless, to live under the benign influence of the Union Jack. The industrial development of the North ensured that some of the greatest developments in the newspapers of Ireland in the 1850s, 1860s and

The printing works of the Meath Chronicle at the close of the nineteenth century.
–Meath Chronicle

1870s took place in the North, helped by the advent, in 1846, of the American Richard Hoe's first rotary newspaper printing press. In 1852, the process for making page moulds from papier maché was invented, so that the printing type only had to be used once, instead of continually.

A remarkable technical advance took place at the *Coleraine Constitution* in 1852, the year that the energetic John McCombie took over as editor from the Rev David Dunlop. McCombie was determined to bring a new look to the paper, so he published its first-ever primitive picture, of a Father Gavazzi, a noted cleric of the day. The Belfast *News Letter* also printed pictures that year, using woodcuts that showed scenes from the Duke of Wellington's funeral.

It was pioneering for an Irish newspaper to publish this type of news

66

picture as opposed to the line drawings of people then in common use. McCombie's new device in Coleraine must have worked with the paper's readers, because by the following year, the newspaper was reporting a circulation of 1,000, a remarkable figure for any Irish provincial newspaper of the day.

As the New Year dawned in Belfast in 1855, two brothers from Antrim, Robert and Daniel Read, cast a critical look over the Belfast newspaper market.

When they arrived in Belfast from Antrim by stage coach over twenty years previously, they both started to serve printing apprenticeships in what was already the wealthiest city in Ireland. Some time after 1834, they succeeded a Mr Slimen in a small printing establishment in Crown Entry in central Belfast. During the next nineteen years or so, their most important productions were of Catholic prayer books and works of devotion. The brothers also printed an edition of the Douai Bible.

Founding manager of the Western People, **Ballina: Terence Devere.**

In that fateful year of 1855, the Belfast *News Letter* had changed from tri-weekly to daily; there were five other tri-weekly newspapers, including the *Northern Whig* (founded in 1824) and the *Belfast Mercury*.

The Reads decided to launch their own newspaper, the *Belfast Morning News* and recruited John Moore, well-known in Belfast literary and musical circles, who had worked on the *Mercury,* as editor of the new paper, which not alone was the first penny newspaper in Ireland, but which was also claimed as the first successful penny newspaper in the United Kingdom.

So successful was the new newspaper that by July, 1856, exactly a year after its launch, it was selling 7,080 copies an issue, far ahead of its next nearest rival, the *Northern Whig,* which had a circulation of 1,795. The *News Letter* was a miserly third, so it came as little surprise to the Reads when that paper made the following virulent attack:

"We warn the people of Belfast that the *Morning News* emanates from the Press which printed the Douai Bible. It has been established on the street hawking system and has as its readers, servants, street-sweepers, pedlars and pot-hogs."

The Reads were unperturbed: their newspaper was selling over 2,000 copies more than all the other Belfast papers put together and took the nastiness of the *News Letter* attack as sufficient proof of the success of their own newspaper. Imitation came from the *Northern Whig,* which went daily in 1858 following the example of both the *Morning News* and the *News Letter*.

The brothers were helped by Government moves that gave the Irish newspaper industry fresh impetus: in the early 1850s, tax on advertisements was finally abolished, along with stamp duty. After 1855, the only copies that had to be stamped were those going out by post.

In 1857, the first issue of the *Skibbereen Eagle* appeared; its founder was

Major Lawrence Knox, who started the present day Irish Times in 1859.

the eighteen year old Eldon Potter, who was also doubling at the time as an auctioneer. He was helped by his father, who had set up the unsuccessful *Bee* in Kinsale in the early 1830s. Eldon Potter began the paper as a monthly sideline, doing virtually everything himself, including writing the copy, setting it, printing it and selling the finished copies, no doubt with the expert assistance of his father, who had had thirty years' experience in the printing and bookbinding trades. The new *Eagle* was so successful that it soon progressed from a four page broadsheet, published monthly, to a weekly. Few copies of the early issues survive, but under the "Town Talk" banner, it detailed the social goings-on of the London scene, far removed from the desolate realities of west Cork, only beginning to recover from the ravages of the Famine. In the future lay Potter's sympathies for very limited Home Rule and more importantly, the remark he is said to have passed in the paper about the *Skibbereen Eagle* keeping its eye on the Czar of Russia.

Two early origins of the legend dated back to the first years of the *Skibbereen Eagle*. In one story, the *Eagle,* or the *Cork County Eagle and Munster Advertiser* to give it its full, later title, was said to have warned Lord Palmerston that it had got its eye both upon him and on the Emperor of Russia. Another version attributed the legend to Father O'Mahony, or "Father Prout" as he was better known, Rome correspondent of the London *Daily News* when Dickens was editor. "Fr Prout" mentioned a Cork editor who was fond of writing on foreign politics and who had his eye particularly on the Czar. The controversy about the *Skibbereen Eagle* probably started about 1860; it still rages today.

There may have been a smell of gunpowder hanging about the Irish press, as an author of the day, Alexander Andrews, remarked, but the times were heady. The final lifting of the duties gave a great impetus to the press. In 1855, Ireland had one hundred newspapers; by 1859, thirty more titles had been added. Just in that one year, 1859, ten new papers were set up, four of them in Dublin.

Yet of all those innumerable titles in 1859, only fifteen survive today, one of them *The Irish Times*.

A young twenty-three year old by name of Major Lawrence E. Knox decided to take his chances in the newspaper boom. He revived *The Irish Times,* first published between 1823 and 1825. On Tuesday, March 29, 1859, *The Irish Times* was launched from modest printing offices at 4, Lower Abbey Street, Dublin.

In the beginning, *The Irish Times* was a tri-weekly, priced at one penny, the second penny newspaper in Ireland. The yearly stamped subscription for the new paper was £2. All the type was set by hand and the paper was printed on a four-feeder flatbed press that could turn out up to 5,000 sheets an hour, printed on one side only. The printing of the second side had to be completed on a second machine.

The tops of the pages of *The Irish Times'* pages (technically called the "bolts") were uncut. Most of the early readers of the paper had their own butlers and it was the duty of the latter to cut the bolts of the paper before placing it upon the master's breakfast table.

The leading article in the first issue of *The Irish Times* saw an ever-increasing proportion of the country's population disgusted at the arts of the demagogues and sincerely desirous of laying aside their mutual prejudices and labouring together for the good of their common country. An advertiser in the first issue urged readers to send a stamped addressed envelope to him: "I will put you in possession of a SECRET by means of which you can win the affection of as many of the opposite sex as your heart may desire. This is suitable for either sex . . . whether of prepossessing appearance or otherwise." The great plunge baths at Beresford Place, plentifully supplied with clear sea water, were advertised as being open for the summer season.

Todd Burns, the drapery firm, was the leading pioneer of newspaper advertising in Ireland, including in the new *Irish Times.* It spaced out the letterpress of its advertisements; most advertisers of the time did not even illustrate their advertisements. Todd Burns even issued advertising Christmas cards with horse omnibus timetables; in one 1859 issue of the *Dublin Local Advertiser,* the firm gave away a map of the war area of Sardinia, Austrian Lombardy and the northern Italian states. In 1859, a pill manufacturer, Thomas Holloway, spent up to £40,000 on newspaper advertising, including Ireland, for his wares.

Just as the newly-founded *Daily Telegraph* in London proved an immensely popular daily newspaper, selling 30,000 copies an issue, so did the immediate success of Major Knox's new Conservative organ persuade him to go daily. Just fourteen weeks after his launching of *The Irish Times,* the paper started coming out on a daily basis. For his printing staff, there was much extra work in bringing out the two daily editions, for each four page edition carried three times as much wordage as the four page editions customary during the Emergency period eighty years later. Fervour of a different kind had attended the *Coleraine Chronicle,* enjoying great popularity under its energetic editor, John McCombie. In the summer of 1859, during the great Ulster religious revival, two compositors and another member of staff from the *Coleraine Chronicle* attended a prayer meeting in the town; they were so overcome by emotion that for some weeks afterwards, they were unfit for work. The week the trio did arrive back at the works, triumphant in their new-found religious beliefs and cured of their sins, they had such a solemnising effect upon the rest of the workforce that with the staunch approval of editor McCombie and the owners of the paper, daily prayer meetings were held on the premises. The *Coleraine Chronicle* was published late that week.

A Scotsman called Andrew Dunlop, who for fifteen years was the only sub-editor on the *Dublin Daily Express* and who then worked for many years on *The Irish Times,* recalled how in the early 1860s, news of the day, sent by telegraph, occupied no more than couple of columns on a Dublin morning paper. Scissors and paste, usually to the detriment of the London *Times*, filled much of the remaining space.

Dunlop recalled how a sub-editor on a Dublin morning paper would have to organise his couple of columns of telegraphic news, his columns of clippings, a column length summary of the day's news and the leading article-single-handedly and between 8 p.m. and 4 a.m. That represented forty-eight columns of type, filling up to eight pages!

Other journalistic feats of that distant era seem equally prodigious by modern standards. Surprisingly, few reporters had any shorthand, yet Maurice Lenihan, owner and editor of the *Limerick Reporter and Tipperary Vindicator*, which died with his death in 1895, used to boast that he could listen to a long speech, or even several speeches, and on returning to his office, write a verbatim report from memory.

The *Freeman's Journal*, under the energetic control of Sir John Gray, even hired special trains on which it sent its reporters to important country events, enabling them to return to Dublin with their copy as quickly as possible.

Reporters working on *The Irish Times* and the other newspapers provided some news copy; their efforts were augmented by the newly-laid submarine telegraph cable that ran on the seabed from Portpatrick in south-west Scotland to Donaghadee in Co Down. The Magnetic Telegraph Company acted as a news agency and sent condensed news copy to the various newspapers. In Cork, Thomas Crosbie of the *Cork Examiner* had his own ingenious system in operation; ships from America were met as they touched Cork Harbour. The American newspapers they carried were collected and brought into Cork, from where Crosbie had the news telegraphed to London a day ahead of anyone else. His system worked well until the telegraph was extended to Kerry and rivals started meeting the American ships off the coast of that county.

Apart from its own foreign news copy, the Magnetic Telegraph Company also summarised the contents of the London newspapers for the benefit of the newspaper owners and editors in Ireland.

Such was the interest in news around 1860 that one wine and spirit merchant in Capel Street, Dublin, posted hourly news telegrams in his shop window. Towards the end of the 1860s, when the Post Office nationalised the telegraph system, news coverage became much more organised. Andrew Dunlop recalled that the Post Office, after its takeover, would send half a dozen telegraph operators out with reporters on major country assignments and send back masses of copy at tremendous speed. The *Irish People* was set up in 1863 as the authentic voice of Fenianism. Curiously, it remained unnoticed by the government for two years.

Major Knox was moving quickly, too. The size of *The Irish Times'* presses hampered expansion of the paper, yet within less than two years of its launch, it squeezed in more copy by running eight 28″

columns to the page. By 1867, Knox managed to fit in nine columns to the page, by which time, the need for a new and bigger press was urgent. New Year's Day, 1870, saw the paper doubled in size to eight pages daily and by 1873, covering the Home Rule conference, the newspaper was up to twelve pages.

Suspensions of publication and sudden death marked the progress of the *Anglo-Celt* in Cavan. In the midst of the great newspaper boom of the late 1850s, the newspaper had to suspend publication because of its feeble financial state. Towards the end of 1864, Martin Kirwan, who started as a typesetter with the paper, took it over and relaunched it after a six year gap in publication. In early February, 1865, just seven weeks after the launch, Kirwan collapsed and died. Salvation was at hand; John O'Hanlon (grandfather of the present owners, Edward and Willie O'Hanlon) bought over the paper. He had been works director of the *Dublin Evening Post* at its Suffolk Street offices; he married a Miss O'Farrell, whose brother, E. French O'Farrell, was the editor, before he fell out with the owner and went off to become assistant editor of the *Daily Telegraph*. O'Farrell's departure must have inspired O'Hanlon to buy his own newspaper.

Similarly strong convictions about the newspaper business were felt in Belfast, when the two Baird brothers decided to start the *Belfast Evening Telegraph*. The rise to prosperity of two brothers in printing, William Savage Baird and his younger brother, George Courtenay Baird, was a remarkable duplication of that enjoyed some years previously by the two Read brothers, founders of the *Belfast Morning News*. The Bairds had joined the small Ulster Printing Company in

Staff of the Impartial Reporter, Enniskillen, **pictured in the printing works, about 1900. Centre is James Preston, forehand.**
–*Impartial Reporter*

The old Theatre Royal, Dublin, burning down in February, 1880. The rebuilt theatre was subsequently demolished to make way for the present day Hawkins House.

Arthur Street, in the centre of Belfast. William became overseer in the jobbing printing department, while George became overseer of the *Daily Mercury*, the Whig Party newspaper that was printed by the firm. In 1861, the Ulster Printing Company went into voluntary liquidation; the two brothers raised £450 and bought the business, although the newspaper plant was bought by an unnamed group that wanted to kill off the *Daily Mercury*.

The two brothers bided their time until 1868, in which year an independent Orangeman called William Johnston was fighting for one of the two Belfast seats at Westminster. The year before, Johnston had been sent to jail for a month for leading a 15,000 strong Orange Twelfth procession from Newtownards to Bangor in defiance of a Government ban. His participation in the election raised vast interest — he went on to win — and when the Baird brothers brought out an election broadsheet, they were pleasantly surprised to find that it sold out.

They decided to enter the newspaper business as soon as possible and announced that on January 1, 1870, the *Belfast Daily Mail* would be launched into an unsuspecting world. The dream remained stillborn, but a few months later, a combination of the Franco-Prussian war and the serious illness of George Baird produced the *Belfast Telegraph*.

George went to Rostrevor to recuperate and while he was there, followed closely the progress of the war; the French army of nearly 100,000 was quick to surrender to the German troops. Then followed the four months siege of Paris, when the inhabitants were reduced to eating rats. "If the war should take any time, there will be a great interest taken at all hours of the day for news. If a halfpenny paper were issued as near three in the afternoon as possible, it should command a good sale," wrote a wise George to his brother, adding a postscript: "I would call it the *Belfast Evening Telegraph.*"

Just two years earlier, the Post Office had taken over the private telegraph service and this meant an enormous improvement in news from abroad. George's idea of same-day reporting of the war news from France could become reality; William was equally enamoured of the idea, so it was with no little shock that three weeks after receiving the prophetic letter from his brother, when he was walking through the Ormeau Park on his way to church with his fifteen year old son Robert, he saw a streamer poster:

"New evening paper will appear shortly".

It was to be called the *Evening Press* and publication date was announced as the following Tuesday week, September 6. That gave the Bairds exactly nine days in which to organise their own evening paper. That Sunday evening, they sat down to plan the first issue of the *Belfast Evening Telegraph* and decided to launch it on the Thursday of that week, so as to come out well in advance of the proposed *Evening Press.* The "Evening" of the Baird's title was subsequently dropped.

On the Monday morning, William Baird and his son Robert were up at 5 a.m. By six, William was busy setting type in the Arthur Street office and a poster was printed stating that the paper would appear on the Thursday, price half a penny. Between the Monday morning and 3.45 p.m. on the Thursday, all sections of the new newspaper, including editorial and advertisement departments, were set up. The first leading article proclaimed that the paper carried reports of business at Belfast Town Council and the Police Court that morning. Among the news items of that first four page issue was one condemning the dangerous Belfast practice of stone throwing.

The proposed *Evening Press* did appear, but only briefly. An *Evening Press* newspaper was published in Dublin in 1932 and again in 1954, the second offspring of the *Irish Press.* That third *Evening Press* survives to the present day.

A few months after the Bairds had successfully propelled the *Belfast Evening Telegraph* into the world, another and rather more well-established Belfast newspaper was also on the move. The *Northern Whig* shifted from its original offices in Callendar Street to the Old Corn Exchange in Victoria Street. The pace of Belfast newspaper life was hotting up, almost by the day. In August ,1872, just under two years since the launch of the *Belfast Evening Telegraph,* the *Belfast Morning News* went daily; its circulation had risen to 12,500 and the pressures on its four pages were immense. The paper was perused all over the northern part of Ireland, as far away as Glenties, Longford and Sligo.

The very week the *Morning News* went daily, the air was thick with the noise of riots. Following attacks on the August 15 Hibernian processions, street battles erupted in Belfast, Lurgan and Portadown. The paper had no shortage of copy for its first daily issues. The change to a daily paper went smoothly enough, under the watchful eye of the publication's new editor, an Englishman called J. P. Swann. He occupied the editorial chair for a mere two years; curiously enough, the *Irish News,* which was the successor to the *Morning News,* also had an English editor, Sydney Redwood, who joined at the end of the 1920s.

Under Swann, the most brilliant member of the editorial staff was Robert A. Wilson, otherwise known as Barney Maglone, the "Bud" Bossence of his time. He had come to the *Morning News* in 1865, bringing both his cloak and his "letters to his cousin in Ammeriky". These proved so popular with the readership that the days they appeared, circulation went up by five to six thousand copies. He also had a strong sympathy for the working people of the North; during the ferocious labour troubles of the Belfast mills in 1874, he did not merely support the mill workers' cause in the paper. When he met groups of the unemployed work people, he ladled out silver to them from the small hoard he possessed. After a lifetime of toiling in the journalistic vineyard, Wilson became editor of the *Belfast Morning News* in 1874 at the age of fifty-four.

His new-found status lasted for just fourteen months. In August, 1875, he was found dying in his garret, where he lived alone, at Wesley Place, Belfast. He had been to Dublin to celebrate (rather too successfully) the centenary of O'Connell's birth and had managed to travel back, in very poor health, to Belfast. A short while before, he had written a poem for the paper, forecasting how the worms would feast on his corpse. With macabre taste, he wrote: "He was mighty poor picking, Maglone!"

Bram Stoker, creator of Gothic horror stories, would have relished the morbid reflections of poor, drunken Robert A. Wilson alias Barney Maglone. As Wilson was coming to an intoxicated end in Belfast, Stoker was just starting his newspaper career in Dublin.

Recipient of an honours degree in science from Trinity College, Dublin, Stoker went to work at Dublin Castle. His job there was uninspiring, the theatre the real love of his life, so when the great actor Henry Irving came to Dublin, Stoker resolved not only to give Irving the notice he felt he deserved, but also to advance his own career. In the Dublin newspapers of the early 1870s, theatre notices were little more than pieces of copy in return for advertisements, or at best, notices of an actor's benefit night. Stoker wrote to Dr Henry Maunsell, editor and joint owner of the *Dublin Mail* and suggested

proper drama reviews. Maunsell agreed at once, but would not pay Stoker. Normally, the theatre notices were done as "extras" by members of the staff and Maunsell had no wish to offend them.

Stoker, however, was quite content with the arrangement and shortly afterwards, paid sixpence for a gallery seat, then wrote a critique of the very first production at the new Gaiety Theatre, Dublin, "She Stoops to Conquer", at the end of November, 1871. Maunsell, who was said to have visited to composing room of his paper only once in his lifetime, when he had to be shown the way back, soon gave Stoker his head in another important production advance. Stoker came back from the theatre, wrote his review and had it set only a couple of hours after the curtain had come down. The appearance of the review in the next day's *Morning Mail* paper was a real revolution for the Dublin newspapers.

A revolution of real prosperity was about to engulf *The Irish Times*. In 1873, Major Knox, its founder, died at the young age of thirty-seven. Ownership of the paper passed to his widow and it was from her some months later that Sir John Arnott bought the publication for £35,000. The paper was then making £7,000 a year and he reckoned that he

First issue of the Roscommon Herald, **1859.**

The facade of the
Brown Thomas store in
Grafton Street, Dublin,
during the nineteenth
century. This engraving
was made about 1878,
when the store was
already popular. Just
across the street,
another famous Dublin
shop, Switzers, was
offering merchandise to
the better-off classes of
the city.
–Brown Thomas

could boost its earnings to £10,000 a year within two to three years.
The *Freeman's Journal* sneered at the purchase and announced that it had
cost the Baronet "a few thousand pounds".

Arnott described himself as a staunch supporter of law and order
and Imperial Government in Ireland. He announced that he would
conduct the opposition to disintegrating forces (i.e. the Nationalists) in
a fair and straightforward spirit, without the shadow of offence to any
person or party in public life. After he had bought *The Irish Times*, he
went to Belfast and won control of the *Northern Whig*; he is said to have
disposed of his interest in the latter paper after it published a scurrilous
attack on Catholics in the North.

He was born in Fife in Scotland in 1814 and came to Cork to seek his
fortune, an ambition in which he succeeded most bountifully. Among

his many achievements in Ireland, where he had arrived without influence or wealth at the age of twenty-one, were the opening of the Cork Park racecourse in 1861 and his vanquishing of the bakers of Limerick in 1884. He opened his own bakery in the city and bread prices, which he had considered too high, soon tumbled. This remarkable man was also Lord Mayor of Cork, Liberal MP for Kinsale, 1859-1861 and founder of Arnott's department store in Henry Street, Dublin.

Sir John Arnott came to a Dublin that was remarkably self-assured. A tram went from the city centre to Rathmines every $3^1/_2$ minutes, a letter could be posted for one penny in one Dublin suburb, Rathmines, up to 6.15 p.m. for delivery within two hours in the neighbouring suburb of Ranelagh. A cup of tea in a city centre hotel cost three pence, while *The Irish Times* at one penny was unchanged in price since its establishment nearly twenty years previously. At 4 p.m. sharp every weekday, for many years, copy for classified advertisements, as well as the cash and any monies for subscriptions, was taken from the two main *Irish Times'* depots, one in Rathmines, the other at Parson's book shop at Baggot Street bridge, and put aboard trams for conveyance to the newspaper's office.

On March 18, 1875, *The Irish Times* reported rather regally that on St Patrick's Day (the day before), "there had been a marked absence of drunkenness by crowds enjoying the day off."

After Sir John Arnott's take-over of *The Irish Times* in 1873, the next major newspaper development in Ireland happened in the North, in Coleraine, where the *Coleraine Constitution and Northern Counties Advertiser* (now the *Northern Constitution*) was launched in December, 1875. The town's first penny newspaper, it had eight pages in its first issue. A steam press churned out 700 copies an hour; a crowd of young boys from the Ragged School in Coleraine pressed their noses to the dirty windows of the *Constitution* printing works in New Row. When the first issue appeared, it was quickly sold out and in the initial years of the newspaper's existence, it sold about 1,700 copies an issue. Seven years after its launch, the owners decided to expand its area of operation from Coleraine and district to the whole northern part of the North of Ireland.

A similar explosion of newspaper interest was about to take place in the South of Ireland, events that were charged with historical interest and importance. Until the late 1870s, few newspapers in Ireland, with notable exceptions like the *Nation,* were Nationalist in sentiment. Tory, or at best Whig, politics occupied the minds of most newspaper owners and editors; *The Irish Times* was an unwavering Conservative organ and the *Freeman's Journal* had only recently escaped from the Castle cloud. But various events moved the received opinions of the newspaper world more in the Nationalist direction: various Education Acts had helped improve literacy, spreading interest in reading newspapers to other sections of society than the gentry and the middle classes, who were almost entirely Protestant.

The growth of the Nationalist Party at Westminster also helped create a new public opinion. So the establishment of Nationalist newspapers, often with the help of the Catholic clergy, starting around 1880, in opposition to the well-entrenched Unionist publications, marked a major watershed in the history of Irish newspaper publishing. Not that newspapers were entirely serious; at this time, Ennis even had a humorous weekly newspaper called the *Man in the Moon;* when its owner was evicted by a landlord called Bernard Greene, the paper ran lampoons about a "Barney Emerald". The *Tuam Herald* had a master printer called William Hawthorne, who in turn had a pet parrot. Every so often, the bird croaked out: "Haw wants copy." One contributor in particular on the *Herald* had no difficulty in keeping up with the parrot's demands: John Glynn, who had come to the paper from the rival *Tuam News.* Glynn, a part-time teacher and a great Irish scholar, made his name as a court reporter for the *Tuam Herald.* The standard of his reporting was so high that his copy was occasionally quoted in the London *Times.*

One of the first of the new breed of nationalist papers was the *Leinster Leader,* set up in Naas, Co Kildare, in August, 1880. It was badly managed and within the first few years of its existence, heavy debts threatened to sink the newspaper. James Carew, MP for North Kildare, bought out the paper in 1886 for £1,100. He went on to set up the *Irish Daily Independent,* forerunner of the present *Irish Independent.* The year that the *Leinster Leader* first appeared, there were seventeen daily newspapers in Ireland.

Terms of imprisonment and libel actions were the two great and ever-present threats faced by the new Nationalist press. The *Midland Tribune* nearly sank under the threat of a libel action. Three priests were the promoters of the *Midland Tribune* in Birr, which took on the powerful Unionist *King's County Chronicle* (in an historical twist, Jimmy Fanning, later owner of the *Tribune,* bought over the *Chronicle* in 1948, but it closed down in 1963).

Birr's three Catholic curates raised just over £1,000 to fund the *Midland Tribune* in 1881; this compared with the £1,500 capital the *Leinster Leader* enjoyed the previous year. The first editor of the *Tribune* was John St George Joyce, a native of New York; he had worked on the *Galway Press,* founded in 1860 and said to have been the first home rule paper in Ireland.

When Joyce joined the *Midland Tribune* in September, 1881, he was aged thirty-five, old enough to have had any radical ideas knocked out of him, according to one biographical source. He stayed with the new paper for three years, moving on to be editor of the *Leinster Leader.* At Christmas, 1884, readers of the *Tribune* had an unexpected bonus from

Joyce, for a free copy of his book, *The King's County, Epitome of its History*, was included with every copy of the newspaper.

Joyce managed to avoid libel actions, but his successor as editor, John Powell, who had joined the new paper as manager in 1881 and who remained as editor until his death in 1901, was in court eight times in connection with libel and intimidation charges. Through the 1880s, the paper made little or no money and in 1888, a Roscrea magistrate and Orangeman called Lloyd Vaughan sued the paper for £1,000. Fortunately, a Protestant jury in Maryborough, now Portlaoise, found that his reputation was worth only £50. Of as much interest to Powell and his staff at the *Tribune* was the progress being made at the *King's County Chronicle,* for it started publishing photographs. It was one of the very first newspapers in the South of Ireland to run regular photographs, yet the *Tribune* did not follow suit until 1898.

Not that progress was confined to the new newspapers supporting

The first offices of the Belfast Telegraph, **in Arthur Street.**
–Belfast Telegraph

the Nationalist Party: there was much life left in the Unionist press. *The Irish Times* was doing so well under the vigorous control of Sir John Arnott that over the weekend of March 18 and 19, 1882, the paper moved from Lower Abbey Street to its new premises at 31 Westmoreland Street, with its famous old-style front office, which captured much of the atmosphere of a rambling country drapery shop. Many legends were to be created in that front office!

Less than two months after *The Irish Times* moved into its new premises on the other side of the Liffey, one of the most dreadful events of nineteenth century Ireland created a sensation that was amply reflected in the newspapers of the time. Lord Frederick Cavendish (nephew of the liberally-minded founder of the *Connaught Telegraph*) had arrived in Dublin earlier in the day on Saturday, May 6, 1882. He was walking to the Viceroy's Lodge in the Phoenix Park with his Under-Secretary, Thomas Burke, when they were set upon by a gang known as the Invincibles and armed with knives. The murder of the two top men in the British administration in Ireland sent waves of revulsion around Ireland and Britain. The sub-editors, the comps and the printers at *The Irish Times* toiled unexpectedly through that Saturday night to bring out a special Sunday edition of the paper, one of the very few in its early history. Later, *The Irish Times,* following the example of the *Freeman's Journal* and the *Irish Independent,* brought out a weekly newspaper which in 1941 was transmogrified into the *Times Pictorial.*

In September, 1882, the eighteen year old John P. Hayden, who had been working on his brother's newspaper, the *Roscommon Messenger,* launched his own newspaper, the *Westmeath Examiner.* Exactly a year later, yet another nationally-inclined newspaper, the *Carlow Nationalist* (later the *Nationalist and Leinster Times*), started publication. Two brothers, John and Patrick Conlan, worked on the *Leinster Leader* in its early months; Patrick had been well trained on the *Dublin Evening Post* by E. French O'Farrell, a relative by marriage. When the Nationalist Party offered to fund a new paper in Carlow, then dominated by such pro-Unionist titles as the *Leinster Express* and the *Carlow Sentinel,* they jumped at the chance. The Carlow *Nationalist* was reasonably well-funded, although when Patrick Conlan, grandfather of Liam Bergin, present managing director and editor, died at the early age of fifty-six, there was only £47 in the kitty, just enough to pay a week's wages to the staff.

Conlan died of TB, thought to have been aggravated by the two months he spent in Kilkenny Jail. The paper was a supporter of the activities of the Land League; at least one letter written by Michael Davitt to his great friend Patrick Conlan, apologising for not being able to attend a meeting, still exists.

When a series of evictions took place in Co Laois, then known as Queen's County, Conlan defied the ban on publishing a resolution passed at a public meeting and was thrown into prison. When he emerged, triumphant but in poor health, the Nationalists presented him with scrolls of welcome. Strangely enough, considering his political views, Conlan also published a newspaper called the *Curragh News,* with the sub-title of "sporting, military and general newspaper". In Liam Bergin's remembrance, it could not have published more than five hundred copies and lasted for a few months in 1891.

Also in 1882, the *Belfast Morning News* changed hands after Daniel Read, one of the co-founders died. Edmund Dwyer Gray, son of Sir John Gray, who took over the *Freeman's Journal* in 1853 and who himself took over the *Freeman* on the death of his father in 1875, bought over the Belfast newspaper.

One man owned two of the great newspapers of Ireland, one in Belfast, the other in Dublin, a feat never before achieved and never since repeated. Under Gray's ownership, the ties between the two papers were close, so much so that Robert Wilson's successor as the *Belfast Morning News'* editor, William J. McDowell, went to the same position on the *Freeman's Journal* in 1883. Gray himself prospered mightily, becoming Lord Mayor of Dublin in 1880 and MP for the Stephen's Green division in 1885.

Soon after buying the *Morning News,* Gray bought up the *Ulster Examiner,* founded in 1868 with the explicit backing of the Catholic Bishop of Down and Connor, Dr Dorrian. Gray moved both papers to new offices at Commercial Court, off Lower Donegall Street, just yards from where the Belfast *News Letter's* offices now stand.

For two years after McDowell went to Dublin, Patrick Kelly was editor of the *Morning News;* he in turn was succeeded by Daniel McAleese, who had been editor of the *Ulster Examiner* for the previous ten years. McAleese was as well-known a journalist in the North of Ireland as Barney Maglone, yet he had followed his father into the family's shoe making business in Randalstown, Co Antrim, before going to Glasgow, where he was active in the shoe makers' trade union. After returning to Belfast, McAleese went into journalism and served the mandatory "training" of many journalists then — jail.

In 1874, McAleese criticised the severity of sentences on two Catholics who had been convicted of taking part in the riots of that year. His outspokenness in the public prints earned him four months in jail.

McAleese came out of jail to find his place filled, so he took himself off to Monaghan to establish the *People's Advocate,* but when Kelly went off to Dublin, Gray appointed McAleese editor of the *Morning News.*

1883 also saw the setting up of the *Western People* in Ballina, Co. Mayo. Like the other new paper of that time, it had a distinctly Catholic and Nationalist hue. The prospectus said that the limited liability company to run it would be formed from the clergy and merchants of Ballina. From this holy alliance came the determination to act as "trusty

Front page of the first issue of the Limerick Leader, **1889.**

sentinels and champions of the rights of the people of the West". It founders were local school teacher, Patrick G. Smyth (who was the first editor) and local printer, Terence Devere. Local rumour later suggested that Devere had "gentrified" his name from Devers, to improve its sound, once he had risen from journeyman printer to newspaper manager. Starting off with a magnificent and impressive canon of Nationalist beliefs, the *Western People* campaigned strongly on behalf of land reform. One of its first subscribers was Michael Davitt, a native of Co Mayo and founder of the Land League, who not only expressed full approval for Smyth's editorial line, but became one of the first subscribers to the paper shortly after it was launched. "The handsome appearance and national tone of your first two numbers will I hope ensure a career of long life and prosperity for your paper," he wrote on July 23, 1883. Two later, he wrote to Smyth again hoping that the paper would rescue the county from the stigma which attaches to its journalism from the ruffianism of some of its "Editors" of unsavoury reputation. In later years, the *Western People* became the stepping-off point for such journalists as Tom Hennigan *(Evening Herald)*, Mick Finlan and John Healy *(Irish Times)*, Brian Barrett *(Irish Independent)*, Jim McGuire *(Kerryman, Western Journal, Drogheda Independent)* and Tom Courell *(Connaught Telegraph)*. Few other provincial papers were to provide such a training ground for the Dublin nationals.

Journalists are usually ready to help one another when in difficulties. That tradition of camaraderie stretches back into the nineteenth century; from then, one of the most extraordinary tales of that journalistic friendship across political and religious divides is told by Eddie Sherry, for long Clones correspondent of the *Impartial Reporter,*

82

Enniskillen and told to him in turn by his father, James, who also worked for that newspaper for many years. In 1883, thousands of Orangemen converged on Rosslea, Co Fermanagh, to protest at the Home Rule meeting, which was to be addressed by Tim Healy. William Copeland Trimble, of the *Impartial Reporter*, arrived by side car, accompanied by Dan McAleese of the nationalist Monaghan *Advocate*. Trimble was resplendent in top hat and morning suit and on his way to Rosslea, the Orange crowd mistook him for Healy. He was pulled from the side car and given a very rough mauling. Only the intervention of McAleese saved the Unionist Trimble from a very nasty fate.

June, 1884, saw a newspaper come and go with remarkable rapidity in Clonmel. Edward McDonald, a printer of Abbey Street in the town, who had worked as foreman printer of the *Tipperary Free Press*, decided to start his own paper, the single sheet *Clonmel Advertiser*. It was the fourth newspaper of this title and only survived for a few months. Nothing more is heard of him — he has disappeared into the oblivion reserved exclusively for expired journalists and newspaper owners.

Serious legal action faced Clonmel's next new newspaper the *Tipperary Nationalist*, which did stay the course and is still published. The paper had been founded under that name in Thurles in 1881; it lasted two years, but was revived in Clonmel in 1886. Its first editor, a Dublin journalist called J. G. McSweeney, was disposed of in quick order and John O'Mahony was recruited from the *Skibbereen Eagle*. The paper was pro-Unionist, but O'Mahony was pro-Nationalist and for reporting details of land agitation in the Clonmel area, was thrown into jail. To make matters worse, a Crown Solicitor called George Bolton brought an action against the paper; a Belfast jury awarded £10,000 damages.

In Belfast, the Unionist *Belfast Evening Telegraph* was making such splendid progress that in 1886, it was able to build brand new premises, still occupied today, in Royal Avenue. They housed two new Victory presses, which brought the paper's production capacity up to 40,000 copies an hour. Anti-Home Rule riots raged in the streets of Belfast as the Baird family moved the newspaper from Arthur Street to Royal Avenue. Sixty-two year old William Savage Baird, one of the founders of the paper, went out on riot duty with the police and troops in his capacity as Justice of the Peace. He collapsed, dying a few days later, little more than three weeks after the newspaper he had helped found had moved into its new Royal Avenue building, visible sign of rapidly growing prosperity, which even a rival evening newspaper, the *Ulster Echo* (1874-1916) could not dent.

William's son, Robert, took over at the age of thirty-one. At his desk before eight o'clock every morning, he drove the paper to new heights. The *Ballymena Weekly Telegraph* started up in 1887, the *Larne Times* in 1891. Two years later, the Bairds had an overdraft of exactly £1,300. From all over the North of Ireland, people were pouring into Belfast to work in the satanic mills and in the shipyards, living in endless rows of back-to-back houses. In twenty years, Belfast's population grew by 100,000 — many more readers for the *Belfast Telegraph*.

Finally, in the great procession of new pro-Nationalist newspapers during the 1880s came the *Limerick Leader* and the *Southern Star*, Skibbereen. The *Leader's* founding owner was one Jeremiah Buckley, a barrister, accountant and dedicated Parnellite. A picture of Parnell always hung in the premises of the newspaper, in silent tribute to the great leader.

Unlike the new *Coleraine Constitution*, with its powerful steam press, the *Limerick Leader* was not ready with its own press for the launch on August 9, 1889. Jeremiah Buckley went across to the other side of Patrick Street, to the printing firm of Macnamara and Brunards, where he had a confession to make to a printer called Nolan:

"We thought we would be ready for our first publication, but our machinery is not ready. Is there any chance you could do the printing of the *Limerick Leader?*"

Although Macnamara and Brunards was principally a music printing firm, the staff set to and printed the first issue of the paper. Helping was a twenty year old in the final year of his apprenticeship as a compositor/machine man, John Gleeson, father of the celebrated Willie Gleeson, long-time compositor at the *Limerick Leader* and grandfather of Joe Gleeson, present day general manager. The first issue rolled off the presses to a nationalist tune: "This journal is intended to be the faithful organ of the National party in the counties of Limerick and Clare. This Journal humbly takes its place as the latest recruit in the hard-fighting ranks of Irish National Journalism."

Strangely enough, the first circulation manager of the *Limerick Leader* was an Englishman called Harry Watson, who worked on the paper from three weeks before it opened until his death in the 1950s. A jolly, rotund man, he never married and lived in "digs" in Limerick for most of his life. Full of sound advice for everyone but himself, he never got round to marrying the girl with whom he was in love.

That year, in June, the papers were filled with news of the train crash just outside Armagh. A train carrying Sunday school excursionists to Warrenpoint failed to make the gradient. It ran back, crashing into another train. Eighty-one people, mostly children, were killed; the Belfast *News Letter* described the "Heartrending and painful scenes."

Three local priests played an important role in founding the *Southern Star* in Skibbereen, Co. Cork, as the Catholic and nationalist paper in opposition to the *Skibbereen Eagle*. They held seventy out of the 200 shares. The Protestant *Eagle* had finally nagged and needled local Nationalists and clergy into forming a newspaper that would represent *their* viewpoint in west Cork. The *Southern Star* did this, moderately, although the founding editor and owner, John O'Sullivan, was bought out for £150 just two years later. It was O'Sullivan's second paper; for some years previously, he had managed the *Tuam Herald*.

After O'Sullivan left Skibbereen to go to Waterford, where he founded the *Waterford Star* (among his competitors there was the twice weekly *Waterford Standard*, a Unionist publication, printed on pink paper), the local parish priest, Rev John O'Leary, continued in the chair. A resolution was passed by the board:

"Nothing shall appear in the *Southern Star*, either editorially or by way of report in any way disparaging to the Bishop."

Parnell and the scandal of his involvement with O'Shea's wife, Katherine, ending in the notorious divorce case, occupied the waking hours of most Irish newspaper editors and journalists through the 1880s and into the following decade. In some cases, Parnell was actually responsible for helping to set up newspapers, such as the *Drogheda Independent* in 1884: he was one of the founding shareholders. Parnell's estate at Avondale was much in the news; the newspapers in Co Wicklow blossomed.

The *Wicklow Newsletter* was the Conservative organ of the county and inimical to Parnell; the *Wicklow People* started in 1883 as a National League broadsheet. Three years later, it went "commercial" and as a nationally minded newspaper for the county, gave the pro-Parnell viewpoint in not-so-delicate counter-balance to the *Wicklow Newsletter*.

The *Freeman's Journal* idolised Parnell; for years, its unashamedly pro-Parnell stance meant uncritical support by one of the country's most influential publications for the leader of the Irish Party. In 1875, the *Freeman's Journal*, in the heyday of its influence, described Parnell as "above all, an Irishman, Irish bred, Irish born, racy of the soil, knowing its (Ireland's) history, devoted to its interests".

In December, 1890, the Irish Party split after the O'Shea divorce case. So too did the press in Ireland, with effects that can be seen to the present day. The *Freeman's Journal* abandoned Parnell with consummate alacrity; after the divorce scandal, its previous years of hero worship fell away like dross. Jasper Tully of the *Roscommon Herald* was also anti-Parnell, but he made some of the most perceptive newspaper comments about Parnell's fall from grace: "He was our own and his faults were those that we ourselves had made for him. If he was ambitious and self-willed, it was because the Irish race spoiled and petted him as they never petted a leader before. "Jasper Tully, the radical of 1879, was turning conservative en route to quite extraordinarily wilful eccentricity.

In Carlow, the *Nationalist* set up in 1883 was proving successful as the town's first nationally inclined newspaper. It too was soon dragged into the Parnellite controversy: Liam Bergin, the present managing director and editor, remembers that his grandfather, Patrick Conlan, one of the two brothers who set up the paper, went against Parnell. For his trouble, he was sometimes chased through the streets by crowds who were pro-Parnell and who made their feelings known by throwing stones at the newspaper's editor. Yet, the newspaper set up about 1890 to propagate the Parnell cause, the *Carlow Vindicator*, only lasted a relatively short time, collapsing in 1898. Ted Kenny of RTE recalls his grandfather the owner, a Dublin printer called Matthew Walker; full of ambitious hopes, Walker went down to Carlow to set up the paper, which he ran virtually single-handed. So high did feelings run in the town over the Parnell issue that Kenny's mother was refused confirmation in Carlow because of her father's attitude to Parnell.

The deep divisions had their odd moments of relief, such as on December 10, 1890, when an anti-Parnellite crowd seized the Dublin offices of the *United Ireland,* the newspaper owned by Parnell. Parnell led the second crowd, the pro-Parnell one, that stormed the building and recaptured it for its owner. Later, Parnell told Katherine O'Shea that it was splendid fun. He wished that he could burgle his own premises every day! He married Katherine the following June, but within less than a year of the *United Ireland* being ransacked by the mob, Parnell was dead.

His death produced an astonishing scoop for the editor of the *Nation*, a man called Sullivan. A stoneman named Lane burst into his office and said that Parnell was dead: Sullivan questioned him and it turned out that a telegram delivery boy, who knew Lane and rushed to tell him, had taken the telegram with the news to the Dublin house of Parnell's sister. He heard someone in the house shriek that Parnell was dead. Sullivan wrote his copy, had it set, the presses made ready and the posters printed. Then he wired the paper's London correspondent to interview Parnell: within ninety minutes, back came the reply: "Parnell is dead". Sullivan had checked in his Dublin club, where among the crowd was a young Tim Harrington, later editor of the *Irish Independent*. No-one else had heard the news, so when Sullivan had the confirmation from London, he had the presses started and soon a tremendous scoop was being noised abroad by the newsboys.

In the North of Ireland, the most far-reaching effects of the Parnellite drama were to be found at the *Belfast Morning News*, founded by the Read brothers in 1855.

The *Morning News* continued to be a successful paper, along with the *Belfast Evening Telegraph,* during the 1870s. But change was coming upon the *Belfast Morning News* more quickly than anyone could imagine.

Gray, its owner, died in 1888 and the paper was sold to a limited liability company, although his son became controller of the Gray family interests in both the *Morning News* and the *Freeman's Journal*. By this time, Daniel McAleese, the editor, had departed once more for Monaghan, where he became MP for the county's Northern division. Patrick Kelly returned to the *Morning News* editorship and precipitated the crisis that split the Belfast newspaper world.

The Evening Press

Vol. III.—No. 520.   BELFAST, THURSDAY, MAY 15, 1873.   [One Halfpenny

The young Gray had even less interest in newspaper management than his father and when the Parnell crisis broke, he was travelling in the southern Pacific. When the O'Shea divorce case was tried in November, 1890, Kelly, the editor of the *Belfast Morning News,* took the anti-Parnell line. The *Freeman's Journal* was still clinging, if tenuously, to the pro-Parnell side.

Kelly must have had few illusions about the danger he was putting himself in and sure enough, when Gray arrived back from his Pacific travels and heard about Kelly's leader vigorously denouncing Parnell, he travelled to Belfast without further delay and sacked Kelly.

Catholic virtue was on Kelly's side and the Hierarchy was strong in its efforts to found a new morning newspaper in Belfast, the *Irish News,* that would adequately reflect its views on the Parnell case. The plan was warmly welcomed by the Bishop of Down and Connor, Dr McAllister, and taken up by two energetic priests of the diocese, Father Hamill and Dr Marner. They were among the directors who attended the first board meeting of the new newspaper company, on May 4, 1891. Its first chairman was appointed soon afterwards, Edward Hughes, owner of Hughes' Bakery in Belfast and renowned for his baps.

That summer, shares were sold throughout the North of Ireland: priests and publicans were among the most active supporters of the canvass for shares and a total of 11,000 £1 shares were sold. Offices were acquired in Upper Donegall Street and on August 15, 1891, the first issue of the anti-Parnell newspaper, the *Irish News,* appeared on the streets of Belfast.

Kelly was the editor; among the staff were T. J. Hanna, later

The Evening Press, **Belfast — an early rival to the** Belfast Telegraph.

James Donohue, who joined the Anglo-Celt, Cavan, as an apprentice compositor in 1898 and who retired in 1967. During his sixty-nine years' service, he set an estimated 200 million words of type, earning him a place in the Guinness Book of Records. **He was reputed never to have read the copy he was setting.**
–*Anglo-Celt*

secretary to John Redmond, leader of the Nationalist Party and a nineteen year old Joe Devlin, later to become the scourge of the House of Commons. The *Irish News* was off to a flying start, with the active support of the Hierarchy. *Morning News'* reporters were barred from meetings of the Nationalist Party; throughout the North, Catholics and Nationalists were urged to boycott the *Belfast Morning News* and support the *Irish News*.

In those intimidating circumstances, the *Morning News* could not last for long and by July of the following year (1892), the owners of the paper, who also owned the *Freeman's Journal,* sold out to the *Irish News,* which was only eleven months in existence. The *Irish Weekly News* took over the *Ulster Examiner*.

On the morning of August 29, 1892, there was no *Morning News* on sale. No public announcement was made: the *Irish News* simply incorporated the *Belfast Morning News* title into its masthead. By 1896, the *Irish News* had recouped the enormous losses it had incurred during the time the *Belfast Morning News* was being bled to death.

The sale of the *Belfast Morning news* in 1892 also marked the beginning of the end for the *Freeman's Journal,* which was sold to Thomas Sexton that year. The two newspapers had been caught the wrong side of

Parnell. The *Freeman's* death came by degrees, hastened by the wrecking of its offices at Easter, 1916 and during the War of Independence. It finally expired in 1924, waked in Bowes' pub in Fleet Street, Dublin.

While the passions and the factions ripped undying divisions in the Nationalist press of Ireland during the downfall, the owners of the Unionist newspapers, amused, amassed fat earnings. By the early 1890s, Sir John Arnott was said to have been earning £30,000 a year from *The Irish Times,* an enormous sum of money, worth up to £1½ million by today's debased monetary standards. *The Irish Times* was said to be the most prosperous newspaper in Ireland.

In 1893, the Home Rule Bill for Ireland was introduced for the second time at Westminster. North of Ireland interest was acute: the day that Gladstone rose in the Commons to move the Bill, the *Belfast Telegraph's* eighth and final edition went on the streets at 10.05 p.m. That day, the newspaper had its biggest ever sale: 70,250 copies.

The *Telegraph* itself was strongly opposed to the measure, but it gleaned its last measure of gold from the Bill when the division was held. At 1 a.m. the following morning, a Home Rule Special was brought out and promptly sold nearly 5,000 copies.

Robert Baird, energetic as ever, listened carefully to complaints from his editorial staff that the football reports in the Saturday night sixth edition were crowding out the rest of the news. This was 1894 and so insistent were the complaints that Baird decided to launch the *Ulster Saturday Night.* Two years later, it spread to Dublin, in competition with the weekly sports paper produced by the *Freeman's Journal.* However, Baird's new sports paper was so well received in Dublin that the anomalous titled was changed to *Ireland's Saturday Night.* So it remains to the present day; strangely enough, the catchphrases, "The Ulster" and the "Pink", the latter because of its paper, lingered on among readers and newsagents for many a long year after 1896.

1893 also saw the establishment of the *Mayo News* in Westport. The newspaper was owned by brother Pat and Willie Doris, who encouraged their compositors to take up journalism as well. Willie had been a reporter on the *Nationalist and Leinster Times,* Carlow. To do so, the local "spoiled priest" taught them small Latin and less Greek, as well as shorthand. John Burke, who worked on the paper as a journeyman printer and who also founded the Burke family dynasty that runs the *Tuam Herald* to this day, edited a journal which chronicled the events of Westport and district. On Sunday afternoons, Burke and the other printing workers, together with their girl friends, repaired to Westport House demesne, where they read poetry, both their own and that of other contemporary poets published elsewhere.

In Dublin, the *Sunday World* was launched in 1895, but it only lasted for just over two years. A name change to *New Sunday World* failed to improved its life expectancy and it only produced eighteen issues under the new banner before folding its tents. Not until 1973 was another newspaper of the same name launched. 1897 saw the founding of the last two great nationalist newspapers to be set up in Ireland during the nineteenth century, the *Longford Leader* and the *Meath Chronicle*. In Longford, Jasper Tully was indirectly responsible for the gestation of the *Longford Leader*. The year was 1884 and J. P. Farrell was nineteen; already he had a great interest in books and reading and when he had a letter from Jasper Tully inviting him to become Longford correspondent of the *Roscommon Herald*, Farrell was only too glad to accept the challenge. In later years, Farrell and Tully continued their association through the stormy years of land league agitation, but for the moment, Farrell had been started down the newspaper road.

That very same year (1884), Farrell had written in his diary: "A new idea had occurred to me and to-day I proceeded to put it in motion, viz., the starting of a National Journal in Longford. Such a thing has long been wanting and this whole day I was occupied writing a circular to twelve of the leading men of the town."In the event, he had to wait for thirteen years before the *Longford Leader* came to fruition. As early as

Banks of Linotypes at the old Dublin Evening Mail **offices in Parliament Street.**

1890, when he was only twenty-five, Farrell made the first of four trips to jail for his land agitation activities. His last imprisonment, at Kilmainham in 1910, was probably responsible for bringing on the illness that killed him in 1921.

The first issue of the *Longford Leader*, in August, 1897, advertised a visiting firm of American dentists, who did sets of teeth for £2. Heavy pigs were 18/- to 22/- a cwt and nurses were offered jobs at the Longford Union for a wage of £30 a year. The paper was an immediate success, yet Farrell continued to throw himself with equal energy into his political work. He was MP first for North Longford and then West Cavan. In one typical week, Farrell travelled 1500 miles in Britain, spoke at four public meetings, asked thirteen question in the House of Commons, dealt with constituents' letters and wrote a 1500 word article.

Yet he was inordinately proud of the fact that his paper was one of the very first in Ireland to put in a Linotype machine when it opened for business in 1897. The Linotype, which set lines of characters in

metal, had been introduced just five years previously and marked the end of dependence on slow hand setting. Not long after the Linotype went into the *Longford Leader,* the O'Hanlon family, greatly daring, introduced one at the *Anglo-Celt.* A young apprentice, James Donohue, was willing to work the new machine, unlike his fellow compositors. By the time he retired in 1967, he had set 200 million words, enough to ensure a place in the *Guinness Book of Records.* In Navan, Tom Daly and his brother Michael started the *Meath Chronicle* in May, 1897; it was something of a gamble, although Tom Daly had much experience on various provincial newspapers; at the time, Meath was a sparsely populated county and Navan was the only town in the county of any size. Then the Dalys espoused the Nationalist cause, which was still not altogether popular or profitable.

By the time Farrell and the Daly brothers were bringing their newspaper projects to fruition, in Longford and Navan respectively, an equal energetic MP was becoming active in Dublin's frenetic newspaper world. Thomas Sexton, son of a Waterford Royal Irish Constabulary man, and one-time Lord Mayor of Dublin, had bought the *Freeman's Journal* in 1892, following "quarrels among the Nationalists", as one contemporary journal so delicately phrased the matter. Sexton, like that other great journalist of the time, Edmund Downey, who later owned the *Waterford News,* had been born and brought up in that city. Such was the power conjured up by the *Freeman's Journal* name, even after the Parnell "split", that Sexton was invited to join the board of such other concerns as the Great Southern Railways, one of the most prestigious directorships to which any businessman could aspire.

Even in the nineteenth century, Dublin had a well-used expression: "Write to the *Mail* about it". The phrase was used to good advantage by James Johnson Abraham, a native of Coleraine. While studying at Trinity College, Dublin, at the end of the century, he wrote a letter to the *Mail* asking whether daughters should have latchkeys. He signed it "Mother of Seven". Then came the reply from "Revolting Daughter". The controversy went on for weeks-shades of that started by Brian O'Nolan and Niall Sheridan in *The Irish Times* forty years later. This controversy too had its desired effect: the young Abraham was called into the *Mail* office and handed £5 for his efforts, which financed a monumental wine party in Trinity and helped launch Abraham on his journalistic and literary career.

The *Dublin Evening Mail* scored a remarkable communications triumph, just as the century was drawing to its close. In July, 1898, details of a regatta organised by the Royal St George Yacht Club at Kingstown (now Dun Laoghaire) were reported to the newspaper by wireless telegraphy, a "first" for a newspaper anywhere in the world. Marconi transmitted over 700 reports of the regatta to a station in the harbour master's house. The messages were printed in Morse code,

Masthead of the Sunday World — not the present version, but that published in Dublin between 1895 and 1897.

decoded and sent by telephone to the *Dublin Evening Mail*, sponsors of the event. The idea had come from the paper's yachting correspondent, whoch had previously found that heavy fog had held up his copy by several days.

By the time the *Mail* scored its communications triumph, there was already a sense of change in the air, marking the turning of one century into the next. On March 28, 1898, Sir John Arnott, owner of *The Irish Times,* died at his home in Montenotte, Cork. At his funeral, one of the hundreds of wreaths, many from the highest in the land, came from H. L. Tivy of the *Dublin Evening Mail.* Arnott's title passed to his son, Lt Col John Alex Arnott, but within two years, major changes were under way at the paper. Little did Tivy of the *Mail* foresee that within a similarly short period of time, change would be on the way at his paper. The century was turning and so too was the tide of fortune in the newspaper world; it had begun with post horses, stage coaches, canal boats and hand-set and printed newspapers and ended with steam trains, vast ocean-going liners, wireless telegraphy and newspapers set by great banks of Linotype machines and printed on rotary presses that could churn out tens of thousands of copies an hour.

CHAPTER IV

William Martin Murphy, a humane man-1900-1915

Gentlemen's suits dry cleaned and tailor pressed in three days. 4s 6d. Prescott's Dye Works, telephone 571.
DUBLIN EVENING MAIL, 1900

Christmas cakes. Ornamented 3s 6d – 30s. Harrisons, 17 Henry Street, 29 Westmoreland Street.
DUBLIN EVENING MAIL, 1902

The new year of 1900 started on a splendidly triumphant note for the loyalists of Ireland: Queen Victoria arrived in Dublin on her State visit in April. Vast crowds thronged the thoroughfares along the course of her route from the landing place at Kingstown into the centre of Dublin. The Union flags were out along the Liffey and the great crowds cheered themselves hoarse. Sixteen years later, almost to the very month, public opinion in the city had changed devastatingly and irrevocably in the aftermath of the Easter Rising.

But this April, for the Queen of the Empire upon which the sun never set, the welcome from her loyal Irish subjects was thunderingly fervent. The *Dublin Evening Mail* reported with an unpardonable typographical error that "the Queen has pissed over O'Connell Bridge".

This same year, the Guinness family bought into the *Mail* and its associated newspapers. Lord Ardilaun, a senior member of the brewing family, took control of the *Mail,* along with the *Dublin Daily Express,* the *Morning Mail* and the weekly *Warder,* for the same reasons as Sheridan Le Fanu sixty years previously. Home Rule for Ireland was perceived as a threat to the well-being of the country, Nationalism was deemed treasonable, so for the second time in just over half a century, financial interest was taken in these papers for the propagation of High Tory views.

Change was also in the air at *The Irish Times*. After the death of Sir John Arnott in 1898, the paper had been held in trust for two years. In 1900, the same year as the Guinness take-over of the *Dublin Evening Mail* newspapers, *The Irish Times* was taken over by a limited company of the same name, with a share capital of £450,000. As chairman of the new company and trustee of the Arnott estate, which controlled nearly all the Ordinary shares, Sir John Arnott, second baronet and son of the first Sir John Arnott, commanded the fortunes of *The Irish Times* until his death in 1940.

Nine months after her visit to Dublin, Queen Victoria died. One Tuesday evening in January, 1901, her death was announced in the *Dublin Evening Mail*. A painter called Richard T. Moynan was walking up

Scenes along the Liffey during Queen Victoria's visit to Dublin in April, 1900. She died nine months later. The *Dublin Evening Mail*, in a famous typographical error, noted that Her Majesty had "pissed over O'Connell Bridge".

95

William Copeland Trimble, son of the Impartial Reporter, **Enniskillen.**

The late "Master Bertie" Trimble of the Impartial Reporter **singing and accompanying himself at the piano.**

Grafton Street that day when he saw a newsboy place the poster announcing the Queen's death at the corner of Trinity College. Then the boy placed a bunch of violets beside the poster. Moynan was so touched that he went straight to his studio and painted the scene exactly as he saw it. In 1936, John Maguire, then chairman of Brown Thomas & Co, presented the painting to the *Mail* owners. For many years after, it hung in the public office of the newspaper.

One winter's day that year was equally remarkable for a young Trinity student, William Egbert Trimble, known to all as "Master Bertie" and son of William Copeland Trimble of the *Impartial Reporter,* Enniskillen. Home on holiday from TCD, Master Bertie found himself at the top of a ladder, helping to try and put out the fire which was to destroy the printing works. Shortly before the fire broke out, a ghost-like figure passed some of the men at work on the paper and disappeared into the furnace; it was regarded as a bad omen. For the next six months, the paper had to be printed in Omagh. The type was locked up in galleys, which were trundled down to the railway station. Long after midnight, the printed sheets would arrive back from Omagh, be loaded back onto the cart, taken to the Trimble house and folded by hand. Young "Master Bertie", together with his cousin Charlie Trimble, later associated with the *Armagh Guardian,* helped in this arduous work. Six months later, the *Impartial Reporter's* printing plant was back in action and "Master Bertie" abandoned his law studies at Trinity College in favour of the family newspaper.

The Queen may have died, but the Empire was still at the height of its crystalline prestige and glory. Dublin resounded to the music of military bands, whose colours and trumpeting enlivened the streets of poor quarters near the various barracks. At the Castle, the city's largely Protestant social elite danced away the evening hours before being whisked away in grand carriages to homes in Donnybrook and Rathgar. When Sir John and Lady Arnott held a grand ball of their own at their Dublin town house, 68 Merrion Square, in February, 1902, the attendance included royalty.

Their country house was at Doneraile Court, Co Cork; periodic residence there, away from the toils of the city, was announced in the social columns of *The Irish Times,* which after all, Sir John did own.

The working classes were not forgotten. In April, 1901, Sir John

Cars at the top of Grafton Street, before the Great War.

William Martin Murphy, founder of Independent Newspapers.
–Irish Independent

Arnott opened the Dining Hall at 23A High Street, Dublin, so that people of little wealth could enjoy a good three course dinner consisting of soup, joint and sweets between the hours of 12 noon and 3 p.m. The cost was fourpence. The following year, Sir John was present at a meeting of the Irish Regiments' Widows and Orphans' Fund, organised by *The Irish Times*. It was reported that 278 widows and 436 orphans had been helped to date. 1902 also saw the inauguration of the Phoenix Park racecourse, in which the Arnott family had a close interest for many subsequent years.

Reporting on the racecourse debut was Charles Frith of the *Irish Field*, itself soon victim of Sir John Arnott's own empire building. This racing paper had been in circulation for some thirty years, but was bankrupt when Arnott bought it for £250. He sent a week's notice of the transaction to his fellow directors, who were understandably aggrieved. It was said that he had bought a bankrupt concern without seeing a properly audited account, yet within three months of its purchase, the *Irish Field* had made a profit for *The Irish Times* of £100.

A brand new name in publishing in 1902 was *Ireland's Own*, born in Wexford as an offspring of the Wexford *People* newspaper. The Walsh family who owned the latter paper believed that there was a market in Ireland for an Irish publication to counteract the flood of English magazines, such as *Tit Bits* and *John O'London's Weekly*, into the country. The homely chat, comment and stories like "Kitty the hare", of *Ireland's Own*, a throwback to simpler times, continues its popularity to this day. So dedicated have been the staff of *Ireland's Own* that one early editor,

(opposite page) Front page of the first issue of the Irish Independent, **1905.**

98

FOOTBALLS,
HOCKEY, HURLEY,
GOLF, BADMINTON.

CATALOGUE FREE.

J. W. ELVERY & Co.,
ELEPHANT HOUSE,
DUBLIN and CORK.
Also at 31 Conduit street, London.

Irish Independent

TELEGRAMS, "INDEPENDENT," DUBLIN.

B. M'GLADE,
BILL POSTER,
POSTER PAINTER,
AND
STREET ADVERTISER.
OFFICE
42 Middle Abbey street, Dublin.

VOL. 14. NO. 1.　　　DUBLIN, MONDAY, JANUARY 2, 1905.　　　PRICE ONE HALFPENNY.

BIRTHS, MARRIAGES, AND DEATHS.

BIRTHS.
MARRIAGES.
DEATHS.
IN MEMORIAM.

WALLER,
41 and 48 DEVILLE STREET,
MERRION SQUARE.

M. McCARTER,
WHOLESALE
COFFIN
MANUFACTURER,
ACADEMY STREET, Belfast.

AN IMPORTANT MATTER!

BEECHAM'S
PILLS

Nervous System,
Cleanse the Bowels,
and Liver,

WORTH A GUINEA A BOX.

PREPARED ONLY BY
THOMAS BEECHAM,
ST HELEN'S, Lancashire.

CANTWELL & McDONALD'S
DUBLIN POT STILL
WHISKEYS

WHOLESALE FROM
CANTWELL & McDONALD,
Wellington Quay, Dublin.

SPECIAL NOTICES.

Alexander Findlay & Co.,
190 Gt. Brunswick Street, Dublin.

Telegrams: "FINDLAY, DUBLIN."

GRAHAM'S CELEBRATED HAT WARE-
HOUSE—Special Variety and Quality.
GRAFTON STREET.

ABBEY LOAN and
DISCOUNT BANK.

110 MIDDLE ABBEY ST., DUBLIN

FINEST TURKISH BATHS IN IRELAND.
HAMMAM, SACKVILLE STREET, DUBLIN.

BUSINESS NOTICES.

The Finest
Whisky
IN THE
WORLD

DWD

Ask for it
and get it.

IF YOU WANT A LOAN
PROMPTLY AND PRIVATELY,
APPLY TO

THE NORTHERN COUNTIES LOAN
AND DISCOUNT BANK

46 Donegall street, Belfast.

Best Portland Cement.

EX-DEPOTS DUBLIN & BELFAST.

CASEBOURNE & Co., Ltd., A)
HAVERTON-ON TEES.

James P. Corry & Co., Ltd.,
CEMENT DEPARTMENT, BELFAST.
Agents Wanted

ROYAL

J. REILLY & SON,
TAILORS,
4 COLLEGE GREEN.

CASH ACCOMMODATION
THE CITY AND COUNTY
LOAN AND DISCOUNT BANK.

CASH ON OWN SECURITY.

Richmond Bros.,
Poultry, Fish,　Fruiterers and
and Game　Green Grocers,
Merchants,
53 North Circular Rd., Phibsborough,
DUBLIN.

HAIRDRESSING.

KANE'S Hairdressing Establishment

21 WICKLOW STREET
AND
19 LOWER O'CONNELL ST.

BUSINESS NOTICES.

McBIRNEY & CO.'S
GREAT
Winter Sale
Commences To-Day.

In addition to their own Immense Stock of
High-class and Fashionable Goods
the Firm have been fortunate in securing
for Cash large quantities of Goods at

Big Discounts off Manufacturers' Prices

all of which have been Marked Down to
a Minimum Price.

CATALOGUES ON APPLICATION.　ORDERS BY POST RECEIVE PROMPT ATTENTION.

McBirney & Co., Ltd., Aston's Quay, Dublin.

A Happy New Year

To all Cyclists, to whom we extend
a cordial invitation to see our 1905

SWIFT
CYCLES

At 34, DAME STREET, DUBLIN, and
86, ROYAL AVENUE, BELFAST.

PRICES from £7 15s. up.　ART CATALOGUE
on Application.

THE OLDEST CYCLE MANUFACTURERS
IN THE WORLD.

D. TOWELL,
THE GREAT IRISH TAILOR.

Upr. Sackville St., DUBLIN.

Irish Bedding and Furniture Factory

CLUNE'S
LIMERICK-MANUFACTURED ROLL
CUT & BAR PLUGS,
LIMERICK FLAKES,
ETC.

All Selected from the Best
Virginia Leaf.

O'Dea & Co., 42 & 43 Stafford Street,
DUBLIN.

Only the Trade supplied.

THE NEW FRENCH REMEDY.
THERAPION.

HOTELS.

THE BEST THAT MONEY CAN BUY.
GALWAY OYSTERS,
FINEST HOME MEATS,
AND VEGETABLES.
NOW OPEN.
LARCHET'S LUNCHEON BAR,
11 COLLEGE GREEN, DUBLIN.

JACOB'S HOTEL,
30 THOMAS STREET.
An Inexpensive House,
MOST SUITABLE FOR TOURISTS.

PUBLIC NOTICES.

PUBLIC NOTICE

Messrs. M. CROWLEY & Co.,
Chartered Accountants,
18 COLLEGE GREEN, DUBLIN.

CHAMBER OF COMMERCE, DUBLIN.
NOTICE OF MEETING.

JOHN MOONEY,
Hon. Secretary.

DUBLIN PHYSICAL CULTURE SOCIETY.
CORPORATION NEW HALL,
TARA STREET BATHS

ROBERT HALL, ETC.
Hon. Secretary.

NOTICE OF PARTNERSHIP.

COUNTY DUBLIN COUNTY COUNCIL.
BOROUGH FUNDS (IRELAND) ACT, 1888.

LEGAL NOTICES.

STATUTORY NOTICE TO CREDITORS.

ELECTION ADDRESS.

TO THE ELECTORS OF THE SOUTH CITY
WARD.

BUSINESS NOTICES.

Kinahan's
CELEBRATED
L.L. Whisky
Known to the Public for over 100 Years.

ESTABLISHED 1779.

KINAHAN & Co., Ltd.,
Dublin & London.

Very Large Holders of
Fine Old
Wines.

Established
Over
100
YEARS.

CATHOLIC NOTICES.

GRAND DRAWING OF PRIZES
IN AID OF
LINDEN CONVALESCENT HOME,
13th DECEMBER, 1904.

SOCIETY OF ST. VINCENT DE PAUL.
CONFERENCE OF ST. PATRICK, ST. KEVIN'S,
HARRINGTON STREET.

PUBLICATIONS.

New Publications of M. H. Gill
and Son, Limited.

M. H. GILL & SON, LIMITED
PUBLISHERS, DUBLIN.

EDUCATION.

DEPARTMENT OF AGRICULTURE AND
TECHNICAL INSTRUCTION FOR
IRELAND
THE IRISH TRAINING SCHOOL
OF DOMESTIC ECONOMY

ST JOSEPH'S SEMINARY,
CLONDALKIN.

RAILWAYS.

GREAT NORTHERN RAILWAY (IRELAND).
BALDOYLE RACES,
MONDAY, JANUARY 2nd, 1905

SHIPPING.

DUBLIN & LIVERPOOL SCREW
STEAM PACKET COMPANY.

FUEL.

THOMAS HEITON & Co.,
LIMITED.

DUBLIN GENERAL STEAM
SHIPPING COMPANY
D'OLIER STREET 15.

WALLACE BROS. LIMITED

Booth Brothers,
UPPER STEPHEN STREET DUBLIN.

GLEESON, O'DEA & Co.,
HOUSE FURNISHING and
BUILDERS IRONMONGERS,
KITCHEN LAMPS, STOVES & GRATES,
21 & 2 CHRISTCHURCH PLACE
and 2 WERBURGH STREET, DUBLIN.

99

crippled by rheumatism and unable to climb the steps to his office of his own accord, had to be carried into work.

The young James Joyce was having his own set of problems with *The Irish Times*. He wrote an article called "The Motor Derby", about the Gordon Bennett race, and sent the copy in to the paper: nothing happened. At the end of February, 1903, he wrote to John Stanislaus Joyce, his father, complaining: "I see that nothing has been done at *The Irish Times* — nothing will be done with its manager who is, I think, very heavy in the head." Eventually, the article was published in early April that year, thanks to the intervention of an *Irish Times'* reporter, Matthew O'Hara, who was a friend of Joyce's father. Joyce got on better with the *Dublin Daily Express* and its editor, Ernest Longworth; he published four reviews by Joyce in 1903.

At the *Freeman's Journal*, Thomas Sexton maintained with scrupulous precision a list of "banned" MPs, whose names were on no account to be mentioned in its pages. He copied his "black list" system from James Gordon Bennett II, the owner of the New York *Herald*, whose other claim to fame was that he had urinated into the grand piano at his fiancée's house during their betrothal party. Sexton's editorial staff dared not dissent from his *dicta*. He was the man, with his middling and muddling ways, who did most to run the *Freeman's Journal* into the ground, apart from the British guns of 1916 and the mob that wrecked its premises in 1922.

Further blackguardism erupted in Limerick in 1904, when the *Limerick Leader* reported a speech made by Fr. Creagh, a Redemptorist priest, on the Jews of that city. He was reported as saying: "Stand at a prominent Jew's house at night and you will be surprised to see the number and class of people who are going in and out, under the cover of shawls, to pay the Jew his usury. "He then went on to accuse the Limerick Jews of preferring to buy their goods from other Jews across the Channel, to the detriment of local trade and industry. The priest's speech marked the beginning of Limerick's "purge" of its Jewish population; over the next two years of boycott, two-thirds of Limerick's Jews left the city.

William Martin Murphy was about to speed the demise of the *Freeman's Journal*. January 2, 1905, saw the first issue of the new-style *Irish Independent*, the first halfpenny popular paper in Ireland. It soon had a devastating effect on the rest of the newspaper industry, but behind its success, in which Murphy had invested "40,000 golden guineas", lay intrigue and duplicity, with its origins in the Parnell split of fifteen years previously. The *Freeman's Journal* had been pro-Parnell; the *National Press* was founded, with Murphy as one of its directors, to be the organ of the anti-Parnellite faction. Later, the *Freeman's Journal* changed its allegiance and supported the anti-Parnell cause.

Murphy had long had an interest in journalism; a native of Bantry in Co Cork, he was sent to school at Belvedere College, Dublin. While still

(opposite page) Lower Grafton Street, Dublin, opposite Trinity College, in the early years of the century.
–Lawrence Collection

100

101

**The Phoenix Park tram
heads down Sackville
Street, Dublin.**
—Lawrence Collection

a schoolboy, he became very friendly with the Sullivans, owners and editors of the *Nation* and often visited their offices at 90 Middle Abbey Street; the site is now part of Independent House. When he left school, Murphy was apprenticed to an architect, John J. Lyons, who also owned the *Irish Builder,* for which he subbed and contributed articles and notes. Thus began Murphy's long involvement with newspapers; he did however have many other interests. He was a director and then chairman of the Dublin Tramway Company for many years; his two legacies to Ireland were the *Irish Independent* and an efficient public transport system in Dublin, although he has long been reviled for his part as the employers' spokesman in the great Dublin lock-out of 1913. Murphy's first major newspaper interest came in the 1890s, when with his friend and fellow-Corkman, Tim Healy, later first Governor-General of the Irish Free State, he bought the *Nation* and turned it into a loss-making daily.

After the change of policy by the *Freeman's Journal,* the *Irish Daily Independent* was set up to put forward the views of the Parnellites. By 1900, the paper was teetering on the verge of bankruptcy. In July of that year, John Redmond, chairman of the Irish Party, wrote to Healy and asked whether there was any way the *Independent* (by then in liquidation) could be saved from the *Freeman's Journal,* which had offered £12,000.

In a prophetic ending to his letter, Redmond wrote: "for all our sakes, don't you think it would be wise for Murphy to step in now and offer to reconstruct the Company, or buy?"

The *Daily Independent* was bought and amalgamated with the *Daily Nation.* The bid in court was made by James Campbell, KC, later the first Baron Glenavy and grandfather of Patrick Campbell, *The Irish Times* and *Sunday Times'* columnist of later years.

John Healy, editor, The Irish Times, **1907-1934.**

William Martin Murphy, then fifty six years old and described as being "by no means ascetic in his personal habits, but habitually frugal", set out on his great newspaper adventure, determined to smash the monopoly held by the *Freeman's Journal.* He ran the *Irish Daily Independent* for four more years, with continuing losses. Two newspaper experts were called in to advise Murphy on what course he should take to save his ailing newspaper.

Before them, the experts had the glowing example of the *Daily Mail* in London, which had become established by Chapelizod-born Alfred Harmsworth, later Lord Northcliffe, as that city's first halfpenny newspaper. Just a short while before Murphy sought expert advice, the success of the *Daily Mail* has been compounded by the equally startling success of the new *Daily Express.* In August, 1904, Murphy called another Corkman to his office, Tim Harrington, news editor of the *Irish Daily Independent* and told him that he wanted to appoint him editor of his new paper, the *Irish Independent,* which was going to rival the successes of the *Daily Mail* and the *Daily Express,* have plenty of photographs (a great innovation for Irish journalism) and be in Murphy's words, a non-partisan newspaper.

Harrington, then in his mid-thirties, accepted the offer with almost indecent enthusiasm. What happened to the existing editor of the *Irish Daily Independent,* at that time unaware of his fate, is not recorded. Not long after, a fellow Corkman, Timothy McCarthy, became editor of the *Irish News,* Belfast.

Tim Harrington then went to London with Murphy and a man called William Chapman, who was works manager and one of the Chapman family which owned the *Westmeath Examiner* in Athlone. The three men inspected the new Linotypes that would be needed for typesetting the new paper and made arrangements for buying a

Carlisle Building,
which used to stand at
the corner of D'Olier
Street and Burgh Quay,
Dublin, and which
housed the commercial
departments of
Independent
Newspapers until 1924.

battery of them, as well as other printing machinery. The reporters'
room of the new paper was the first on any Irish newspaper to make
extensive use of that recent invention, the telephone.

New staff were taken on including Andy McEvoy, father of Dermot
McEvoy; Andy had served his time with the notorious Jasper Tully on
the *Roscommon Herald,* an experience that at least ensured he had first-
class shorthand. An old-timer on the staff was Martin Joseph Pender,
chief proof reader, who had joined the *Irish Daily Independent* in 1892 and
who was also a journalist until the proof readers became unionised,
forcing Pender to choose between the two jobs. A fellow proof reader
was Arthur Griffith, notable for his thick glasses, even as a young
man. Pender later recalled how the two of them used to walk out to
Johnny Fox's pub in Glencullen, some ten miles south of Dublin, to
enjoy the "crack" and the pint at fourpence. Pender's son, Aidan, was
Irish Independent editor until his retirement in 1982.

In October, 1904, the lease on the *Irish Daily Independent* offices in
Trinity Street, off Dame Street, ran out. Murphy refused to pay the
greatly increased rental sought by the landlord, so a feverish hunt
began for new premises. A four storey house at 111 Middle Abbey
Street was found; no doubt William Martin Murphy reflected, even

fleetingly, on its closeness to the *Nation* office where he had spent so much spare time as a schoolboy.

Murphy announced that the new-look *Irish Independent* would be launched on January 2, 1905. That gave less than three months in which to rebuild and convert the premises to house newspaper offices and printing presses. In early December, the Trinity Street landlord decided to eject Murphy and his paper forthwith, but a close friend of Murphy's, John Clancy, Sheriff of Dublin, managed to have the ejectment put back until the end of December.

For the last fortnight of December, the editorial staff of the *Irish Daily Independent* worked out of Trinity Street, while the printing staff started work in Middle Abbey Street. The first of the new Goss presses was installed and tested by the end of December, but by itself did not have enough capacity to print the new newspaper. The second Goss arrived late, only days before the launch.

Tom Stobie, the mechanical engineer, never left the office for the week prior to the launch. At 2.30 on the morning of January 2, 1905, the first Goss was running smoothly, turning out thousands of copies of the first issues of the *Irish Independent*. The entire staff, led by Harrington, the editor, watched from the gallery overlooking the machine room and cheered the first copies off the press. Stobie and his staff still could not get the second Goss to work properly; its "kicking" was tearing the reels of newsprint, but later that morning, this second press was running smoothly. Until about 1933, one of these presses was still in use, printing the old *Weekly Independent*.

That day, Harrington and the rest of the editorial staff took a slight breather from their toils. Over 50,000 copies of the first issue of the *Irish Independent* had been printed; the old *Irish Daily Independent* had sold a mere 8,000 copies daily. Murphy himself was an old man, over sixty years of age, yet his boyish enthusiasm at the success of the new paper inspired the rest of the staff.

Rival journals and journalists regarded the new *Irish Independent* as a flash in the pan, but as a report in the Golden Jubilee issue of the *Irish Independent* stated:

"The reading public of Ireland, slow as a rule to take to any innovation, quickly recognised in the *Irish Independent* an almost entirely new departure in Irish journalism. They were fascinated by its clever make-up and were delighted by its literary style. They were impressed, above all, by its strict adherence to the highest canons of decent journalism. It won respect and admiration for its scorning of sensationalism and for the honourable, impartial treatment it gave to every school of thought in Ireland."

On January 19, just a fortnight after its launch, James Joyce said that the poetry in the *Irish Independent* was "really awful".

William Martin Murphy was undeterred; as sales climbed spectacularly, he introduced the concept of audited net daily sales.

Previously, newspapers produced gross circulation figures, which took no account of the up to fifteen per cent of copies given out free, damaged or returned unsold. The *Irish Independent* claimed it was the first newspaper anywhere to bring in the new idea of audited actual sales. Some London newspapers adopted the practice three years later.

Rumours had to be put down, however. Harmsworth was making a great success of the *Daily Mail*. Initially, he had been asked by Murphy about the possibility of publishing the *Mail* in Dublin. Then, as Murphy was setting up his plans for the *Irish Independent*, he discussed them with the *Daily Mail* owner. Harmsworth's visit to Dublin included dinner at the Murphy home in Dartry.

It was freely suggested in Dublin that the owner of the *Daily Mail* was the real man behind the *Irish Independent*. Not until 1909 did Murphy admit in print (the *Irish Independent*, naturally) that Harmsworth had freely placed his great experience at his disposal. The suggestions that Harmsworth owned the *Irish Independent* and that the new paper was staffed by English journalists continued; the rumours enjoyed remarkable longevity, even by Dublin standards. A further four years passed before Murphy again went into print, stating that not a penny of anyone's money but his own had gone to the building up of the paper.

Within weeks of the launch of the *Irish Independent*, sales had settled down at about 25,000 a day, but within three years, the new paper was selling around 40,000 copies daily. The *Evening Herald*, which dated back to 1891 and which was the fifth newspaper of that title, together with the infant *Sunday Independent*, launched in December, 1905, were also

(left) An off-duty soldier from the British Army enjoying a stroll with his girl friend in Westmoreland Street, 1915.
–*Lady of the House*

(right) The "White Coons" band entertains Edwardian holidaymakers on the promenade at Bray.

going well. No 111 Middle Abbey Street soon became far too cramped for the staff of the three newspapers, so Murphy acquired Carlisle Building by O'Connell Bridge. O'Connell Bridge House stands on the site today. Under the auspices of Independent Newspapers' first manager, T. W. Brewster, an Englishman, with gold glasses and a bullet-shaped head, the commercial sections of the firm were moved from Middle Abbey Street into Carlisle Building.

One major innovation pioneered by the *Independent* was in the organisation of its advertisement sales department, under Galway man Thomas À Kempis Grehan, father of Independent Newspapers' columnist Ida Grehan.

Assistant to the general manager, Brewster, was a man called Joseph

'Scabs' at work in Guinness' brewery during the great Dublin strike of 1913.
–*Guinness*

Edward Walsh, one-
time owner of the
Munster Express,
**Mayor of Waterford
and father of J. J.
Walsh.**
–Munster Express

**Sir John Arnott, Second
Baronet, chairman of
the board of** The Irish
Times, **1900-1940.**

Henderson; he carried out an enormous variety of tasks in the office, yet had no exact job title. When the move was made to Carlisle Building, Brewster and Grehan were at a loss for a sign to put on the door. In the end, they compromised with just "Mr Henderson". Grehan later recalled the characters he had working under him, men like Edward Hollywood, who regaled his advertising clients with a vast store of tales about Dublin musical and theatrical life, "Martin" Lacey, whose head was so big that he could never get a hard hat to fit him exactly and who never kept an appointment and Tommy Barden, who had an encyclopaedic knowledge of Dublin personalities. None was too far removed from the fabled character of Leopold Bloom in *"Ulysses"*, whose "job" was advertisement canvasser on the *Freeman's Journal*.

Soon, the effects of the competition from the *Irish Independent* were being felt not only in Dublin, but in many larger towns and cities throughout Ireland. Waterford, for instance, had five newspapers, two of them evenings. Until the launch of the *Irish Independent*, competition from Dublin newspapers was of little account: the *Freeman's Journal* and *The Irish Times* did not arrive in Waterford until late afternoon. The new

Irish Independent started arriving in the city at 11 a.m. Edward Walsh, father of J.J. Walsh, owned a morning paper called the *Waterford Daily Mail* and four weekly newspapers. He bought new premises at The Quay, in 1907, moved in his printing plant and to meet the new competition, merged all his newspaper interests into one of his titles, the *Munster Express,* which continues to this day.

Walsh had to compete with another brilliant Waterford newspaper publisher: Edmund Downey, who was the son of a shipbroker and owner in the city. Downey went to London at an early age and spent thirty years there. He helped T. P. O'Connor found *T. P.'s Weekly* in 1903, he wrote extensively and published many books. Among the authors with whom he was personally acquainted were Canon Sheehan, George Moore and Katherine Tynan. In 1906, Downey returned to his native city and bought the *Waterford News,* which had been founded in 1848 (five years before the neighbouring Wexford *People).* The previous owner of the *Waterford News* had been a schoolfriend of Downey's, Banquo Redmond, who died in mysterious circumstances in Cairo. Downey ran the *Waterford News* easily and without fuss; in 1914, he published one of his best-known books, *The Story of Waterford.*

Edmund Downey, who returned home to Waterford after a successful publishing career in London, to take over the Waterford News.

In the early years of the century, the launch of the *Irish Independent* may have made most of the headlines, but important provincial weeklies were being set up, too. In 1902, the *Echo and South Leinster Advertiser* started publication in Enniscorthy. A group of local businessmen, politicians and a solicitor funded the newspaper, which was among the first to propagate the more militant nationalism of the time. Its first editor was William Sears, later a TD for Mayo in the first Dáil. Larry de Lacy, noted Republican and later a sub-editor on *The Irish Times* and editor of the *Drogheda Argus* and *Clare Champion* started his newspaper career with the *Enniscorthy Echo* just six years after it was launched.

The year after the *Enniscorthy Echo* came into existence, a major nationalist paper emerged in Co Clare from the ruins of another paper. The Banner County had a remarkable tradition of newspaper publishing dating back to 1778, with the *Clare Journal.* All but two of its eighteen or so newspapers have been published in the county town, Ennis. The exceptions came from Kilrush; one of its newspapers, the *Kilrush Herald and Kilkee Gazette* (1877-1922) followed the popular turn-of-the-century custom of having two of its four pages printed in England. The remaining two were printed with local news in the town. Early this century, the *Clareman* was an energetic nationalist newspaper in the county.

In 1904, £600 damages were awarded against the *Clareman* in a libel action. To raise the money, the sub-sheriff and his bailiffs seized equipment from the newspaper office. Later that day, the premises

The Sligo Independent office decorated for the visit to the town by the Lord Lieutenant of Ireland and his wife in June, 1903.

were sold to a man called Elliot, described as a swarthy Jewish-looking stranger; in fact, he was from the Landlord's Defence Association. Thousands of nationalists marched on the town, bands played; it was the sale of the early twentieth century as far as Ennis was concerned.

Staff outside the
Southern Star **office in
Skibbereen, Co Cork
about eighty years ago.**
–*Southern Star*

Tom Galvin, owner and editor of the *Clareman*, put in an unsuccessful
bid for what had been his own property. The night before the sale, one
of the comps and some of his friends, climbed through the window and
rescued bags of type. With this type and other meagre equipment, the
Clare Champion was born within a couple of days of the enforced demise
of the *Clareman*. The new paper was printed in Limerick; editor Tom
Galvin said in the first issue: "The *Champion* will stand as the inveterate
foe of landlordism, shoneenism, grabbers and Castle hacks.
"Tragically, Galvin died just eight months later.

The year following the fiery birth of the *Clare Champion,* a newspaper
of diametrically opposed views was born at the other end of the
country: the *Co Down Spectator* in Bangor. Its "father", David Alexander,
described as a genial and kind-hearted man, and a prominent Mason,
had been born and brought up in Scotland. He was regarded as a great
disappointment to his father when he decided to enter journalism, but
he worked on the *Scottish Leader* in Edinburgh, said to have been the first
newspaper in the United Kingdom to introduce Linotypes. The *Leader*
paid the penalty for pioneering — it closed down in 1894. Alexander
transferred to a sister paper, which also closed down, three months
later. Instead of going to bed when the paper itself had been put to bed,
he waited up for the public library in the centre of Edinburgh to open.
Studying the "situations vacant" notices in the morning papers, he saw
one for editor of the *Leitrim Advertiser*. He promptly sent a telegram:
"Don't fill situation. Application by letter following. "He got the job,

The men who founded the Kerryman in 1904, from left: Daniel Nolan, Maurice Griffin (first managing director) and Tom Nolan (first editor and father of the present Dan Nolan). Maurice Griffin came from Dingle and was correspondent there for the Kerry Weekly Reporter. Between them, Griffin and Tom Nolan wrote all the copy for the first issue of the Kerryman, which had ten pages and cost 1d.

spent four years with the paper and then moved North to take over the editorial chair at the *North Down Herald,* vacated by the death of W. G. Lyttle, who was also the author of *Betsy Gray.*

Some of Alexander's leisure interests seem peculiar by today's standards. He was described as being "an authority on the pockets throughout England, Scotland, Wales and Ireland where blending has not been complete and where the various races which go to make up British stock are to be found today in a state of comparative purity."

Be that as it may, Alexander's energetic mind soon turned to setting up his own newspaper in Bangor, then a sleepy little town with a winter population of 7,000. The body copy in the first issue of the paper, on June 3, 1904, was set entirely on a Linotype. The machine and operator were placed in a window, amazing the public of Bangor. A separate edition, known as the *Newtownards Spectator and Donaghadee Review* was published from the very outset, using a small office at High Street, Newtownards.

The very same year that Alexander created his new newspapers in Co Down, the *Kerryman* was established in Tralee, along similar political lines to the new *Clare Champion* on the other side of the Shannon estuary. Like Waterford, Tralee was a veritable warren of newspaper titles, some pro-Unionist like the *Kerry Evening Post* and the *Kerry Weekly Reporter,* others pro-Land League, like the *Kerry Sentinel.* Three young men, Daniel Nolan, Tom Nolan and Maurice Griffin, all had humble jobs as clerks in various firms in Tralee. They had great ambitions, however, and set up the Kerryman Printing Company in 1902 with a very modest capital of £500 and an equally modest first year turnover of £900. When the *Kerryman* made its first appearance, at one penny for ten pages, one of the other Tralee papers said that it looked forward to the prompt sale of the machinery. Although the new paper espoused what was then the still-minority cause of Sinn Fein, it ended up by outlasting all its rivals in the county.

Despite the growing newspaper competition in the first decade of the century, humorous moments provided relief. In 1906, a French newspaper offered £10,000 to the inventor of the machine that would fly from Paris to London. Not to be outdone, a columnist on the *Northern Constitution,* Coleraine, said that the paper should put up a £5,000 prize for the first Ulster inventor to fly from Garvagh to Swatragh in Co Derry.

The editor, in an unusually generous mood, wrote: "We cordially accept the suggestion but would prefer to double the amount of the prize as a still more substantial inducement to the inventive genius of

One of the great news stories carried by the Belfast Telegraph — **the launching of the "Titanic" at Harland and Wolff on May 31, 1911.**
–Belfast Telegraph

A remarkable advertisement from the Golden Jubilee issue of the Skibbereen Eagle in 1907.

Ulster." At the time, the Rev Aubrey Foster was building a machine based on the principle of a floating bird at his rectory in Newtowncunningham, Co Donegal. It looked a good contender for the aerial contest, but fortunately for the financial standing of the *Northern Constitution,* never did the short flight from Garvagh to Swatragh.

Dublin remained a city of great elegance; many newspaper reporters wore morning coats and striped trousers. They doffed their top hats to ladies of their acquaintance whom they passed in the street. Every afternoon in Grafton Street, a procession of ladies of wealth and leisure paraded up and down the pavements, occasionally stepping into one of the many cafés that then lined the street, such as Mitchells, the Café Cairo and Robert Roberts. Bewleys had not yet extended from South Great George's Street into Grafton Street. A pound of tea cost half a crown, a cup of tea four pence. Sailing ships still tied up by the Custom House. Into this elegant atmosphere in 1907 came the new occupant of the editorial chair at *The Irish Times.* The polished John Healy, complete with neat moustache, took up the position at the instigation of Sir John Arnott. Healy, who was said to have written like a savage angel on occasion, remained aloof from the rest of the staff at the paper. Closeted away in the editor's room, he conversed only with other senior members of staff. His austere and impeccably dressed figure, complete with bowler hat and walking stick, struck fear bordering on terror into the more junior members of the firm. Healy was an unwavering Unionist and in his convictions, mirrored the loyalties of his employer. So close were the two that practically every Sunday evening for many years, Healy went to dinner with the Arnotts.

The year that John Healy became editor of *The Irish Times,* another notable newspaper, the *Skibbereen Eagle,* commemorated its Golden Jubilee. Its anniversary issue had sixty four columns of type in eight pages, but its self-congratulatory tone was muted by the death of the paper's founder, Eldon Potter, just a few months before the special issue, which came out on Saturday, May 4, 1907. Very curiously, the *Skibbereen Eagle* made no mention itself of the remark carried in its columns about keeping its eye on the Czar of Russia, the basis for the most famous apocryphal remark ever passed in an Irish newspaper. In this issue, however, tributes were paid to the longevity of the *Skibbereen Eagle,* but the London *Tribune* said: "We have scrutinised the *Eagle's* strenuous political activity during the past fifty years and have found not a hint of the awe-inspiring admonition to which it owes its name." All the files of the *Skibbereen Eagle* were destroyed in an IRA raid on its premises in 1920, but from copies of the paper in the British Newspaper Library, Colindale, London and the National Library, Dublin, references have been found in the year 1898 and 1899 to the paper *still* keeping its eye on the Emperor of Russia, which implies an

114

John Caughey (top right), who joined the Belfast Telegraph in 1909 after writing a paragraph about a cow falling into the river at Donegall Quay. Also in this family photograph are his wife "Mollie" and son John, also a journalist (top left), his daughter-in-law Valerie and his grand-daughter Laura, now Mrs Laura Hoy, managing director of one of Northern Ireland's leading public relations firms.

earlier and original use of the famous phrase in the paper. When was the first mention of the famous phrase in the paper? It may be unclear, but the paper enjoyed unprecedented world-wide publicity.

When Churchill came to Belfast in 1908 to address a Nationalist meeting as a Home Ruler, he barely escaped with his life. When he left his Royal Avenue hotel, a 10,000 strong mob tried to overturn his car. Churchill did manage to address his meeting at Celtic Park, then the RIC smuggled him onto the cross-channel steamer at Larne. These tumultuous events were covered by Joe Anderson, then a reporter with the *Belfast Telegraph,* later editor of the *Dublin Evening Mail.*

Also in Belfast, John Caughey found a most unusual means of joining the *Belfast Telegraph.* In 1909, he was a messenger boy in the *Ulster Guardian* office in Royal Avenue (this Liberal paper closed down in the early 1920s). Every night, the *Belfast Telegraph* published a "Seen and

Davy Adams, who joined the Belfast Telegraph **in 1904; not long after, he saved the then editor, Andy Stewart, from further injury when a suffragette knocked him flying.**
–Belfast Telegraph

Heard" column; readers who had a paragraph published about something he or she had seen in the city received payment of 2/6d. One day, the young Caughey was watching drovers load cattle onto the cross-channel steamers at Donegall Quay. One of the animals slipped and fell into the water.

His humorous paragraph describing the incident appeared in the *Belfast Telegraph* an evening or two later, but for weeks, there was no sign of the 2/6d arriving at his house in Pollard Street off the Springfield Road. Then a letter came from the editor, a man called Andy Stewart, asking John Caughey to come and see him. Even as an adult, Caughey never measured more than 5' 4" in height, so he had trouble getting past the *Telegraph* doorman. When he got to the "Holy of Holies", the conversation went something like this:

Editor: Could your father not come?
Caughey: I thought you wanted to see me.
Editor: Did you write the story about the cow falling in the water?
Caughey: I did.
Editor: Where do you work?
Caughey: In the *Ulster Guardian* office down the road.
Editor: Would you like to work here?
Caughey: I certainly would.
Editor: You're too young at fifteen. I thought you were older.
Caughey: Give me any sort of a job now. I'll eventually get older.

The young John Caughey became a copy boy on the *Telegraph;* two years later, he became an apprentice reporter for a seven year period. His starting wages as a young reporter were 7/6d a week. He started learning shorthand; eventually, his speed was up to 200 words a minute. John Caughey (whose son, also John, is also a journalist in Belfast) went on to spend fifty-one years with the *Belfast Telegraph*, and became one of Ireland's best-known (teetotal) sports writers.

Serving with Caughey on the *Belfast Telegraph* was another youngster, who had joined the paper five years before Caughey under equally improbable circumstances. Davy Adams was walking past the newspaper office when someone popped out and asked him to run a "wee message". He received a penny for his trouble; when he left school at fourteen, he went straight into the newspaper, where he worked for sixty-eight years, first as copy boy, then in a variety of jobs, including personal assistant to the great Stephen Williamson, chief sub-editor. Adams also saved Stewart, the editor, from a Lisburn suffragette at about the time the young John Caughey joined the firm. The woman, protesting about a news report, knocked the editor flying; Davy stopped her from kicking him.

In 1910, a medical scandal rocked the nation. Periodic outbreaks of typhus happened in parts of Connemara for years past and accounts were toned down in the newspapers. In 1910, Father Healy, the parish priest of Carraroe sent a private letter to the *Independent* editor, Tim

Harrington, telling him that a severe outbreak had occurred and begging him to send down a reporter. Several deaths had already occurred. A reporter was sent: he took the Clifden train as far as Maam Cross and from there hired a side car to do the remaining twenty-five miles to Carraroe. Harrington had given typically brief instructions: "Be sure of your facts, give the situation a good write-up — and take care of yourself." The series of articles that followed in the *Irish Independent* caused uproar; other newspapers complained that the reports were exaggerated and local hoteliers complained about loss of business. During a further outbreak, three years later, the *Independent* organised a relief fund.

The *Irish Independent* put its first three motor vans on the road in 1911; previously, Dublin distribution had been by horse-drawn van and bicycle. The Ford vans had brass fittings, acetylene lamps and no protection for the driver, so it was with some apprehension that Frederick Brannigan drove the first-ever newspaper lorry from Dublin to Cork.

One of the earliest Belfast Telegraph **delivery vans, about 1914.**
–Belfast Telegraph

The *Sunday Independent* missed the night mail train from Kingsbridge one winter's Saturday night in 1912; a volunteer driver was called for and Brannigan stepped forward. A temporary windshield was put up and Brannigan and his helper wrapped themselves in heavy greatcoats and caps with protective ear flaps. Twelve gallons of spare petrol, as well as two spare tyres, were loaded aboard. Leaving Dublin at 11.30 that Saturday night, the lorry travelled roads that were covered in ice. Few signposts existed then, but somehow, amid the howling winter weather, Brannigan and his helper drove into Cork after lunch on the Sunday. They turned round after a short break and arrived back in Dublin after noon on the Monday — the driver and his helper had pioneered the "Dawn Patrol" of years yet to come.

The *Independent* was pioneering another distribution "first" — the introduction of "shoppers" to liaise between the paper and the newsboys. Until the *Independent's* revolution, the newsboys, often in bare feet, sold papers, hawked studs and laces in the streets, held horses outside hotels and carried bags at railway stations, any kind of humble job to keep destitution at bay.

William Ryan, the first "shopper", who acted as go-between from the circulation and despatch departments to the newsboys, had started at the old *Irish Daily Independent*. He recalled years later that the scheme immediately bore fruit, giving the newsboys some security of livelihood. William Martin Murphy was described as a man of progressive ideas.

While he was continuing his humane efforts, many attempts were made to organise journalists, of whom it was estimated there were about six hundred throughout Ireland in 1910. In December of the preceding year, there had been a meeting of the promoters of the Irish Journalists' Association. Maurice Linnane, the famous chief reporter of the *Irish Independent*, was among the unsuccessful nominations to the committee. Journalists in 1912 were complaining that £3 10s a week was hardly a living wage, but they were doing rather better than Bulmer Hobson, the founding editor of *Irish Freedom*, set up at the end of 1911. His leaders may have been marvellously graphic, but he remained as unpaid editor for several years. Ill-paid contributions to other publications kept him going.

As Murphy was establishing his newspaper empire in Dublin, Tom Kenny was doing likewise in Galway. Born in Cork (hence his lifetime "nickname" of Tom Cork), he went into journalism in Manchester, then became chief reporter on the Unionist *Kilkenny Moderator*. In the early years of the century, Galway had four newspapers, including the remarkable *Galway Observer*, run by the Scott family. Into the maelstrom of the *Connacht Champion*, the *Galway Express*, the *Observer* and the *Galway Pilot*, Kenny, as first editor, together with A. F. O'Reilly, set up the *Connacht Tribune* in May, 1909. Soon, the new paper began to succeed, not that the Scott family at the *Observer* were too bothered by

the competition, although it was less frenzied than twenty years previously, when the city had a dozen newspapers.

Alexander Gaffney Scott had set up the *Observer* in 1881; he, his wife and later his six daughters and son John, ran the paper entirely on a family basis. Gaffney Scott was known as one of the old-time characters around Galway, exclusively devoted to the paper, rarely venturing out of the office and printing works.

On the *Anglo-Celt* in Cavan, rather more rumbustious mementoes were being forged. Bob Green, the chief reporter at this time, was a Kerryman and an alcoholic — a combination that led to much spontaneous gaiety.

He stayed in "digs" in Cavan and often demented his landlady by playing traditional Irish music all night long. He was an expert musician, but his skills were not appreciated at four in the morning. However, on one occasion, the landlady enjoyed a respite: Green went off to the workhouse, as an inmate, for two nights and then wrote up his experiences. His most memorable exploits took place at Belturbet council meetings; not only did Green report them, but if he took exception to points raised, joined in the discussion. All participants in the debate (including of course Green himself) were duly reported in that week's newspaper.

The machine room of the Connacht Tribune, **Galway, as the paper was being launched in 1909.**

119

John Walsh, who
founded Ireland's Own
in 1903, as an offshoot
of the Wexford People.

The *Anglo-Celt* was mechanically innovative; James Donohue was setting away on the Linotype and the firm was printing on the rotary press it had put in during the course of 1905 and which enabled it to produce a twelve sheet broadsheet newspaper. Cavan, with the *Anglo-Celt*, must have seemed a thriving place to the Bairds of the *Belfast Telegraph.*

In 1904, they had launched the *Irish Daily Telegraph;* for two years previously, it had been the ninth edition of the *Belfast Telegraph.* Published in Derry, it covered the western counties of the North of Ireland. Remarkably, the *Irish Daily Telegraph* survived until 1951. But in 1910, the Bairds went further, by establishing the Orange-inclined *Irish Post* newspaper to cater for a largely Protestant readership in and around Cavan. This somewhat improbable newspaper venture (the only one ever launched by the *Belfast Telegraph* organisation outside what is now Northern Ireland) lasted until 1920, when the troubles of the time saw it off. One reporter on the *Irish Post* is still remembered: he must have been the cause of the legends about Cavan meanness. In all his forty years of covering court cases and other events in the country, first for the *Irish Post* and then for the *Belfast Telegraph* and *Irish Daily Telegraph*, this reporter, a man called Arthur Tanney, is said never to have offered anyone a cigarette. To make matters worse, he had the reputation of cutting his own cigarettes in half so that they would go further.

The same year that the *Irish Post* was launched, James Lynch decided to leave the *Drogheda Independent.* He cast around Ireland for a suitable town in which to launch his own newspaper and lighted upon Dungarvan, since it was seat of the county council, meaning plenty of jobbing printing work. He founded the *Dungarvan Observer.* According to the records of the time, "it immediately had a large circulation, the proprietor's efforts being appreciated." It succeeded the *Dungarvan Journal,* set up by a man called R. Edward Brennan, who had been the Postmaster in Dungarvan for thirty years and who also ran a printing office. The *Journal* was described as being very chatty and of a high order of merit. However, the proprietor found it difficult to devote sufficient time to its publication and after the issue of twelve numbers, it ceased. Mr Lynch stepped neatly into the breach and his paper serves Dungarvan to the present day, run by his son Paddy.

More stirring events were happening in the North, culminating in the signing of the Ulster Covenant in Belfast in 1912. It was a momentous occasion for the Loyalist side in the North, duly reported by the Unionist newspapers of the city in all its detail. No paper gave the event more sympathetic coverage than the *Belfast Telegraph;* Thomas Moles, at this period, the paper's leader writer (he was appointed editor in 1924) had the ear of the loyalist politicians and indeed wrote many of the propaganda pieces issued in the Loyalist cause. He was so close to these events that he was the only journalist to have had advance knowledge of the Larne gun running in 1914.

Sir Edward Carson
signing the Ulster
Covenant at City Hall,
Belfast, in 1912.
–*Belfast Telegraph*

It provided more exciting copy that the signing of the Covenant. One Belfast reporter, from the *Irish News,* thought he had a great exclusive when Captain Craig as he was then, later the first Prime Minister of Northern Ireland, agreed to be interviewed as one of the main participants in the signing. The "scoop" proved to be shallow indeed; Craig blew down the length of his very long nose and passed the illuminating comment: "O God". End of interview. Yet despite the rising political tension of the North, journalistic ethics still prevailed. Patrick Pearse, later to lead the Easter Rising in Dublin in 1916, came to Belfast and made a speech at the Ulster Hall that was regarded in Unionist circles as seditious. Reporting the event was a noted Orange journalist, R. M. Sibbett of the Belfast *News Letter,* who was also *Irish Times'* Belfast correspondent for many years. After the meeting was over, the police called on Sibbett and demanded to see his notes. He refused to hand them over. Much as the great political events of the day, such as the signing of the Ulster Covenant, occupied column after column in most newspapers of Ireland, matters of social importance did surface from time to time. The great Irish literary revival, particularly the majestic opening nights at the recently founded Abbey Theatre, also provided many column inches of copy, while at Coole Demesne in Co Galway, great Irish writers such as Sean O'Casey, G. B. Shaw and W. B. Yeats often held literary court under Lady Gregory's roof. After dinner, they carved their initials on the historic tree in the garden.

The great Dublin lockout of 1913 produced its own set of bitter working class memories: the food kitchens which helped relieve the distress are remembered even to this day. Joe Anderson, that great newspaperman, saw Jim Larkin, dressed as a priest, appear in a window and try to address the prohibited meeting, which was broken up by a DMP baton charge. That acclaimed photograph of Jim Larkin, hands raised to heaven, was taken by Joe Cashman, who eight years previously had been doing coloured half-tones for the *Cork Examiner* and who was later one of the founding photographers of the *Irish Press*. *The Irish Times* denounced Larkinism as an "intolerable tyranny" (par for the course amongst Unionist newspapers of the day), but curiously enough, went on in almost the same breath to give full vent to AE's magnificent letter to the "masters of Dublin", in which he remarked that "if every unskilled labourer in Dublin were the tenant of three or even two rooms, the city would not be divided today into two hostile camps." In February of the following year, *The Irish Times* ran a leader saying that the slum conditions of Dublin could be compared to Dante's Inferno.

The tocsins of war were ringing; August 1914 saw the start of World War I. Thousands upon thousands of young Irishmen enlisted for the British Army in support of what they believed was the freedom of small nations.

Soon after the declaration of war in 1914, a compositor on the *Midland Tribune*, Jim Mulhern, tossed his apron onto the "stone" in the printing works at Birr and after a few bracing pints in Jane Kenneally's pub, marched off to the military barracks at nearby Crinkle. He signed up for the war as one of half a million recruits from Ireland. 50,000 Irishmen were buried beneath foreign fields by the time the holocaust was over, including Francis Ledwidge, the Co Meath poet, who had already won a degree of recognition, helped by his local newspaper, the *Drogheda Independent*. Mulhern was one of the lucky soldiers of the King. He returned, unscathed, in 1918, put on his printer's apron and set to work once more, almost as if he had been away four days, rather than four years.

1915 saw a disastrous fire at the *Anglo-Celt* in Cavan, when the whole printing works was burned down. For the following fortnight, the paper by printed by the *Belfast Telegraph*, then for the next six years by the printing firm of Cahills. With the Great War in progress, the Cavan paper was unable to obtain replacement machinery. Newsprint was also in short supply and newspapers found themselves under military censorship; the *Nationalist and Leinster Times* had to send page proofs up to the Curragh Camp from Carlow to have them cleared by the military authorities. For Irish newspapers, the Great War period of 1914-1918 was a dry run for the far greater stringencies of the World War II emergency. The first year of the Great War was a time of euphoria; it had no major and direct impact on daily life in Ireland, apart from the recruiting of soldiers. Ahead lay the massacres of the Somme and Easter, 1916; the course of Irish history was soon to change dramatically and irrevocably.

CHAPTER V

Closed by proclamation
1916-1923

*Clonskeagh Hospital, Co Dublin. Required, a Probationer for
fever duty. Salary £12 (per annum), with uniform.*
THE IRISH TIMES, 1916

*Enlarged glands in the neck. Your blood is calling for help.
Clarke's Blood Mixture. 3/- per bottle.*
THE WEEKLY IRISH TIMES, 1922

When the New Year dawned in 1916, who in the newspaper world, or indeed in Ireland at large, could have foreseen the dramatic change of events and political fortunes in the country. From Easter of 1916, until the ending of the civil war seven years later, the newspaper industry of Ireland endured the most hazardous and difficult period of its entire existence.

On Easter Monday, April 23, 1916, Maurice Linnane of the *Irish Independent* lived up to his nickname of Maurice the Good, given to him because of his impeccable newsroom habits. His brother, Mick, also on the *Independent,* was called the Bad because of his prolific drinking and tendency to "lift" other journalists' copy. In keeping with his self-ordained image, Maurice Linnane arrived at work punctually that Monday morning, despite it being a Bank Holiday. Some of the reporting staff were going away to the country by train that afternoon, while others had city stories to cover. One reporter rushed in early that morning with an exciting story that armed men had seized a considerable quantity of dynamite at Brittas, Co. Dublin.

Linnane was well aware of the scare the previous week about the Volunteers mobilising; he knew equally well that the day before, the Sunday, this call-up under the leadership of Professor Eoin MacNeill had been abandoned. Calmly, the early sporting edition of the *Evening Herald* went to press, containing little more than the racing

Crowds gaze at Dublin city centre ruins in the aftermath of 1916.
–National Library

Official Government notice concerning the 1916 Easter Rising in The Irish Times.

programmes for Fairyhouse and Cork Park. In Dublin city centre, the crowds were preparing to leave for Fairyhouse; a caretaker at the *Irish Independent,* a heavily-built man called Pat Gaffney rushed up the stairs and literally fell in through the door of the reporters' room.

He shouted: "The Volunteers have gone into the GPO; they are breaking the glass with the butt of their rifles and sandbagging the windows." The reporters rushed wildly downstairs and out into Middle Abbey Street.

When Maurice Linnane started to run with the rest of the crowd, he bumped into Dr Louis Byrne, the City Coroner. When Byrne was told the news about the GPO, he said: "Ah, go to blazes!" Dr Byrne was enjoying a day off from his duties as a visiting surgeon at the nearby Jervis Street hospital, but later that day, as the dead and the dying arrived there, he was called in. Until the insurrection was over, a week later, he never left the hospital.

The Irish Times.

LVIII. NO.— 18,444.   DUBLIN, WEDNESDAY, APRIL 26, 1916.   PRICE O

A PROCLAMATION.

WHEREAS, in the City of Dublin and County of Dublin certain evil-disposed persons and Associations, with the intention of subverting the supremacy of the Crown in Ireland, have committed divers acts of violence, and have with deadly weapons attacked the forces of the Crown, and have resisted by armed force the lawful authority of His Majesty's Police and Military forces; and WHEREAS by reason thereof several of His Majesty's liege subjects have been killed and many others severely injured, and much damage to property has been caused; and WHEREAS such armed resistance to His Majesty's Authority still continues:

NOW WE, Ivor Churchill Baron Wimborne, Lord Lieutenant-General and General Governor of Ireland, by virtue of all the powers thereunto enabling us, do hereby proclaim that from and after the date of this Proclamation, and for the period of one month thereafter, unless otherwise ordered, the City of Dublin and County of Dublin are under and subject to Martial Law; and WE do hereby call on all loyal and well-affected subjects of the Crown to aid in upholding and maintaining the peace of the Realm and the supremacy and authority of the Crown; and WE warn all peaceable and law-abiding subjects within such area of the danger of frequenting or being in any place in or in the vicinity of which His Majesty's forces are engaged in the suppression of disorder; and WE do hereby enjoin upon such subjects the duty and necessity, so far as practicable, of remaining within their own homes so long as these dangerous conditions prevail; and WE do hereby proclaim that all persons found carrying arms without lawful authority are liable to be dealt with by virtue of this Proclamation.

Given at Dublin

This 25th day of April, 1916.

WIMBORNE.

GOD SAVE THE KING.

LICENSED PREMISES TO BE CLOSED.

The following Military Order was issued last night:—

I, as the Competent Military Authority, do, in pursuance of the powers conferred under the Defence of the Realm (Consolidation) Regulations, 1914, order and require all premises licensed for the sale of intoxicating liquors for consumption on the premises, and situated within the Area of the A, B, C, D, E Divisions of the Dublin Metropolitan Police District, to be closed until further order, except between the hours of 2 p.m. and 5 p.m.

H. G. KENNARD, Colonel,
Competent Military Authority.

Dated this 25th day of April, 1916.

Just after 11.30 a.m., Linnane saw copies of the Proclamation being handed out to the crowd gathering outside the GPO. One was handed to him by Professor Hugh MacNeill, who said that he was on his way to the *Evening Telegraph* office in Prince's Street, at the side of the GPO, to give some to the editor, Paddy Meade and his staff.

The crowds were unable to quite comprehend what was going on inside the GPO. Equalled baffled was Lord Powerscourt, seen strolling down Sackville Street in the uniform of a British staff officer. He stood for a moment trying to unravel the mystery, then passed on. Within minutes, the first shots in the war against British rule would be fired. Linnane went back to the office to see about producing an edition of the *Evening Herald*, or if that failed, an edition of the *Irish Independent* for the following morning, but all hope of further publication had already been ruled out. Linnane returned to the GPO with a colleague from the *Independent* newsroom, Michael Knightly, who joined in the fighting that night as a Volunteer and stayed in the GPO until the bitter end. During World War II, Knightly fought another kind of battle — against the newspapers, in his capacity as chief censor.

Another man who heard about the Easter Rising was Matthew Walker, founder of the unsuccessful *Carlow Vindicator* over twenty years previously. He had returned to Dublin after its collapse and founded the Tower Press; although sixty-eight years of age, he walked from his home in Sandycove to the GPO as soon as he received the news. He is said to have met Patrick Pearse. One of the journalists who took part in the Easter Rising only had to a step a matter of yards into the GPO — Piaras Beaslai. Like so many Nationalists (he was a founder member of the Volunteers in 1913), he was born outside Ireland, in Liverpool. He came to Ireland when he was twenty-four to work on the *Evening Telegraph*.

Soon, the Lancers arrived from the direction of Parnell Square; Volunteers opened fire, killing two of the Lancers and their horses. They then retreated, but no further shots were fired from the GPO as they departed. A lull settled over the centre of Dublin; that afternoon, an attempt was made to blow up the rails under a tram abandoned in Earl Street. It failed. That night, there were abortive attempts to blow up the railway bridges at Cabra Road and North Circular Road, near Phibsborough Church. No issue of the *Irish Independent* was produced that night, but over in Westmoreland Street, the lights blazed on at *The Irish Times*.

Every available reporter was marshalled to cover the Rising for both the Dublin papers and those further afield. "Master Bertie" Trimble, of the *Impartial Reporter*, Enniskillen, was one of the first out-of-town journalists to arrive. Later that week, he found that his wife's family was isolated at their home near St Stephen's Green and took them food and drink. His teetotal father-in-law was highly relieved to see a bottle of whiskey included for medicinal purposes!

About midday on the Tuesday, Maurice Linnane met Francis Sheehy Skeffington, the pacifist, on O'Connell Bridge. Many times that week, he confronted gangs of looters ransacking city centre shops and warned them of their disgraceful conduct while men were fighting and dying for the freedom of their country. Also on the Tuesday, a company of the Citizen's Army occupied the *Dublin Evening Mail* and *Dublin Daily Express* building at the top of Parliament Street, opposite City Hall. The newspaper offices were retaken the next day by British forces.

On the Wednesday morning, *The Irish Times* carried three lines about the Sinn Fein Rising. The official proclamation said that evilly disposed persons had disturbed the peace and that the situation was well in hand. The rest of the country was described as quiet, but no English or country papers were available in Dublin. Pubs were to be closed until further notice, except between the hours of 2 p.m. and 5 p.m.

On the Wednesday evening, when Sheehy Skeffington was walking to his home in Rathmines, he was arrested by British troops from Portobello barracks. The next morning, he was taken out to the

Ruins of the Freeman's Journal **office in Prince's Street, beside the GPO, after the Easter Rising, 1916.**

127

barrack square with two prominent Dublin journalists, Patrick McIntyre, editor of the Labour paper, *Searchlight* and Thomas Dickson, editor of a controversial weekly, *The Eye-Opener*. All three were killed by firing squad, without any formal charges having been brought against them. Later, Captain Bowen Colthurst, in charge of the firing squad, was tried by court-martial and found guilty but insane.

Tim Harrington, the editor of the *Irish Independent*, managed to reach his office on the Wednesday, but had nothing to do. The next day, Maurice Linnane tried to come to work, but could only get as far as Phibsborough, where even hearses for the nearby Glasnevin cemetery were being stopped by British troops. In some cases, coffins were opened to make sure they carried neither guns nor ammunition in addition to their usual cargo. Some members of staff did manage to get into the *Independent* offices, but still there was no sign of the firm's three papers being able to resume production. That day, gas and electricity

A reference to the famous Czar of Russia story in the Golden Jubilee issue of the Skibbereen Eagle, **1907.**

THE "TRIBUNE," LONDON.

Westminster has witnessed the rise and fall of many Governments since the memorable day when the "*Skibbereen Eagle*"—or, strictly speaking, the "*Cork County Eagle and Munster Advertiser*," published at Skibbereen—solemnly warned Lord Palmerston that it had "got its eye both upon him and on the Emperor of Russia." What effect that terrible warning had upon the distinguished statesman and the Tsar of all the Russias history does not say; but the little town of Skibbereen, on the south-west coast of Ireland, awoke to find itself famous. Not without reason, therefore, should the "*Skibbereen Eagle*" now rejoice on the celebration of its Jubilee. But, strange to say, carefully though we have scrutinized the leading article which surveys the "*Eagle's*" strenuous political activity during the last fifty years, we have found not a hint of the awe-inspiring admonition to which it owes its fame.

supplies to the building were cut off and on the Thursday evening, a squad of Volunteers took over the premises.

They were in possession of the *Irish Independent* offices until the Saturday night, but even though they barricaded the front windows of the sub-editors' office with tables and reference books, not a shot was fired from or at the building. Machinery and plant were undamaged during the occupation.

At about the same time that the group of Volunteers took over the *Irish Independent* on the Thursday evening, the Crown forces started firing incendiary shells into O'Connell Street. The Hotel Metropole (later the site of the Metropole cinema where the British Home Stores now stands) was one of the first buildings to catch fire, followed by much property in Abbey Street. Despite the destruction in Middle Abbey Street, No III, home of the *Irish Independent,* came through the Easter Rising virtually unscathed. Ironically, three years later, much of its plant was destroyed by IRA men complaining about a news report. Shortly afterwards, William Martin Murphy was to pick four adjoining sites, in ruins after Easter Week, as the location of what is now Independent House. *The Irish Times,* too, was lucky, unmarked by the 1916 fighting; later its weekly paper published its famous handbook of the "Sinn Fein Rebellion".

The *Freeman's Journal* offices in Prince's Street, going through to Middle Abbey Street, were destroyed; they also housed its sister papers, the *Evening Telegraph* and *Sport.* All printing equipment and records were destroyed, but within a short space of time, its papers were back in circulation, from temporary premises in Fleet Street, but they had been dealt a mortal blow from which they never recovered.

The Volunteers surrendered on the Sunday and on the Monday, staff began to arrive back at the *Independent,* although some had been arrested for their part in the Easter Rising and at least two had been marooned in the country. Every available man (there were no women reporters in those days), including sub-editors and sports writers, was sent out to cover the aftermath of the Rising.

Strange stories were procured, of bodies of civilians buried in backyards and cellars, of arrests, burnings and lootings. When the *Irish Independent* appeared on the Tuesday morning, there was tremendous interest, for news was scarce and well filtered. Official bulletins, censored by the British military, appeared in one or two papers, but gave few facts. The *Independent* had the first substantial news of the Rising and many people waited up half the night until the first copies came off the presses. Some newsboys sold copies for half a crown each. For the rest of that week, the *Independent* presses could not keep up with the demand; the ringing leader, written by Harrington himself, denouncing the rebellion, did not strike a discordant note with readers, since it reflected the popular mood. Not until after the 1916 leaders had been shot did popular sentiment change abruptly and dramatically.

DOOMED LEADER'S WEDDING.

A PATHETIC INCIDENT.

A pathetic incident has to be recorded in connection with the execution of Mr. Joseph Plunkett, one of the insurgent leaders, who was shot yesterday morning in accordance with the sentence of the Court martial.

On Wednesday evening an attractive-looking young lady entered Mr. Stoker's jewellery establishment, 22 Grafton street, and said she wished to purchase a wedding ring. Mr. Stoker, observing that she seemed to be labouring under some strong emotion, expressed the hope that she was not in any trouble. The young lady, who made a gallant attempt to preserve her composure, replied that she was the fiancee of Mr. Plunkett, who was under sentence of death, and was to be shot the following morning, and her marriage to him was to take place on the morning of his death.

Mr. Stoker, who was thunderstruck by such a startling statement, expressed his deep sympathy, and the young lady having quietly thanked him, selected a ring and departed. The marriage was to have taken place at an early hour yesterday morning, a short time before the condemned man met his death.

The Sinn Feiners who had possession of the "Irish Independent" premises in Mid. Abbey street converted the sporting editor's room into a kitchen, where they provided themselves with cooking utensils. In the hurry of escaping they left behind them parts of loaves of bread and some tinned foods. Three prisoners were taken by the military when they retook possession, and some brand new rifles were seized by them.

The editor and manager of the "Irish Independent," who performed long journeys through the city and suburbs during the most trying week-end Dublin has ever experienced, had their permits examined in one day at different points by over fifty sentries. It took them several hours to perform a small circuit of the city on bicycles. Several members of our staff were repeatedly under heavy fire.

Burned fragments of notepaper blown as far as Sandford conveyed the first news to this suburb of the fires in the "Freeman's Journal" and Hugh Moore and Alexanders.

Rev. Fathers Rooney and M'Clorey, Banbridge, at the Masses on Sunday denounced the rising as "impious and unpatriotic," and as "a grave crime against God, as well as a most deadly blow against the best interests of the country." Reference was made to the progress made under constitutional agitation, and the congregation were advised to stand by Mr. Redmond and the Irish Party.

The only portion of the "Freeman's Journal" offices intact are parts of one outwall on which still hang the names of the Company's publications.

Dublin newspapers will be hampered for want of telegraphic, telephonic, and postal facilities for some time to come.

News snippets about the Easter Rising from the Irish Independent, **May 5, 1916.**

MESSRS
JOSEPH DOWNES
AND SONS.

NTH. EARL STREET,

Beg to announce that, in spite of the extensive fire in part of their Bakery premises last week, they are now in a position to turn out all the usual supplies of Bread.

All the vans of the Firm are now delivering in the city and suburbs as heretofore.

BOLAND'S LTD.

Beg to inform their Customers, and the Public generally, that their

USUAL DELIVERIES OF BREAD

have been resumed.

Two advertisements from the May 5, 1916, issue of the Irish Independent.

Very soon, the censorship spread. On April 24, 1916, the *Enniscorthy Echo,* already noted for its pro-Sinn Fein editorial policy, had suffered the dubious distinction of being first paper in the country to be banned. The British military authorities, by the simple expedient of padlocking the printing works in Millpark Road, Enniscorthy, prevented the newspaper being published until early the following year. The place had been a hive of nationalist sentiment and one of its clerks, Dick King, was a signatory to the Enniscorthy 1916 proclamation. He was sentenced to death, but the verdict was commuted and he was later released.

The economic problems of the next few years caused the demise of many newspapers; in Tralee alone; three papers, the *Kerry Evening Post,* the *Kerry Sentinel* and *Kerry People* ceased publication. So too did the *Kerryman* — on the orders of the British military authorities. One day in 1916, the young Dan Nolan, later managing director, was coming out of the convent school in Tralee to go home for his lunch when he saw a military squad in full battle dress outside the works of the *Kerryman.* They had arrested Maurice Griffin, one of the founders of the paper and were busy tucking into their own lunch, emptying bully beef tins into their upturned tins hats with a bayonet. Then they took vital parts from the printing presses, nailed the formal order of suppression to the door of the works and marched off.

One of the other founders of the paper, Tom Nolan, first editor of the *Kerryman* and father of Dan, quickly decided that the paper would not be allowed to go out of circulation. He went to Dublin and made an arrangement for its printing with the Gaelic Press in the Proby's Lane area of the city centre. Copies were brought down to Tralee by sympathetic railwaymen in the tenders of the locomotives. Then the emergency issues of the *Kerryman* were sold over the counter of the Nolan family pub in Tralee.

"Bolger" O'Donoghue, brother of Con O'Donoghue, who went from the *Kerryman* to run the new Linotypes at the *Drogheda Independent* in 1917, thus starting the O'Donoghue dynasty at that paper, was one of the "friendly" locomotive drivers.

During one journey from Dublin to Tralee, with the tender filled with "illicit" copies of the *Kerryman,* "Bolger" had a premonition and stopped the train at a small station just outside Tralee. As the train halted briefly, he and the fireman unloaded all the copies (later he arranged for their collection). Minutes later, as they steamed into Tralee station, they saw the platform crowded with RIC men and British soldiers. Somehow, the authorities had got wind of the special shipments, courtesy of the Great Southern Railways. The fireman was ordered to unload the coal from the tender, but he refused, so the RIC men had to undertake the task. That night, in a pub in Tralee, according to Dan Nolan's recollection, the soldiers were heard to remark that they were glad the black bastards had got nothing! That first suppression of the *Kerryman* lasted about two months.

In the North, the start of the Somme offensive on July 1, 1916, which involved the 36th Ulster Regiment, was marked by tremendous massacres. On the very first day alone, 20,000 men were killed and scarcely a home in Belfast remained untouched by the tragedy. The headlines in the Belfast papers were far more pertinent for their readers than the news stories from Dublin. Down in Co Cork, the *Southern Star* was suppressed in November, 1916. The ban lasted for just over a month; its increasingly nationalistic tone did not meet with the authorities' approval. Elsewhere in the town, the Unionist *Skibbereen Eagle,* under the control of local solicitor and MP for West Cork, Jasper Wolfe, since the death of its founder, Eldon Potter, in 1907, suffered the first of several raids on its premises by armed Republicans.

The following year, 1917, saw an amnesty for prisoners captured by the British during the Easter Week rebellion. Among those freed was Piaras Beaslai of the *Evening Telegraph;* he never returned to that paper, becoming instead head of the IRA publicity department and for a six year period, prior to the death of Michael Collins, editor of *An t-Oglach.*

In 1917, the *Kilkenny People* gave rise to some interesting newspaper history, enlivened by a comic touch from its owner/editor, E. T. Keane. In 1892, he had established the nationalist newspaper tradition in the city and in the run-up to the parliamentary election in Kilkenny in August, 1917, the decision of de Valera to nominate W. T. Cosgrave as the Sinn Fein candidate was made in the offices of the *Kilkenny People* in High Street. Cosgrave went on to win with the election, gaining twice as many votes as the Irish Parliamentary Party candidate. After this significant urban breakthrough for Sinn Fein, the *Kilkenny People* was suppressed.

Ned Lawler, then a young journalist with the paper (he went on to be political correspondent of the *Irish Independent* and then the first public relations manager at the Electricity Supply Board in 1927) temporarily saved the day. When a British Army squad arrived to remove parts of the printing press, the officer asked Lawler to point out the press. The man knew nothing of printing, so when the journalist showed him an old poster press, the soldiers dismantled that! It provided the shortest of reprieves.

E. T. Keane used to relish one story about himself during those acutely troubled years; he went to London on a business trip, but since he was on the wanted list, he was worried about getting back safely. A friend of his, a fellow Kerryman, was on the staff of the Metropolitan Police in London and arranged for Keane to have a police pass, which guaranteed his safe passage. When he reached Holyhead, the police escorted him to the first-class section of the mailboat to Kingstown, blissfully unaware that Keane was on their wanted list!

Ernest Blythe, later a Free State Government Minister who gained notoriety for slashing a shilling from the old age pension, was unable to

Ned Lawler, one-time political correspondent of the Irish Independent made public relations manager at the Electricity Supply Board, the first such public utility appointment in Europe, in 1927. The ESB was a safe haven after his many adventures during the War of Independence.
–Anne Lawler

Ernest Blythe in *Dublin Opinion.*

Staff of the Connacht Tribune **pictured outside the premises in 1911. Included are Tom Kenny ("Tom Cork") the editor, fifth from left and James Pringle, linotype operator, fourth from left. Pringle's son Jimmy became a distinguished war photographer during World War II, working for Associated Press of America.**

keep the RIC from the door of the *Southern Star* in Skibbereen in 1917. The paper had been reorganised in January of that year; among the shareholders was Michael Collins, although he did not take an active interest in the paper. In the February, Blythe, a Northern Protestant and ardent Sinn Fein supporter, was appointed editor, but he only worked in the west Cork newspaper for a short while before being removed to prison in Britain.

The young Billy King had more youthful and innocent preoccupations that year at the *Irish Independent*. He had wanted to become a journalist and asked J. P. Rice, the editor of the *Evening Herald,* about his chances. The great majority of the editorial staff had graduated from the provinces, so he didn't see much chance for the young Dublin lad, replied Rice. William Chapman, the works manager, didn't have anything to offer either, but Tom Grehan, the advertisement manager, said that he would be in touch. Some months later, Grehan *did* write offering a job. Billy King started work in the advertisement department, first on the telephone side, then taking copy, before being promoted to advertisement representative.

The senior reporters were concerned about being picked up by the military authorities for their clandestine activities. The teenage employees on the advertisement side were more terrified of Joe Mooney, the cattle dealer friend of William Martin Murphy. Mooney was a director of the paper and after board meetings, would come down to the advertisement offices in Carlisle Building and write out reams of copy for his cattle sales. Then he totted up the cost of the classified advertisements; the staff were scared witless in case their tots were different from Mooney's. His son, incidentally, worked on the paper for years as an advertisement canvasser; Leo's son, also Leo, a journalist of the present day, needs little introduction in the Dublin press world.

Outspoken as they were against the British authorities, the Nationalist press remained suitably obsequious on purely local matters. In February, 1917, the *Westmeath Independent* in Athlone ran an obituary on Joseph Sweeney, a merchant in Mardyke Street: "Docile as a child, true and sincere, as good men are, he was a friend without equal to be consulted and relied upon at times when true friendship is most valued." In Athlone that year, the *Westmeath Independent* further reported that milk cost 4d a quart and that it took £1 9s 6d a week for a labourer to keep a household of six people.

Next to be suppressed were the *Clare Champion* in Ennis and the *Meath Chronicle*. In April, 1918, a detachment of the military arrived at the works of the *Clare Champion* and removed sections of the press. In control of the paper were Josephine Maguire, sister of Tom Galvin, founding editor, who had died so tragically soon after its launch and Josephine's husband, Sarsfield, who was editor. The Maguires were given an ultimatum: if they guaranteed not to publish subversive and seditious articles, undermining the official Dublin Castle line, they could continue publishing. They refused, so the *Clare Champion* remained silent until September that year. The *Meath Chronicle* was similarly outspoken: after 1916, it called repeatedly for full independence for Ireland. It suffered the same fate as the *Clare Champion,* in the same year, 1918. Its printing factory at Newmarket Street, Kells, was raided and pieces of the press were taken away, but the paper soon reappeared. The first issue after the "ban" apologised for the first failure to appear since the paper was founded twenty-one years previously and took a few sideswipes at the authorities. In September, the *Southern Star* was suppressed again, this time for six months.

One of the most remarkable newspaper stories of the 1916-1923 period emerged from the *Belfast Telegraph.* In keeping with its then strongly Unionist beliefs, the paper employed an almost entirely

Protestant workforce. It had a lone Catholic reporter, Hugh P. Allen. Towards the end of 1918, he was covering a General Election meeting in Belfast; he decided that the tone of the speeches was too weak, so he jumped up on the stage and delivered a strongly nationalistic speech himself. It was a big improvement on the previous efforts and went down well with the audience. Belfast being almost as notorious for gossip as Dublin, the word quickly got back to the *Belfast Telegraph* about Allen's fire-raising oratory.

Sir Robert Baird himself called Allen into his inner sanctum, told him that the paper had received complaints about the young reporter's performance the previous night and said he would have to sack him. The blow was softened by a letter of introduction to the editor of the *Western Morning News,* Plymouth (Baird was a great friend of its owner, Lord Northcliffe) and £50 in travelling expenses.

The following day, Allen crossed over to England and took the train to Plymouth. He was taken on the staff of the morning newspaper without quibble, since he was a good reporter with excellent shorthand. The introduction from Baird hazed over the events of that infamous night. One of Allen's jobs, some eighteen months later, was to cover the Assizes in Penzance, about a hundred miles south-west of Plymouth, at the very tip of England. Taking a breather from the court one lunch-time, he walked along the great promenade at Penzance and as he did so, spotted a warship several miles out to sea. A pinnace left the warship and headed for the small harbour at the eastern end of the promenade.

The boat was tied up and Allen saw a figure on a stretcher being brought ashore. He recognised the face as that of Archbishop Mannix of Melbourne. Mannix, with strong Cork conections, had been president of St Patrick's College, Maynooth, before being appointed to the see of Melbourne. He was a great supporter of the Land League and as he grew older, so did his sense of Irish nationalism grow fiercer. On his way from New York to Liverpool aboard the "Baltic", he had been taken off the liner when it was three miles out of Queenstown (now Cobh) to prevent him speaking in Ireland in favour of the Irish cause. To confirm his story, Allen snatched a few hasty words with Archbishop Mannix and told him, jokingly, that the British had just won the greatest naval victory since Jutland! Allen then went to the main post office in Penzance, just a few hundred yards away, and using his pressman's telegraph pass, wired the story to every newspaper he could think of in the USA, on the Continent, in Argentina even. It was a tremendous scoop that earned Allen hundreds of pounds, but his main interest was in dealing a blow to British prestige.

The *Western Morning News* did not approve of the liberal use of its telegraph pass: Allen found himself back in Ireland, working on one of the comparatively few newspapers sympathetic to someone of his

(opposite page) Ruined buildings in the centre of Cork, 1920.

strongly Republican viewpoint, the *Enniscorthy Echo,* under its founding editor, William Sears. He was soon fired from that newspaper for writing a leader that attacked a prominent local Orangeman, Herbert Moore Pim, who had converted to the Sinn Fein cause. Allen forecast that Pim would soon revert to form; after his dismissal, Allen must have taken a morsel of comfort from seeing Pim becoming a born-again Orangeman. As for the pugnacious reporter, he came to Dublin to work for the *Freeman's Journal* and after that paper closed, was last heard of on the *Irish Independent,* a curiously muffled ending for the career of this Republican-minded journalist.

The various elections during 1918 proved hazardous in other ways for newspaper people. John F. O'Hanlon of the *Anglo-Celt* in Cavan stood as a candidate in the East Cavan by-election on behalf of the Irish Parliamentary Party; Sinn Fein's Arthur Griffith won by a landslide. The *Anglo-Celt* was one of the few papers described at the time as having given election coverage fair to all sides. Despite the political leanings of O'Hanlon, the Sinn Fein people were well pleased with the local coverage they got in the paper. O'Hanlon himself had a remarkable escape in the election: he was driving from Bailieborough to Shercock in east Cavan to address an election meeting there when he had a sudden premonition that he should go no further.

He could put no concrete reason on his decision to turn back, although he was expected in Shercock. It took nearly twenty years before he found out that his premonition had been amply justified; one day in 1936, two men came to his house in Cavan and while one stayed silent, the other insisted on begging forgiveness for something that had happened years before. The night that O'Hanlon had turned back from Shercock, these two men, together with a third man, who had died in the meantime, lay in wait at a crossroads for the O'Hanlon car. "We had instructions to kill everyone in the car. We waited with our guns and we were saying the rosary that you would never come." John O'Hanlon had been right. The two men left his house: he never found out who they were or who had given them instructions to kill him and his party on their way to Shercock.

Other journalists had their own problems, too. Robert Smyllie, a Scottish journalist and father of the famous R. M. Smyllie, editor of *The Irish Times,* who sometimes referred in public to the fact that he had been born in Glasgow, had been left £15,000 by an uncle in Scotland. For the time (around 1909) it was a great deal of money, worth around twenty times that much today. It enabled Smyllie senior to fulfill his lifetime ambition of owning his own newspaper, so he started up the *Sligo Times,* a suitably Tory paper. Not being much of a businessman, Smyllie appointed a manager to run it for him; this man, said to have been a relation by marriage of the Maguire family who owned the Brown Thomas department store in Grafton Street, Dublin, simply

The funeral procession of Terence MacSwiney in Cork in 1920. Lord Mayor of Cork and IRA veteran, he was arrested in August of that year on a charge of possessing revolutionary documents. In protest, he went on hunger strike and died at the end of October.
–Cork Examiner

137

Riots at the corner of York Street and Donegall Street, Belfast, in 1920.
–Belfast Telegraph

pocketed most of the cash that came in for classified advertisements and subscriptions.

At the time, Smyllie blamed his bank manager for not spotting the discrepancies in the newspaper's account, but the damage had been done. The manager fled the country with around £15,000, equivalent to Smyllie's entire starting capital. The manager went to America, yet Smyllie, despite his friendship with the RIC county inspector, refused to let the police take up the case and have the man extradited from the United States.

Smyllie, who was known in Sligo as the "workman's friend," despite his Tory views, and who had succeeded in getting elected to the local corporation, went bankrupt. After the collapse of his newspaper, he went to the Belfast *News Letter* as assistant editor and stayed in Belfast for the rest of his life. Not long after he arrived in that city, he was seen on New Year's Eve, 1921, taking a leading part in the merriment at the Albert Memorial, so the Smyllie joviality must have emerged quickly from the traumatic events of Sligo.

Smyllie's son, R.M., faced an equally traumatic homecoming when he was released from the German prisoner-of-war camp at the end of the Great War in 1918. He went to Sligo to find his father's paper collapsed and the family virtually destitute. Four years in the German camp had helped improve the young Smyllie's fluency in that language even further, so he wrote to *The Irish Times'* editor, John Healy, and suggested that he would have the ideal qualifications for covering the 1919 Versailles peace conference. Smyllie's reports were so good that when he returned to Dublin, he was offered a permanent job on *The Irish Times*, becoming assistant editor not long afterwards.

With the Armistice in late 1918, some Nationalist newspaper editors were villified by Unionists who had opposed their coverage of the war. In Birr, Co Offaly, then a strongly Unionist town, James Pike, the dour, walrus-moustached editor of the *Midland Tribune*, found that when local loyalists started a bonfire in Cumberland Square (now Emmet Square) to celebrate the end of the Great War, they added his effigy to that of the Kaiser. More serious troubles were on their way; an influenza epidemic swept Europe, killing millions. At the *Midland Tribune*, several compositors went down with the virus and parts of the paper had to be set in Dublin to ensure its appearance.

On New Year's Day, 1919, a fault occurred in the press at the *Impartial Reporter*, Enniskillen, while the paper was being printed; "Master Bertie" Trimble was trying to repair the breakdown when his clothing got caught up in the shafting. He was whirled upwards into the machinery and left hanging upside down against the ceiling. The engine of the press was still running, but the shafting had stopped. Later, it turned out that a vital steel pin had snapped and to that miracle, he owed his life. As it was, the printers spent half an hour frantically cutting him down with penknives. He spent the next six months in hospital with a broken thigh and as soon as he was able to leave on crutches, went to a fancy dress dance as an "old soldier". Coming out of the hall, he fell down the steps and broke the same thigh again! For the rest of his life, he walked with a limp.

That same month, January, 1919, saw the first shots fired in the War of Independence, at Soloheadbeg, Co Tipperary. News reporting became much more difficult, with physical dangers faced by reporters, many of whom were involved themselves in the struggle for independence. One weekend, Ned Lawler, by then working for the *Irish Independent* in Dublin, took a bag of ammunition home with him to Kilkenny. When he got off the train, the guard starting chatting to him; Lawler couldn't put down the bag, because of the noise it would make. Then he met a friend who insisted on accompanying him home,

John Downey, who founded the Donegal Democrat **in 1919 with C. A. Stephens.**

the long way, across the Green in Kilkenny. One of Lawler's arms must have have been longer than the other that evening! In October the following year, 1920, Lawler was sent just down the road from the *Independent* to cover the fatal shooting of IRA man Sean Treacy (a top man in the Tipperary Brigade) in Talbot Street, Dublin, by the Black and Tans. He turned in graphic copy about the gangs of Black and Tans running up and down the street and the corpses in the gutter, including that of Treacy. He rushed back to Middle Abbey Street and in the space of a few minutes, wrote his copy for a special late edition of the *Evening Herald* that came on the streets at 6 p.m. Also at the *Irish Independent*, David Sears was the noted drama critic. His foppish appearance, made more extreme by a fedora hat, belied his sympathy for the Republican cause. Once, when drinking in a nearby bar, he is said to have become suspicious of a man who claimed he was a journalist with a cross-channel paper, since he knew little of newspaper terminology. It turned out that the man had no newspaper connections at all — he had been sent to spy on Michael Collins.

Martin Pender, father of Aidan, chief proof reader in the *Irish Independent* was strongly committed to the national cause and was chairman of the AOH Irish-American alliance. A machine man who worked in the *Independent* acted as a runner for Martin Pender and was said to have carried at least two execution orders for him.

The publishing of advertisements for Dáil Bonds in 1919 also meant harrassment for nationally-inclined newspapers. The money raised for them in America also, unwittingly, helped to fund the start of the *Irish Press* twelve years later. James Pike of the *Midland Tribune*, had actively canvassed for the Sinn Fein candidate for King's County in the 1918 general election. In September 1919, he had little trouble making up his mind to publish a full page advertisement for the Irish National Loan, in contravention of a British Government order. The paper was promptly suppressed, for a week. At one stage, while members of the RIC and military were guarding the exit gate of the newspaper printing works, Pike had the staff pass bundles of copies through rear windows into a garden that lead into fields and away for clandestine distribution. Police seized type and printing equipment at the *Freeman's Journal* during the course of 1919, putting the paper off the streets for over a month.

Amid all the turmoil and confusion of 1919, one newspaper was launched, the *Donegal Democrat* of Ballyshannon. John Downey had been a printer with the venerable *Donegal Vindicator*, founded some thirty years previously and run by the McAdam family in support of the Irish Parliamentary party. That latter fact alone helped render the paper obsolete, since the Party was a spent force after the crushing victory of Sinn Fein in the 1918 General Election. The energetic young printer, Downey, decided that the district needed a more Republican-minded

newspaper, so with his friend, C. A. Stephens, he started up the *Democrat*. Its first small premises in Ballyshannon now form the town's ESB office. For years, the paper was handset and its circulation confined to Ballyshannon and district; Bundoran and Belleek represented the ends of the earth. The paper survived and prospered, reporting its own tragedy not long after it started when a member of staff, Thomas Rooney, was shot by a military patrol for failing to halt.

Others felt as Downey did and they too came to prominence in Irish journalism and publishing. Like so many other journalists of note, Frank Gallagher (first editor of the *Irish Press*) came from Cork. He had started on the *Cork Free Press*, owned by MP William O'Brien. As a teenager, Gallagher had reported on the Westminster Home Rule debates before the outbreak of World War I. Gallagher was active in

First meeting of the Northern Ireland Parliament at City Hall, Belfast, on June 7, 1921. Sir James Craig arrived late for one early meeting of the Parliament; he asked an Irish News reporter whether prayers were finished. "No, they're just on the last decade of the rosary," quipped the reporter. Craig is said to have roared with laughter at the joke.

the War of Independence and worked on the *Irish Bulletin* from the very start; it owed its origins to Desmond FitzGerald (father of the present Taoiseach, Dr Garret FitzGerald), the director of publicity in the first Dáil. Gallagher himself suffered internment; later during the 1920s, he was editor of the weekly *Nation,* named in tribute to the first *Nation* newspaper.

Working closely with Frank Gallagher on the *Irish Bulletin* was Anna Kelly, mother of Ruth Kelly, the *RTE Guide* columnist. After Easter Week, 1916, Anna Kelly was on the staff of Sinn Fein; it was said that for nearly two particularly troubled years, the *Irish Bulletin* never missed an issue largely thanks to her work. On one occasion during a raid when she was at No 6 Harcourt Street (Sinn Fein headquarters), she watched Michael Collins standing at the open window of a third floor room, wondering whether to leap to safety (and possible death) in the yard below.

In Belfast, the young Michael Rooney (editor, *Irish Independent,* 1960-1968) was also having a hard time. Given a job on the *Irish News* by its editor, Tim McCarthy, Rooney was soon caught up in Republican activities; they provided a respite from the relatively humdrum work on the newspaper, where McCarthy's golden rule was that reporters should be read but not seen.

Newsmen also had to cope with the machinations of the British military publicity machine. After the Black and Tans arrived in Ireland in the summer of 1920, convicts emptied out of British prisons to quell the Irish rebellion, a press officer operated on their behalf out of Dublin Castle. Basil Clarke was known to the Dublin and overseas pressmen who went to the twice daily briefings in the Castle as the "Black and Tan publicity man." At one briefing, at the request of the IRA source, Ned Lawler of the *Irish Independent* asked questions about a top ranking British general. As it turned out, a short while previously, the general had been fired at while travelling along the quays. Thereafter, Lawler remained under suspicion, which was compounded when he refused to stand for the British national anthem at an official ceremony he was covering at St Stephen's Green during the War of Independence. Still, Lawler's luck always held, even when he and a member of the Black and Tans in Dublin became personal friends!

In Dublin and many areas of the country, the Black and Tans roared through in their lorries, creating great fear and alarm, which were compounded by their habit of knocking at random on doors. A young girl in Dublin's Liberties used to lie in bed at night, trembling. The family lived above their shop and most nights, the Black and Tans banged their rifles on the door; eventually, they did decide to break in, but without harming the family. A young Dublin man, coming home from a concert with his violin, was hauled up on one of the Black and

Tan lorries, but he too escaped. Many transport difficulties were created for the newspapers; the sole reporter of the *Longford Leader*, George Mulvey, often had to help out delivering copies of the newspaper by bicycle to outlying areas of the county because roads had been blocked by trees.

In September, 1920, the *Skibbereen Eagle* was put off the streets by an IRA gang which raided its works and smashed the machinery, dumping some of it in the nearby River Ilen. All the files were destroyed, making it difficult for subsequent historians to prove the absolute authenticity of the story about the paper and the Czar of Russia. The offices of the *Eagle* had the only complete file in existence of copies of the paper since it was first published in 1857.

In a claim for £500 damages, the *Eagle* was unable to prove that the damage had been caused maliciously, despite derogatory references in its columns to de Valera and Countess Markievicz. No-one would print the paper, not even the Eagle Printing Company in Cork, which had been founded by Eldon Potter, creator of the *Skibbereen Eagle*. The manager of the Cork firm said that he would be afraid of undertaking the job, since his windows would be smashed. The *Eagle* remained silent for six years.

Light relief was provided for readers of the *Westmeath Independent* that year, 1920; one advertiser promised them that deafness and head noises could be banished. A news item recorded the proposition that Athlone's undesirables should be deported for five years. No wonder that not many years after, the editor of the later combined *Westmeath-Offaly Independent*, John E. Glennon (father of present-day *Irish Times'* journalist Tom Glennon) was able to come up with a cure for that perpetual problem on the provincial press, that of people wishing to keep court reports out of the paper. One night he was caught after hours in a pub. Following the custom of the time, the names of all those "found on" were published when the case came to court. Glennon included his own name and for ever afterwards, when he was pestered by people trying to keep *out* of the paper, he whipped out the cutting of the pub raid case and remarked: "I can't even keep my own name out of my own paper."

On a more serious note, the Athlone paper had said as early as June, 1920: "English rule is broken in Ireland. No English policies, good or bad, will stand. The Irish people will govern themselves." Remarks of that calibre ensured that four months later, the *Westmeath Independent* it self was the cause of the most exciting news story the paper ever carried.

That October, the printing works of the paper that stood for peaceful settlement in Ireland was attached by the Black and Tans. The founding managing director of the firm, Thomas Chapman, was described as being in a delicate state of health and had been away from

J. P. Hayden, founder editor of the Westmeath Examiner **— still going strong in 1940 after fifty-eight years' service.**

E. T. Keane of the
Kilkenny People, who
returned to Ireland
from London during
the War of
Independence on a
forged Metropolitan
Police pass.

Athlone, convalescing, for some considerable time, so it was left to Chapman's wife and the maid, alone in Garden Vale House next to the printing works, to raise the alarm. About 1 a.m. one Sunday morning that October, Mrs Chapman saw flames coming from the end section of the works. She rushed out towards Mardyke Street to try and get some of the printing workers to help tackle the blaze; then she saw about a dozen dark figures (Black and Tans) moving away from the building.

Many people in the town wanted to help put out the fire, but were afraid to break the early evening curfew then widespread in Ireland and run the risk of being shot, so it was left to the two ladies to tackle the blaze as best they could. During Athlone's night of terror, they worked to quench the flames; fortunately, they had access to unlimited water supplies. As dawn broke on the Sunday morning, James Martin, the works manager and a storekeeper called O'Brien, managed to get through to the printing works to relieve Mrs Chapman and her maid. Later still that morning, many townspeople came to congratulate the two women on their heroism.

Despite the partial wrecking of the premises and the destruction of some printing equipment, the *Westmeath Independent* came out as usual the following Saturday, with the lead story on its own disaster. Thomas Chapman's health never recovered; he died in 1922.

The Black and Tans were also held to have made their mark on *The Irish Times;* for years after the Tans left Ireland, marks on the counter of the old office in Westmoreland Street were said to have been made by the boots of a Black and Tan soldier. Another Black and Tan rumour also circulated in *The Irish Times* in later years; "Pussy" O'Mahony, father of Dave Allen, the comedian, was general manager of the paper in the late 1940s. He was said to have been involved in the Black and Tans in Co Meath; when he was taken on a tour to visit favourite spots in the county just before he died, he met up with a sweetheart in Trim. The friendship was said to have dated from around 1920, when the Black and Tans sacked the town. O'Mahony himself neither confirmed nor denied the suggestions about his past.

Ireland's state of terror was aptly described in the daily publication brought out by the *Connacht Tribune* in Galway at the end of November, 1920. Railwaymen were refusing to carry armed troops on the trains, so the consequent delays meant that the Dublin morning papers were not reaching Galway until after six in the evening. The miniature tabloid, a rare feat in Irish provincial journalism, selling for one penny, carried as much news as it could about the war.

"Mortimer Duggan, a teacher, was shot dead in a public house in Broadford, Co Limerick. The tragedy occurred when two lorries containing armed forces raided the licensed premises of Mr O'Riordan ... Constable Cronin died as a result of wounds received at Castlemartyr, Co Cork ... Brigadier-General Cameron was fired

upon while leaving New Barracks, Limerick. In consequence, the military authority has forbidden all fairs and markets in the city."

The weekend of terror in Cork, when many of that city's finest shops and stores were destroyed, was also highlighted in the first issue of the daily *Connacht Tribune* on November 20, 1920.

The Black and Tans were even more active in Tralee; by the start of the War of Independence, the town had just two papers left, the *Kerryman* and the *Kerry Weekly Reporter*, the latter edited by John Moynihan (who eventually became involved with the launch of the *Irish Press* in 1931 and then became secretary to the Fianna Fail Government elected in 1932). The *Reporter's* offices in Russell Street and the Market, Tralee, were burned out by the Black and Tans in 1920. The *Kerryman* came in for similar treatment; on various occasions prior to 1920, it had been suppressed, for refusing to print recruitment advertisements for the British army and for carrying advertisements for the famous Dáil bonds in 1919.

In April, 1921, after the local commander of the Auxiliaries had been killed by the IRA at the old golf links in Tralee, the paper's position became even more difficult. Armed soldiers of the Auxiliaries burst into the office and demanded that the paper be printed with black

Military action at the corner of Henry Street and Sackville Street (now O'Connell Street), Dublin, July, 1922.

A smashed Linotype machine at the Cork Examiner **office, after an IRA raid in 1922.**
–*Cork Examiner*

bordered columns as a mark of respect for their murdered commander. The editorial staff refused; the Auxiliaries burned down the printing works and put the *Kerryman* out of action until the summer of 1923. Whereas the *Kerryman* premises had been burned as a malicious reprisal, the Black and Tans were said to have burned down the *Kerry Weekly Reporter* offices (owned by the Unionist Quinnell family) out of sheer devilment.

Also burned down by the Black and Tans was the *Leitrim Observer* in Carrick-on-Shannon. The paper had been bought for a (borrowed) £5 in 1910 by an extraordinary character, Pat Dunne, the Jasper Tully of Co Leitrim. He did time in Ballykinlar internment camp in Co Down, where he claimed to have perfected the technique of distilling whiskey from old tea leaves. During the six months he was at Ballykinlar, his sister, Eliza, ran the place. The ultimate torture came in 1921, when the Black and Tans set fire to the printing works.

In the early years of the national movement, Pat Dunne was renowned locally for his Model T Ford, which he delighted in running without the benefit of lights, licence or tax. When the races were on in Co Fermanagh, he used to delight in taking "loads" for the lads; try as they could, the RIC were never able to get their man. Pat Dunne was also said to have taken various fatal means of persuasion with him when he confronted particularly difficult advertisers who refused to settle accounts.

Soon however, Dunne had the *Leitrim Observer* running again, with the help of itinerant typesetters who wandered from town to town and from job to job as late as the 1920s. Dunne also brought in Patrick Hyland, who had served his time at the *Nationalist and Leinster Times,* Carlow, as his manager. From Jasper Tully's *Roscommon Herald,* he brought in Pat Moran of Boyle as his reporter. Moran had had extensive experience both with Tully and in various British Army regiments during the Great War, so that he was well able to keep up the editorial side of the *Leitrim Observer.* With the help of Hyland and Moran, Dunne soon overcome the problems imposed on him by the Black and Tans.

1921 saw a young Wexford man called Francis Carty join the Republican movement. He became commandant of the South Wexford Battalion; as a supporter of de Valera, he spent some time in prison after the civil war, until April, 1924. In his teens, he had written stories for *Ireland's Own,* the Wexford-published paper, and ended up as editor of first the *Irish Press* and then the *Sunday Press.* Another young journalist making his mark was Pat Murphy, who now lives in retirement at Crookhaven, Co Cork. For years foreign news editor of the *Daily Mail,* London, he had been educated in pre-Revolution Russia, where he had become acquainted with the peculiar sexual tastes of Rasputin ("he liked to go to bed with three girls and a black dog"). He returned home briefly, did two pieces for the *Irish Independent* (by-lined "From our Russian correspondent") and claims he was told by one of the Murphys when he went looking for his fee, "Nonsense, you should be doing it for the experience". The *Freeman's Journal* then took him on, at three guineas a week. 1921 also saw a young reporter on the *Sligo Independent* made the bold step of buying the newspaper from its then owner, Alexander Gillmor. William Peebles (father of Ivan Peebles of the *Belfast Telegraph)* had started in newspapers as a "printer's devil" in the *Mid-Ulster Mail* at Cookstown, Co Tyrone, graduating to junior reporter. Before the Great War, he joined the *Sligo Independent.*

1921 saw the *Connacht Tribune* produce a special fight bulletin — on the great Dempsey-Carpentier world heavyweight championship. Before 9 p.m. on the Saturday night of the fight, a Press Association telegram arrived at the newspaper with news of Dempsey's win and a special one sheet edition was run off. A more detailed edition appeared

W. D. Peebles, who bought over the Sligo Independent **in 1921; he closed down the newspaper forty years later.**

147

THE
EYE-OPENER.

Registered as a Newspaper under the "Newspaper Libel and Registration Act, 1881."

NO. 7.   VOL. I.   APRIL 1, 1916.   ONE PENNY

ENGLISH COWARDS AND SLACKERS

The Howling Mob that Insulted Irishmen

THEIR INVASION OF IRELAND

Some months ago, in England, a great outcry was raised against the Irish harvesters who were returning to their homes in Ireland. At the ... which the boats for Ireland depart, howling mobs crowded these and attacked the Irishmen; and among the ... insulting remarks used ... men were

that of England, the British Army contains more Irish than English. This is a solid fact that def... contradiction ... ... the streets of Dublin a... ... large numbers of these English cowards and slackers, who are of military age and fit for ser... who ...ve in... ...reland, ...

fleeing from the fight are hold up to the same scorn and abuse that they meted out to the Irish ... ... allowed to forget that they are cowards and slackers, and that they are part of the howling mob who some few months ago, ...ese names. ...ress a...

Thomas Dickson, editor of the Eye-Opener, **a controversial weekly newspaper, was executed by Crown forces only three weeks after this issue appeared.**

the next day, Sunday. One paper, however, closed down that year, the *Evening Irish Times,* after forty-one years in existence.

Trade was so bad early the following year, 1922, that Irish printers agreed to a five shilling weekly reduction in their wages, which ranged as high as £4 7s 6d a week. Much worse was to come. April, 1922, saw a devastating attack on the *Freeman's Journal* offices in Dublin. Supporters of de Valera burst into the printing works and smashed up the presses. The morning after the raid, a single sheet issue was run off on a duplicator, not more than a few hundred copies, more an act of defiance than a serious attempt at bringing out a newspaper. It went on display in the paper's Fleet Street, London, offices and a facsimile was reproduced in the London *Times.*

Said the *Freeman's Journal* a couple of days after the raid: "The sledge is not all-powerful. On the night it demolished our machines, we managed to produce one sheet. Today, we have seven. Why did Mr

O'Connor and his fellow mutineers order the wrecking of the *Freeman's Journal* – because they allege we published statements prejudicial to the discipline of the Army. Their press agent and apologist is Mr Childers and they presume to dictate what Irish journalists shall say or leave unsaid!" The raid came 2½ years after the disabling raid on the paper by the police.

The same day that the *Freeman's Journal* produced its famous single sheet issue, its sister paper, the *Evening Telegraph* turned out a special edition for sale at the Leopardstown races run that day in aid of the Press Fund for widows and orphans of journalists, as well as at a Mansion House concert that night.

In 1922, a popular paper, the *North Antrim Standard*, published in Ballymoney, died. At the turn of the century, the *Standard* had linked up with the *Northern Constitution*, preserved its own identity through such features as "Fun for the fireside", mostly jokes. Living in the shadow of the *Constitution*, it was eventually eclipsed by that paper and in November, 1922, the title of the *North Antrim Standard* was incorporated into that of the *Northern Constitution*.

On Easter Sunday of 1922 William Peebles of the *Sligo Independent* enjoyed a "scoop" at the expense of his rival, the *Sligo Champion*, which was unable to publish because its machinery had been badly damaged by "bandits". Peebles reported Griffiths' famous Sligo speech while a machine gun was trained on the platform. Sligo was rushed by the Irregulars, including Eamon de Valera. Twelve armed men seized the *Sligo Independent* offices and Peebles had to run the risk of being shot on his way to and from his premises.

In Belfast, Michael Rooney from the *Irish News*, already nearly bald because of beatings he had suffered from British forces, was commander of the Republican prisoners in Crumlin Road jail, Belfast. He was just nineteen years of age. When he was let out of prison, he returned to the *Irish News*, where as he moved up the reporting scale, he continued to be puzzled by a frequent entry in the markings' book kept by the chief reporter, so that reporters would know which stories they were due to cover. One reporter's initials appeared time and time again, "E. P." Only later did Rooney discover the key to the mystery — E. P. stood for evening paper. The *Irish News*, chronically under-funded, was "lifting" much copy from the *Belfast Telegraph*.

Cork journalists had their own share of troubles; dark as were the days of the Black and Tans, worse was to come with the civil war in 1922. Irishmen fought fellow Irishmen with even more viciousness than they fought the British forces. On the *Cork Examiner*, military raids by the Black and Tans had disrupted production. Military censorship compelled the paper to publish the official version of ambushes and shootings. Two brothers who were reporters in the city, Michael and George Harrington, (their brother Tim was editor of the *Irish Independent*), were arrested on a trumped-up charge and landed up in the

"On Cave Hill we took a solemn obligation NEVER TO REST in our efforts until we had subverted the authority of England over our Country and asserted our Independence."
WOLFE TONE

Poblacht na h-Eireann

SOUTHERN EDITION.

"That Tone's teaching is true and great and that no other teaching as to Ireland has any truth or worthiness at all, is a thing upon which I stake all my mortal and immortal hopes."—PEARSE.

"It is not those who can inflict most, but those who can endure most, who will conquer."—Terence MacSwiney.

No. 25.   Thursday, 23rd November, 7th Year of the Republic.   Price 2d.

Frightfulness.

We heard this term first in English propaganda. We did not believe it of those to whom it applied. We did not think it very important that we should consider it at all. But it is no longer propaganda. It is naked Truth, and of all people in the world it is true of Irishmen. There can be nothing but disgust for men, drunk with power, who on a sudden access of unwonted strength exercise it in brutal and cruel acts, in acts negatory of their manhood, and in acts negatory of their National status and reputation. To any man or woman who holds the name of Ireland dear, it is heart-rending to see our reputation dragged through the dirt by these men. Within five months they had placed to their record a terrible account, viz. in the shooting of Brugha and Boland, the shelling of Irishmen in the streets of Dublin, the jailing of upwards of ten thousand of their countrymen, the outlawing of every man and woman who had the pluck and honour to stand by an unequivocal oath to Irish Freedom, the establishing of a system of lettres de cachet, espionage and the giving over to military courtsmartial of the liberty and the lives of the individual. Now they must needs go farther.

They are killing by slow starvation the sister of Terence MacSwiney. They emulate Englishmen's treatment of Roger Casement by their mock trial of Erskine Childers. They have hanged four young Irishmen in Dublin. By these men's latest acts the F.S. they represent has become a still more repulsive thing, if that were possible. Hitherto we had hoped to keep uppermost in our minds the thought that England was our sole enemy whom we could meet UNITED. It will be a terrible thing if these men's actions make their persons so repugnant to true Irishmen that the necessity for their removal overshadow the vital issue of England the Enemy.

The Wise Words of Eoin MacNeill.

The following is from Eoin MacNeill's pamphlet "Daniel O'Connell and Sinn Fein."

"The fatal weakness of Grattan's Irish Constitution was that, IT OPENLY TOLERATED FROM THE BEGINNING THE EXERCISE OF INTERFERENCE FROM ENGLAND . . . . The one great political necessity of Ireland is to get rid of interference from England. Any measure that secures the freedom of Ireland from English interference, by what name soever that measure may be called, whatsoever may be its draughtmanship and its details will solve the Irish political problem ; and any measure even the Repeal of the Union, that leaves interference from England a thing practicable with impunity, will leave the problem still unsolved. That is the test. IF ENGLISH POLITICIANS CLAIM THE RIGHT TO INTERFERE OR RESERVE THE POWER TO INTERFERE, then we know where we stand and what we have to expect. We know from history and experience that, in that case, THE STATE OF IRELAND CAN NEVER BE SETTLED OR SAFE OR WHOLESOME. The ancient wound will remain unhealed, the ancient hostility unappeased."

Treatment of Prisoners.

Any Republicans captured and taken prisoners to Wellington Barracks, Dublin, under circumstances which appear to connect them with any ambush or armed attack on Free State troops are put through the form of torture one reads of as taking place in the days of the Spanish Inquisition. Brought to an office, popularly known as the "knocking out" shop, these unfortunate men are examined by a barbarian known as Dolan (or Dolain). Any answer they make is treated as a deliberate lie. A small platoon of C.I.D. men gathered around strike or kick the prisoner, according as to whether he is on the ground or standing up. Many prisoners have been kicked into the stomach. Others have had a revolver muzzle forced down their throat and then twisted around to make a severe wound. Others have had their arms twisted almost to breaking point, while the man who escapes with one black eye is indeed lucky.

The most brutal case of all concerns a Republican named Tom Hendrick. Elected O.C. of the prisoners on Thursday, November 9th, he was called down to the "knockout" shop on the following day and informed that he must act as a spy on certain comrades or be shot. On indignantly refusing such work, he was treated to an utterly inhuman beating. Struck repeatedly with revolvers, he was rendered semi-conscious, and then his clothes being partially removed he was lashed with the butt-end of rifles till the lower portion of his body was a mass of bruises. On falling to the ground he was kicked in the stomach, when he fainted with pain. He was then carried back to the prisoners' room, where he suffered two or three severe fits, and had eventually to be attended by a doctor.

News of this beating reached the ears of the officers' mess (who are gentlemen in comparison with this Dolan), half a dozen of the latter, including Brig. McNeill, Captain O'Byrne, O.C. Wellington Barracks, Lt. Kennedy, O.C. Prisoners, and the barrack doctor came upstairs. McNeill was intensely affected by Hendrick's condition. He sent for a clerk, and in presence of officers and prisoners, took a statement from Tom Hendrick of his beating. He promised to work for an inquiry into the whole occurence. On Saturday, November 11th, Hendrick was still in a weak condition.

P.S.—Hendrick was a prisoner without charge. He was not arrested for taking part in any ambush or attack.

Barrister-at-Law

Prophecy.

The Free State, no doubt,
    When its life ebbs out,
Will ride in a blazing chariot,
    And sit in state
    On a red-hot plate
'Twixt Pilate and Judas Iscariot.

    Ananias that day
    To the devil will say:
My claim to precedence fails,
    So I'll move up higher
    To make room by the fire
For the "tools" of the Wizard of Wales."

WORKERS' REPUBLIC.

Bridewell. Not that Tim Harrington fared much better — for several months during 1921 and 1922, because of his editorial policies, he was forced to live in the *Irish Independent* offices in Dublin, for fear of assassination. Colleagues remembered him coming to the front door when the coast was clear, a pale-faced man snatching a quick breath of fresh air.

The *Cork Examiner's* support of the Treaty also caused reporters from the paper to be regarded strangely in some quarters. One reporter who was threatened had been served with a deportation order with the Black and Tans not long before!

For three months in 1922, because of damage to its printing works, the *Cork Examiner* had to be set just up the road in Guy's old factory. Every day, trolleys containing the formes of type were wheeled up the street, protected by an escort of Free State soldiers. In the June of that year, the first shots were fired in the civil war. With the destruction of the railway bridge at Mallow, Cork became the *de facto* capital of the Republican part of the country. Two months later, the Free State forces started their advance on Cork.

In the besieged city, workers at the *Cork Examiner* waited uneasily. Then, one morning, a squad of Republicans came thundering up the stairs from Patrick Street. The officer in charge had a revolver; each of the men carried a fourteen pound sledge hammer like a rifle at the slope. "Everybody out" they shouted as the gang went to the printing floor and started breaking up the banks of Linotype machines. The Republican plan, as the Free State forces advanced on Cork, was to resort to guerilla warfare; the Republicans planned to put the *Cork Examiner* and Parnell Bridge out of action. Fortunately, quick repairs to the rotary presses and improvisation with the setting enabled the *Examiner* to be published again next day.

One young reporter was to have Cork etched in his memory for ever: Frank Geary, who had joined the *Irish Independent* in 1922 from the *Kilkenny People*. Geary was covering the civil war fighting in Kilmallock, Co Limerick, when he got a message from "H" (Harrington the editor in Dublin). He was told to return to the office immediately.

Geary passed a long, tedious journey to Dublin wondering what he had done to deserve this sudden recall. That Sunday night, he was called to Harrington's room in the *Independent*. Harrington, never one for either pleasantries or preliminaries, said: "Geary, I want you to got to Cork. Lie low when you get there. There should be some good copy in it soon. When the Free State army arrives, we will have a man with them on the outside and you will have the story from the inside."

When the young reporter protested that he couldn't get to Cork since there were no trains and the roads were blocked, he was told: "Get there as best you can. Meet our man on the outside. And now, Geary, I am busy." Geary sailed to Liverpool and from there to Cork, where he stayed for about ten days before the Free State forces

Barefoot boys imitate soldiers on the Dublin quays after the 1916 Easter Rising.

arrived. He got his story; it was as big a scoop as Harrington had promised.

For another newspaperman Cork that year was equally memorable. John O'Sullivan, who became a reporter on the *Cork Examiner* in 1923, saw Michael Collins outside the Imperial Hotel, then the temporary headquarters of Southern Command, the afternoon before he was killed at Beal na mBlath. Collins made a striking figure in uniform, with a shock of hair falling across his forehead; his eyes sparkled as he talked with Emmet Dalton and other officers.

Somehow, the *Cork Examiner* scraped through, although the effects of the troubles lingered on long in the South. As late as 1932, the *Cork Examiner* had a van burned by activists on the Cork/Kerry border. Denis McGrath, the paper's manager, was shot in the back during the civil war; he never fully recovered from his wounds and died in 1931. Yet relations on the paper itself were remarkably free of the bitterness engendered during the war between Irishmen. Some staff had been active in the Republican cause, while a few Free State soldiers joined the firm as van drivers after 1923. There was never any friction but other papers in the city were not so fortunate. The *Cork Constitution*, for long the bulwark of Unionism in the city, and fat with advertising, was reduced to a single sheet measuring 8" x 4" in 1924. It staggered through that year in that form, before finally expiring, an ignominious end for the newspaper that once drew vast comfort from Cork's merchants.

In Waterford, the offices of the *Munster Express* had the unwelcome distinction of being the only newspaper offices anywhere in the country to be used as a fort during the hostilities. Considerable damage was caused, to the total of £3,000, but Edward Walsh, the proprietor, only claimed for and received the nominal sum of £35.

With his late brother Patrick, J. J. Walsh had some hair-raising escapades getting through Republican lines by bicycle to ensure that readers of the paper in Carrick-on-Suir received their weekly copies, as expected. In Dublin, Anna Kelly had a close shave while she was printing an issue of the *Republican War News* in a garage in Appian Way at Ranelagh, Dublin, during the civil war. Free State forces raided the place: Anna slipped out through the back door, ran across a field and in through the open window of a large house. It was a maternity home and to the surprised nurse, she said: "It's not twins, it's politics." Free State forces caught up with and arrested Anna Kelly in 1923.

The troubles of the War of Independence and the civil war in the southern part of Ireland, as well as the troubles in the North of Ireland, were compounded by the great slump in world trade that followed World War I. Business was so bad for Andrew Clarke, owner of the *Coleraine Chronicle,* that he had to considerably reduce the size of the paper before selling it off.

After the end of the civil war, when the country settled into a period of economic desolation, journalists like Anna Kelly and Frank Gallagher were released from internment and Unionist newspapers in the South of Ireland either collapsed or began the slow change to adapt to the new political realities of the Irish Free State. The newspapers of Ireland had just come through a tremendous challenge. Such testing times would never again happen and neither would journalists enjoy quite so much excitement.

Special bulletins published by the Connacht Tribune **in 1921 and 1922.**

CHAPTER VI

Rising star of the Irish Press
1924-1939

*Lady with private touring car takes orders for drives and
excursions. 6d a mile. Box G945 this office.*

THE IRISH TIMES, 1925

*For Christmas. Fruit cake (about 3lbs) and bottle of wine, 3/-.
L & N Tea Co., Nenagh.*

NENAGH GUARDIAN, 1938

Mrs Pearse, mother of
Patrick and Willie
Pearse, starts the press
for the final trial run of
the Irish Press in 1931.
Also in the photograph,
from left: Robert
Brennan (first general
manager), Eamon de
Valera, Seamus McCall
(art editor), Fr Albert,
Paddy McGrath (works
manager), Jim Ryan
(later a Fianna Fail
Government Minister)
and Frank Gallagher
(editor).

–Irish Press

As the country slipped into the uneasy, post-civil warm calm, and
Ireland's lifeblood, Nationalist and Unionist people alike,
haemorrhaged away by the tens of thousands to find new lives
overseas, that great newspaper institution, the *Freeman's Journal,* was
slipping inexorably into oblivion.

In the early 1920s, it was owned by a publican called Martin
Fitzgerald, who always carried a gun because of the threats on his life.
On one occasion, he is said to have brandished the weapon in order to
settle a threatened strike by caseroom staff. The evening before the
strike was due to start, he went into the caseroom and announced:

"Good evening, gentlemen. My name is Fitzgerald; I own this
newspaper. Will all those in favour of the strike stand up. "Then he
produced his gun.

In the two years before the closure of the paper in 1924, the staff
knew instinctively that they were aboard a doomed ship. Changing
political fortunes and the wrecking of its offices, in 1916 and 1922,
made its failure inevitable. No-one was more aware of impending
disaster than its editor, Paddy Hooper; nevertheless, he hoped,
forlornly, that some totally unexpected miracle would emerge. He
smoked dozens of "Sweet Afton" cigarettes a day and eventually
became so ill that the young J. J. McCann, later of *Radio Review* and *Irish
Times'* fame, had to go out to Hooper's house in Morehampton Road,
Donnybrook, to take his dictation.

Desperate measures were taken to try and save the paper. In an anti-vice campaign, the *Freeman's Journal* condemned the brothels of the Railway Street area in no uncertain fashion. All went well until the police raided one such brothel and found a senior journalist from the *Freeman* using its facilities!

There were other notable characters, too, in the newspaper's offices almost next door to the Theatre Royal (Hawkins House now stands on the site). Mick Tobin, star of the reporting staff, had a voice of such strength that when he was on the telephone in the reporters' room, he

Irish Press **sports department and contributors with the editor, Frank Gallagher and his wife Celia and daughter Anne. At front, Charlie Perry and Sean Coughlan. Back row, left to right: Arthur McGahon, Mitchel Cogley (father of Fred Cogley), Paddy McKenna, John Joe White, Joe Sherwood ("In the soup"), Des Burke and Tom Bissett.**

could be heard in the hallway. One of the MacWeeney family was Night Town reporter, while Barry Tynan O'Mahony, the barrister brother of "Pussy" of *Irish Times'* fame, also worked for the paper for a while. Later, Barry developed three addictions — to borrowing money, to morphine and to his pet dog.

Paddy Montford, the advertisement manager and associate of *Dublin Opinion's* Charlie Kelly, had one great gift. Although he never touched a drop of alcoholic drink, he took much pleasure in doing perfect imitations of a drunk. He was said to have been thrown out of more pubs in Dublin than most very drunk journalists! When the end came for the *Freeman's Journal,* days before Christmas, 1924, the paper was "waked" in Bowes' pub in Fleet Street, just across D'Olier Street from its offices.

The staff on the three papers (the *Freeman's Journal*, the *Evening Telegraph* and *Sport)* were scattered far and wide. Larry Morrow, the literary editor, was a relation of Robert Lynd, the Northern writer, and joined him on the staff of the London *Star*. Charlie Kelly, the editor of the *Evening Telegraph,* went to the Cork *Evening Echo.* Mick "Sport" Byrne, who worked on the weekly *Sport* newspaper, went to work for the *Irish Independent* and then the *Irish Press* when it started in 1931. Sean Lester, who was Douglas Gageby's father-in-law, had started on the *North Down Herald* and was news editor of the *Freeman's Journal* during the War of Independence. Then he joined the new Irish Diplomatic Service. He became secretary-general of the League of Nations.

By a strange coincidence, the *Irish Independent* had moved into its new headquarters in Middle Abbey Street just a short while before the *Freeman's Journal* died. After the Easter Week Rising of 1916, William Martin Murphy acquired four burned-out sites in Middle Abbey Street; before he died in 1919, he had outlined the plans for the impressive new building.

Murphy's son, Dr William Lombard Murphy, was brought home from the Royal Army Medical Corps in Greece to run the firm and it was he who supervised the building of Independent Newspapers' new headquarters. William Martin Murphy had left instructions that he wanted the building to be designed with an eye to the health and comfort of those who were to work in it. After the *Freeman's Journal* closed down, Dr William Lombard Murphy bought the titles of the

Cearbhall O Dálaigh, first Irish language editor of the Irish Press. Later, he was President of Ireland. The original purpose of the photograph, taken in 1931, was to get an illustration of hand-writing to illustrate an article. The rest of the photograph was not published.
–Irish Press

paper and its associated publications, together with printing machinery, for £24,000, not to continue in publication, but to prevent others carrying on the *Freeman* tradition. A group of Republicans, later associated with the formation of the *Irish Press,* tried unsuccessfully to raise a bid against Murphy.

In the *Independent* then was one of the finest journalistic characters it ever produced: George MacDonagh, a Limerickman and chief reporter. A small, fragile man, he had joined the paper about two years after its launch in 1905; in the early 1920s, he was remembered by Frank Geary as being a man with "a big, big heart made of the purest gold". Very often, he was in the wars with Harrington, the editor, over the errors and omissions of the reporting staff. Similarly, the chief sub, a Donegal man called Pat Aikens, who died at a comparatively young age, bore the scathing criticism of Harrington in the subs' room night after night. Aikens took it quite impassively, knowing through the wisdom of his experience that rows in newspaper offices rarely last long. Aikens did not approve of the impetuous young subs who took a malicious delight in answering Harrington back.

A great change came upon the *Northern Standard,* Monaghan, in 1924. The paper had been in the Swan family for the previous fifty-two years and was being run by Philip McMinn, grandson of William Swan, who had bought the firm in 1872. In the 1920s, religious differences between Catholics and Protestants still ran deep in Monaghan. McMinn ran the paper along strictly Presbyterian lines: no advertisements for dancing, no coverage of Sunday sport. So to general surprise, he appointed Joe Turley as editor; Turley was

Eamon de Valera with Frank Gallagher (left), first editor of the Irish Press.
–Irish Press

Catholic and the paper was Orange by inclination. Contemporaries of Turley included Alfred Shannon, who later owned and edited the *Portadown Times*, Robert Hamilton and a man called Cousins, who both went to work on the Belfast *News Letter*. Under Turley's influence, the paper began to broaden its outlook, becoming one of the first Unionist papers in the new Irish Free State to adapt — and survive.

In 1925, newspaper expansion came to Galway with the launching by the *Connacht Tribune* of the *Connacht Sentinel;* two years later, the firm bought a new Cossar press which enabled it to print its newspaper from reels rather than flat sheets. The new *Connacht Sentinel,* which still survives today, gave an early opportunity of publication to Padraic O Conaire, that celebrated modern writer in Irish whose statue today

Eamon de Valera on his American tour just before launching the Irish Press. De Valera spent some six months visiting American newspapers to study production techniques, together with Frank Gallagher (right), first editor.

**The late Paddy Clare,
who joined the** Irish
Press **as it started in
1931 and spent many
years as Night Town
reporter.**
–Irish Press

adorns Eyre Square. His reputation then in the Galway newspaper office was of a different kind: he was said to have been promiscuous in his relations with the opposite sex and older members of staff recalled that there was great concern in the *Connacht Tribune* offices that O Conaire would spread disease there. Not far away, the Scott family continued their almost private existence, locked into the weekly production of their newspaper, the *Galway Observer.*

The Scott family, by themselves, ran the paper. As his parents became old, John Scott took charge of the newspaper, which had a circulation of about four thousand in and around the city. Since Galway in the 1920s was a much smaller city than today, that gave the *Observer* a very respectable sale to one in four of its inhabitants. John Scott was devoted to the production of the paper, which was printed downstairs at their premises in Abbeygate Street. The family lived upstairs. The only excursion for John, apart from Mass with the rest of the family, was for his regulation two bottles of stout after 9 p.m. every night. In those days, the fisherwomen of Galway carried baskets of fish on their heads and they used to come in to the Scotts to buy scrap paper for wrapping up the fish.

A valiant and ill-fated attempt was made in 1926 to revive the *Skibbereen Eagle,* silent since the IRA raid on its premises six years previously, but the paper was past its time. Principal behind the revival was Jasper Wolfe, but his efforts at resuscitation were unsuccessful and in 1929, its deadly enemy, the Nationalist *Southern Star* bought it out for a total of £1,400.

In Tralee, the *Kerryman* bought over its one-time rival, the *Kerry Weekly Reporter* and the burned-out premises of the latter paper were used as the site for the new printing works and offices for the *Kerryman.* Many of the *Weekly Reporter's* staff dispersed. John Moynihan, the editor, went to Dublin, where he worked on the *Nation* and then briefly on the new *Irish Press.* Joe Harrington went to the *Kerryman* and later became editor of the *Sligo Champion.* Tommy Lynch and Paddy Cahill went off to found the *Kerry Champion* in 1928. During the *Champion's* thirty year lifespan, one of its editors was the father of Tony O'Riordan, the book reviewer and quiz compiler. Some of the *Kerry Weekly Reporter* staff were anti-Treaty, while the *Kerryman* was pro. The two factions blended well enough on the latter paper. Con Casey, who went from the *Reporter* to the *Kerryman* and who spent forty-eight years at the latter newspaper, culminating in his editorship, was carted off to Mountjoy in 1926 for his anti-Treaty activities. When he returned to the *Kerryman* three weeks later, no questions were asked and no undertakings were demanded. Considering the economic plight of the country, the new Free State government was generous towards the press. In 1928, it spent £80,756 on advertising in newspapers and periodicals.

All over Ireland, as a respite from the political turmoil of the civil

FÁILTE ROMAIB SO LÉIR
Ó MUINCIR DROMACÁIN
ANNSO A RUSAÓ COMAS RUISÉL

war, the picture houses blossomed. The Ritz, the Coliseum, the Electric and the Grand Central, these and a hundred other cinemas the length and breadth of Ireland showed silent films with such stars as Charlie Chaplin, Lillian Gish, Mary Pickford, Buster Keaton and Gloria Swanson in the latest Hollywood epics. A pianist, usually female, provided the musical accompaniment, switching from "Moonlight and Roses" to the William Tell overture when the flickering images on the silver screen demanded music for the inevitable horse chase. Young and old alike queued for the often makeshift bench seats with just as much enthusiasm as working people queued for hours for tickets in the "gods" for the opera at the Gaiety Theatre, Dublin.

The cinema also provided great tragedy and the news story of 1926. When the cinema at Drumcollogher, Co Limerick, went on fire, burning to death many of the audience, after the reels of film flared up, newsmen came from Belfast, Cork, Dublin and further afield. Frank Geary arrived hotfoot on behalf of the *Irish Independent* and started his copy in his usual florid style, "Coffins, coffins, coffins . . ."

The blessing ceremony for the Mallow, Co Cork, sugar factory, 1934. Eamon de Valera, president of the Executive Council of Saor Stáit Éireann, is second from the left, front row.
–*Irish Sugar Company*

161

The *Limerick Leader* really broke out; for the first time, in the recollection of Mainchin Seoighe, it ran a headline the full width of the page.

Another fire occurred, with less tragic consequences. The office of E. T. O'Hanlon, editor of the *Anglo-Celt*, Cavan and uncle of the present editor, Edward O'Hanlon, caught fire. Having decided that there was nothing he could do personally to help matters, and determined not to miss his daily "constitutional", he went for a walk at the height of the blaze. The neighbouring *Northern Standard* in Monaghan caught fire three years later, in 1930. The fire was far more serious and while the damage was being repaired, the paper was printed at the *Belfast Telegraph*.

Meanwhile, Smyllie, assistant editor of *The Irish Times*, between belching smoke from his pipe, introduced a great brainwave in 1927: "An Irishman's Diary", the daily column on the leader page. For many years after the Second World War, it was the domain of Seamus Kelly, the Belfast-born journalist who was by turn tetchy and charming, largely depending on the company he was keeping. Before the war, the Diary was filled with paragraphs from an assorted variety of freelance sources, to whom the half-crown per par was much-needed manna.

Children on their way to Mass in Dublin during the great Eucharistic Congress of 1932.

On Saturdays, Smyllie himself monopolised the column, even after he became editor, writing under the pseudonym of "Nichevo". Friends were tolerant of Smyllie's ramblings; enemies said that the column never moved far from Grafton Street on a Saturday and that its contents merely "puffed" Smyllie's friends and drinking acquaintances.

Smyllie had some strange journalistic bedfellows on *The Irish Times*, most notably Cyril Bretherton, who had been the notoriously anti-Irish correspondent in Ireland during the "troubles" for the ultra-conservative *Morning Post*, London, swallowed up by the *Daily Telegraph* during the 1930s. Bretherton had acquired an unsavoury reputation among nationally-inclined journalists, but he and Smyllie worked together on the *The Irish Times* to produce a magazine-type page that was the forerunner of the Diary. Healy himself, the long-serving editor, was utterly inflexible in his Unionism, although the paper had welcomed the appointment of Tim Healy as the first Governor-General of the Irish Free State. Relations between the new regime and the paper were not always cordial; in 1926, a furious row broke out between Healy and one of the paper's reporters, W. P. B. Buttimer. Healy alleged that a meeting at which he spoke had been incorrectly reported. This particular source of friction remained unresolved. *The Irish Times* continued to set all foreign language words, including those in Irish such as "Dáil" in italics until as late as 1934. In the midlands, the *King's County Chronicle* refused to change the name of the county in which it was located until the end of 1922, two years after "King's County" became "Offaly".

As Smyllie was consolidating his position as heir-apparent to Healy, a young school master joined the staff in 1930. Alec Newman had been a Classics scholar at Trinity College, Dublin, after which he spent two unhappy years as senior classical master at the High School in Harcourt Street. He joined as a leader writer and when Smyllie was made editor in 1934, moved up to become assistant editor. Appearing a little remote and austere in the classical mould, Newman nevertheless had a penchant for colourful and vituperative language when drunk.

While the editorial machinations continued upstairs, below stairs life at the paper had many hilarious moments, well remembered by such venerable characters as Benny Green, who joined the paper as a clerk in 1921 and who was once told by Smyllie in a moment of anger to "get back to his ghetto on the South Circular Road" (Benny is Jewish). Alec Newman rang down on one occasion and said so politely: "Benny, you're a bollox!" Down amid the Linotypes, the bowler-hatted comps, male chauvinists to a man, regarded themselves as the elite of Dublin craftsmen. For comps who were late for work, a cab driver used to wait at the works entrance in Fleet Street. The driver would then be sent to collect the missing man and 2/6d was deducted from his wages. One *Irish Times'* comp, Paddy Cullen, always wore a top hat, which he raised religiously at every street corner. One day at Leonard's Corner, he was

Jasper Tully of the Roscommon Herald **and his wife; after she died, he readdressed letters sent to her with the legend: "Not known at this address. Try Hell."**

stopped by two women he knew and asked why he pursued this peculiar custom. "Well, whichever direction you look, you will find a church. I raise my hat to them all." In the austere days before the war, another comp, who was on duty until six in the morning, always took the first tram home. A number 15 or 16 tram would stop outside the office and if the man wasn't there, the driver or conductor would nip into *The Irish Times* and fetch him. Another employee left his bicycle on the footpath outside the offices in Westmoreland Street; he came back two days later to find it in perfect condition.

Other printing workers also considered themselves a cut above the ordinary Dublin craft workers: one *Irish Times'* proofreader, a man called Baker, who lived in the then highly exclusive suburb of Rathmines, wore gaiters into work, emulating the Church of Ireland Archbishop. He also brought a pie in every evening and heated it up on the stove in the reading room. Then there was the case of a printer at the paper who missed a funeral at Westland Row: the time had been printed as 11 a.m. instead of 10 a.m. All dressed up for the occasion, he went down to O'Connell Bridge and asked a guard: "Find me a funeral, any funeral."

Other mistakes happened, causing much merriment among the more junior echelons. In the 1920s, *The Irish Times* still had its own horse and cart; one day a junior was instructed to get the horse shod. Thinking he had been told to get it shot, he promptly took it to Keeffes the knackers (known by smell if not by sight) in Blackpitts and had the unfortunate animal dispatched to an untimely end.

Well after the civil war troubles had subsided, people were nervous of imaginary gunfire. The remarkable George Leitch, who had been an airman in the Great War, to Smyllie's eternal delight, was taking photographs in the Gresham Hotel for *The Irish Times*. Old-fashioned magnesium trays provided the lighting; one was accidentally lit and everyone dived to the floor! Conditions for reporters were equally primitive. At the Ireland-Scotland rugby match at Lansdowne Road, Dublin, in February, 1927, the East stand (since demolished) had no roof. In the merciless gale, not alone were the spectators soaked to the skin, but many of the players had to be helped from the playing area after the match. The reporters had to try and take notes, in the open, on saturated paper. Vincent Gill, then a schoolboy in Longford, was producing the *Canal Herald* for a penny a look, with his great friend, Vincent Mulligan.

1927 saw an attempt on the life of Jasper Tully of the *Roscommon Herald* by Free Staters: he survived, but the shooting only heightened his already extravagant eccentricity. He was the very image of outward respectability, with his bowler hat and cravat fastened with a diamond pin. As a young man, he had been an avowed Parnellite; in 1881, at the age of twenty-two, he was locked up in Kilmainham Jail as the authorities tried to "break" the *Roscommon Herald*. Parnell sent two

Billy King, veteran of the newspaper industry, who started work with the Irish Independent in 1917.

editors to stand in for Tully, who was to spend many years as a Westminster MP. One of the first provincial newspaper owners to install a Linotype (1898), he sat at the keyboard himself after the day operator went off about 6 p.m., in order to save money. On the lead stove of the machine, he kept a coffee pot bubbling during the silent hours of the night. Next morning, when the day man returned, Tully would still be there, setting the Roscommon County Works Book, in the remembrance of Cahir Healy, who once worked as a reporter on the *Roscommon Herald* and who was later a director of the *Irish News,* Belfast, and a Stormont MP.

Tully's attitude to trade unions and other interferring busybodies was equally blunt; he saw a gang of heavily armed auxiliaries off his premises in the War of Independence. They had arrived to warn him to tone down his comments about the Black and Tan atrocities, but received such a tongue lashing from Tully that they fled! When a member of the Typographical Union arrived from Dublin to try to organise Tully's workers, he lay in wait behind the works door with a metal ems rule and knocked the poor union official senseless before having him put on the next train back to Dublin.

His wife, the former Mary Ellen Monson, fared no better. Her

Frank Geary, appointed
editor of the Irish
Independent in 1935 in
succession to Tim
Quilty.

family ran the Royal Hotel in Boyle; she was well educated and good
looking, but as strong-willed as her husband was unpredictable. The
two clashed so severely that for years they led separate lives. When
Tully installed one of the first telephones in the West of Ireland, it was
said at the time that he only used it once a day, to ring up his wife from
the printing works and order his breakfast. When she died in 1932, the
ritual gestures in the *Roscommon Herald* stated that the couple were
devoted to each other. Local people in Boyle knew better; after his
wife's death, Tully used to readdress letters to her with the legend
"Not known at this address — try Hell." His domestic arrangements
were strange: his house was shared by his secretary, Rebecca Murray
and her sister. As the *Roscommon Herald* put it years later, with curious
tact: "Mr Tully was a tireless worker and a rather exacting and at times
difficult employer. As Miss Murray resided in his private house, her
working day extended late into the night." She later married a *Herald*
reporter, Martin Coffey; in 1936, they moved to Dublin, when he
joined the *Irish Independent.*

Coffey later recalled that litigation was the elixir of Tully's life. For
weeks before a battle in the courts, he prepared for action with
meticulous care and thoroughness. During the 1920s, he fought an
abusive, vitriolic campaign against fellow editor Tom Kenny of the
Connacht Tribune. Kenny was active in the Galway Harbour
Commissioners and to the forefront of the campaign to improve the
harbour for use by trans-Atlantic liners. Funds were raised from the
County Councils of the West of Ireland to finance the project, but
Tully objected strongly to Roscommon helping to finance port
development in Galway and he thoroughly abused those local
councillors who supported the scheme.

(opposite page)
Correspondence
between Billy King and
George Bernard Shaw
in 1937. King obtained
permission to publish
from Shaw and sold the
rights to Frank Geary,
editor of the Irish
Independent, for £5.

Envelope 1 (left):

William G. King
Independent Newspapers Ltd
90 Middle Abbey St
Dublin

Irish Free State

Envelope 2 (right):

A. J. King
Independent House
90 Middle Abbey St
Dublin

Irish Free State

Irish Independent.
WEEKLY INDEPENDENT
SUNDAY INDEPENDENT
EVENING HERALD

ADVERTISEMENTS ALSO RECEIVED
AT ALL BRANCH OFFICES.

BRANCH OFFICES
LONDON—118 FLEET STREET, E.C.4.
MANCHESTER—2 CHESTER ST. OXFORD RD.
BELFAST—33 DONEGALL STREET
CORK—37 PATRICK STREET.
DERRY—43 BISHOP STREET
DUNDALK—3 & 4 EARL STREET.
KILKENNY—28 ST. KIERAN STREET.
LIMERICK—7A CATHERINE STREET.
WATERFORD—28 O'CONNELL STREET

TELEGRAMS
"INDEPENDENT DUBLIN"
TELEPHONE NUMBERS
COMMERCIAL & EDITORIAL
21035.7.8.9

REPORTING 23065-6-7-8

DIRECTOR and MANAGER
J. DONOHOE

SECRETARY
J. DUNNE

Independent Newspapers, Ltd.

Head Offices, Independent House.

(90. Middle Abbey Street.)

Dublin November 26 19 37.

Confidential.

G. Bernard Shaw, Esq.,
4, Whitehall Court,
London, S.W.I.

Dear Mr King

I authorize you personally to exercise the "first serial right" in this questionaire in the Irish newspapers until the 31st Dec. next.

G. Bernard Shaw
30th Nov. 1937.

---

1. Would you accept the position of President of the Irish Free State
(or Eire) if you were offered same?

   I am too old.

2. Who else would you consider as suitable among the Public figures
in Ireland (leaving out the Politicians) i.e. Yeats, Dunsany, etc?

   I do not know enough about contemporary public life in Ireland to have an opinion. Certainly not anyone with a record in the unhappy past. To put it another way, not anyone old enough for me to know anything about him — or her

3. Under the New Constitution the fundamental duty of the President
is to be "The guardian of the Peoples Rights". What do you
regard as the most important aspect of that right.

   Whichever happens for the moment to be menaced. In a high wind the most important thing is to prevent your hat being blown off. Unless you take it off voluntarily.

4. What is your opinion of the new Royalist Party, do you consider
the Irish Republican or Royalists at heart — Would you be in
favour of a King of Ireland.

   I never heard of the new royalist party. All the arguments which induced the Cromwellians to prefer Charles II to the mess they are making themselves still hold good.

   G. Bernard Shaw
   28/11/37

Gracie Fields singing "Sally" on the roof of the Independent House, Dublin, 1933.
Billy King

Like James Gordon Bennett II of the New York *Herald*, Jasper Tully kept a "taboo" list of people whose names were on no account to be mentioned in the paper. Tully was so strict that one day, his reporters were astonished when he ordered his review of a book by a local solicitor on the banned list to be set in type for the paper. Said Tully's review in part: "We are happy to welcome back to Boyle Mr Greene (the solicitor), who has been on his holidays in Douglas. We are willing to bet Westminster cathedral to a hayseed that a map of the Isle of Man will be found under his wig."

Mercury injections were the cure for syphilis, but they caused baldness. Greene the solicitor sued for libel; in his turn, Tully sued for the alleged libel of himself in Greene's book. The two injured parties were each awarded one farthing's damages.

In Roscommon Town, some thirty miles to the south of Boyle (far enough away for Jasper Tully to be fascinating legend), James Quigley saw the message on the wall for the *Roscommon Messenger*; the paper folded in 1935, but the young Quigley had started his own paper, the *Roscommon Champion* two years previously. It continues to this day, as does the *Roscommon Herald*, but while the *Herald* under Tully enjoyed a remarkable notoriety, the *Champion* proved the very opposite: quiet and inoffensive. Perhaps the most newsworthy event ever to happen on the *Roscommon Champion* was Niall Hanley, editor of the tabloid *Evening Herald*, worked on it for a couple of years.

During the late 1920s, a famous figure worked on the *Morning Post* in London. Sean MacBride, later Minister for External Affairs and winner of the Nobel and Lenin peace prizes, among a host of glittering achievements, was on the run at the time. By his own admission, he secured a sub-editing job on the *Morning Post*, but under an assumed name. He spent some six months with the paper; his real identity was never discovered. MacBride was sharing a house in London with a chef at one of the great London hotels, who brought home vast helpings of left-over food from the kitchens when he finished work, so those six months passed pleasantly enough.

The 1920s started with gunfire and bloodshed in many parts of Ireland, the battles for Independence and the Black and Tans in many southern areas, pogroms and street riots in Belfast. The decade ended on the drab note of depression, triggered by the Wall Street crash in 1929. At the best of times, long before the present troubles, Derry was a drab city, so hardly surprisingly, the *Londonderry Sentinel's* special edition in 1929 to mark the centenary of its foundation, captured all the inherent dreariness of the place. To modern eyes, prices were the redeeming feature: a bottle of Irish whiskey was 15s 6d, ten "Park Drive" cigarettes were 4d and it was 3d into the Opera House. The Midland Cinema at Bond's Hill showed the musical, "Lights of New York", while Harold Lloyd starred at the Rialto, which had its own orchestra. Wreaths were laid on the new war memorial in the

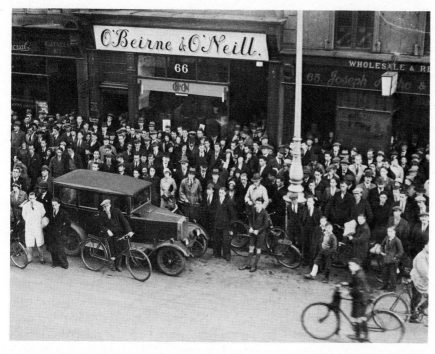

Crowds in Middle Abbey Street, Dublin, hear Gracie Fields.
–Billy King

Diamond in honour of city sportsmen who had died in World War I, ended eleven years previously.

James Colhoun, owner of the *Sentinel,* had himself won the Military Cross in that war; he was also president of the City of Londonderry and Foyle Unionist Association. His politics and his newspaper ambitions were inextricably mixed.

In Tuam, Co Galway, ambition outran financial ability for Gabriel Diskin. During the 1920s, the *Tuam Herald* had been run and edited by a Dublin Senior Counsel, Richard J. Kelly, who decided in 1930 that he could no longer afford to run the paper. When he died, he left £77,000. For a few weeks, publication was suspended. Then Diskin, who had a yen to get into journalism, bought the paper for a small sum. Unable to raise the capital to re-equip the office, he sold out to the Burke family. Diskin did however realise his ambition; he became a sub-editor on the *Irish Press.*

During the dreary, Depression days in 1931, the *Irish Press* was launched, an event that proved as momentous for newspaper history in this country as the launching of the *Irish Independent* twenty-six years previously. As early as the mid-1920s, Eamon de Valera and members of Fianna Fail had been determined to publish a daily national paper that would reflect their views. Sean T. O'Kelly (later President) founded a weekly paper called the *Nation* (after the publication started in 1842 by Davis and Gavan Duffy); its editor was Frank Gallagher, who had joined the Volunteers after 1916, had helped run the *Irish Bulletin* from 1919 with Erskine Childers, had taken part in the Mountjoy Jail hunger strike in 1920 and who was interned at Gormanston Camp in Co Meath after the civil war.

His Republican credentials were impeccable; he used to recall with much amusement in later years how he had gone to a DBC restaurant in Dublin's city centre swathed in gelignite, which he had been told to keep warm. Underneath his shirt seemed as good a place as any. Over his tea, he discussed Irish politics with the Church of Ireland Archbishop of Armagh. Gallagher remarked: "I expressed my dissent with such deference that he went away marvelling at the tolerance and courtesy in the Republican movement." While Gallagher was editing the *Nation*, a frantic but unsuccessful attempt had been made by Republicans to raise cash to buy the assets and titles of the *Freeman's Journal*.

De Valera did not stand still; at the second Fianna Fail Ard-Fheis in 1927, it was announced for the first time, and reported in the *Nation*, that it was intended to launch a new newspaper. A campaign to raise the capital needed, £200,000, was put in train and Robert Brennan got the subscriptions campaign under way in Ireland. De Valera went to America; on his return in February the following year, he announced

Anyone for tennis? A fancy dress party at Malahide Tennis Club in 1937. Third from left, back row, is author and former Irish Times **journalist, Brian Inglis. Far right, front row, is Nigel Beamish, now noted in the Irish drinks trade.**

that he had been successful. He had been assured of half a million dollars. He stated that a similar amount needed to be subscribed at home.

With America heading for the Wall Street crash, the 1927/28 trip there by de Valera was not nearly as fruitful in fundraising as his earlier visit in 1919/20, when he raised over five million dollars for the first Dáil loan. But by September, 1928, enough money had been subscribed to incorporate the *Irish Press* company. A prospectus published in the *Nation* set out the share capital as £200,000 in £1 shares.

Fund raising continued as far away as Australia, where Archbishop Mannix of Melbourne urged support. In America, the minimum subscription of 500 dollars was becoming more difficult for would-be supporters, so de Valera decided to accept smaller amounts. He had an ace up his sleeve: just over half the money raised in America in 1919 for the Dáil loan had been remitted to Ireland and used for the purposes for which it was intended. The remaining two and a half million dollars remained on deposit in New York banks. In August, 1922, the Cosgrave Government applied for and won an injunction restraining the banks from paying out the money to de Valera and his associates.

The Dublin Government then applied to the New York Supreme Court for a declaration that it was entitled to the funds, a claim contested by de Valera on behalf of the Republican party. In May, 1927, it was ruled that neither the Dublin Government nor the Republican Party in Ireland was entitled to the money, which the judge ordered should be returned to the original subscribers. The holders of some of these bonds instead assigned them to de Valera to promote the *Irish Press* and a corporation was formed in America to invest this money in the new newspaper company. The financing of the *Irish Press* has been the source of continuing controversy down through the years; allegations that de Valera and later other members of his family controlled the *Irish Press* financially were persistently denied. There is no doubt, however, that a reasonable portion of the initial capital of the newspaper came from money originally subscribed to the first Dáil loan of 1919.

As well as fund raising in America, de Valera also went to gain practical newspaper experience, of which he had little. In March, 1929, the new company bought the Tivoli Theatre at Burgh Quay; once a music hall it was then being used as a cinema. It had originally been the Conciliation Hall from where O'Connell led the Repeal Movement. The Young Ireland movement had also been based there, so the building was a firm historical base for the new Republican-minded newspaper. Reconstruction of the building began in August, 1930. Later, when things went wrong, staff used to say it was *still* a music hall. Staff began to be recruited; Frank Gallagher, editor of the *Nation* was appointed editor. Gallagher was not the automatic choice for

Anna Kelly, first woman's editor of the Irish Press and mother of RTE Guide columnist Ruth Kelly.
–*Ruth Kelly*

George Crosbie,
chairman of the Cork
Examiner in the 1930s.
–*Cork Examiner*

editor; another journalist, Seamus O'Farrell, was in line for the job, but as the launching deadline drew nearer, he was edged out in favour of Gallagher. Among those who advised on setting up the paper was Michael Rooney, who had been working on the *Irish News* in Belfast and who ended up as editor of the *Irish Independent*.

Once Gallagher was appointed, other staff positions were filled. The young William Sweetman, who already had some London experience, was made London editor, a more junior position than was the case with the other Dublin newspapers, because the *Irish Press* considered London far more peripheral than either the *Irish Independent* or *The Irish Times*. He also had the embarrassing situation of being in charge of a journalist far older than himself. Bob Egan from the *Connacht Tribune*, Galway, was the news editor. M. J. McManus was appointed literary editor, a position he held until his sudden death on holidays in Co Donegal in 1951. The circumstances of his birth amused him: he was born in the workhouse at Carrick-on-Shannon, where his father was master. John Moynihan, who had been editor of the *Kerry Weekly Reporter* and had worked with Gallagher on the *Nation,* joined as assistant editor and leader writer.

James Kelly, who was the first correspondent of the *Irish Press* in the North, recalled how coverage there was organised, with the last-minute frenzied gallop with which the whole paper was stitched together. Kelly was working on the *Irish News* in Belfast, under its English editor, Redwood, a barking tyrant. Kelly read in the *Dundalk Examiner* about the new paper and wrote off; back came a letter from Frank Gallagher regretting that there were no vacancies. By the same post came a letter from Bob Egan, the news editor, asking him to come to Dublin for an interview.

Kelly got the job of Belfast staff reporter, working from a converted bookie's premises in Garfield Street, off Royal Avenue. When he stepped off the train in Belfast that night and went into the *Irish News'* office, he was greeted by the chief reporter, who congratulated him on escaping from the captivity of Upper Donegall Street. It turned out that the chief reporter himself had also applied for the *Irish Press* job! Every *Irish News* correspondent in the North of Ireland received a letter of appointment from Kelly, along with books of press telegraph passes. Sammy Troy of Coleraine was amused to have been appointed to the job of local correspondent for the *Irish Press* — a lucrative sideline in those days-without even applying!

Joe Sherwood joined as sports editor; of the founding members of the *Irish Press,* he was to become one of its most notorious staffers. Born in Workington, Cumbria (which accounted for the strange accent), he was apprenticed to the *Workington News* at the age of thirteen. He served in the Royal Navy in World War I and was severely wounded at Gallipoli. After that war, he went to South Africa, where he was sports editor of the *Cape Times* in Capetown. Returning to England, he saw an

advertisement in a Liverpool paper for jobs on the *Irish Press* and applied. To everyone's astonishment, including his own, he found himself working in Dublin.

His prior knowledge of Ireland, the Irish and Irish games was non-existent, but he is credited with having given the first decent coverage in an Irish newspaper to Gaelic games. His deputy was Herbert Moxley, a fine journalist from Cardiff, who ran the racing page. Racing correspondent was Mick "Sport" Byrne, whose sons and daughters, including Frankie, also became renowned in journalism, mostly sporting. He was noted for his winning tips, which benefitted everyone except himself. A junior on the sports staff at the launch of the *Irish Press* was Mitchel Cogley, later to become sports editor of the *Irish Independent*.

Cearbhall O Dálaigh was appointed Irish editor; this mild, gentle, learned man later became President of Ireland. His brother, Aonghus, an even more saintly figure, was appointed librarian. He helped Dorothy MacArdle with the proof reading and indexing on her monumental work, *The Irish Republic* and had trained in the Co Dublin libraries, bringing his bookish skills to the *Irish Press;* he also brought a saintly asceticism to his job that is normally quite foreign to the world of newspapers. Many tales were told of how he would wait for hours in the evenings so that he could run colleagues home in his car after functions. On one occasion, a journalist is said to have borrowed his car

A conference in the early 1920s in the boardroom at Carlisle Building on the corner of D'Olier Street and Burgh Quay. Left to right: Mr Sexton, manager, Limerick office, Billy King, Thomas A'Kempis Grehan, advertisement manager, T. W. Brewster (an Englishman who had been appointed manager of the company by W. M. Murphy), Joseph Henderson, chief clerk, Jack Bushe, Mr Brewster's son, Theo (manager of the Cork office), and A. J. Cox, London manager.
–Billy King

— permanently, knowing full well that Aonghus was too polite to ask for his property back.

Jack Dempsey joined the new paper well before it was launched, to work on the advertisement side; he had been working in Kenny's advertising agency in Dublin. In 1934, he became advertisement manager; in 1948, general manager. Other appointments were made on the entirely casual and off-hand basis so beloved of the industry: Paddy Clare, who was Night Town reporter for twenty years, was a young fellow at the time. He knew Frank Gallagher from civil war days (they shared a prison camp). Clare claimed that he was walking past the Tivoli.building one day when Gallagher saw him peeping in, called him inside and told Bob Egan to find him a job. Since Clare had no newspaper experience, apart from writing paragraphs for weekly political newspapers, he was given a job as a junior "fixer", organising such things as telegram arrangements for the reporters, at a shilling for eighty words. A competition to find a title for the paper produced many suggestions, but the directors had already decided upon that used by the Irish-American newspaper founded in Philadelphia in 1918.

One print worker who later spent many years at Burgh Quay, Paddy Farrell, came to the paper from the *Longford Leader*. When de Valera visited Longford, Farrell asked him for a job on the new paper, which in the event he was unable to take for a considerable time because of union difficulties. de Valera replied, in answer to Farrell's question about profit sharing if the *Irish Press* turned out to be a success,

The Independent Newspapers' sports club dinner at the Metropole on December 30, 1933, with, from left to right: Don Chance (son of Sir Arthur Chance), Miss Eva Murphy (sister of Lombard Murphy), Alfie Byrne, Lord Mayor of Dublin, Tim Quilty, editor, Irish Independent, **W. Lombard Murphy,** chairman, Independent Newspapers, Mrs Quilty and Billy King, who proposed the toast of the firm.
–Billy King

*William G. King
The world is at our feet
Best Regards Anna May Wong*

Billy King shows the sights of Dublin to 1930s film star Anna May Wong from the roof of Independent House.
–Billy King

that he didn't believe in it; you would be sharing your profits with the next fellow who wouldn't work as hard.

Recruiting of printing, advertisement and editorial staff went on at a fine pace, but the first of several serious strikes at Burgh Quay threatened the existence of the *Irish Press* before it was even born. A Dublin building dispute brought work on the conversion of the Tivoli to a halt; as it dragged on for weeks, and funds to pay the people already recruited to the *Irish Press* dwindled, an appeal was made to the building workers to go back. Amazingly, they did, at the old rate of pay. September 5, 1931, was fixed as launch date.

On the evening before the first day, the staff of 400 worked frantically to produce the Number One issue of the *Irish Press*. Several dummy runs were printed, not as many as planned; the button to start the press rolling for the final trial run was pressed by Mrs Pearse, mother of Patrick and Willie, the 1916 leaders. So many people were crowded into the machine room as the 300,000 copies of the first issue were being printed that the newspaper train taking copies South was missed. Many country readers of that first *Irish Press* did not receive their copies until late the following afternoon.

In the Dáil, the new paper came under fire; a T.D. asked W. T. Cosgrave if he intended to suppress this "Republican rag". Cosgrave replied gravely that he did not, that it would suppress itself shortly.

Distribution for the new paper was a major problem. Three years previously, the *Independent* had offered shares worth £200,000 to the public. Many were said to have been allocated to newsagents and other business people at a discount, in order to encourage their advertising business in the paper. Prior to the *Irish Press* launch, both the *Independent* and *The Irish Times* had made arrangements with many newsagents for the exclusive sale of their newspapers. Many new accounts had to be opened by the *Irish Press* for the sale of copies. Advertising, too, was a great difficulty. The first issue went well, but subsequently, advertising was hard to come by.

Many British-controlled firms were reluctant to advertise in the new paper, given its Republican leanings. Claims were even made at the time that detergent and soap advertisements in *The Irish Times* were not aimed so much at keeping its readers clean as subsidising its pro-Unionist views. Erskine Childers, later a President of Ireland, worked miracles on the advertising side. On evenings when little or no advertising had been booked for the next morning's paper, Childers would stay in the office until eight or nine o'clock at night, wheedling advertisements out of his business contacts. To make its death notices' column more inviting, the *Irish Press* often "lifted" death advertisements from other papers and ran them for nothing. Once in the early days, one man with an English accent working in the *Irish Press* advertisement department borrowed one such notice concerning a man called Murphy; he assumed that because it was such a common name, there would be no problem. It turned out to be one of the Murphy family who owned the *Irish Independent* and Frank Gallagher himself had to make a personal, grovelling apology.

The feud between the *Independent* and the new *Irish Press* ran deep and bitter, for many subsequent years. When Tom Samways, the Belfast journalist, was freelancing in Dublin, he remembers being told by a senior editorial man on the "Indo" that they didn't mind him blacking copy for the *Mail*, but that if he did the same for the *Press*, he would be out on his ear. That feud spilled over into the distribution of the new paper. Dr Lombard Murphy, chairman of the *Irish Independent*, was also a director of the Great Southern Railways. The *Irish Press* was excluded from the newspaper train. The Railway Tribunal ruled that the new paper should have equal access to the special train, but early in 1932, the *Independent* took the case to the High Court, which ruled in its favour. The *Irish Press* was forced into hiring its own train, which added £30,000 a year to its costs. Not until 1937 was the paper able to use the newspaper train run for the *Independent* and *Irish Times*. It was done by bluff, remembered circulation man Padraig O Criogáin: "A van was bought. It was photographed in a different location every day, giving the impression that the *Irish Press* was building up a huge distribution fleet of its own."

The circulation of the *Irish Press*, which presented a breathtakingly fresh view on Irish affairs, breaking the monopoly of the other daily newspapers with its Republican viewpoint, soon settled down to a circulation of around 150,000. Even after de Valera's Fianna Fail Government came to power in 1932, it was the only daily paper giving credence to the views of Ireland's new political masters. On the *Cork Examiner,* leader writer David Ryan was always vitriolic about de Valera. The Crosbies wanted to tone down his comments; the embarrassing predicament of what to do with the veteran journalist was solved when he became seriously ill. The Eucharistic Congress in Dublin that year was manna from heaven for the newspapers. The *Irish Press* did a special congress supplement. At the *Irish Independent,* where a quiet Monaghan man called Tim Quilty was settling in for a spell as editor that only lasted in the event until 1935, a special Congress issue was published. The paper was in its element: the story at the time was that visitors to the *Independent* boardroom had to genuflect before entering. Even *The Irish Times* played its part, with the proceedings of the Congress relayed on loudspeakers outside its Westmoreland Street offices. Smyllie, then assistant editor, made a great name for himself and his paper with his masterly reporting of the events, keeping up his note-taking for hours on end.

Schoolchildren tropped obediently through the city centre on their way to the Phoenix Park. Returning pilgrims had special teas in Bewleys, the DBC or even the exclusive Mitchell's café in Grafton Street. Dublin was thronged with the trappings of religious fervour. The young Dermot McEvoy was working on the *Irish Press,* along with his father, Andy, and was sent up to the Archbishop's Palace in Drumcondra: an Italian Monsignor gave him an envelope to deliver at the GPO. McEvoy couldn't read the telegram, which was in Italian, so he knocked up one of the Cafolla family in Talbot Street and had it translated. It was an excellent account of what the Monsignor thought of the Eucharistic Congress proceedings, but the *Irish Press* would not use his copy. Correspondents from the London papers were in town, including H. V. Morton for the *Daily Herald.* McEvoy met the *Daily Mail* man, who told him that he would have paid £5,000 for the story. Three days after collecting the telegram from Drumcondra, every paper had the story from the Vatican. McEvoy was suitably aggrieved about what he regarded as the cowardice shown in running a good story by Bob Egan, news editor of the *Irish Press* and his assistant, Jack Grealish.

Not long after this episode, a Co Longford businessman sued a parish priest for allegedly seducing his wife. The case made pages of copy in some of the cross-channel papers; not a line appeared in the Irish press. Still, the journalists on the *Irish Press* did have the fun and excitement of working on the new newspaper. Anna Kelly was first woman's page editor; she had the capacity for work of two or three people and soon after the paper started, she was sent down south to write up a different town each day. She started in Waterford, where she received a telegram from Bob Brennan, the general manager:

When the American flyer Douglas ("Wrong Way") Corrigan landed his 'plane in Ireland, allegedly by mistake, in July, 1938, he created many headlines in the local press. He is seen here 'phoning in the American Legation, Dublin.
–*The Irish Times*

"Good man, Fitz, I knew you had it in you." In Tullow, Co Carlow, where its inhabitants woke up late to the milkman, Kelly caused fury by writing about "Sleepy Valley".

Unusually for a Dublin newspaper, the *Irish Press* had at least one other women reporter, a strange lady called Kathleen O'Brennan, a sister of Eamon Ceannt, one of the 1916 leaders. Her political background was an immediate passport into the newspaper; she is remembered as very mannishly dressed, complete with pince nez, at one side of which hung a shoe lace for antique style and support.

Perhaps the most popular column of all on the paper was "Roddy the Rover", written by Aodh de Blacam, a man of great professional ability, who could write a column in Robert Robert's café at the top of Grafton Street in thirty-five minutes flat, complete with setting instructions for the printer. After the war, de Blacam, who was able to write virtually any kind of copy at a moment's notice, resigned from the *Irish Press* and stood as an Independent candidate in a by-election in Co Louth. He garnered only a few hundred votes and disappeared into that oblivion reserved for retired newspapermen and failed politicians.

A brave experiment took place at the *Derry Standard* in 1932; the paper had been set up in 1836 and had a powerful reputation, but when its owner, J. C. Glendinning, retired, the publication faced closure. The employees, including Robert Thompson, foreman printer, decided to establish a co-operative to run the newspaper: it was the first one ever set up in the newspaper industry in Ireland. Deductions were made from the employees' wages until the sum of £100 was saved, which was then converted into shares in the company. Tom Parke, who had joined the paper as a reporter in 1914, later becoming chief reporter and sub-editor, was made editor. The workers on the newspaper saved what was then the tri-weekly publication, which lasted until 1964, when the company was wound up. The employees who had made such a brave gesture in 1932 had become old men, no longer able to keep the paper going.

Derry in 1932 was the scene of one of the great "scoops" of the decade. Cecil A. King, the chief reporter of the *Derry Journal*, had the "scoop" of his life. He was sitting having his lunch one day, reading in the *Irish Independent* about the American flyer Amelia Earhart taking off from the United States on her epic solo flight across the Atlantic the previous day. He heard a 'plane going over, realised it must be the woman flyer, rushed out and commandeered a taxi. Shortly afterwards, he found the field four miles on the Donegal side of Derry where Earhart's 'plane had landed. She had flown over Arranmore island, west Donegal, seen by Patrick Bonner of Meenmore, Dungloe, among others. He remembers watching the one o'clock train making its way to Burtonport; the drone of the engine was muffled by the train.

When King walked into the field near Derry, he met Earhart; she gave him an interview, later turning away other pressmen, saying she was too tired. She had brought with her a copy of the *New Brunswick Telegraph Journal*, the first air delivered newspaper from America to arrive in Ireland the day after publication. Eventually, other reporters representing Belfast, Dublin, London and American papers arrived in Derry; they offered copious five pound notes to Cecil King for the story. He declined, but helped them anyway. King was delighted enough with the story; he was also delighted to meet Amelia Earhart, saying that her girlish simplicity won over the hearts of all who met her. Five years later, she died when her 'plane crashed into the Pacific. Cecil King went on to take over the *Donegal Democrat* newspaper in Ballyshannon.

Two other Derry reporters covered the story: Cecil Milligan, then the chief reporter of the *Londonderry Sentinel*. That very year, 1932, he took over as editor, following the retirement of J. C. Orr. Milligan also covered the story for British and American news agencies, as well as for a number of Irish and British newspapers. Later, he also had a post as shorthand writer at Stormont. Milligan was assisted on the Earhart story by another noted Sentinel reporter, David Ruddock. 1932 also saw a Derryman taking up a major position in a leading Irish weekly.

Bob Donaghy had worked on the *Derry Journal*, the *Anglo-Celt* and the *Donegal People's Press*; in 1932, he was made manager of the *Leinster Leader*, Naas, becoming managing director in 1947, a position he held until his

The late Jasper Travers Wolfe, solicitor and one-time M.P. for West Cork, who was the last managing director of the Skibbereen Eagle. Following raids by the IRA, the Eagle ceased publication in 1920 but it was revived in 1926 when Wolfe formed The Skibbereen Eagle 1926 Ltd. This, however, was a last despairing fling for by now the paper was an anachronism and when it finally failed in 1929, its assets and machinery were sold to the Southern Star.
–Southern Star

Cecil A. King (third
from right), then chief
reporter of the Derry
Journal at the landing
site near Derry in 1932
of solo American flyer,
Amelia Earhart. Also in
the photograph are
members of the
Gallagher family on
whose farm Earhart's
'plane landed and a
member of the RUC.
–Cecil A. King

death seven years later. He played an important role in Associated Irish
Newspapers during the war, being president in 1943-44.

The *Irish Press* took a brave but disastrous step in 1932; the paper had
published evening editions during the great Eucharistic Congress,
calling them the *Evening Press.* Then in July, de Valera decided to launch a
full scale evening paper, titled, inexplicably, the *Evening Telegraph,* the
name of the evening paper that had been run by the *Freeman's Journal.*
The title was still owned by the *Irish Independent* and only the paper's
collapse in October prevented the *Independent* bringing an action for
breach of copyright. Bob Egan was promoted from news editor of the
Irish Press to editor of the *Evening Telegraph;* Joe Anderson, later editor of
the *Dublin Evening Mail,* was chief sub-editor.

An amusing misprint on the *Evening Telegraph* caused some chagrin
among the paper's staff, including Sean MacBride. Once, the front
page was remade three times in the course of three hours; during the
Economic War between Ireland and Britain, de Valera and the British
Prime Minister, Neville Chamberlain, were both making speeches to

their respective Houses of Parliament in Dublin and London. The two speeches were being reported under double headings, de Valera's on the left hand side, Chamberlain's on the right. As the London copy came off the teleprinter, it was hastily subbed and then set. Only after the last edition of the *Evening Telegraph* had been put to bed was it discovered that three inches of de Valera's speech had been transposed into that of Chamberlain's and vice versa.

Egan, the editor, was in favour of telephoning de Valera immediately; Anderson meditated on his pipe for a few minutes and advised doing nothing for a couple of days. No-one noticed the error outside the office and when de Valera was told a few days later, during one of his periodic visits to Burgh Quay, he actually made a joke about it. On the *Irish Press* about this time, an equally amusing "mistake" also caused pandemonium. Paddy Clare was covering the removal of the remains of a well-known Dublin businessman; a woman pushed in when he was getting the names of his daughters. The "extra" name she gave went into print and apparently turned out to be that of the man's illegitimate daughter.

Less happily though, the *Evening Telegraph* only lasted a short while, before a thirteen week strike put it off the streets for good. The newsboys downed papers; Jim Larkin had organised the badly clad and poorly paid lads into the Transport and General Workers' Union. They picketed Burgh Quay and won the support of the despatch department workers; the National Union of Journalists did not support the action. After the newsboys' strike had brought the *Evening Telegraph* to a halt, the management simply closed down the paper. Not until twenty-two years later did the *Irish Press* group make a second and more successful attempt to launch an evening paper.

In Sligo, too, change was in the air. The *Sligo Champion* had been owned from 1885 by P. A. McHugh, then after his death in 1909, in trust for members of his family. About 1920, it was taken over by McHugh's son, Alfred. In the autumn of 1932, McHugh had to go abroad for health reasons, so he sold the paper to a consortium of three — Senator McLoughlin, Martin Roddy and William Townsend. They also took over the *Donegal People's Press,* established some years earlier in Lifford, Co Donegal; printing of both papers was at Sligo, although the Lifford office was kept on. Today, the Townsend family still controls the firm.

Jasper Tully had his flashes of brilliance, too, like the occasion in 1932 when he ran a cartoon in the *Roscommon Herald* showing the money-lenders of the world gleefully preparing for another world war. He did not live long enough to see the brilliance of his perception. In the meantime, he carried on his usual harrassment. Edward MacSweeney, better known to RTE radio listeners as Maxwell Sweeney, was a young reporter learning his craft with *The Irish Times* in the early 1930s. He was sent to Roscommon to file copy on reported drilling in

John Caughey, "The Timekeeper" of the Belfast Telegraph, **who used "blue black vitriol" in his boxing column towards fans who spat out bad language, drawn by the paper's staff cartoonist in the 1930s, William Glenn.**

Roscommon Castle by IRA members.

When he arrived, he found that the IRA men *had* taken over the castle ruins; Jasper Tully went on to write a piece in his paper about the young reporter from Dublin with the Oxford accent and said that he wouldn't dare show his face in the locality. Tully made serious accusations against MacSweeney, who must have been deeply hurt by the unfair and untrue remarks. Wiser counsels in *The Irish Times* decided against legal action.

As the *Irish Press* was getting into its stride, a youthful recruit joined *The Irish Times*, Lionel Fleming, who later became a noted BBC correspondent and who returned to the Dublin paper as foreign editor in 1964. The young Fleming went in search of Smyllie in the Palace Bar, where he and his group were discussing the arguments for and against the Resurrection. "Bring your arse to an anchor, boy," Smyllie instructed Fleming, before ordering him to come for a formal

The Patrick Street, Cork, entrance to the Cork Examiner, **1931.**
Cork Examiner

182

interview at 1 a.m. As Fleming climbed the stairs in *The Irish Times*, he heard singing in the distance; when he moved nearer, he discovered Smyllie, then assistant editor, correcting proofs with one hand and playing dominoes with the other. To the tune of the last movement of Beethoven's Choral Symphony, Smyllie was singing:

Down the hall the butler wandered
Bent on sodomistic crime,
For the parlourmaid was pregnant
For the forty-second time.

Smyllie paused a second or two to bark out instructions to the youthful Fleming, newly emerged from Trinity College, Dublin: "Be here tomorrow. Three guineas a week." *The Irish Times* had its newest reporter, soon to discover that Smyllie also sang his leaders, on occasion, before sending them for setting. During the early 1930s, vicious communal rioting erupted in Belfast. Tension in the city was electric; on one occasion, a Protestant funeral, followed by an enormous crowd, came down through the Catholic area of York Street. At the corner of Upper Donegall Street, the mob was incited to run riot — in the direction of the *Irish News'* office. The crowd, several hundred strong, pushed menacingly towards the newspaper office, determined on its destruction. A reporter who was standing nearby remembers now that the mob was only halted when an armoured car, machine gun mounted on the front, sidled out of Union Street, opposite the *Irish News,* and halted the crowd in its tracks. Amid the bleak violence of Belfast in the hungry Thirties, as grass grew over the shipyards, the *Irish Weekly News* created a sensation among its overseas readers by putting news on the front page. Its sister paper, the *Irish News,* was simultaneously claiming to be the first daily newspaper in Ireland to follow this revolutionary practice. The influence of its new editor, Belfast man Robert Kirkwood, appointed in 1933, was being felt after five years of its English editor, Sydney Redwood. Perhaps the most popular feature between the two papers was the most homely imaginable — "Mrs Twigglety", based on the city's gossip and which brought to the *Weekly News* floods of letters from Belfast exiles all over the world.

The *Independent* had a neat line in publicity in 1933. In poverty-stricken Dublin, the arrival of Gracie Fields caused a great sensation. On the roof of Independent House, she sang her Lancashire heart out, to the crowds gathered in Middle Abbey Street below. Of all the acts brought to Dublin by the paper, Gracie was the greatest.

At the *Connacht Tribune* one wet, windy night towards the end of 1933, Jack Fitzgerald, a bluff, retiring man with a prizefighter's nose, joined as Connemara correspondent, based in Clifden. He had worked on the *Kilkenny Journal,* the *Kilkenny People* (under the great but crusty E. T. Keane) and the *Southern Star.* In Clifden, his transport was a bicycle, a source of constant anecdotes in later years. However, he was

The old Tivoli music hall, Burgh Quay, Dublin, before its conversion into the premises of the Irish Press.

only in Clifden a week before being recalled to Galway to replace the previous Clifden correspondent, who had been likewise transferred but who had then left the paper. Fitzgerald thought he was called to Galway on a "help out" basis, working under Tom Kenny and his daughter, Peggy, the chief reporter, who married novelist Walter Macken. Fitzgerald's stay became permanent; eventually, in 1950, he was made editor. Then he had an embarrassing encounter with a Bishop in 1934. The Bishop disliked the press, because of coverage given to his remarks, critical of Wolfe Tone, which had offended local Republicans. Fitzgerald had to cover a confirmation service at Oranmore; he was well up the church. The Bishop then announced that he would not start the service until any reporters present had left. There followed a long, long walk up the aisle by Fitzgerald, all eyes upon him.

Joe Anderson returned from the *Irish Press* to the *Dublin Evening Mail,* this time as chief sub-editor, at a salary of £6 a week. Born in Ballymoney, Co Antrim, he had come to Dublin, after working in Coleraine, Belfast and the North of England, to join the *Irish Independent.* The genial figure of Joe Anderson presided over the fortunes of the *Evening Mail* for over twenty years, until he retired in 1958.

After he was appointed editor two years later, he began building up the Letters to the Editor page. For years, it was a saying in Dublin "that you should write to the *Mail* about it" and readers who wanted to write to the paper had every encouragement from Joe, who subbed most of the letters himself. He also had a soft spot for animals and any reader sending in details of a lost pet could be sure of a place in the *Mail.* Scarlet fever was one of the scourges of the time; the *Mail* published details of people's progress in combating the disease. Anderson even ran a "lonely hearts" column. Limericks were another popular item.

The same year that Anderson left the *Irish Press* for the *Evening Mail*, 1934, John Healy, editor of *The Irish Times* since 1907, died. The immaculate and remote figure was gone and with him went the inflexible Unionism of the paper; the shambling Smyllie became editor. The succession was automatic. In his twenty years as editor, he tucked and turned by small degrees to bring the paper more into line with the political realities of the day. As Smyllie sat expansively in the editor's chair, Alec Newman also stepped up, to become assistant editor. Newman tapped into Powers; he was said to have kept a barrel full of the whiskey in his office, so that he and his colleagues always had their small ones to hand. More serious drinking was done in George Ryan's Palace Bar in Fleet Street, the far side of Westmoreland Street. Here Smyllie, aided and abetted by Newman, ran the branch office of *The Irish Times*; a clique surrounded Smyllie. Cogitation and rumination were the order of the day; Smyllie had the reputation of being able to drink more than virtually any other journalist in Dublin, yet he had a remarkable capacity of concealment. In the warm, foetid atmosphere of the Palace Bar, described so aptly by Cyril Connolly as being like a warm alligator tank, members of the clique polished their bons mots off one another. Outsiders were scrupulously barred from entering the magic circle, as Paddy Kavanagh found out. On one occasion as a young man, newly arrived in Dublin, he attempted to inveigle himself with Smyllie, only to be rebuffed by the venerable editor. Kavanagh retaliated by deliberately hitting the underside of the table with his knee, tipping over a glass of Guinness.

The golden days of the newspaper and literary clique at the Palace Bar included such worthies as Leslie Montgomery (bank manager by day, "Lynn Doyle" of *Ballygullion* fame by night; he was also father of Alan Montgomery, who himself became an editor of *The Irish Times*, Sean O'Sullivan, the painter, Donagh MacDonagh, the writer and District Justice and Cathal O'Shannon (senior). Those warm, cosy nights lasted until the end of the 1930s; George Ryan, its owner, died in 1938 and the running of the bar was taken over by his widow, Sheila and a friend, Jack Murphy. Subsequently, they sold out to Bill Ahern, but by the time this happened, the custom of the Smyllie clique was ebbing away to "Gus" Weldon's new Pearl Bar.

Smyllie was expert in slipping into his office; daily, he was pestered and plagued by aspirant reporters, painters trying to sell him their works and elderly writers seeking favours. He had a great reputation in *The Irish Times* for dodging and tacking, making his entrance a secretive rush so as to avoid the hangers-on. One unfortunate man, "Twitchy" Doyle, was put off for years; he had given Smyllie the manuscript of his master work on Dickens. Smyllie persistently avoided giving an opinion, fobbing off the man with the purchase of

The late Joseph O'Regan who first became a director of the Southern Star in 1919, during which time the paper was very active in supporting the independence movement and was suppressed on five occasions, once for a six month period in 1918. Mr. O'Regan in later years acquired the majority shareholding in the paper and remained managing director until his death in 1975, at which time he was succeeded in that position by his eldest son, Liam.

Jack Hilton and his band playing on the roof of Independent House, May, 1933.
–*Billy King*

odd paragraphs for the paper. Smyllie's endless procrastination merely concealed his loss of the manuscript. For years, the manuscript could not be found; it turned up when Smyllie took over as editor in 1934 and changed offices. With a triumphant whoop, he produced the long-vanished script, decided that he couldn't possibly return it to its long-suffering author and dumped it in the waste paper basket. "An Irishman's Diary" on *The Irish Times* was compiled at this time by Alec Newman; he paid Brian Inglis 3/6d for each two hundred word paragraph; one decrepit old man collected his 3/6d every month for writing a paragraph on the night sky, transcribed word for word from an almanac. Saturday's column was reserved for "Nichevo" (Smyllie) and his friends.

Matt Farrell started in *The Irish Times*. A quiet, down-to-earth man, he began in the humblest of jobs; while he was night watchman one weekend, he wrote to Smyllie and asked if there was any chance of promotion to editorial. On the Monday, Smyllie met him on the stairs and simply said, very gruffly, "We're taking you on as a sub." Later on, he became a reporter. He was always astonished by Smyllie meeting his (Farrell's) wife outside Whitefriars Street church one day and asking her how their two sons were, by name. He had never met them. Matt Farrell, who died recently, ended his career with a long stint on the *Evening Press*.

Social pleasures on *The Irish Times* then were simple: the staff club was located in Middle Abbey Street (the site is now occupied by the Adelphi cinema). Billiards, cards and drinks — those were the pastimes of the night. On Saturday nights, when *The Irish Times'* reporters' room was deserted, artistes belonging to the Rathmines and Rathgar Musical Society came down to the club to give impromptu concerts. Charles Mullock, who joined the paper in 1929 and who retired as assistant manager, also remembered some of the other simple pleasures of those days, like the ritual visit to Cafollas for ice cream after the pictures.

Down in the basement of *The Irish Times* lurked a Union Jack. Despite the presence on the staff of one or two people said to have had subversive Republican ideas, like Mick Clarke, the advertisement manager, the paper was still a bastion in Dublin of Empire loyalism. Bill "Windy" Coyne, a porter in the front office, who had been a batman to Sir Lauriston Arnott in the First World War, kept this prize possession of the flag as a memento of obviously happy times amid the mud-filled trenches of the Somme. When a youth of different disposition threatened to put the flag to another use, Coyne saw a highly inflammatory red and shouted out: "You are disgracing my King's flag. Step outside for a bout of fisticuffs."

Behind the travado of the Palace Bar, Smyllie concealed a remarkable editorial shrewdness. He saw instinctively that the old-style Unionism of Healy was finished, that to pursue it further would bring down the paper. During the Spanish Civil War, Smyllie sent Lionel Fleming to cover it, telling him: "I don't give a bugger what your conclusions are, as long as they are honest. "For failing to support Franco in Spain, the paper lost many advertisements from Catholic schools.

Frank Geary, who took over as editor of the *Irish Independent* in 1935 after its short-reigning editor, Tim Quilty, had been dumped with conspicuous lack of ceremony, brought a more forceful and Catholic approach to the running of his paper for a total of twenty-five years. He was much more ruthless and organised than Smyllie, but ultimately, far more lacking in character. A sharp dresser, he was long remembered for his superb overcoats and perpetual homburg hat. On one occasion, a lady of leisure was in the main hallway of Independent Newspapers to see some of the reporters. The lift descended and out stepped that man of high moral purpose and sharply pressed trousers, Frank Geary. The woman spotted a "catch", rushed over and threw her arms round Geary, saying as she did so, "Oh, I don't half fancy you." Subsequently, it was said among the *Independent* reporters that

Anthony Mulvey of the Omagh Herald **series . . . stopped the press when a wedding report had "Requiem Mass" instead of "Nuptial Mass".**

Tommy O'Brien of "Your Choice and Mine" radio fame, who learned shorthand as a lad in order to join the Clonmel Chronicle as an apprentice reporter for 7/6d a week.
–RTE

their editor had made the fastest exit on record from the building.

From *Queen* magazine in London, Geary recruited a rather mannish looking woman journalist called Gertie Gaffney, born in Co Armagh. She was said, years after, to have had a remarkably close professional relationship with Geary. Gaffney was sent to Spain, with strict instructions to cover the fearful threat to Christianity being countered by Franco. Franco's opponents had little coverage in the *Independent,* and no advertising was lost.

Alan Montgomery, later to be editor, came in as a learner reporter at *The Irish Times* in 1936. He remembers that in those days, newspapers were not unionised. The Institute of Journalists was pro-management and the National Union of Journalists was only just starting in Ireland. When Montgomery started, reporters had just won a great victory on the Dublin papers; a six day week instead of a seven day week. He had to come into work at 11 a.m. and get his markings, or assignments, for the day. As a fledgling reporter, he was sent to cover such events of breathtaking interest as Dublin rotary club lunches and inquests. He had to work on through the day and into the evening, catching the 11.35 p.m. bus home to Skerries.

Just a week after Montgomery joined the paper, Dublin had a ten week newspaper strike. There was no alternative news service, as on radio, but no-one minded. At *The Irish Times,* the reporters had a great "holiday", keeping a record of the news as best they could, playing dominoes and bringing over jugs of iced lager from Wynn's Hotel in Lower Abbey Street. They were hard days before the war, but Montgomery believes he learned good journalistic English. The reporters' room, in common with the sub-editors' room, boasted an enormous style book, even Latin dictionaries. Newman waged war on split infinitives, while Smyllie insisted that NT had to be spelled out as National Teacher, while "street" and "quay" were always lower case. The only commencement in this life, thundered Smyllie, is at Trinity College.

The linguistically brilliant Smyllie sometimes left off his smelly, shapeless pullover. At Punchestown Races, near Naas, he was to be seen immaculate in grey top hat and heavy black overcoat (despite the summer weather), race glasses at the ready.

Meanwhile, the *Mayo News* claimed a "scoop" in 1936 with the great abdication scandal in Britain; it was covered up by British papers, but not in the rest of the world. An Australian newspaper arrived in Westport by post; it had full details of the abdication, which the *Mayo News* promptly printed. An English linotype operator called Gerry Gillette was one of two compositors setting the paper. He took a light-hearted view of the story and said: "I'll never get to tell my father quickly enough!"

Relations between Geary at the *Irish Independent* and the various *Irish Press* editors were non-existent. Each paper chose to ignore the

HAVE YOU ANYTHING
TO BUY OR SELL ?

*OUR "SMALL ADS." BRING
EXCELLENT RESULTS*

EVENING TELEGRAPH
AND EVENING PRESS

Vol. I., No. 53.   DUBLIN, WEDNESDAY, AUGUST 3, 1932.   PRICE ONE PENNY

CITY

CONSULT
E. J. KEARNEY
OPHTHALMIC
OPTICIAN
SIGHT-TESTING
ROOMS,
26 - 27 ESSEX QUAY, DUBLIN
'PHONE 21403.

Possible Extension of the Dundalk Rail Strike

Brilliant Second Day at the Horse Show

BUS REPAIRERS MAY CEASE WORK TO-NIGHT

ROAD SERVICES LIKELY TO BE AFFECTED

PICKETS ON WATCH

Possible extension of the railway strike in Dundalk is foreshadowed by the statement to-day that it is likely that the workers in the road garage who repair the 'buses will cease work this evening.

FIFTY-FIVE road repair and overhaulage men are already out, and it is feared that the addition of 40 to their number will mean that all road services in the area will be greatly affected.

TRADE UNION LEADER'S COURT APPEAL

Fight To Retain Presidency

APPLICATION FOR AN INJUNCTION SUCCEEDS

MR. JUSTICE GODDARD in the Vacation Court, in London, to-day, granted an interim injunction over next Wednesday on the ex parte application of Mr. Wm. Harold Hutchinson, President of the Amalgamated Engineering Union, restraining the Union from seeking to remove him from his office as President.

Mr. Arthur Capewell said the grounds of the application were that the rules of the Union had not been complied with; that the Executive Council's attitude was ultra vires, and that Mr. Hutchinson had had no opportunity of defending himself, no

Some of the spectators watching the judging at the Dublin Horse Show.

PIER DESTROYED IN A

SCENES OF GAIETY AND COLOUR

FIRST PARADE OF PRIZE ANIMALS

SUNSHINE ATTRACTS A GREAT CROWD

BRILLIANT sunshine stimulated the great crowds who attended at Ballsbridge to-day for the second stage of the Horse Show.

The scene in the show yard, and also in the jumping enclosure, was bright with colour, and many foreign visitors were impressed with the brilliance of the spectacle.

existence of the other. After the mysterious translation of Frank Gallagher from the *Irish Press* to Radio Eireann in 1935, the Burgh Quay morning paper had to endure two years of constant shifts in the editorial chair. Star personalities like Anna Kelly left in sympathy with Gallagher, but returned later. Andy McEvoy left and went back to edit the *Clare Champion*. Peadar O'Curry who had joined in 1932 as a leader writer also left, for the less wearing pastures of the *Evening Herald*. Later, he became editor of the *Standard*.

Stability did not return until Sweetman was promoted to editor in 1937. Bob Brennan, the general manager, had left just before Gallagher. Joe Sherwood left, some say after one of his blazing rows, to work for Herbert Moxley, who had himself left the *Irish Press* to run a sports news agency in Birmingham. Erskine Childers also departed, but as he was going his brother, Robert, came in. He survived at the *Irish Press*, with a break for Emergency service, until 1947. But with all these departures in the mid-1930s, the paper found it hard to recover its early vitality. After Gallagher departed, much of the hard editorial work was done by Paddy Kirwan, the assistant editor. Kirwan had been a third year medical student until an operation for a duodenal ulcer prompted him to gravitate in the direction of the arts. For 30/- a week, he became assistant editor, art critic, music critic and drama critic all rolled into one. Often described as the *eminence grise* of the *Irish Press* editorial department in the 1930s, Kirwan kept the paper rolling. Of one subsequent editor it was said that all he sent down for setting were the crosswords; Kirwan filled in.

Evening Telegraph and Evening Press — **the ill-fated attempt at a Burgh Quay evening newspaper in 1932.**

189

At lower levels, however, the japes continued. Paddy Fennessy, a sub, was also one of the city's most prolific drunks. He had been arrested by Free State forces in Clonmel during the civil war; they had found him acting suspiciously. A friend discovered him awaiting execution and managed to save him, saying that Fennessy always looked suspicious. Ever after, he celebrated his narrow escape from death most energetically. Time after time he was sacked from the *Irish Press;* on one occasion, he was so intoxicated that he had to be removed from the office and charged with drunk and disorderly behaviour. "I was only celebrating Fianna Fail winning the election," he was said to have told the judge. Another time, when Fennessy was passing a fishmonger's shop, he asked the price of crabs. 2/6d, he was told. "In that case, I'm a millionaire." He once put a report of a twenty-year-old military ambush in the subs' tray; it was stopped in time. For all his drunken jesting, Fennessy was considered one of the best subs in Dublin.

A week before Christmas during this editorial *interregnum* at the *Irish Press,* a permanent casual was sacked. Another reporter bought up every scrap of drink and turkey he could find in the city centre, loaded them aboard a taxi and ordered the driver to take them to the home of the sacked man and his mother. All the accounts were charged to Mr de Valera.

Still, the *Irish Press* recruited more staff. Maire Comerford had had an active War of Independence, where among her tasks in Cumann na mBan was acting as driver to Frank Aiken, later Minister for External Affairs. She carried despatches for him as Commander of the IRA's fourth Northern Division. After her imprisonment in the civil war, she ran a poultry farm in Co Wexford; it was not successful and by the time she joined the *Irish Press* as a journalist in 1935, she had accumulated a mountainous ten years of debt. For most of the thirty years she was at work on the paper, she was paying back most scrupulously the money she owed.

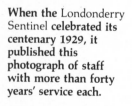

When the Londonderry Sentinel **celebrated its centenary 1929, it published this photograph of staff with more than forty years' service each.**

Millicent Trimble of the Impartial Reporter, Enniskillen, brought her ample-girthed charms to social reporting for the paper and the BBC in Belfast. The photograph was taken about 1928.
–Impartial Reporter

Liam MacGabhann joined the Irish Press just a year before Maire Comerford; he had had his baptism of journalistic fire on such publications as An Caman. After the IRA split, Frank Ryan (later to die aboard a German submarine) quit the editorship of An Poblacht. Sean MacBride, who had himself left the Irish Press, took over and appointed MacGabhann and a young Derry journalist with strongly Republican leanings, Terry Ward, later to be London editor of the Irish Press, to the staff of the Republican paper.

Early in January, 1934, the Government banned that week's issue of An Poblacht. MacGabhann went down to Longford, where it was printed at the Longford Leader, to find the Market Square lined with police and Lucius Farrell, owner of the Leader, ready with his shotgun. To beat the ban on the paper, dated January 5, MacGabhann changed the publication date to the following day. While the guards hurried out to get new instructions, the staff at the Leader printed away. Two doors away from the entrance to the Leader, a van was loaded up with copies. "Go to Dublin and drive like hell, "Lucius Farrell told the driver.

Then during the Dublin newspaper strike, while Alan Montgomery and his colleagues were playing dominoes at The Irish Times, MacGabhann and Ward struck a deal with the striking printers. Republican propaganda was kept to the leader columns, while the rest of the paper was sympathetic to the union cause! For a very short time, Longford became almost the press capital of Ireland, for in addition to An Poblacht, Ryan was in the town producing a paper for the breakaway Republican Congress and several Catholic weeklies were also being printed there. By the time Liam MacGabhann joined the Irish Press, to work with people like Brian O'Neill and Joe Dennigan, he had had plenty of newspaper experience. MacGabhann, hat perched on the back of his head, turned out to be one of the most perceptive journalists the paper ever produced.

Another journalist to change jobs at this time was Tommy O'Brien, of RTE's "Your Choice and Mine" fame. He had started as an apprentice reporter with the Protestant *Clonmel Chronicle* as a sixteen year old. He had spent the summer learning shorthand and when he joined the paper, he was paid at the grand rate of 7/6d a week.

On the *Chronicle,* he graduated to writing a humorous column under the by-line of "Scrutator". When the *Chronicle* folded in 1935, he transferred to the *Nationalist* newspaper in the town, eventually becoming editor. Under him trained such journalists as Maurice Hickey, retired political correspondent of the *Evening Herald* and Tommy Cleary, the retired *Irish Independent* sub-editor.

Pay was so poor that Tommy O'Brien had to double job in order to live and pay for his pre-war trips to the opera at Covent Garden, London. He is said to be the only person ever to have bluffed their way into the dress circle wearing a lounge suit instead of the customary dress suit, keeping his coat and scarf on until he was seated. Reporting for the *Nationalist,* he also became official stenographer for the Co Tipperary circuit court. It was absolute slavery, remembers Tommy, but he needed the money.

Tommy Cleary was working on the *Offaly Chronicle* (known jokingly as the Offaly Comical) for 35/- a week. Four reporters, including himself, all from separate papers, met up one day in Roscrea court house and ended up trying to form the Irish Journalists' Association. The weekly contributions to the NUJ and Institute of Journalists were too heavy for most country reporters, so there was good support for the new organisation. However, it never materialised, because the supporters could not afford the Government fee of £500 demanded of new trade unions. Cleary then went to work on the *Limerick Leader* and while there, helped in forming what he describes as the first provincial branch of the NUJ in Ireland. On the *Drogheda Independent,* George Hussey remembered three reporters sharing two ancient typewriters. Penny poker was played after the week's copy was written. Those pre-war union stirrings were a sign of the more successful union organisation that came after the war. Everyone on *The Irish Times* was underpaid. Smyllie used to say: "It's a privilege, gentlemen, to be on the staff of a literate newspaper."

In Belfast, John Caughey was belligerent towards boxing fans who used strong language at fights. For years, he wrote a boxing column for the *Belfast Telegraph* under the by-line "The Timekeeper". He also became unofficial press agent for Jimmy Warnock, the great Northern boxer; Caughey had recognised his talent when he was a mere booth fighter. The Shankill Road southpaw never won the world title because of a series of unfortunate occurrences, including his own ill-health, but he was acknowledged as the uncrowned world flyweight champion.

"SUNDAY INDEPENDENT" PRINTS ALL THE NEWS WORTH PRINTING

SATURDAY HERALD
INCORPORATING THE "EVENING TELEGRAPH"
Vol. 48, No. 209 Telegrams: "HERALD DUBLIN" DUBLIN, SATURDAY, SEPTEMBER 2, 1939. PRICE ONE PENNY.
FINAL

LOANS ON JEWELLERY, ANTIQUE and MODERN SILVER. KELLY'S 8 WESTMORELAND ST. (CORNER OF FLEET ST.)

No Reply So Far From Germany to Ultimatum by Britain and France

"MERELY RECTIFYING EASTERN FRONTIER," SAYS BERLIN

Poland Says She Will Defend To The End

BRITISH WAR CABINET

Germany has not yet replied to the ultimatum delivered by Britain and France last night. The ultimatum told Germany that unless her troops were immediately withdrawn from Poland, Britain and France would go to Poland's aid.

IT IS LEARNT IN PARIS THAT WHEN THE FRENCH AMBASSADOR HANDED IN HIS GOVERNMENT'S ULTIMATUM HERR VON RIBBENTROP, THE GERMAN FOREIGN MINISTER, REPLIED THAT GERMANY HAD NOT BEEN GUILTY OF AN ACT OF AGGRESSION. HE ADDED THAT HE WOULD INFORM HERR HITLER AND WOULD REPLY LATER. THE BRITISH AMBASSADOR WAS RECEIVED SEPARATELY. THE PRESENT WHEREABOUTS OF HERR HITLER ARE UNKNOWN.

THE STAND GERMANY TAKES TO-DAY IS THAT WAR AGAINST POLAND HAS NOT BEEN DECLARED AND, THEREFORE, A STATE OF WAR DOES NOT EXIST.

Reuter was informed in Berlin that other Powers were not officially notified of Germany's action "because it was quite clearly stated by the Fuehrer at the Reichstag meeting, which was attended by the diplomatic representatives of other great Powers." It is stated in Berlin that there is no intention on the part of Germany to bring about a complete change in Poland. Germany would merely "rectify" the eastern frontier.

IT IS ANNOUNCED THAT THE BRITISH PARLIAMENT WILL MEET AT NOON TO-MORROW.

Slovakia Appeals To Poland

The following communication has been handed to Col. Beck, Polish Foreign Minister, by Dr. Szathmary, Minister of Slovakia in Warsaw:

"In the name of the Slovak people and its representatives, who under the pressure of the Third Reich, have been reduced to silence and have been reproached for penetrations exclusively in the interest of Germany, I protest as the representative of the State of Slovakia in Poland against the brutal disarmament of the Slovak Army; against the arbitrary occupation of Slovakia by the troops of the Third Reich; against the use of Slovakia as a base for warlike action against the brotherly Polish people.

VIOLENCE

"The Slovak people, whether they be at home or abroad, will never submit to the violence of the Third Reich.

"It associates itself with armed resistance against the aggressor to regain its freedom in collaboration with the civilised nations of the world and in order that it may freely decide its own destiny."

The statement begs Poland and her allies to support the fight of the Slovak people to win true independence.

Slovakia declared its independence on March 14 last and sent a telegram to Hitler asking for aid against the Czechs. These actions brought about the dismemberment of the Republic of Czecho-Slovakia.

MORE CROWDS IN DOWNING STREET

The crowds were so great in Downing St., London, to-day that the police moved the people on.

Viscount Gort, Chief of the Imperial General Staff, was seen in Whitehall in uniform and carrying his gas-mask.

Sir Thomas Inskip again received representatives of the Dominions at his office keeping them in touch with the latest developments in the situation.

"TREACHEROUS AGGRESSION"

An official communique issued in Warsaw, after mentioning yesterday's land and air attacks, says:—"This treacherous aggression was launched a few hours after the Polish Ambassador in Berlin had informed the Government of the Reich of the Polish Government's attitude of goodwill towards the efforts of the British Government aiming at the maintenance of peace.

"This aggression, unparalleled in its brutality, will meet with the firm will of the whole Polish nation, which will defend its liberty, rights, and honour to the end."

The communique goes on:—"Contrary to German statements issued to justify further acts of aggression, there was not a single case of violation of the German frontier by Poles last night.

"A train evacuating women and children from Warsaw was bombed by German military 'planes near Kutno, 60 miles west of Warsaw, causing many casualties in killed and wounded."

UNFORTIFIED TOWNS BOMBED

The Polish Embassy in London, in an announcement, emphasises that the sole responsibility for the hostilities taking place rests exclusively with Germany and that Germany stands before the world as a wanton aggressor.

Contrary to the announcement of Hitler, it is not only military objectives which are being bombed by the German military air force, says the Embassy announcement, but unfortified towns, claiming many victims among the civilian population.

The announcement adds that in consequence of terror directed in Danzig against Polish inhabitants, many Danzig-Poles sought refuge in Poland and are forming Danzigers' units of the Polish Army.

BRITISH CABINET WIDENED

The British Cabinet has been widened, it is learned in London. Most probably four new Ministers will be included, among these Mr. Winston Churchill. The National Executive of the British Labour Party have decided not to join the War Cabinet at this stage. Although supporting the Government on the main lines of its policy, the Executive has some reservations.

The British Ambassador at Ankara is reported to have received assurances that Turkey will remain faithful to the Peace Front and at the side of Great Britain and France.

Mr. Chamberlain to-day received from Mr. Mackenzie King, Canadian Prime Minister, a message stating that the Canadian Government had unanimously decided to seek Parliamentary authority on Thursday for effective co-operation by Canada at the side of Britain. Canada's military, naval, and air forces have been placed on a war footing. New Zealand has proclaimed her unity with Britain. Eighteen more Indian Princes have pledged their support.

GERMAN INTERESTS IN POLAND

At the request of the German Government, it was an-

(Continued on Page Three)

A steel-helmeted member of the Danzig SS-Heimwehr observing activities on the other side of the frontier at Zoppot. In front of him can be seen an anti-tank entanglement.

TO KEEP COUNTRY OUT OF WAR

MR. DE VALERA'S SPEECH

Eire's Attitude Defined: New Ministry May Be Set Up

The Dail met specially to-day in a subdued but tense atmosphere to give the Government emergency powers to protect the interests of this country in view of the international situation.

In the course of his statement, Mr. de Valera foreshadowed the establishment of a Ministry of Supply.

Mr. de Valera indicated that an amendment would be introduced before the Emergency Bill became law, to make it clear that there was no intention of having compulsory military service under the Bill.

Mr. de Valera rose and referred to the anxiety of the European situation and the fact that the Government put off as long as possible the calling of the Dail until the last moment.

It was now, therefore, necessary to act with speed. There was now extreme urgency for the passage of the measures before the House.

The policy of the Government had already decided to keep the country out of a European war.

They had set that policy before them, and they intended to pursue it.

They had to protect their own interests and give none of the belligerents proper cause for complaint.

"SYMPATHIES"

The policy of neutrality was one that could be pursued only if they had a determined people, determined to stand by their own rights, conscious of the fact that they did not wish to enter the war.

They had their sympathies in this struggle. In this country there were very strong sympathies in regard to the present issue, but he did not think anybody, no matter what his feelings were, would suggest that the official policy of the State should be other than the one suggested by the Government.

IRELAND'S EXPERIENCE

The Irish, of all nations, had known what force as applied by a stronger nation against a weaker one meant.

They knew what invasion and partition meant but they did not ignore existing facts, and as long as their own country or any part of it was subject to force and the application of force by a stronger nation it was only natural that their people, whatever sympathies they might have in a conflict like the present one, looked at their own country first, and accordingly considered what their own interests should be and were.

The Government stood before the people as the guardians of their interests, and it was to guard these as best they could that they proposed their present policy.

The first measure before the House was an amendment to the Constitution—a very simple one—which made it clear that "time of war," as referred to in the Constitution, meant a crisis such as that.

The other measures undoubtedly placed on the Government considerable powers.

MILITARY SERVICE

The Emergency Bill powers could not be asked for except in a general form, for nobody could see all the possible causes which would require prompt action.

There was no power in the Emergency Bill to introduce compulsory military service.

That would be made clear by amendment before the Bill was passed.

Any propery taken would be paid for.

The Government would not use the powers in an arbitrary way.

They would always meet any reasonable demands made by the House.

The burden of responsibility on the Government was heavy. The provision of essential supplies would provide many problems.

A Ministry of Supply might be established in re-arrangement of the present Ministries.

The work of supply might, on the other hand, be delegated to a Parliamentary Secretary or a Civil Servant with a Minister responsible.

The First Readings of the First Constitutional Amendment Bill and the Emergency Powers Bill were passed without discussion.

MR. COSGRAVE

Mr. Cosgrave, speaking to the Second Reading of the Constitutional Amendment Bill, said he would like it to contain some provision providing for a proof that an armed conflict existed affecting the vital interests of this country. There might be an armed conflict on the other side of the globe which did not affect our vital interests, and yet, as the Bill stood, all the citizens' constitutional rights could be put in cold storage.

It might be possible to include in the amendment a provision making it necessary to have a message from the President to the effect that in his view a national emergency existed and that he thought it desirable that the Houses of the Oireachtas should take that into consideration.

Mr. Dillon said he believed the vast majority of the Irish people placed their sympathy on the side

(CONTINUED ON PAGE THREE.)

GERMAN OFFENSIVE IN POLAND

Women Among Raid Victims: Bombs on Hospital

(Reuter Telegram.)

Warsaw, Saturday.

Three women and two men were among the victims of a German air-raid over Warsaw yesterday, according to a statement issued by the semi-official Polish Agency. They were injured by debris caused by bombs.

The raid was one of a number made on Polish towns, including Cracow, Gdynia, Zukow, in Polish Pomerania, and Biala, Podlaska, 100 miles east of Warsaw, where there is an aircraft factory.

ALTOGETHER, IT IS CLAIMED, NINE GERMAN MACHINES WERE SHOT DOWN. FULL DETAILS OF CASUALTIES AND DAMAGE IN WARSAW ARE NOT YET KNOWN, BUT THE DAMAGE CAUSED BY THE RAID WAS NOT EXTENSIVE.

FIRES ARE BELIEVED TO HAVE BEEN CAUSED IN SEVERAL HOUSES, AND POLISH OFFICIAL QUARTERS STATE THAT THE 'PLANES BOMBED AND WRECKED A HOSPITAL FOR JEWISH DEFECTIVE CHILDREN.

Polish sources state that raids on other towns caused "numerous deaths, including many women and children."

According to the same sources, an evacuation train filled with women and children was bombed from the air near Kutno, about 60 miles west of Warsaw.

A number of women and children are reported to have been killed and many injured.

A German armoured train is claimed to have been captured near Danzig.

Referring to these raids and the invasion of Poland from East Prussia by land forces, a semi-official statement issued here declares:

"Thus the German aggression against Poland is an accomplished fact."

AN OFFICIAL GERMAN COMMUNIQUE ISSUED AT MID-DAY SAYS THAT EARLY THIS MORNING GERMAN TROOPS CONTINUED ADVANCES AT ALL POINTS.

(Continued on Page 2.)

You'll like SWEET AFTON BETTER THAN EVER
The Proof is in the Packet

Fred (above) and Vincent Devere, of the Western People, **Ballina, two of the best-known "characters" in Irish provincial newspapers earlier this century.**

Sporting prowess in the Gaelic code did not come easily to Joe Sherwood, the founding sports editor on the *Irish Press.* Described by Mitchel Cogley as "not a nice person to know", Sherwood never lived down an early report on a GAA final, when he wrote "Kick-off, 3.15". Later, he was to confess that he didn't know whether it was kick-off, bully-off or bugger off! No wonder that whenever Dorothy MacArdle, the first drama critic on the *Irish Press,* heard foul language one day at Burgh Quay, she remarked: "Have I by any chance strayed into the sports department?" Paste pots, even the occasional typewriter, became airborne in Sherwood's office.

Dr Dan McSparran ordered a clean up in the reporters' room at the *Irish News* in Belfast, not of language, but of the desk drawers. No missing files were found, as was the case in the big *Irish Times'* clear-out in 1934, but empty bottles in abundance. A junior member of staff made four trips over to McGlade's bar on the other side of the street and collected £2 17s, a good sum of money for the mid-1930s. Reporters also did a great line in swopping copy.

Community tensions were high in Northern Ireland during the decade, but on many weekly newspapers, reporters simply swapped blacks, making slight alterations in copy, so that a report of a Unionist meeting could be "doctored" for a Nationalist newspaper and vice versa. On one famous occasion, recalls veteran Northern journalist, Tom Samways, the sub didn't have time to make substantial changes to the copy borrowed from a reporter on a rival newspaper of the opposite political persuasion. All he could do was change "loud applause" to "cries of derision". In the days when Monaghan had both Nationalist and Unionist newspapers, the two editors were so friendly that they were reputed to write each other's leader, easier than it sounds, since the formula was entirely repetitive. Perhaps the most famous case of copy swopping came from the inimitable Maurice Liston of the *Irish Press,* handicapped by a slight speech defect, but great fun. Once, he was sent to Sligo to cover the Feis Cheoil there, which incidentally was always dutifully covered in detail for *The Irish Times,* since Smyllie had been brought up in the town.

A gang of reporters from the Dublin papers had drawn lots for the man to cover the musical proceedings for the day while the remainder went off to their spiritual celebrations. Liston drew the unlucky number, so while he slaved for the day taking notes, the others went on a grand drinking spree, later claimed on expenses. On the train back to Dublin that night, one of the very drunk reporters asked Maurice if he could have a look at the copy. Said Maurice, very thoughtfully patting his back pocket, "I've a dreadful suspicion that I've used it in there", pointing to the lavatory. Forty years and more later, devotees of Maurice Liston still savoured that story, told as with so many hundreds more, in the rich accent of his native Co Limerick. He never confirmed the ending of that particular tale.

The special Sunday edition of the Cork Evening Echo on September 3, 1939, heralded the start of war.

Newspaper rivalry in north Cork was a more serious affair in the 1930s. The *Kerryman* was building up its circulation in its native county; then came the decision to run a separate edition for Co Cork, although the title was not changed to the *Corkman* until many years later. The rotund character of Dan Griffin, a skilled shorthand taker, deservedly took much of the credit for building up the *Kerryman* in north Cork. He had told Dan Nolan's father that if he were appointed in Mallow, he would guarantee the sale of hundreds of copies in the locality. Griffin was true to his pledge and at a time when hundreds of pounds in bribes were paid to secure jobs such as that of rent collector, he stood up to the local bodies. At one meeting of the old and corrupt North Cork Board of Health and Public Assistance, Griffin refused to leave when the Board decided to go into private committee session.

He said that he would only leave the press table when the proposal to go into committee had been voted on, in accordance with the law. While standing up to the local administrators, Griffin also had to respect the wishes of readers, particularly with regard to coverage of funerals. Very often, the list of mourners was so long that it filled an entire column of the *Kerryman*. Still, Dan Griffin was so good at his job in Mallow that the *Kerryman* beat the competition from the other weekly papers in the area; it was one instance in the 1930s when rivalry between local reporters was far from friendly, but deadly competitive.

The boredom of such local coverage, with all its detail, was relieved by the occasional mistake. The *Irish Independent* caused much mirth among the knowing when it printed a death notice for a priest. "Father ---- is survived by a sister and five brothels." Frank Geary, later confidant of Dermot Ryan, now Archbishop of Dublin and many others in the Catholic Hierarchy, cannot have been pleased.

While John Healy was editor at *The Irish Times* until his death in 1934, his namesake, J. C. (Jack) Healy (no relative) was editor of the *Cork Examiner*. Healy became editor of the Cork morning paper not long after the turn of the century; with his amazing skills as a raconteur, he was rooted very firmly in the editorial seat. He also had an uncanny knack of spotting subs' mistakes and was as ruthless over reprimanding the culprits as Harrington and Geary were at the *Irish Independent*. At this time, the *Cork Examiner* had a remarkable London editor, Louis McQuilland, who held celebrated "At Homes" in his Chelsea residence, where young reporters delighted in meeting some of the best-known men of letters of the day. L. C. Blennerhassett, moved from publicity manager of Independent Newspapers to London manager; a flamboyant character, in the style of McQuilland, he became London's resident authority on Ireland. Ask for a contact or information, and Blennerhassett had it all to hand.

In succession to the first London editor of the *Irish Press*, Bill Sweetman, came a Co Waterford man called Liam McLoughlin. He remained in London for five years, before making an abrupt change of career, eventually becoming Mayo county manager. In Waterford in 1937, Edmund Downey, owner and editor of the *Waterford News*, died. The *Waterford News* staff passed a special resolution, in respectful silence: "We have learned with profound sorrow of the lamented death of a beloved employer and wish to place on record our deep appreciation of his many acts of generosity and kindness." When Edmund Downey died, his son, Alan, was aged fifty-five. All his life he lived in the shadow of his father's literary achievements; he led a recluse's existence, rarely going to functions, but staying at home and living life at second-hand. He had little experience of newspaper management, but was a good writer, especially of leaders; the equipment at the *Waterford News* gradually deteriorated and circulation fell away. Somehow, he managed to pull the paper through the war years, but the decline continued. Eventually, the *Cork Examiner* Crosbies bought both the *News* and its rival, the *Waterford Star,* and merged them into one paper, the *Waterford News and Star* in January, 1959.

Another "absentee", but for entirely different reasons, was Anthony Mulvey, M.P. at Westminster for Tyrone-Fermanagh; he never took his seat. He started on the *Leitrim Observer* and went on to Boyle to work with Tully on the *Roscommon Herald*. From there, he went to Wexford, where he worked on both the *Free Press* and the *People*. Mulvey became editor of the *Ulster Herald* series of newspapers, based in Omagh, Co Tyrone. At that time, besides the *Herald,* it included the *Fermanagh Herald,* the *Derry People,* the *Strabane Chronicle* and the *Frontier Sentinel,* Newry. While Mulvey was editor, Louis Lynch was managing director. Lynch used to love telling a story about the Northern customs; in the 1930s, customs searches were particularly vigilant:

Coming back by train from Dublin one day, he shared a compartment with a young man, who had a bulky case, and a young lady, both strangers to one another. When the Customs' man opened the case, it contained much ladies' clothing and underwear. "Who owns this?" he asked. Quick as a flash, the young man replied: "The two of us". Later, amid much amusement, he apologised to the woman for his presumption.

Mulvey himself once had his own spot of embarrassment on the *Ulster Herald:* he took a special interest in one wedding report, writing it himself and then proofreading the setting. When the machines were running, he barked out the order to stop the press: "Nuptial Mass" had been described as "Requiem Mass."

Just as the young man on the Dublin-Omagh train had a caseful of ladies' clothing, so too did similar garments attract a noted writer, curiously enough also from Co Tyrone, Brian O'Nolan, later Myles na gCopaleen, born in Strabane. When he was working in the Dublin civil service, he met up with a Belfast traveller in ladies' underclothes. He became more and more curious; the two men ended up in a snug in Ryans' pub in Bath Avenue, where Myles was spotted prancing around trying on one of the voluminous ladies' corsets so popular in the 1930s!

A peculiar story emerged from the *Sunday Independent;* the *Irish Independent* ran a medical queries column. For this feature, a woman reader had sent in a sample of her urine in a baby Power's bottle. By some chance, the accompanying note became detached from the bottle, which ended up on the desk of the *Sunday Independent* editor. A passing journalist spotted the bottle and promptly took a swig. His illusions of refreshment were swiftly destroyed. Another journalist of the period had a strong aversion to water in his whiskey; he used to say "Look what water does to the soles of your shoes, rots them."He went to his eternal rest and the priest, having said the prayers, started to pour holy water over the coffin. A wag in the congregation whispered: "Don't pour too much on him. He wasn't used to it."

Few journalists went abroad, although Liam Bergin from the *Nationalist and Leinster Times,* Carlow, spent much time in pre-civil war Spain and J. J. Walsh of the *Munster Express,* Waterford, went to his first Olympic games, in Berlin, in 1936. Hitler, three years in power, refused to present the black American athlete, Jesse Owens, with the four gold medals he had won.

A young employee of the *Irish Independent,* Billy King, conducted a protracted correspondence with George Bernard Shaw. King, an advertisement representative, wrote to Shaw after he had ordered his complete works from the *Daily Herald.* Offers of books, free insurance and the like were made in abundance by the English papers of the 1930s as circulation building efforts. The Irish customs impounded the volumes until duty had been paid. So began a correspondence between

Mrs Nell O'Reilly, long-serving manager of the Connacht Tribune, **a well-known Galway businesswoman. She took over the position after the death of her husband Sam in 1935.**
–Connacht Tribune

Sam O'Reilly, manager of the Connacht Tribune **until his death in 1935.**
–Connacht Tribune.

the two men over such matters as whether Shaw would accept the position of President of the Irish Free State ("No, I am too old"). Eventually, Shaw gave copyright clearance on the letters to King, who then sold it to Geary for a mere fiver.

Another up-and-coming young man was Earl Connolly, the jolly, bow-tied veteran of the *Limerick Leader,* who joined the staff just before the war and as advertisement manager, is the newspaper's only surviving employee from those far-off days. He recalls how the paper was printed then at premises in Patrick Street. The press, in the basement, was controlled by the state of tides on the nearby River Shannon.

Douglas Hyde, with the seal-like moustache, was the first President of Ireland. Not long after he had taken up residence at Áras an Uachtaráin in Dublin's Phoenix Park, Hyde threw a garden party. On behalf of the *Irish Press,* Anna Kelly, who had recently returned to the fold, wrote up the proceedings. She is said to have compared his moustache (the great seal of Ireland) with certain inhabitants of the next-door zoo. The report did not go down at all well with the Fianna

Fail faithful, some of whom threatened to burn down Burgh Quay. Anna Kelly survived; so did Douglas Hyde.

On a more serious note, one of the finest pieces of Irish journalism in the 1930s was written by Liam MacGabhann and like all good news copy, had its origins in tragedy. In 1937, Irish migrant workers were burned to death in a bothy at Kirkintilloch in Scotland. MacGabhann heard a brief mention of the story on the lunchtime Radio Eireann news; he rushed in to see Jack Grealish, *Irish Press* news editor, who had taken over the job two years previously following the sudden death of Bob Egan. MacGabhann said to Grealish: "It's a big story" and off he went to Scotland.

Tom Barrett also worked for the *Irish Press* then; he remembers MacGabhann rushing through the office, thrusting a note in his hand and collapsing into a taxi waiting outside. The note was for his wife, Phenie; they had been due to go to the Savoy. It read: "Phenie a Gradh, gone to Scotland — hope you enjoy the film. Liam". When he got to Kirkintilloch, he established an immediate rapport with the surviving potato pickers (he had fluent Irish), stayed with them until all the formalities were completed, travelled back to Ireland with them and helped to lay the dead to rest in their native Donegal. His description of the tragedy, his interviews with the survivors and his story of the sad journey home made memorable reading — and Liam MacGabhann's reputation. The *World's Press News* said of his feat: "He is a writer of outstanding ability, courage and sympathy."

1938 saw the death of Jasper Tully of the *Roscommon Herald;* quiet relief must have been breathed by the unfortunate workers on the paper, badgered almost daily by Tully until shortly before he died. Only then, when he was safely buried, could the legends multiply and the *Roscommon Herald* slip into a quiet respectability, led by Tully's manager, Paddy Nerney, whose widow, Lillie, now runs the firm. Paddy had joined the paper as a teenager, so he had had the best part of twenty years during which to sample the dreadful waywardness of Tully.

They were dull days, too, at the *Irish Independent.* Its sub-editors' room before the war was large and unfriendly, with about as much cheer as a morgue. Up to twenty subs at a time worked in the room and there was little interruption, apart from when the chief sub barked "Clear", meaning that he was clear of copy. The first time one newcomer to the *Irish Independent,* from a country paper, heard this message, he was so surprised that he nearly left the room in a hurry. The *Independent,* too, had its dynasties, in common with other well-established newspapers. In Middle Abbey Street, the Flynns, father and two sons, were noted characters in the sports department, already augmented at this stage by the able Arthur MacWeeney, one of the great family of sporting journalists.

Slowly, the dreary pre-war days were ending; the country had

Douglas Hyde, first President of Ireland, who came under written assault from Anna Kelly in the Irish Press.

enjoyed sixteen years of comparative peace since the ending of the civil war. Now came global war, although Ireland stayed neutral. The war-time circumstances provided their own set of difficulties for newspapers, so just as the 1916-1923 period provided the greatest-ever challenge for Irish newspapers, a great test for the industry was set by the Emergency.

One of the last noted recruits to *The Irish Times* before war broke out was Patrick Campbell. "Never begin a sentence with a shuddering preposition and remember that the semi-colon is the prerogative of the senior practitioner, "Smyllie told Campbell after he had written his first faltering leader. Soon Campbell graduated to be the Parliamentary Sketch Writer; he whizzed round town in a bull-nosed Morris Cowley, said to have been owned previously by Nurse Cadden, later convicted for performing an abortion. From Leinster House, Campbell wrote: "Deputy C...... addressed the Dáil yesterday in what he called the "tongue of the sthranger". Sthrange it was indeed."

"You'll be getting us all shot," laughed Smyllie. As for Campbell, later, much later, he was said to have developed his famous stutter just for television.

Poachers turned gamekeepers. In 1939, Frank Gallagher, the founding editor of the *Irish Press,* was removed from the stuffy confines of Radio Eireann to the equally stuffy confines of the Government Information Bureau. For the duration of the war, in close consultation with de Valera, he remained its head. Another well-known journalist, Michael Knightly from the *Irish Independent,* later to work with the shorthand writers of Leinster House, was appointed to take charge of the wartime censorship. A young man took up a casual position with the *Irish Press* just before war broke out — Francis Carty, later to be editor of that paper and then of the *Sunday Press.* He had spent most of the decade writing novels and freelance writing, having been unable to get into the *Irish Press* in its early days. As war drew closer, the newspapers started their special editions. In Cork, on the first Saturday night in September, 1939, staff at the Cork *Evening Echo* laboured to produce its first and last Sunday edition, bringing the momentous news of the declaration of war to the people of Munster, although readers of the *Saturday Herald* and the *Dublin Evening Mail* that Saturday evening were equally well informed.

CHAPTER VII

War Town
1940-April, 1945

Avoid flatulence after meals. Milk of Magnesia tablets.
NORTHERN WHIG, 1940

Westport Boot Workers' second annual dance, Grand Central Hall, Westport, Friday, January 15th. Garvey's Radio Orchestra. Admission 3/-.
MAYO NEWS, 1943

Long term loans for farmers 4½%. Agricultural Credit Corporation, Kildare St., Dublin.
CORK EXAMINER, February, 1945

War could not interrupt the more serious pleasures of life, like drinking. As the world drifted into war, the newspaper crowd floated away from the Palace Bar. In April, 1940, "Gus" Weldon took over Moore's pub in Fleet Street and rechristened it the Pearl Bar. In the thirty-three years of its existence under Weldon's benign rule, some of Ireland's best, unpublished quips were manufactured. Before taking over the Pearl Bar, Weldon's family had been closely involved with the Boot Inn at Cloghran, north Co Dublin. Smyllie used to drop in for refreshment to and from the golf course at Malahide, so he already knew the family well. After the death of George Ryan, owner of the Palace, it was inevitable that the focus of attention should shift to the Pearl. Myles na gCopaleen was more fortunate; he was said to have laid in his own stocks of whiskey for the duration of the Emergency and emergency it would have been for Myles without his whiskey. His column progressed from its humble start in 1940, becoming almost daily.

One of the most famous stories of the war concerned an *Irish Times'* leader writer, John A. Robinson. He had joined the Royal Navy and was aboard HMS Repulse when it was sunk by Japanese torpedoes in 1941; he was rescued. Smyllie wanted to let readers know of Robinson's great good fortune, but the censor refused; to beat the ban, a paragraph appeared in the paper saying that Mr Robinson's many

201

(Opposite page): At the launching of the Times Pictorial, George Burrows, the editor (pointing finger, at rear) and a group of wives celebrate the new paper.

Group at the launching of the Times Pictorial in 1941.

At the launching of the Times Pictorial in December, 1941: Frank Lowe (centre) examines a matrix for the paper. Also in photograph are from left, Mrs Lowe, Mrs Campbell (wife of the works manager) and Mrs Kathlyn Smyllie, wife of The Irish Times' editor.

friends would be glad to hear he had survived his recent boating accident. The knowing knew, but to the unknowing, including the censor, the few sentences were meaningless. In the *Irish Independent,* early in the war, the death of an IRA hunger striker merited a short single column story. The death of an eighty-nine year old Bishop warranted 104 lines.

In Tralee, the young Dan Nolan, the new managing director of the *Kerryman,* supervised the stockpiling of paper. Up in Ballina, the crafty Fred Devere of the *Western People* did the same; by every train and lorry, supplies of newsprint came in and he supervised the packing of it into every nook and cranny of the firm's new premises at Francis Street. At the *Munster Express* in Waterford, J. J. Walsh had shown unusual foresight in buying up property for storing the extra newsprint. He acquired so much that when one Midlands paper was on the verge of closing down because it was fast running out of paper, he was able to save their press day. Later in the war, a freak flood on the River Suir wiped out most of the *Munster Express* stock, but the newspaper somehow survived. The provincial newspaper association also organised its own scheme for importing newsprint. In Dublin, *The Irish Times* packed warehouses near Pearse Street railway bridge with newsprint. When supplies ran dangerously low, Smyllie made a personal appeal to de Valera, with whom he was on surprisingly good personal terms. De Valera immediately had a cart-load of newsprint sent over from the *Irish Press.* Shortages of lead and brass for the Linotype machines were even more serious. Constant recycling took place. Formally, the Government was at odds more with *The Irish Times* than any other newspaper, mainly because of Smyllie's natural desire to support the Allied cause in the war. *The Irish Times* was subjected to far greater censorship than any other paper in Ireland, so much so that as the war wore on, even the small advertisements had to be censored. On one occasion, much amusement was caused when a church advertisement for "Kingstown Presbyterian Church" slipped through; "Kingstown" was not an officially acceptable name for Dun Laoghaire. Smyllie had running battles with the chief censor, Michael Knightly and his political boss, Frank Aiken, who was Minister for Co-ordination of Defence and whom Smyllie disliked intensely. Like all the other occasions of war, the censorship did provide moments of amusement. One Dublin messenger boy, taking approved galley proofs back from Dublin Castle to one of the newspapers, stopped to watch Jack Doyle, the prize-fighter (prize drinker and prize womaniser, too) have a splendid punch-up with his wife Movita on the pavement outside the old Jurys Hotel in Dame Street.

The Irish Times was held up going to press one night because all its approved galley proofs had blown away in Dame Street. Paddy McDonald, in the remembrance of Matt Farrell, who worked in *The Irish Times'* newsroom throughout the war, had stuffed all the passed

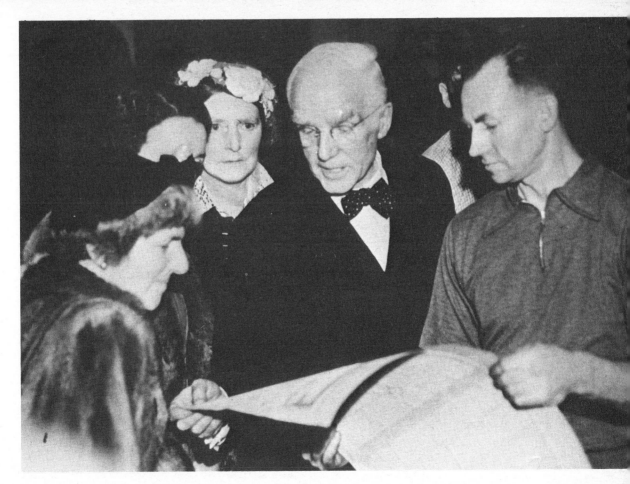

A young Cork lad gets a taste of the Emergency.
–Cork Examiner

proofs in his overcoat pocket. A gust of wind carried them all over the street. Smyllie carried on, oblivious even of the IRA threats made against him during the war. Slightly more latitude was enjoyed by Hector Legge, the new editor at *Sunday Independent*. He employed Major Eamon Rooney (brother of Michael Rooney, assistant editor of the *Irish Independent*) to write a military affairs column charting the progress of the war. Strangely enough, Major Rooney refused all blandishments to write the column for the daily paper instead of the Sunday publication. After the war, Major Rooney played an important part in building up Aer Lingus. He was not always the most popular of men; neither was Myles na gCopaleen, who had progressed sufficiently by the middle of the war to write an almost daily column. Starting off mainly in Irish, after March, 1943, the column was written almost invariably in English. Despite his linguistic brilliance, the author was disliked. Remembers Charles Mullock: "He was not a funny person to deal with, very uncouth and rough. Most people in the office would scarper when Myles arrived."

In 1940, a Limerick editor, Paddy Fitzgibbon, enjoyed seeing his play, *The Fire Burns Late* produced at the Abbey Theatre, Dublin. He had been appointed acting editor of the *Limerick Chronicle* in 1938 and with P. J. Moroney, the circulation manager and Harry Pickford, the printing manager, went on to own the paper, which later still was sold off to the *Limerick Leader*. Then, and until twenty years ago, the *Chronicle* was very much Limerick's Church of Ireland newspaper and even through the war years, a Canon would come into the *Chronicle* office every week and write out the copy for Church service advertisements. The rival *Limerick Weekly Echo* was taken over the same year that Fitzgibbon enjoyed his Abbey triumph by a young Limerick man called Ivan Morris. Only ten years previously, he had gone to Dublin to be articled to an accountancy firm for £3 10s a week. Now, when he returned in triumph to his native city, he also took over the editorial chair at the paper. At the rival *Limerick Leader,* the fires also burned late; to beat the electricity rationing, the manager, E. B. Duggan, organised a battery of blow lamps to heat the metal for the Linotypes.

Towards the end of 1940, most of the English dancing girls in Dublin went home: for the remainder of the war, the theatres depended upon local talent. May Devitt, Josef Locke, Ria Mooney, the whole Happy Gang at the Queen's Theatre, all came into their own. So too did Ernie Murray, at this time still working as a sub on the *Irish Independent,* although he transferred shortly afterwards to the *Evening Mail.* Not only was he commander of the LDF unit set up for Dublin newspaper workers, but he was also churning out gags as fast as he could for the Happy Gang in the Queen's Theatre. The shortage of talent in the theatre benefitted that great comic actor, Wilfred Brambell, who worked as assistant to Ernie Branson, the editor of the *Irish Field,* the weekly racing paper published by *The Irish Times.* Branson was an Englishman and a bachelor; he was said to be so well off in his own right that he had no need of his salary from the paper. The safe in his office was reputed to be full of unopened wage packets, the only use for which was as loans for his fellow workers. Bewley's cafe on the opposite side of Westmoreland Street was (and still is) a popular rendezvous for *Irish Times'* staff: Brambell was often seen there.

However, Brambell had more pressing matters on his mind than the *Irish Field:* that was just the day job. His real interest was in the theatre; such was the shortage of actors that the ambitious Thespian had the run of the Dublin theatres, the Gaiety, the Gate and so on; once, he even did pantomime, which caused great astonishment and amusement to his *Irish Times'* colleagues. As the war went on, so did Brambell's theatrical career progress. In 1944, he was reported as playing leading roles with a theatrical company touring the North of Ireland. After the war, he went to London to pursue his stage career, becoming best known for the part of the dirty, irate father in "Steptoe and Son", the BBC television comedy series.

Brambell must have had one of the most exciting wars for a Dublin newspaperman. At the *Sunday Independent,* eventually reduced to one sheet, Hector Legge, had precious little to do putting the paper together. Jack Grealish, news editor of the *Irish Press,* recalled that life in the reporters' room during the war was dull. Most of the news was foreign; home news was strictly censored, so much so that a story could be held up for ten days, by which time any "scoops" were well out of date. Reporters twiddled their thumbs, with not much to do; local

Paddy Fitzgibbon, editor of the Limerick Chronicle, **had his play, The Fire Burns Late, produced at the Abbey in 1940.**

Bill Coyne, a porter at
The Irish Times — **one
of the great characters
produced by the paper.**

correspondents round the country, dependent on selling copy to the Dublin papers, had a lean time indeed.

All through the dark days of the war, through the London blitz even, the wire from the *Irish Press* London office kept functioning, with little disruption. Thomas P. Rowan was its London editor. Through the blitz, he never missed a night at Ludgate House at the bottom of Fleet Street, even though bombs fell all around and parts of Fleet Street were often closed while unexploded bombs were defused. All through the war, the private wires of the London offices of the three Dublin newspapers and the *Cork Examiner* were allowed to operate unimpeded, with the exception of a small number of news items, which were submitted voluntarily to the censorship department of the Ministry of Information. The press censorship back home in Ireland was far more stringent. In Ballybay, Co Monaghan, in 1941, the bridge was mined because invasion was expected from across the nearby border. One mine slipped and the entire village had to be evacuated. The story never appeared in the press. When a garda was killed during shooting at a Mountnugent, Co Cavan, wedding party that involved IRA members, two lines appeared in the press to the effect that a member of the Gardai had been killed in an "accident" at Mountnugent.

In all parts of Ireland, weather details could not be used. In the North, during a visit by the American chief of staff, a UTA bus driver was shot dead by a member of his escort; the bus driver had not responded to an unfamiliar signal, but it was days before the official report of the incident was released to newspapers.

In London, *The Irish Times'* London editor, Bill Sheedy, kept functioning, but later had to be recalled back to Dublin, he was so shell-shocked after the blitz. Tom Samways recalled Sheedy giving a performance in a Mooney's pub in Fleet Street once: his trousers were rolled up, he was dancing on the counter and singing to the top of his voice about Phil the Fluter's Ball!

In the subs' room at the *Irish Press* in Dublin, electricity rationing meant that lighting was restricted. The sub-editors had to work in small pools of light from reading lamps on their tables; the night watchman was under strict orders to save electricity, and he took his instructions seriously. Lurking in the darkness, he would leap out when no-one was around and switch off as many lights as he could. A sub who left his desk would have to grope his way back in semi-darkness; when the electric light bulbs became so scarce that they started vanishing, they were caged in with wire. Then wire began to get scarce.

A weakness of Sweetman, the *Irish Press* editor, was to have copy read out to him: backwards and forwards the arguments flowed between himself and Paddy Kirwan, the assistant editor. Once, in exasperation, a reporter was told by Sweetman: "You know that Kirwan failed in every faculty at UCD? They had to make him a

Mr. Burrowes (Photo Dept. Irish Times)
and Mr. McSweeney (Photo Dept. Times
Pictorial) approached Mr. F. O'Carroll
who consulted Mr. Binnie with the
result that the above photograph was
taken on the understanding that there
was to be no publication without our
permission. I should not have granted
permission for publication though the
photograph is not without humour.
Fortunately the photographer himself
has decided that the matter should be
dropped.
Photo taken 26/7/42.
    On left   Robert Grey,
    On right Ignatius Kelly.
                    E. F. MANNING.

**This photograph was
organised in 1942 by
George Burrows and
Eddie MacSweeney of
the** Times Pictorial, **but
never published because
of the wartime
censorship.**
–*Guinness*

207

One of the legendary Bundoran golf outings; included in this group are R. M. Smyllie (editor, Irish Times, centre with cup). "Pussy" O'Mahony (general manager, Irish Times, **extreme left, front row)** and Charlie McConnell of McConnell's Advertising (immediate right of Smyllie). Immediately behind Smyllie is Alan Montgomery. Next to O'Mahony is J. J. Walsh of the Munster Express.

lawyer." Sweetman himself was a barrister. Anna Kelly, the sharp and sometimes foul-tongued woman's editor, used to refer to Sweetman and Kirwan as "Lo and Behold", but in which order, no-one was quite sure. Kelly poured verbal vitriol round the office; not even her own daughter, Ruth, soon to start her own journalistic career at the *Irish Press,* was immune.

In Dublin, advertising was strictly rationed and many was the bottle of whiskey passed under the counter from advertiser to clerk. Despite the rationing of food (½ lb of sugar a week) and of gas and electricity, the war was very phoney to most Dubliners. The glimmerman, checking to see that cookers were not left on after the gas supply had been turned off for the day, was a much more serious threat. One *Irish Times'* employee, Garry Redmond, found the solution; more than once, he cooked kippers for his lunch on the foundry stove.

The Belfast papers had their own baptism of fire, an ordeal not shared by newspapers anywhere else in Ireland. In April, 1941, just a month before the bombs were dropped on Dublin's North Strand, Belfast was pounded by the Luftwaffe bombers. Many areas of north and central Belfast were devastated by the bombs; there were thousands of casualties, with over 700 people killed. In Royal Avenue, on the night of April 15, two 500 lbs German bombs landed in front of the *Belfast Telegraph* building. The damage was extensive, with every window in the building blown out, offices wrecked and printing equipment distorted. In the hours after the editorial staff joined with the fire watchers and others in clearing away the debris, the piles of broken glass, the twisted typewriters, the scattered papers. Advertising staff went to work in the despatch department, while the leader writers went to the photographic darkroom, the most windproof place in the buliding. Casting of stereo plates was a major problem, overcome by reverting to the old-fashioned hand boxes. The *Telegraph's* clock, as famous in its own way as that on *The Irish Times,* was shattered into fragments by the blast, but the most delicate instrument in the house, the Creed telegraphic apparatus connecting the newspaper with its London office, was undamaged. One curious fact about the library made a neat line for the *Belfast Telegraph's* own reporting of the story: the library was undamaged, except for one drawer, which the blast shot open. It contained the wallet full of Hitler's speeches since he came to power in 1933.

Dermot Barry, a photographer at The Irish Times; **his son Norman is well-known in the Dublin publishing business.**

The day after the raid, the *Belfast Telegraph* not only produced its own editions, but also those of the Belfast *News Letter,* the *Northern Whig* and the *Irish News.* These papers were all housed in buildings within a 500 yard radius of the *Belfast Telegraph* and all had suffered much more severe bomb damage than the *Telegraph.* The other papers soon reverted to their own production, while the *Belfast Telegraph* continued with its four page editions, reduced because of the effects of the bomb blast and the severe shortage of newsprint. On one occasion the following month, when a bombing raid on the harbour power station cut off electricity supplies to central Belfast, the *News Letter* was reduced to turning out a single sheet issue, using paper for bill printing, on a treadle-driven press. When several thousand copies were run off, copies were then printed using the same contents but the *Northern Whig* masthead. Later in the war, the *Belfast Telegraph* was also printing rather larger special editions — for the US armed forces based in Northern Ireland.

The printing works of the *Spectator* in Bangor, Co. Down, had contingency plans for printing the Belfast newspapers, during the war, but these were never needed. The main problem faced by the *Spectator,* remembers its present editor, Annie Roycroft, was that if the advertisement manager went into Belfast once a week to collect copy, that used up most of the company's petrol allocation. For the rest of the week, out came the bicycles.

Throughout Ireland, such train services as ran were used

Loftus Arnott, chairman of the board of The Irish Times, **1940-1945.**

extensively for distributing newspaper copies. In Dublin, the war without bloodshed came to an abrupt end in May, 1941, the night of the North Strand bombings. True, there had been fatalities with bombings in Co Wexford, but the horror being endured elsewhere in Europe only hit home to Dubliners with the destruction on the North Strand. Liam MacGabhann covered the story for the *Irish Press;* also there was a young reporter called Seamus Brady, who much later uncovered many excellent "scoops" as Irish correspondent of the *Daily Express.* Maurice Hickey, recently retired political correspondent of the *Evening Herald,* is one of the few surviving reporters of the group who covered the story of the 1941 North Strand bombing.

MacGabhann remembered the rescue parties pulling the bodies out from the burning rubble at North Strand: "Some were so badly burned as to be unrecognisable." The next morning, the reporters on the story were taken to the city morgue in Amiens Street.

MacGabhann again: "The man in charge pulled the covers off the bodies. 'There they are', he said. After some of the things I had seen during the night, these terrible sights did not upset me so much until I came to two babies, a boy and a girl, huddled in each other's arms. They were completely untouched, but dead from concussion. I had to leave." Michael Rooney of the *Independent* was nearly jailed, for sending the story by wire to the Press Association.

Newsprint rationing by the Government (under the aegis of Sean Lemass' Department) did not begin until 1941, the year of the air raids on Dublin and Belfast. But somehow, in December of that year, *The Irish Times* managed to procure enough newsprint to launch a new paper, the *Times Pictorial,* although it was in effect a complete overhaul of the old *Weekly Irish Times,* rather than a brand new publication. It was the first new project at *The Irish Times* since the acquisition of the *Irish Field* nearly forty years previously. Appropriately, the lead story in the first issue of the *Times Pictorial* was on bread, increasingly in short supply and getting greyer by the day. The emphasis in the "Pic" was on feature coverage and news and feature photographs: during the war, two of its stalwarts were George Burrows, its editor, now *Irish Times'* angling correspondent and Eddie MacSweeney. The paper managed to survive until 1958, although it was never an outstanding financial success. Another of the myriad MacWeeneys, Cecil, worked as advertisement manager of the *Times Pictorial.* Nicknamed "Mufti", he was said to glide, rather than walk.

The city had other press characters during the war, like Seamus G. O'Kelly, who did snippets on Irish history for the *Irish Independent.* He was paralysed, so his crab-like progress along Middle Abbey Street was tortuous both for himself and for onlookers. He was also a life-long member of the IRA and when he was interned for a while during the war, he was far from well treated, despite his disability, because he refused to support either faction in the Curragh.

Wandering in and out of *The Irish Times*, overseen by the telephonist, Harry Sullivan, who had lost most of his right hand in an accident with a band saw in one of the printing departments, was "Pussy" O'Mahony's brother, Barry, quite as disfigured mentally as Seamus G. O'Kelly was physically. Barry O'Mahony, a barrister by profession, wore his LDF uniform, riding breeches and a top hat for his forays into *The Irish Times*. Ceaselessly trying to borrow money from staff members, oblivious to memos warning them against the practice, he was addicted in equal proportions to Dr Collis Browne's "Chlorodyne"

A group of Cork Examiner **directors and employees during the presentation to Jack Healy (editor,** Cork Examiner, **fourth from left, front row) in the Imperial Hotel on May 8, 1943.**

Kevin Collins when art editor of The Irish Times, **about 1941.**

mixture and to his pet dog, "Mr Fox". When he wasn't in *The Irish Times'* office, he was to be found across the road in Bewleys, where the wartime rations resulted in such confections as "Crunchettes", made from oatmeal and syrup, neither of which was rationed. Shortly after the dog was killed by a tram in Westmoreland Street, Barry O'Mahony himself died, it is said of a broken heart.

When Matt Farrell was a junior reporter on *The Irish Times* during the war, he often used to meet a prostitute at Portobello on his way home to Rathmines. She would tell him, Matt recalled with glee, that if she wasn't in bed inside an hour, she was going home. One day, when she was in court on a street walking charge, she waved across the dock at Matt in the reporters' gallery as a long lost friend, much to the amusement of his colleagues.

Becoming better-known by the year as the war progressed was Northern journalist, Billy Morrow. Early in the war, he had been appointed editor of the *Portadown News* at the age of twenty-one making him the youngest editor anywhere in Ireland. By 1943, he had taken part in many broadcasts on both Radio Eireann and the BBC in Belfast, as a baritone soloist.

The war was not all serious; despite the shortages and the difficulties of transport, the famous golf outings to Bundoran brought together members of the Dublin advertising fraternity and the newspaper world; Charlie McConnell, the founder of McConnell's advertising agency, was keenly involved. So too was Smyllie. J. J. Walsh of the *Munster Express* also participated and he has vivid stories of how on one occasion, Patrick Campbell's trousers were hidden. He was not amused.

During one of these golf trips to Bundoran, Paddy Campbell got so drunk that he spoke without a stutter. Once, he brought the house down by welcoming R. C. Ferguson, secretary of the Department of Industry and Commerce, a Presbyterian teetotaller and non-smoker, who happened to be one of de Valera's key men, with the following words: "Now we have a baldy headed old Presbyterian with the extraordinary initials R.C." Collapse of many stout parties, including Smyllie.

Lighter relief was also remembered by Paddy Clare of the *Irish Press*. A French artist, who had escaped from France to London at the height of the blitz there, wanted to live in Ireland, but was refused a permit. A plaster cast, destined for a sculpture exhibition in Dublin, was shipped from Liverpool in a huge box full of straw. The Frenchman joined the cast for the journey across the Irish Sea; Dublin dockers heard faint cries from the crate and found the Frenchman inside. He was taken to Jervis Street hospital, where Paddy Clare sneaked in and got a photograph of the man in bed. A detective chased Clare out and confiscated his camera. Two weeks later, his camera and film were returned, minus the offending photograph. The Frenchman did rather better than Paddy Clare — he was allowed to stay in Ireland and spent the rest of the war painting the society ladies of Dublin.

As the *Irish Press* shrank in size, down to six pages an issue, compared with sixteen or more before the war, editorial copy was cut remorselessly under the eager supervision of chief sub-editor Arthur Hunter. Dáil reports went from pages to inches and no court cases were included, unless they were of outstanding national interest. Yet as Bill Sweetman later observed, the paper was greatly improved for being produced so tightly. All the padding copy that had filled out the pages of the *Irish Press* before the war fell away. Perhaps one of the most interesting jobs for an *Irish Press* reporter then was manning the radio set in the building in order to monitor foreign news broadcasts. Outside, half the population of Dublin was listening to Lord Haw-Haw on the German radio.

Arthur Hunter found relaxaton in his bee-keeping; later, he was to write a memorable column on the subject, as the *Irish Press'* resident expert. Geoffrey Coulter, a sub-editor, used the most popular form of wartime transport, a bicycle. He used to cycle between the office and his home at Sutton and astonished colleagues in the *Irish Press* would sometimes see him dismantling and repairing the bicycle on his desk. One morning, at 4 a.m., after he had finished his shift at Burgh Quay,

Seamus Brady — saw the aftermath of the North Strand bombings in Dublin in 1941 as a young Dublin reporter. Over twenty years later, he had many notable "scoops" as Dublin correspondent of the Daily Express.

High Street, Belfast as it looked on the morning after the German bombing raids in April, 1941.

–Belfast Telegraph

he caused equal astonishment to a Local Defence Force unit when they saw him bowling along the coast road towards Sutton, his bicycle propelled by a small sail.

Towards the end of the war, public transport in Dublin petered out almost entirely. *The Irish Times'* basement was filled with bicycles. One country newspaper worker beat the transport troubles. Willie ("Wacker") Gleeson, of the *Limerick Leader,* walked at least once from Limerick to Dublin. 1942, the year after the big air raids, the *Belfast Telegraph* published a book of photographs called *Bombs on Belfast,* which earned itself a deal of fame. The *Belfast Telegraph* made its own contribution the war effort, most notably through its "Spitfire" fund, which collected enough money to build seventeen Spitfire planes for the RAF. The paper also ran a "Lonely Outposts" fund for troops serving in foreign stations. John Caughey ran a column called "Calling all exiles", which served as a link between families in Northern Ireland and their relations serving in the British forces all over the world. The *Belfast Weekly Telegraph* carried these messages, passed on by Caughey;

214

The Belfast Telegraph
office devastated after
the German air raids of
April, 1941.
–Belfast Telegraph

after the war, the column, which was to run for a total of twenty-one years, developed into a link between local families and exiled relations. Black flags flew in Belfast's Catholic enclaves that year, to commemorate the first Republican prisoner executed for killing an RUC policeman. That same year also, death overtook a legendary newspaper figure, Thomas F. McGahon, who had been editor and manager of the *Dundalk Democrat* since the early years of the century. His son Owen had joined the paper as a journalist nearly twenty years previously and is still working there today, probably Ireland's oldest working journalist.

Gerry Kelly, a machine minder, had a remarkable escape from death at the *Anglo-Celt* in Cavan one day in 1942. A great flywheel drove the pulleys that in turn worked the press; a lever on the gas pressure bottle was pulled the wrong way and Kelly got caught up in the flywheel and thrown onto the pulleys. These went through a nine inch gap in the wall to the press room. Kelly sailed through the gap and landed on the press. Fortunately, his companion, ignoring the dangers of leaving the

THE CORK EXAMINER, WEDNESDAY, MAY 9, 1945.

Front page of the Cork Examiner **at the end of the war.**

pressure bottle, rushed to turn off the press. Kelly escaped shaken but unhurt, but then he never admitted to getting hurt, even when as a young man, he lost the tops of three fingers in a mangle at the Cavan works.

Mrs McCarroll of the *Derry Journal* must have enjoyed the comparative peace of that city. She lived in Buncrana and travelled into the newspaper's office in Shipquay Street every day; the paper had quite a reputation, particularly since it had the unique record of being the only newspaper at the time to have been banned in both parts of Ireland. She also shared another distinction with a Tipperary woman, Kathleen Long, owner of the *Tipperary Star*. During the war years, these two ladies were the sole female newspaper owners in Ireland, Mrs McCarroll having taken over on the death of her husband, James J. McCarroll and Miss Long on the death of her father, Ed J. Long, in 1925. The death of another noted newspaper character took place in 1943. Charles Carey, owner of the *Leinster Express* in Portlaoise, had been fighting a rearguard action to keep the *Express* Loyalist.

In the late spring of 1943, just as *The Irish Times* was urging the virtues of severe bread rationing on its readers, the lakes in the Phoenix Park were frozen over while the city had a foot of snow; this remarkable happening went unreported by the papers, since it would have given away vital details of the weather. The Minister for Posts and Telegraphs, P. J. Little, was photographed skating on the ice in Herbert Park — the caption possibilities were considerable! — but the print went unpublished until after the war.

Virtue had its own reward; in common with most other papers, the *Westmeath Examiner* in Mullingar collected and paid for scrap paper. The provincial newspapers had a scheme for organised scrap paper collection to help the local papermaking effort. Micheál O'Callaghan

216

remembers the *Roscommon Herald* appealing to its readers for waste paper, while the Mullingar paper did likewise. Pat Layde, the actor who was brought up in the town and who died recently, recollected taking scrap paper from his family shop, going over to the *Examiner* office and receiving sixpence a bundle.

Sometimes, he would catch a glimpse of the august and Olympian figure of the owner and editor, J. P. Hayden, clothed in an enormous scraggy beard, seated at his desk. Hayden was then aged about seventy-nine and must have seemed positively terrifying to the young boy. On one of his trips to the *Westmeath Examiner,* Layde saw another famous figure, destined to be portly and persuasive on television, John (later Sir) Betjeman, who was press attaché for a year during the war to the UK representative in Ireland, Sir John Loader Maffey. Betjeman prepared several books of poetry during his stay here; they were printed by the Mullingar firm and Pat Layde remembers seeing him tipping the used metal type that had been used to print the books, back into the furnace.

The first issue of the *Roscommon Herald* that Micheál O'Callaghan, long since made editor, worked on was dated May 9, 1943. He remembers cycling the twenty-two miles from home. All the signposts had been taken down for the Emergency. On arriving at the *Herald* office for the first time, he was greeted by the three stalwart owners of the company: Paddy Nerney, the manager, Surgeon J. T. O'Hanrahan and C. E. Callan. They were a very respectable, God-fearing trio after the bluster and bigotry of Jasper Tully; the young O'Callaghan quickly settled in. The *Herald* then ran to four pages an issue.

He recalls the trappings of life in war-time Ireland: the wet and dry batteries for the wireless, the weekly butter ration of ½ lb per person, eggs at 2/9d a score and womens' outer garments forbidden by law to have pleats, epaulettes and turn-back cuffs. A cook could earn £30 a year and it was 2/- into a local dance for women, 2/6d for men.

1943 saw the only provincial newspaper launch in Ireland during the war. The *Drogheda Argus* had been a staunch Unionist newspaper, run by a Newry man called R. H. Taylor, who had taken over the Unionist *Drogheda Advertiser* from the two McKeown sisters in 1926 and merged the two titles three years later. The *Argus* closed in 1936. The *Drogheda Independent* — in the heyday of the O'Donoghue ownership and edited by Peter Casey, the third member of the family to occupy the editorial chair — was going strong as the dominant newspaper in the Boyneside town. Joe Stanley, a great friend of de Valera, bought the title of the *Argus.* He had already started up the *Argus* printing works just before the war and relaunched the newspaper in 1943, with a strong Republican slant.

Since newsprint had gone on strict allocation two years previously, ensuring that even those papers with sufficient stocks had to observe the drastic cutback in pagination, there was surprise and anger in

Larry de Lacy, made editor of the Drogheda Argus **when it was revived in 1943.**

Billy Morrow, the Portadown editor, already noted for his singing on the BBC and Radio Eireann.

newspaper circles when the *Drogheda Argus* did the impossible, by securing enough newsprint to start publication. Stanley, who was a prominent printer and publisher in Dublin, put his de Valera connection to good use. Stanley was said to have played an active part in the 1916 Easter Rising; better still, the first editor of the revived paper, Larry de Lacy, also had impeccable Republican connections. De Lacy had started on the *Enniscorthy Echo,* going on to work for newspapers as diverse as the *Kilkenny Journal, Connacht Tribune, Leinster Leader* and *Irish Times.* When he was working in the USA after 1916, ostensibly he was a reporter on the *San Francisco Leader;* he also wrote up reports of speeches said to have been made by de Valera. In fact, these speeches were cover for de Valera's return to Ireland, concocted to fool British Intelligence. De Lacy had also helped to smuggle arms to Ireland from the USA. With the credentials of Stanley and de Lacy, there could be little real surprise about the source of the *Drogheda Argus'* newsprint!

De Lacy came to the paper from the subs' desk in *The Irish Times;* he was described as a great nature lover with a keen interest in farming. De Lacy's brother-in-law was Stephen Hayes, the IRA chief of staff who was abducted with de Lacy himself in the summer of 1941. George A. O'Gorman, a retired Drogheda journalist, remembers going into de Lacy's room at the *Argus* one day and seeing his revolver on the table, a hardly surprising precaution. The previous owner of the *Argus,* Bertie Taylor, had a taste for westerns and had books by Zane Grey and others bound in the covers of Shakespearian titles, so that when visitors came in, they thought he was reading to improve himself! De Lacy wrote stirring leaders in the best Republican tradition: these helped to build the paper's circulation.

Overnight, the old Ascendancy *Drogheda Argus* became the new Republican paper. Larry de Lacy was the first of many characters associated with the new-look paper; among the first to arrive after he took over as editor was Paddy Mathews, a great man for the sing-song and story-telling. He later worked on the subs' desk in *The Irish Times,* exactly reversing De Lacy's progress.

Stanley brought in one of his sons, called Heuston after one of the 1916 leaders, to act as manager. He was described at the time as being "full of the enthusiasm of youth". The O'Donoghues at the *Drogheda Independent* just down the street were far from pleased at the paper starting up and obtaining newsprint so easily. Staff on the two papers were friendly (Drogheda is too small for relations to be otherwise), but the management of the *Drogheda Independent* frowned on the exchange of "blacks" (copies of stories) between the papers. Ironically, both newspapers, the *Independent* in Drogheda, the *Argus* in Dundalk, are now owned by Independent Newspapers.

Also in 1943, Hector Legge of the *Sunday Independent* gave a desperately needed chance to Frank O'Connor, the writer and

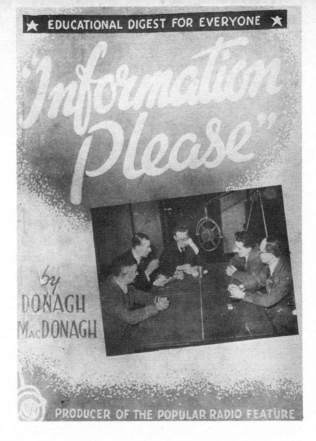

★ EDUCATIONAL DIGEST FOR EVERYONE ★

"Information Please"

by
DONAGH MacDONAGH

PRODUCER OF THE POPULAR RADIO FEATURE

One of the Radio Eireann's most popular programmes during the Emergency, "Information Please". In the Henry Street studio are, from left to right, Hugh Houlihan, Kenneth Deale, Niall Sheridan and Alec Newman (Irish Times). –RTE

broadcaster, who was denied work at every turn. For two years, Legge gave him a weekly column on the paper, under the name of "Ben Mayo". Every Tuesday, Legge and O'Connor would meet in Fuller's cafe in Grafton Street to decide the subject; every following Friday, Legge would pick up the copy. No-one found out O'Connor's identity, although several people came close. Another extraordinary character was working for the *Irish Independent* at the time, a Dutch journalist called Kees van Hoek, (nicknamed the "Hoek of Holland"), who had come to Ireland well before the war to work on films. He decided to stay and spent the war years as a feature writer with the "Indo"; his style was said to have been culled from *Time* magazine. After the war, he joined the *Irish Times* for a period, amid protests from staff on the paper, who believed that van Hoek's approach was too light.

1943 was also the year of the terrible orphanage fire in Cavan: some forty-five youngsters were burned to death. They had been locked into an impregnable room and when the boiler went on fire and set the rest of the building ablaze, they couldn't get out; the rescuers who couldn't get in had to watch them burn to death. Reporters from far and wide converged on Cavan; it was one of the few major domestic events of the war that caused little upset with the censor, but the shortage of newsprint forced the newspapers to curtail their coverage of the dreadful event. The *Anglo-Celt* in Cavan was down as small as six tabloid pages towards the end of the war, with all body copy set in 8pt., while the *Enniscorthy Echo* in Co Wexford used to run four pages, with an additional half-page, nicknamed a "pup", for carrying extra

A Publicity Club dinner
in the Shelbourne Hotel
forty years ago. Included
in the group are "Pussy"
O'Mahony, The Irish
Times (second left) and
Jack Dempsey, Irish
Press (extreme right).
Third from right is
Mick Clarke, Irish
Times' advertisement
manager. Third from
left is Billy King.
–Billy King

advertisements. Some advertisers used to object, however, saying that if they had wanted a handbill, they would have asked for one!

During 1944, the *Coleraine Chronicle* had to let slip the opportunity of celebrating its centenary because of the newsprint shortage, but somehow, the *Tyrone Constitution* in Omagh, the oldest newspaper in Co Tyrone, managed to celebrate its centenary. S. S. Wilson was recently appointed managing director, while Robert A. Parke, the editor, was described as having spent his entire forty year journalistic career with the paper. Norman Armstrong, the present editor, also took over as managing director on Wilson's death in 1981.

Terry Spillane married a young lady called Eileen from *The Irish Times,* where Terry himself worked. It was a brave step for the young lady; in those days, remembers Charles Mullock, women working in *The Irish Times* were most reluctant to get married. The work was prestigious, if not well paid, and the young ladies were not keen to get married and abandon their careers. Slowly, slowly, the war petered out and the newspapers of Ireland were able to resume a kind of normality, although Annie Roycroft of the *Spectator* in Bangor, Co Down, remembers that newsprint rationing did not end for them until 1951.

Ben Kiely decided to opt for the easier life after the war, most of which had been spent at the *Standard,* edited by the inimitable Peadar O'Curry, who spent considerable time boxing and shadow boxing with the paper's board of directors, described by one source then as "being like a crowd of rat-catchers." The *Irish Independent* must have seemed a safe haven, so Kiely got a job as a leader writer. "There were five of us, including Professor James Meenan. We worked from 7.15 p.m. until 11.15 p.m. When they had a Catholic problem, they turned to me," remembers Kiely, who adds that the piece he once wrote about earning his living on the "Indo" by the sweat of his brow causes laughs to the knowing even to this day.

M. J. McManus, literary editor of the *Irish Press* offered Ben Kiely more money, so he crossed the river without compunction. Smyllie said: "I hear you are slumming it."

At the *Irish Press,* he met up with the notorious Maurice Liston one day. Between writing leaders for the "Indo", Kiely had started novel writing. Liston picked up Kiely, literally, so that his feet were quite off the ground and said to him lispingly, "You hoor you, you've put me in a book." Kiely had indeed picked out the good points of the lovable Liston for the book character, but Liston was not seriously put out.

Another new recruit to the *Irish Press* was Douglas Gageby; he joined the paper on June 25, 1945, the day that Sean T. O'Kelly was inaugurated as president. Gageby, brought up in Belfast, liked the perspective on history shown by the *Irish Press* and he liked the family-

Micheál O'Callaghan, **editor of the** Roscommon Herald. **He joined the paper in 1943.** –*The Irish Times*

BLACK & WHITE *It's the Scotch!*

Established 1720
WEST & SON
Jewellers, Silversmiths, and Watchmakers. Gifts for Weddings, Anniversaries and all occasions.
Grafton House,
102-103 Grafton Street · Dublin

The Irish Times

CITY

Boys' Shirts 8/11
Well made and hard wearing with attached collars and long sleeves. White Union shirts at this price. Also available in smaller sizes worn by GALLIGAN'S
HENRY STREET, DUBLIN

BM
BRADMOLA MILLS,
BLACK ROCK, CO. DU

PRICE 3d.   **DUBLIN, SATURDAY, MAY 12, 1945.**   No. 27,395

CENSORSHIP AND MANY EMERGENCY RESTRICTIONS ABOLISHED

British-U.S. Attitude On Polish Crux

REUTER'S Special Correspondent at the San Francisco Conference states that there is no intention by Great Britain or the United States of allowing the Polish question to be dropped or standing by while the Warsaw Government stampedes its position and the whole issue goes by default.

This interpretation was put on the statement made yesterday by Mr. Anthony Eden, British Foreign Minister, on the breakdown of the Three-Powers' discussions of the Polish situation.

It is stated that Mr. Eden's declaration that it is now for the Governments, rather than the Foreign Ministers, of the three nations to determine what should be the next step appears to foreshadow new joint Anglo-American action on the whole subject.

DIFFERENCES

On being questioned at a Press conference, Mr. Eden replied that there were differences on the interpretation of the Yalta Agreement between the Soviet Union, on the one hand, and Great Britain and the United States, on the other.

Mr. Eden, however, stressed that the difficulties had arisen, not out of the interpretation of the Yalta Conference, but as a result of the action of the Polish leaders.

Strong and intensely vocal blocks of small nations are engaged in drives along three different lines in efforts to increase their power under the proposed World Charter, but final "showdowns" are still in the offing, states a San Francisco (Reuter) cable.

Three members of the British Commonwealth — Canada, New Zealand and Australia—seem to be taking the lead in efforts to gain more power for the smaller nations. New Zealand is demanding that the General Assembly should be allowed to accept or reject major decisions of the Security Council, without referral to the Great Powers.

The Big Five Powers flatly opposed this proposal on the grounds that action to prevent war might have to be taken quickly, and this could best be done by a small and powerful group.

Hitler's Bomb-proof Cellar

When U.S. troops opened Hitler's safe in his former private home in Prinz Regentenstrasse in Munich, yesterday, he found instead of important documents, only twelve copies of the 1st edition of "Mein Kampf."

Under the home, however, was a bomb-proof cellar, with a ceiling of seven-inch steel plates embedded in four feet of concrete. Every room was separated from the next by steel doors, and there was a modern electric kitchen, a small bedroom and several living rooms.

Like everything else affecting Hitler his dwellinghouse in Munich had costly furnishings, modern "gadgets" and expensive paintings, says an A.P. correspondent. The upholstery of the chairs and chairs in his bedroom had delicate, light colours, such as the average man would not choose. No wall was found.

Where He Was Wounded

DECORATING a young officer of the Royal Air Force at the investiture at Buckingham Palace yesterday, the King noticed that his arm was in plaster.

"Where were you wounded?" asked the King, and the pilot replied, with a grin, "In Trafalgar Square on VE-night."

Hitler's Bomb-proof Cellar

[columns of small print continue]

THE Censorship Order was revoked yesterday at a meeting of the Government. The staff of the Censorship Office has ceased to function, and to-day's Irish newspapers have been produced without submitting any of their contents to Dublin Castle.

A large number of other Emergency restrictions, imposed under the Emergency Powers Act, 1939, were removed at the same time.

In addition to the Press Censorship, the following is a list of the other Orders which have been revoked:—

Restriction of movements and activities of suspected persons.
Postal, telegraph and wireless censorship.
Power of police to prohibit processions and meetings.
Temporary special police force.
Power to arrest and search without warrant.
Identification of persons in custody.
Control of street collections.
Registration of foreign residents.
Dispensation from sealing of documents by President, Government and Ministers.
Exercise of functions of Taoiseach and members of Government in case of disability.
Sittings of Courts in camera.
Military Courts.
Postponement of execution of certain sentences of Military Courts.
Holding of inquests without juries in certain cases.
Control of collections other than street collections.
Appointment of Bank Holidays, etc.
Acquisition and requisition of goods, vehicles, etc.
Report of military casualties at civilian hospitals.
Appointment and powers of General

SALE OF SUPPLIES

The Minister for Supplies has revoked Orders made in 1941 and 1942 which were originally made to enable the authorities to keep a check on the disposal of forces, with a view, particularly, to preventing the sale of forces for the purpose of illegal exportation. It has now been found possible to dispense with this check, and the effect of the revoking Order is that persons may now buy or sell forces without obtaining a permit from the Gárda Síochána.

The removal of restrictions on the sale and purchase of forces does not involve any change in the emergency regulations governing the issue of ration permits and petrol allowances for commercial vehicles, nor does it affect the restrictions on the sale and purchase of new private cars.

Cabinet's Loss Country's Gain

"When Mr. Seán T. O'Kelly was nominated for the Presidency his colleagues realised that his departure from the Cabinet, where he had been such an outstanding success as Minister for Finance and Minister for Local Government and Public Health, would be a very great loss; but the Government's loss here would be the country's gain," said Mr. G. Boland, Minister for Justice, referring to the Presidential election at a Fianna Fáil meeting at Clara, Co. Roscommon, yesterday.

"Some of us felt sorry that he was a candidate because of his status in the Cabinet, where it will not be easy to fill his place. But we did not know of anyone in public life more suitable for the post," he added.

Mayo Farmer's Will Contested

THE hearing was begun before Mr. Justice Haugh and a jury in the High Court, Dublin, yesterday, and adjourned until Monday, of an action brought by John McGarry, Claremorris, an executor, to establish the last will dated October 1st, 1944, of Denis Sweeney, farmer, Carramore, Claremorris, who died on October 1st, 1944, aged 73, leaving about £3,000, most of which he bequeathed to charities.

The will was contested on the three usual statutory grounds by the cousins of the testator—Mrs. Katie Killeen, Miss Delia M. Sweeney, Miss Mary Sweeney and Miss Nora Sweeney, all of Claremorris, and William Kelly, Fairview avenue, Dublin.

Irish News in Brief

Clergyman's Appointment.—Canon Wm. Sentkit Harvey has been appointed by the Government as one of the Commissioners of Charitable Donations and Bequests for Ireland.

Larceny by a Trick.—Philip Walsh, Church street, Dublin, was, in the Circuit Criminal Court, yesterday, sent to prison for 15 months, with hard labour, in date from January 27th, for larceny by a trick, of furniture valued at £42 10s.

Reef Theft Fine.—For theft of beef yesterday, Thomas Lyndon, Pembroke street, Dublin, was fined £3 and ordered to pay £6 9½ compensation for wasting rail, valued at £6 10s.; the property of Philip Reynolds, N.C.R., Dublin.

Jail for Receivers.—Mrs. Bridget Mooney, Henrietta street, Dublin, and Mrs. Christina Farrell, 18b Parnell street, Dublin, were, in the Circuit Criminal Court, Dublin, yesterday sent to jail for six months for receiving wearing apparel, valued at £45, the property of Harry Jacobs, Ltd., Christchurch place, Dublin.

Theft of £1,959 Alleged.—Charged, in the Dublin District Court yesterday, with conspiracy, breaking and entering the Mantle and Costume Factory, 43 Dame street, Dublin, the property of Messrs. Verby and Co. Ltd., and stealing £1,959 in cash. Robert Murphy (21), Fishamble street, Dublin, and James Campbell (20), High street, Dublin, were remanded in custody for one week. Detective-Sergeant J. P. Moran said that all the money had been recovered, but not with the assistance of the accused men.

Goering Says Hitler Refused His Advice

Goering, perspiring and uneasy before a battery of war correspondents in Augsburg, yesterday admitted that he had ordered the bombing of Coventry.

The order to bomb Canterbury came from higher headquarters as a reprisal for the British bombing of a German cathedral city, Goering said.

He spoke bitterly of Hitler refusing to take his advice in military matters. "When Hitler decided to attack Russia," said Goering, "I referred him to Mein Kampf, where he said that it was dangerous to fight a war on two fronts was dangerous."—(Associated Press.)

Office of the Controller of Censorship
Dublin Castle.

—This is to notify you that, pursuant to the decision of the Government which has been publicly announced, the censorship of the press has now terminated.

Michael Knightly

11 Bealtaine, 1945.

RUMOURED JAPANESE PEACE FEELERS

Rumours of Japanese peace offers circulated in diplomatic quarters in Washington yesterday. It was strongly believed in reliable quarters that soon such feelers from certain Japanese elements have been put out in the last few weeks, but all Allied officials in a position to give authoritative information on this subject are maintaining strict silence, says a Reuter message from Washington.

It was generally understood that the Japanese have as yet made nothing like an offer of unconditional surrender, which is the only offer acceptable to the Allies.

According to reports certain unspecified political elements have offered to surrender the Fleet and Air Force and to withdraw from all exterior territory if the nations at war with Japan will renounce the right to occupy Japan itself. This offer—rejected by Britain and the United States—is said to have been verified at San Francisco by statesmen whose countries have big stakes in East Asia.

The truth is that the Allies have no intention of altering the unconditional surrender stand which brought Germany to her knees.

On this point there are those facts to be taken into consideration—First—Japanese feelers in the past —especially towards China—have been put out frequently and have been uniformly insincere. Secondly —The main aspiration behind any approaches is believed to come from Japanese agents in Europe, who have seen for themselves Allied power in the full flush of victory. Thirdly—Experts who have studied the recent military and political reshuffle in Japan are of opinion that any attempt at peace-making by the politicians would meet with strenuous opposition from the extremists, who are in full control of the army.

These experts point out that recent developments may be signs of weakness—weakness which bombing, guns and propaganda may well be successful in exploiting.

RAGING BATTLE

Heavy coast-to-coast fighting is raging on Okinawa Island, according to the Japanese News Agency. "Powerful enemy units," it said, "supported by tanks have been attacking since Thursday morning in the forefront of Suri." The news agency said that the Americans crossed the Asa stream under cover of intense artillery and air bombardment and with the aid of amphibious tanks.

For biggest air mishap operations in history are paralysing Japan's entire waterborne commerce, it was stated last night, says Reuter's special correspondent at Guam. Super Fortresses, each dropping ten tons of mines, began operations on the night of March 27 to seal off the three entrances to the inland

THEY CAN BE PUBLISHED NOW—I.

Pictures That Were Stopped by the Censor During the War

Air raid damage in London. Masonry falling during bombing. St. Paul's Cathedral is in the background.

Woman Found Guilty Of Murder, But Insane

Mrs. Elizabeth Rogers, Oldtown, Co. Dublin, was found guilty, but insane, in the Central Criminal Court, Dublin, yesterday, on a charge of murdering her infant daughter, Mary, at the Rotunda Hospital, Dublin, on January 25th, 1945.

Mr. Justice Davitt ordered her to be kept in custody pending the pleasure of the Government concerning her.

The case for the State was that Mrs. Rogers was born in the hospital on January 20th. Five days later Mrs. Rogers was seen beside the baby's cot in the hospital with a bathed paper. The cot was up in flames and, although a nurse took the baby out, it died from burns next day.

Dr. John Dunne, Resident Medical Superintendent, Grangegorman Mental Hospital, stated that after an examination he came to the conclusion that Mrs. Rogers was not capable of knowing what she was doing at the time on account of the disorder of her mind.

Dr. Bethel Solomons said he had formed the opinion that the woman was not responsible at the time.

Camp "Break" Disclosed Invasion Plot

A REPORTED German plot to invade Britain last December was discovered by two U.S. intelligence officers in February, says A.P., and the news has just been released by the Allied censors.

The German officers, Captain Joseph Hoefel, of Louisville, Kentucky, and Captain Frank Brandmeier, of Lake Champlain, New York, who landed in Normandy on D-day, returned to Britain to help train intelligence officers from the

T.D.'s Story in Appeal Against £100 Fine

Judgment was reserved until Monday next by Judge McCarthy in the Dublin Circuit Civil Court yesterday, when the hearing was resumed of the appeal by Patrick J. Fogarty, T.D., against a conviction and fine of £100, imposed in the Dublin District Court for furnishing false information at Luck Garda Station.

Mr. Fogarty was fined £100, in order to get a permit for Poor Rooney, Ballyboughal, Lusk, in the name of Robert Savage, Ballyboughal. Co. Dublin, to purchase a motorlorry from Joseph Harford, Swords. The alleged false information was to the effect that the motor lorry was purchased by Robert Savage, whereas in fact it was purchased by Poor Rooney, in contravention of Emergency Powers Order No. 177 (1943).

The appellant, giving evidence, said he knew Peter Rooney for 15 years. He never saw Robert Savage until the particular day on which they went to Luck Garda Station. Referring to the conversation with Savage in the Luck Garda Station, he said he had at the time no idea that he was doing anything wrong or that he was being used to get extra petrol for Rooney.

Clerk Honorary Commanders.— Major-General Mark Clark yesterday presented the U.S. Legion of Merit of the degree of commander to Lieutenant-General Sir Bernard Freyberg, V.C., and Major-General Dudley Russell.—(Reuter.)

G.N.R. Defence in Train Meals Case

There was not a shred of evidence to show that the company had been guilty of the smallest degree of negligence, Mr. J. A. Costello, S.C., told the jury that sat with the President at the High Court yesterday, before the case on behalf of the defence, Mrs. Martha Farrell, 19 Ash st., and Miss Teresa Walsh, Carmen's Hall, Dublin, who each had taken an action against the Great Northern Railway Company, for damages for meals served.

The actions were for damages for alleged breach of warranty in the sale of a meal in the restaurant car of a Dundalk to Dublin train on June 29th, when Miss Farrell and Miss Walsh were both unwell, it was alleged, as a result of eating meals served on the train.

The further hearing was adjourned until next Monday.

Mr. Costello said that the outbreak of typhoid fever which had given rise to this action had been unprecedented, in this country. A large number of people who had travelled on the train had shown in the buffet-car. So far as he was concerned typhoid or food poisoning, or anything else. On June 29th last, 57 meals had been served in the car, and 25 people contracted typhoid, on the following days, 71 people were served, and four people were taken ill; 57 meals were served, and 1,037 on July 3rd. 50 were served, and nobody got it; on July 4th, 77 were served, and two got it; on July 5th, 59 were served, and nobody got it; and on July 6th, 105 were served, and two got it.

No individual meal had been due to a carrier, then there had been no negligence on the part of the company.

Patrick Casey, assistant manager, catering departments, Great Northern Railway Company, stated that the dining-cars were supplied with all the necessary materials for the staff to use for washing. During 1944, a total of 195,052 meals had been supplied on trains running through the buffet-cars. In the Dublin refreshment rooms, 482,359 meals had been supplied, and 14,043 in the staff dining club; and, with the exception of this particular outbreak, there had been no incidence, in so far as he knew typhoid fever. He had charge of the restaurant-car, and he had never suffered from typhoid fever. He had been medically examined four times since the outbreak, and each test had been satisfactory.

German Prisoners To See Atrocity Films

The U.S. Army authorities are insisting that every German prisoner in the United States should see films depicting the atrocities in Nazi concentration camps. Booklets of pictures showing details of the Nazi mass murder "assembly lines" will also be distributed in prison camps.—(A.P.)

Allied Move To Stamp O Nazi System

AN intelligence section, to detect and ruthlessly suppress any Nazi underground activities, will be part of the U.S. Military Government in the American zone of occupation inside Germany, the War Department announced yesterday in Washington.

The American Government unit will be divided into 12 major divisions, corresponding generally to the Ministries of the German Central Government.

General Eisenhower will be the U.S. representative on the Four-Power Control Council, as agreed at Yalta, with Lieut.-General Lucius Clay as his deputy, as well as Deputy Military Governor for Germany.

The War Department added— "U.S. Army, Navy and Air Forces have perfected, over a period of many months, and in co-ordination with the British, Russians and Americans to preserve a modern a stern Military Government all over Germany and to carry out the policies agreed on at Yalta."

The public information section will control all forms of public expression, including newspapers, radio, magazines and films, and will deal with the dissolution of Goebbels' Propaganda Ministry and the establishment of an unbiassed and truthful Press and radio system.

"The three military divisions will deal with the demobilisation of the German armed forces and disarmament."

An Allied token force of British and Americans is being prepared to go to Berlin as soon as arrangements with the Russians have been completed, it was announced in Paris yesterday.

Brigadier Hilton, Chief of the Allied Military Mission to Norway, announced yesterday that the Russians will occupy only the northern part of Norway, which they already hold, and will leave the rest to the British and Americans.—(A.P.)

HENLEIN'S SUICIDE

Konrad Henlein, one time leader of the Sudeten German supporters of the Nazis, who was captured by the Americans, has killed himself in a prisoner-of-war cage. He was sentenced to death by the Czechs in 1938.

Yugoslav partisans, moving into Southern Carinthia and Styria, in an apparent attempt to claim parts of the two provinces for General Tito, set up a block on one main road on Thursday, forcing the 8th Army to redirect traffic for a time.—

Fourteen U-Boats In British Harbours

Up to a late hour last night nine U-boats had surrendered in British harbours. Another two were approaching Loch Eriboll, on the north coast of Sutherlandshire, to give themselves up, and two others were nearing Londonderry. Yesterday these were swelled by the arrival of two in Loch Alsh.

With late arrivals, the totals will be:—Loch Eriboll, 6; Weymouth, 2; Londonderry, 2; Loch Alsh, 2. R.A.F. Coastal Command aircraft are according surrendering U-boats, states the Air Ministry. News service. A large number of U-boats have now flashed "surrender signals," but not all the submarines are accessible to Coastal Command aircraft.

Mines Off Wex

MASTERS of ships an are warned that a are drifting mines were Wexford, says a notice Department of Industrial

SEVEN V WON B IRISHMEN

UP to November last, from five serving Irish forces had decorations for brave included seven Victoria which were won by—

Captain Edward Stephen Fegen, R.N., Ballinterry, perary, who, in 1940, convoy by attacking a cruiser with his ship, merchantman, Jervis Bay this war, his ship, Je third Irishman to win the

Lieutenant-Command perary, was killed in act when challenging hostile boats near the German ports, Scharnhorst, Gneisenau, cruiser Prinz Eugen.

Major Harold Marcus Andrews, East Lancs., Co. Wexford, one of the main part of their forces direction of Pilsen, head of the Skoda armaments works, which is in American hands.

The most troublesome groups north and east of Prague, they have dug in around the mountain towns and easily defended hill positions. Although the Germans have no line in front, they have several hundred tanks as well as ammunition, and are giving considerable trouble —(A.P.)

The Red Army High Command has despatched two of its toughest tank commanders, Colonel-General Lelyushenko and Colonel-General Rybalko, to deal with operations in Czechoslovakia and parts of Austria, states an Associated Press message from Moscow.

Appeal To T Union

AN appeal "to the seceding unions seriously before taking along while they were kept in interests of the work objective," was made t executive committee of a of trade unions and to w affiliated to the Irish Trades Congress, held in Dublin y

The conference," continued resolution, "while deplored the unreasonable the dissension with the seceding unions in seeking to set up minority organisations Ireland Irish Trade Union Congress had become and international affairs representative authority organised workers of the over fifty years."

The places of Mr. O'Brien, General Sec Irish Transport and W Workers' Union; Senator Kennedy, General Presiden same union; Mr. W. O'Brien, and Treasurer, the gradually Society, and Senator J O'Farrell, Railway Clerks of Dublin: S. Larkin, Ex Irish Municipal Employ Union; J. Keohane, national Union of Distrib the Allied, and Mr. Bennett, Irish Wom

German Prisoners To See Atrocity Films

German prisoners who were in the plot were informed that it had been postponed.

The whole fantastic scheme is unfolded by three prisoners who made a suicide venture for these participating, but the Nazi High Command was hopeful of causing maximum confusion among the British at a time when they supposedly would be caught off guard in the midst of Christmas holiday preparations.

PEACE

[decorative illustration of a dove and "BREAKFAST"]

Matrimony are supplied on deferred payments extending to one or two years at Cavendish

CAVENDISH FURNITURE CO., LTD.

THE IRISH ASSURANCE COMPANY L
and
THE INDUSTRIAL AND LIFE ASSURANCE AMALGAMATION Co.,

Principal Figures from the combined Accounts for 1944

NEW LIFE POLICIES IN 1
    Ordinary Branch   7,1
    Industrial Branch   162,8
NEW SUMS ASSURED IN 1
    Ordinary Branch   £3,151,2
    Industrial Branch   £4,495,4

Total Income   £2,30
Life Funds   £7,26
Investments in Government and of Eire Securities   £4,12
Investments in and Loans to Municipal, County and Public Boards in Eire £1,2
Total Assets   £7,7
Claims paid since 1939   £4,95
Total Assurances in force £35,2

THE IRISH ASSURAN

Relief for Smyllie — the wartime censorship is lifted. The Irish Times, May 12, 1945.

R. M. Smyllie, former editor of The Irish Times **and one of the most famous of all Irish newspaper editors.**
–*The Irish Times*

type atmosphere in the paper: "great bonds of warmth encompassed people in every department," he was to recall later. Sweetman was still editor, having held the paper together during the war; he often came into the office in Wellington boots and overcoat and continued to wear them while working at his desk. Over at *The Irish Times*, Smyllie still came to work on occasions dressed in his pyjamas.

Smyllie had the last laugh, both against himself and the censors. Not long after the war, when he went to his cottage in the Greystones area, he tapped his pipe into the Elsan, which promptly exploded, blowing him off his pedestal. No personal damage was done, but Smyllie enjoyed the joke as much as his various relatives. When the censorship restrictions were lifted some time after the end of the war, Smyllie made his own Churchillian gesture in the direction of Frank Aiken and Michael Knightly. He had the photographic department gather together all the major news photographs he had been banned from using during the war; they were then published in the paper over a fortnight.

CHAPTER VIII

Dinner at Jammets
May, 1945-1961

*Metropole Ballroom. House Dance. Music by
Jack Murtagh and his Sweet Rhythm Orchestra. 5/-.*
EVENING HERALD, 1949

Austin Cambridge, two tone blue/black. New. £744.
THE IRISH TIMES, 1959

*Wanted – Protestant Lad as trainee houseboy. Major O'Brien,
Kilbrittain, Co Cork.*
THE IRISH TIMES, 1959

With the end of the war, newspaper life inched back to normal. Looking back on those grey, impoverished years just after the end of the war, they seem in retrospect surprisingly well coloured by characters and pungent events. Many noted people joined the newspaper world, many stirring developments began a period of profound change. Symptomatic of the change was the ending of the Arnott rule at *The Irish Times;* from 1940 until 1945, Loftus Arnott had been chairman. Frank A. Lowe headed a "ginger" group of shareholders who complained about the ineffectual way the paper was being run. Lowe won the day; he had much experience as managing director of Helys, the Dublin printing and stationery firm. He also brought in his nephew, George Hetherington. Lowe's tactic had been to persuade the more difficult of the Arnotts to sell their shares after some of Sir Lauriston Arnott's shares came on the market; eventually, Lowe, Philip Walker and Ralph Walker each held a quarter of the equity. After Lowe was made chairman of *The Irish Times,* Smyllie used to say "now we have grocers on the board", a reference to Lowe's directorship of Findlaters, the now-defunct Dublin grocery firm.

New editorial blood surfaced; Samuel Beckett was one of the first new contributors to *The Irish Times* in the months following the outbreak of peace in 1945. Beckett had spent most of the war years in the South of France, playing an active part in the French Resistance. In

Seamus Kelly, ballet and theatre critic of The Irish Times. **He was also Quidnunc of "An Irishman's Diary" for many years. In 1954, he played in Huston's film of "Moby Dick", the harbour scenes of which were shot in Youghal, Co Cork.**
–The Irish Times

the early summer of 1945, he was able to make his first visit to Dublin since before the war. His great friend, Thomas McGreevy, by now director of the National Gallery, Dublin, asked him to write a review of his essay on Yeats. Beckett duly obliged. It appeared in The Irish Times less than two months after a poem called simply "Dieppe". Once he had finished his visit to Dublin, Beckett worked with the Irish Red Cross in the ruined Normandy town of St Lô in order to secure readmission to France.

Some of the editorial staff who joined The Irish Times just after the war were university graduates; their entry foretold a time twenty years into the future, when a university degree would be as essential as shorthand for starting on a newspaper. The most outstanding Trinity graduate to join The Irish Times after the war was Bruce Williamson. His academic career counted for nought with Smyllie, who might have appeared to have been over-fond of the Pearl Bar, but he had his lines out nevertheless. It was there that Smyllie asked the young Williamson how he defined the word "bags"; Williamson cannot remember now how he answered, but he presumes it was to Smyllie's satisfaction. Williamson soon began writing on all manner of subjects, film reviews, books (as literary editor), leaders. He remembers that his first political leader was on Siam. At Smyllie's insistence, he had to look up the map to see what he was writing about. Williamson also checked the copy of Myles na gCopaleen for possible libel; "his prose was limpid and clear, but he could be dangerous". In subsequent years, Williamson

Group from the Irish
News Agency in the
Palace Bar about 1951.
From left: Jack Smyth,
Redmond Walsh,
Douglas Duggan,
Dolores Rockett, Wolf
Schuster, Kevin
Collins, Gerry Keenan-
Hall, Bill Aherne
(Palace Bar owner) and
Peter Byrne.

has acquired a formidable reputation on the subject of libel, the bane of every newspaperman's life.

Another newcomer was Seamus Kelly, who came from a poor background in Belfast, but who had graduated from Queen's University there. Full of life, he was very prickly, but defended his friends to death. Enemies were ostracised for life. Kelly was said to have been taken on as drama critic of *The Irish Times* entirely by accident; after the resignation of Brinsley McNamara (*Valley of the Squinting Windows*), Smyllie was so overwhelmed by the number of applications for the job that he decided to choose the first man he saw when he arrived in the office one afternoon. Kelly had come to the office about something entirely different and left having been appointed to the job of drama critic. He went on to add ballet criticism to his duties and most famously of all, authorship of "An Irishman's Diary". After his death in 1979, his by-line, "Quidnunc", was never used again.

When Kelly was young and new at *The Irish Times*, he had to good humouredly demolish a myth about himself. He was widely considered to have established the world meringue eating record at Bewley's café in Westmoreland Street. In fact, by his own admission, he set up this gargantuan gastronomic title at Mitchell's in Grafton Street, that superbly refined establishment now the site of McDonald's hamburger restaurant. Kelly, who was a young recruit in the Army at the time, crunched his way through thirty-one meringues. His verbal put-downs were blunt, as expected of the pugnacious Belfast man. Once, he attended an Abbey premiere with a distinguished Dublin man of letters and design, together with a second friend. After the performance, the black tie trio showed every sign of continuing the evening's merriment. Instead, when they came near the newspaper office, Kelly shouted at his friends: "Fuck off, will youse, I've work to do," turned his back on them and went inside to write his critique. Dan Duffy came to the paper from the *Northern Constitution* and was instrumental in organising the NUJ at the newspaper. Before 1947, reporters were at the beck and call of their news editors. Up to fourteen hours' work a day was common; so insecure was the profession that many journalists remained unmarried. Work, meals and the pub were the Holy Trinity around which reporters' entire existence revolved. The 1947 agreement between the NUJ and Dublin newspaper managements brought in the revolutionary eight hour working day and a minimum rate of pay. The Dublin newspaper world did not collapse, as feared by some of the more reactionary managers. Instead, journalists were encouraged to begin more specialised reporting.

June Levine, who joined The Irish Times as a precocious teenager, just after her fifteenth birthday.
–The Irish Times

Gerry Mulvey, later to be deputy news editor under Donal Foley and then news editor, came to the paper from a North of Ireland publication. Tony Gray, that chirpy soul, who had come in during the war, following in the footsteps of John A. Robinson, was moved at the end of the war to the *Times Pictorial*, as Number Three to George Burrows and Eddie MacSweeney. Tony Kelly, joining *The Irish Times* at the age of eighteen, started as a trainee reporter, working under Donald Smyllie, who was chief sub and coincidentally, a brother of Bertie Smyllie. Cathal O'Shannon joined the crew as well, like Seamus Kelly, almost by accident. Smyllie was guarded by an old dragon of a secretary; between her security and his own ability to vanish like a puff of lightning, despite his eighteen stone weight, Smyllie was well able to avoid the continual crowd of supplicants. O'Shannon might have suffered the same fate, except that Smyllie thought the son was the father, with whom he was very friendly. O'Shannon junior got the job, was sent to Skerries College to learn shorthand and joined the reporters, numbering seventeen in all.

June Levine joined the paper as a trainee reporter not long after her fifteenth birthday. By her own admission, she was very forward with the fellows. She was a rare creature among the seventeen-strong

Included in a group at the Shelbourne Hotel, Dublin, in the early 1950s are Alan Montgomery (Irish Times — **far left**), George Burrows (Times Pictorial — **third from left**) and Peadar O'Curry (Standard — **second from right**). Second from left is Jack Webb.

Frank A. Lowe, made chairman of The Irish Times in 1945.
–The Irish Times

reporting staff; women were virtually unknown in Irish journalism, although *The Irish Times* did have the well-established Barbara Dickson, who did the "Candida" column; later, she was the editor of *Woman's Way*. Mia ffrench-Mullen was there, too.

Altogether, *The Irish Times* had a splendid crew; no other newspaper could match the immediate post-war intake into Westmoreland Street. A young Michael McInerney was there, that most humane Limerick man who harboured the best of intentions about everyone and who was deeply hurt if his trust in the good faith of human nature was betrayed. He was instrumental, along with Dan Duffy, in organising the NUJ at the paper. A Belfast journalist called Jimmy Kennedy provided much amusement: his speciality was walking along the upstairs window ledges *outside* the building, out one window, in another. He was husband of the ubiquitous Kay Kennedy, once such a mainstay of the Belfast *News Letter* and a popular figure in the Duke of York pub.

What was claimed to be the first news story ever published in *The Irish Times* with the reporter's by-line came when the "Muirchu" (formerly the British gunboat Helga, used in the 1916 bombardment of Dublin by the British forces) was on its last voyage, after the war, from Cork to Dublin, where it was due to be broken up for scrap. Brian Inglis and other Dublin reporters were aboard. The ship never made Dublin, sinking en route, but not before all on board were rescued. Inglis claimed that by-line "first" for *The Irish Times*.

A noted outside contributor to *The Irish Times* was Tommy Woods of the then Department of External Affairs. He worked there until his tragic, solitary death in the Hotel Terminus, Strasbourg, over twenty years later, when he was permanent representative of Ireland to the Council of Europe. A total of six people were in love with the wrong partners in Tommy Woods' set; he was one of them, yet he wrote brilliantly week after week for the paper, a literary column under the nom de plume of "Thersites". In *The Irish Times,* despite the sense of change in the air, the atmosphere was cosy. In winter, a good coal fire was kept burning in the reporters' room. The whole building, or series of buildings was however like a rabbit warren. One reporter of the time even called it "Dante's Inferno".

Larry de Lacy, editor of the *Drogheda Argus,* once had a brilliant solution to the eternal copy shortage problem. One week the paper was about three columns short of setting, he told a young lad at the firm to go down to the newsagents' shop in the Bull Ring and buy a western. The young man came back with a "pulp" novel. At the top of the first page, de Lacy wrote: "This week, we begin the first episode of our thrilling new serial. Now read on . . . "He marked up the copy for setting, tearing out about a quarter of the book. The *Drogheda Argus* looked as immaculate as ever that week. Dave Allen went on from tying up the bundles of newspapers and getting people of the town to fill in the pre-printed forms with details of births, marriages and deaths for the *Drogheda Argus,* to become a remarkably successful comedian in Britain. His brother Peter Tynan O'Mahony also worked on the paper, as a reporter/photographer in the days before unions issued strict instructions for separation of the two functions. Later, he went to work for his father's old paper, *The Irish Times.*

The O'Mahonys' father, G.J.C., more commonly known as "Pussy", because one night, he was said to have been seen returning to the office exceptionally drunk and to have taken a sup from the saucer of milk left out for the works cat, was general manager at *The Irish Times.* He had sold advertisements and written editorial feature copy and was said to have risen by levity to the position of general manager, following the death of Simington, the man who wrote thousands of notes to himself.

O'Mahony had a wooden leg, but whether this was a result of his alleged involvement in the Black and Tans or the consequence of a lift accident in London, when he is said to have amputated his leg with his penknife, no-one was quite sure, perhaps not even "Pussy" himself.

Once, he announced that he was going to a fancy dress ball, as a toffee apple.

Habits were catching. Smyllie had a long pause between opening his mouth and speaking. O'Mahony, the general manager, adopted the same style out of reverence to the editor, who was placed only marginally below God in the order of existence to most *Irish Times'* employees. Finally, at the foot of the hierarchy, Sullivan the porter,

Following the death of M. J. McManus, Ben Kiely was literary editor of the Irish Press for much of the 1950s and 1960s.
–Irish Press

Eamon de Valera
signing copies of the
first issue of the
Sunday Press for
members of the staff,
September, 1949.
–Irish Press

Newsboy selling copies
of one of the last issues
of the Irish Pictorial
(formerly the Times
Pictorial), which closed
down in 1958.

decided that he too should have this ponderous style of speaking. "Pussy" was a man with a heart of gold, but there were legendary stories about his deeds and misdeeds, like the time he was taking a short cut one night to his home the far side of Templeogue. He fell into a newly-cut grave; because of his wooden leg, he was unable to climb out. A second drunk fell in the hole. O'Mahony roared in the darkness: "You'll never get out of here", after which the second drunk left with remarkable alacrity. On another occasion in a country hotel, "Pussy" is said to have sat down on the side of the narrow spring bed to take his leg off. A certain part of his anatomy caught between the springs and the wooden edge of the bed and there he stayed all night, rather than run the risk of being gelded, until the maid found him the next morning. Once, he went to fetch Smyllie from a Masonic meeting in Molesworth Street. O'Mahony burst in saying: "Gentlemen, I bring you fraternal greetings from his Holiness the Pope". O'Mahony was also said to have enjoyed chewing lumps out of his whiskey glasses. Many of the stories now told on TV by Dave Allen seem to have their basis in the legends of his father.

Paddy Mathews, a sub on *The Irish Times,* often dozed off in his chair, which no-one else dared sit in. Donald Smyllie had his own way of reviving Mathews from his reveries. He screwed up hard wads of copy and threw them at the sub at the other end of the table with devastating accuracy. Mathews used a crutch to walk and on the famous night that the gardai carried out an after-hours raid on the Pearl Bar, he was ensconced upstairs with a group of people who included Donagh MacDonagh. The raid was particularly embarrassing for MacDonagh because he was a District Justice in addition to writing for *The Irish Times*. The matter took some sorting out, but the story that later circulated about Paddy Mathews was that he left so fast he was on the pavement to catch his crutch, thrown out of the first floor window!

Much speculation in the late 1940s arose from the unexplained death of the sports editor at *The Irish Times*, Harold Brown. A small, dapper man, rather stout in build, he died when his car filled with exhaust fumes late one night. He had driven home from a function, but stayed in the car in the garage. No satisfactory explanation of his death was ever forthcoming.

Scarcely had the echoes of the war died away in January, 1946, when the *Londonderry Sentinel* had a world-wide scoop about the new nuclear arms threat, from the Soviet Union. A West African doctor called Armattoe was working in Derry during the war; he claimed to the paper that the Soviet Union had followed the American example in perfecting the atomic bomb. Within twenty-four hours of the story appearing in the *Sentinel*, American president Harry Truman was denying the story. The *Sentinel* reporter who got the "scoop", now editor, although soon to retire, Sidney Buchanan, still remembers the telephone calls flooding into the newspaper office (then in Pump Street) from American news agencies. The learned doctor stood by his original statement and three weeks later, the official announcement was made by the Russians about "discoveries in the field of atomic energy." Dr Armattoe and the *Londonderry Sentinel* had been proved right. Later, Buchanan used to quote Bismarck: "A statement is never true politically, unless it is denied. "When the final confirmation of the story came through from Moscow, the White House had nothing to say.

Change was also the order of the day at the *Irish Press*. Perceptively, Terry Ward was made London editor in 1946. He had a great affection for London, despite his Republican upbringing in Derry and he used to delight in taking guests on vivid and learned tours of selected London hostelries. Two years later, Ward was joined by his new assistant, Jim McGuinness, later to be editor of the *Irish Press*. The office junior was Donal Foley.

Not long after his London appointment, there was a brief royal visit to Northern Ireland, which Ward covered. For security reasons, the royal train from Belfast to Derry was not used; at the last minute, the Royal party was driven to Derry, but the journalists covering the tour were still allowed to travel on the Royal train. Hospitality was generous, so much so that when it arrived at Derry's Waterside station, few of the reporters were able to walk straight. Terry Ward

Four famous photographers seen at the Royal Dublin Society. Front to back: George Leitch (Irish Times), Mick Loftus, Tommy Lavery and Fred Ludlow (all Irish Press).

ERRY SENTINEL, TUESDAY MORNING, JANUARY 8, 1946.

Ulster Administrations. from these material they have been so everything else Bri- anathema to them, ceaselessly scheming hen they can vote he United Kingdom nd into the Eire

f their policy they me the application of ge to Local Govern- stration in Ulster, and been done in Britain ddenly become very tish system. What nt! And because ernment is not fol- the people who have led everything British Britain's jobs and s untouchable are for Britain's lead to be

Ulster Government has here to the old Local ystem of franchise, difications, and it is tions that have made its and Republi-

DERRY SCIENTIST AND ATOM BOMB RESEARCH

Believes Present Anglo-U.S. A.B. Rendered Obsolete

BY NEW RUSSIAN DISCOVERIES

Use of Energy for Engineering Projects

Interviewed yesterday by a "Londonderry Sentinel" repre- sentative regarding atomic research, Dr. R. E. G. Armattoe, the noted scientist of the Lomeshie Research Centre in London- derry, made some striking revelations regarding the Soviet Union's activities.

Dr. Armattoe stated that following the announcement of the discovery of the atomic bomb without the participation of the So Union, the Soviet Council of Defence appointed the scientists: Joffe, Semyonow, Vavilov

NO Not Peopl

All Jour another, when cov asked speakers parts of st made with at least p The su leave a mind of obliges t cused by who were incomplet With t it

Londonderry Sentinel's **Soviet nuclear bomb "scoop", 1946.**

got off the train and walked, unsteadily, along the red carpet placed along the platform, to be greeted by an RUC inspector as a distinguished visitor to the city. Had his Derry Republican antecedents been realised, the RUC man might have greeted Ward less cordially.

At the *Irish Press* then, recalls Alan (Sammy) Bestic, who worked there from 1944 for some five years, calling the Six Counties "Northern Ireland" was tantamount to excommunication. Éire was considered a terrible vulgarism, but no man was better able to play the rules as Eamon de Valera laid them down than Bill Sweetman, the editor. Once, when there was a great danger that the *Irish Press* would have to go to press without the text of a speech by de Valera, one of the staff, Liam Skinner, paced up and down shouting: "The fecking paper can't come out". It did come out — without de Valera's speech and the world didn't fall in. At a board meeting, there was uproar when someone said that every death announcement in the paper meant one reader less and what did the board propose should be done? Anna Kelly, the woman's editor, provided moments of blazing anger. On occasion, remembers Ruth Kelly, Douglas Gageby had to step in and rescue her from her mother's wrath.

Light relief was provided at the *Irish Press* by Paddy Kavanagh, the poet. He was film critic on the *Standard,* which was then printed at

Burgh Quay. Down there one afternoon to correct proofs, he watched scornfully as a group of nuns wound its way through the caseroom on a guided tour. Profanities had been extinguished for the afternoon. Suddenly, excitement mounted as news came through on the wire of the death of Cardinal MacRory, Archbishop of Armagh and Primate of All Ireland. Kavanagh turned to the nuns with the slightest hint of scorn in his voice and murmured in that fractured voice: "Now the Cardinal is finding out what I've known all along — there is no God."

Paddy Kavanagh was also a man of notoriously dirty habits, no doubt engendered by his upbringing in poor and primitive circumstances on a small Monaghan farm. Once at a film preview he attended on behalf of the *Standard,* he took off a shoe and a stocking, raised his bare foot in the air and proceeded to pare his toenails with his penknife.

Quips were unkind: a man called John Devereux was a porter at *The Irish Times* and was said to have been a great rival of Bill Coyne, Sir Lauriston Arnott's batman in the Great War and who often walked round the office shouting "We've got them", i.e. the Germans. Anyway, Devereux looked in particularly bad health one day he went to the funeral of a colleague at Glasnevin and was told it was hardly worthwhile him coming back to the office.

Alan Reeve, one-time caricaturist at The Irish Times.

The Irish Times' sideline in those days was an agency for domestic servants, called after a Mrs Synnott. A procession of young, unknowing country girls had to take the lift to the agency's office in the top of the building. So often did the lift break down between floors that many bold quips passed from mouth to mouth. A printer used to enjoy standing under the grill in the Westmoreland Street pavement, especially when crowds gathered to look at photographs on display in the office window. Buckets of cold water poured down the grill by colleagues one day terminated the practice. One well-known Dublin actor at this time, taking grave offence at a theatre critique in the paper, heaved a milk bottle through the front window early one morning. He was forgiven easily enough.

Donal MacMonagle, who enjoyed many vintage moments as an Irish Press **photographer in the late 1940s and 1950s.**

While these ferocious strategies were being played out, the most deadly of chemicals were used daily in newspaper production. Etching department staff were strict, but surprisingly nonchalant, about the use of cyanide and nitric acid. One production man, Danny Cregan, who was very deaf and almost blind and who retired from *The Irish Times* at the age of eighty, used to etch plates with nitric acid, working by feel rather than sight. At 10.30 p.m., when production was finished, he would nip out for a quick one, come back, crawl under the bench in a foetal-like position, have two or three hours' sleep and finally go home.

Tommy Cleary, who had worked on a succession of provincial papers, such as the *Clonmel Chronicle,* the *Clare Champion,* the *Offaly Chronicle* and the *Limerick Leader,* made his transition to the city with the end of the war. He joined the *Irish Independent* as a sub-editor at almost

In The Irish Times'
newsroom in the 1950s,
left to right: Tom
Burnes, Barbara
Dickson, Cathal
O'Shannon, Tony
Kelly, Michael
McInerney, Jimmy
Meagan and Tom
McCaughren, now RTE
security correspondent.

(right) Joe Anderson,
editor with J. C. Dann
of the Dublin Evening
Mail.

the same time that Ben Kiely came to the paper. With Frank Geary in full swing as a conservative, Catholic editor, the *Irish Independent* must have seemed dull enough. Michael Rooney, the assistant editor, went off on several visits to Germany and Austria after the war. In Germany, he visited Berlin before that city had had any chance to recover from the devastation of the war. In the Kurfürstendamm in Berlin, few buildings were left; heaps of mud and rubble marked the once elegant shops and restaurants of pre-war. Pipes poking through the rubble indicated make-shift homes fashioned from blocks and girders. The poverty and desolation of twentieth century Berlin were similar to the degradation of nineteenth century Ireland during the Famine. Rooney and Alec Newman, of *The Irish Times,* both dressed in Allied uniform, passed on from the black scenes of post-war Berlin to the Austrian Alps. When Aer Lingus inaugurated its service to Paris, Donal MacMonagle, the photographer, remembers attending the pre-launch press "junket" in the Gresham Hotel. Someone got up on stage (later, he was revealed as a conman) and said that the flight had been postponed for technical reasons. No-one from the press turned up, except MacMonagle, who took two dozen copies of the *Irish Press,* thus engineering a minor "scoop" that won editor Sweetman's approval. Press trips to the Continent just after the war were unusually interesting and those to America were better still. The American airlines were extraordinarily generous with trans-Atlantic tickets from Shannon. On one of the memorable visits to the Hollywood film studios, Alec Newman was most disappointed to receive a telephone call on the fifteenth day instructing him to return home because Smyllie had been taken ill.

In Co Mayo in 1946, there was much more tongue-wagging about the change of interest in the *Mayo News,* bought over by the directors of *Inniu,* the Irish language paper. One of the directors was Ciaran, brother of Briain O Nuallain, alias Myles na gCopaleen. Ciaran, an Irish language enthusiast, spent some forty years working on *Inniu* until his recent death.

At the *Leinster Express* in Portlaoise, Paddy Montford, who had once been advertisement manager of the *Freeman's Journal,* acquired a controlling interest in the paper from a relative of the Careys, who had been owners from 1859 until 1943. Montford set about revitalising the *Express* with the help of his nephew, Gordon Clark, who later died in tragic circumstances. Montford himself died suddenly in 1947, when the paper was taken over yet again, this time by Fred Townsend senior, whose family is still closely associated with the *Sligo Champion.*

A frozen event took place at Jammet's, that missing and missed restaurant in Nassau Street: W. R. Rodgers, the Armagh poet clergyman, took the young Bruce Williamson to dinner. Rodgers was full of wine and poetic vigour, as stimulating as he was during his BBC broadcasts; accompanying him was Louis MacNeice, that other North of Ireland poet, sardonic in appearance and eyes full of melancholy. For the two hours of that dinner during the great winter blizzard of 1947, punctuated by breakdowns in the electricity, the cold MacNeice was as silent as Rodgers was voluble, almost as if he wanted to talk to someone who was not in the company. Williamson was timid of MacNeice, whom he now places in almost the same pantheon as Auden. While Rodgers burbled on, Williamson died many deaths of youthful embarrassment and wished fervently to be back before the coal fire in the newsroom of *The Irish Times.*

Brendan Malin, from the Irish Press **via the Irish News Agency to the Boston** Globe.

Heading for the emigrant ship — queues for the boat at Dun Laoghaire about 1947.
–Irish Railway Record Society

Centenary celebrations for the Redemptorists in Limerick, 1954. Representing the press are from left: **Sean Clancy** (Irish Independent), **Donal MacMonagle, Joe Shakespeare** (both Irish Press), **Redmond Walsh** (Irish Independent) and **Louis MacMonagle** (Cork Examiner).

In the Red Bank restaurant in D'Olier Street (now a centre of worship), lunch at 6/6d was marginally cheaper than Jammets. Half a dozen oysters cost 3/6d.

The Almighty must have reacted to Kavanagh's blasphemy at the *Irish Press* with the winter weather of 1947; for months, the streets of Dublin and towns throughout Ireland were piled high with decayed snow and lumpy ice. Cautious slithering was the order of the day as pedestrians and traffic scrambled around. Harry White, the retired transport manager for Easons, remembers one newspaper lorry in the south-east that drove over the top of the snow on a country road for quite some distance before the driver realised that he was at tree top height! In Monkstown, Co Dublin, another newspaper lorry skidded over the protecting wall at Seapoint Avenue. Only the rear wheels of the lorry held it while the driver wormed his way out. In the North West, *Belfast Telegraph* vans could only get as far as Bellarena in Co Derry. The newspaper copies completed their journey to Derry by train. The blind, mean publisher John Flynn, who had brought out the *East Coast Express* before the war and who was now producing magazines and books, did not turn on the heating. His comps sat shivering in their overcoats, trying to set copy with blue fingers. Only a few years previously, he had been lauded to the skies as president of the Master Printers' Association.

Light relief from these miseries was provided by Donal

MacMonagle, the new photographer at the *Irish Press*. Free turf was given to the needy; he photographed one young Dublin lad with his bag of turf. "Put it down and go and get another," the young fellow was told. One bag of turf per person was the rule; no wonder the lad smiled so broadly for the *Irish Press,* because he ended up with four bags of turf. Still, MacMonagle was renowned for his pranks. He was sent to cover an Ireland-Wales rugby match in Cardiff just after the end of the war. No press tickets were being issued, so he crept into the printing department of a local newspaper, found paper blanks the same size and colour as the official tickets for the game, set up the type and printed a couple of perfect tickets for himself and the other *Irish Press* man with him. George Leitch, *The Irish Times* photographer, who travelled with the Irish team, expressed considerable amazement that MacMonagle had got into the grounds!

It was the season of good writing and "scoops". First of all, in the bleak winter of 1947 came Liam MacGabhann's account for the *Irish Press* of Jim Larkin's funeral moving through a drab, frozen city. The spirit of Larkin is still revered today by poorer sections of the community and MacGabhann's funeral copy is still revered in journalistic circles. Also still remembered is Jack Grealish's "scoop" at the *Irish Press*. A young American politician called John F. Kennedy arrived at the office; Grealish had to borrow 2/6d to take the man for a drink in Mulligans. Still, the government was generous that year. Frank Aiken introduced the first subsidies for journals in Irish.

A Germany spy made a good "scoop" for *The Irish Times*. Hermann

Dan Duffy, one of the NUJ stalwarts at The Irish Times, **who joined the paper at the end of the war.**
–The Irish Times

Pictured in the Dublin Evening Mail **office the afternoon of the fire at** The Irish Times, **in 1951, are Donald Smyllie (man with moustache behind desk. Smyllie's brother and chief sub-editor of** The Irish Times), **then from left to right: Michael Devine, Noel Fee, Tony Kelly and Morrison Milne, deputy chief sub-editor,** The Irish Times).

J. Doran O'Reilly, star columnist with the Dublin Evening Mail.

After Bill Sweetman left the Irish Press in 1951, Jim McGuinness (later with RTE) was editor for much of the 1950s.
–Film and Illustrations Library RTE

Goertz had been captured and interned in Ireland during the war. Two years after the end of the war, he had been asked to report to the Aliens' Office at Dublin Castle. Fearing expulsion to Germany, despite assurances about his safety, he swallowed a cyanide tablet he had concealed in his clothing; by the time that Dick Dowling of *The Irish Times* (to which paper he had transferred from the *Waterford Star,* where his son, also Dick, also went to work), Goertz had been rushed to Mercer's Hospital, where he died. Dowling was in luck, however; Goertz's solicitor agreed to let Dowling have a glimpse of the German's diaries. He quickly transcribed them; his notes made an engrossing series for *The Irish Times,* under the title "Mission to Ireland".

Honours for the best "scoop" of all in those immediate post-war years went to the *Irish Press,* for its month-long coverage of the Aga Muller story. The German girl and her father had decided to set sail from the destruction of Germany after the war. Their boat was shipwrecked in Liberia in West Africa; her father died. Interest in their story was world-wide, but Sean Lemass, then *Irish Press* managing director, was far-sighted enough to give Liam MacGabhann sufficient licence to sign the "scoop". Aga and her family were brought to Ireland and for a month, Liam MacGabhann, with the able assistance of Terry Ward, sat in Bewley's café in Westmoreland Street writing up the saga of the Muller family. Sean Lemass gave the serial the run of the *Irish Press* and for the month that it was published, sales of the newspaper soared to the 200,000 mark. Never before or since has the paper repeated that performance; today, its sales are just under half that figure. As for Aga herself, she was employed in the art department of the *Irish Press,* married a fellow employee, Jim Cantwell and lives quietly in south Dublin.

In the run-up to the 1948 general election, the *Anglo-Celt* in Cavan made a grievous typesetting error. It printed an advertisement for the Protestant candidate, a man called Cole; between the foot of this advertisement and the next, for a play called *A Dark Stranger,* a rule should have been set. To call a Protestant in the border counties "Black" is the worst possible insult, so that when the rule was omitted and the two advertisements ran on from "J. J. Cole" to *A Dark Stranger,* Mr Cole was most displeased. He also lost the election. Above the entrance to *The Irish Times* office in Westmoreland Street, beneath the famous old clock, a running tally of the parties was kept as the results came in.

Sean Lemass was also responsible for the greatest newspaper launch in the immediate post-war years, that of the *Sunday Press* in 1949. In May of that year, he called a meeting of circulation representatives and told them that a new Sunday paper, the *Sunday Press,* would be launched on the first Sunday of September. "We will knock the guts out of the *Sunday Independent,* " Lemass told the assembled multitude. Padraig O Criogáin remembers that they went through all the Catholic

directories and assembled the names of every parish priest in the country. They were roped in to help with the distribution of the new paper after Sunday Mass; in more remote parts of the country, the priests agreed to carry the bundles of newspapers in their cars, to be dumped outside their churches so as to be ready for the crowds coming out of Mass. In this way, the enormous rural readership of the *Sunday Press* was built up; to this day, the readership and influence of the paper lies much more in the country than in Dublin.

Lemass, remembers one source in the *Sunday Press,* was much more interested in circulation matters than in editorial content or advertising. His circulation manager was Liam Pedlar, who was a personal friend of de Valera and who always used to say that he had come home from Glasgow to take part in the 1916 Easter Rising. Pedlar also used to say: "Some people in this organisation think I am employed solely to go to funerals and race meetings." He was held in great esteem at Burgh Quay and it was common for him to be rung up on a Bank Holiday by newsagents looking for more copies of the *Irish Press.* Pedlar would then wrap up the bundle himself and go across to the bus station and put it aboard the appropriate bus. With the imminent launching of the *Sunday Press,* Pedlar threw himself into the organisation of its distribution with a zeal only surpassed by Lemass himself.

Editorial appointments were made: the young Douglas Gageby was promoted to assistant editor. Lt Col Matt Feehan was made editor, a

Pearl Bar group, from left: Alan Montgomery, Leslie Luke, Alan Bestic, Kevin Collins, Tony Gray, Desmond Fricker and John Ross. Serving the drinks is "Gus" Weldon.

239

Liam MacGabhann
brings Aga Muller to
Dublin, ready for the
remarkable "scoop" in
the Irish Press.
–Irish Press

John J. Dunne of
Independent
Newspapers

post he was to hold for some thirteen years; he had been in business
before the war and in the Army during the Emergency. He knew little
about newspapers, but everything about Fianna Fail, perhaps the most
important asset of all for a Burgh Quay editor. He did something,
however, that Douglas Gageby had never seen done before: he
brought a military precision to his new job and costed every item in the
new paper, right down to the slightest paragraph from a country
correspondent, so that he knew the editorial cost of the whole paper
down to the last shilling.

The Saturday night the *Sunday Press* was launched, crowds gathered
at the rear of the Burgh Quay premises to see the lorries carrying off
the first copies to distant parts. One drunk wanted to accompany the
copies going to Belfast. The first issue was a great success and printing
did not stop until about 10 a.m. on the Sunday; subsequent issues
proved equally successful. The hunches of Sean Lemass had been
right.

The circulation men, remembers one of them, Tom Barrett, had a
hard time. Most of the lorry drivers were Dublin men, unused to the
intimate geographical details of the country dropping-off points. For
the first six weeks of the *Sunday Press,* the circulation men had to go with
the lorry drivers to show them the way — for no extra pay. On one of
the runs to Limerick, Barrett remembers that their lorry got stuck in a
snowstorm near Nenagh. The driver, his helper and Barrett huddled in
the back of the lorry for the night while the snowstorm raged outside.
The *Sunday Press* was rather late reaching Limerick that week.

"On the Road" was reckoned to be the most successful feature of the new *Sunday Press*. Terry O'Sullivan (real name Tomas O Faolain) had an Army background like his editor, Matt Feehan and also brought the clipped tones and precision of Army life to his newspaper work. Before he ever started writing "On the Road", he was well known to Radio Eireann listeners; writing about the highways and byways of rural Ireland made his newspaper career. His photographer was usually Dick Shakespeare and a colleague of the time recalls that the enterprising duo literally drank their way round Ireland. It made great copy. Also working on the *Sunday Press,* as well as on the *Irish Press,* was agricultural correspondent Maurice Liston, a lisping giant. A lovely story of the period concerns the Limerick Agricultural Show, which Liston was covering with Donal MacMonagle, the *Irish Press* photographer in the city. Liston was said to have had many whiskies before he arrived at the showgrounds; a lady in a tent gave him a programme and told him that if he came back at the end of the day, she would have it marked up with the results, leaving him free to attend to more pressing needs for the remainder of the day.

In the Pearl Bar in 1950, from left: Tony Gray, Kevin Collins (George Burrows, peeping over Collins' head), R. M. Smyllie, Alan Montgomery, Cathal O'Shannon, Edgar Brennan, Matt Farrell, Michael McInerney, Des O'Leary (Irish Times' advertisement department), Dermot Barry and Tony Kelly. Lying on the floor is George Leitch, The Irish Times' photographer.

Sam Edgar
(representing the
Empire News) with
Thomas Keogh, a
Wexford sailor.

Taking part in a 1954
Radio Eireann "Press
Conference"
programme were, from
left to right: Michael
Clarke, Alfie Byrne,
Matt Farrell and
Seamus Kelly (then
"Quidnunc" of The
Irish Times).
–RTE

Liston went back for the programme, raced to the railway station with MacMonagle at the wheel, got as far as the station entrance and saw that the winner of the *Irish Press* cup had been left off the list. They did an about-turn, hurtled through the streets of Limerick, collected the vital result and drove back to the station leaving Liston with a second or two to catch the train. Writing up the copy was the least of his problems; once, he wrote up a desolate Cavan farm in prose so glowing that its owners must have thought they inhabited Shangri-La.

Limerick and Shannon were particularly vital sources of news for the Dublin papers just after the war. One of the reasons was the spate of air crashes at Shannon; Donal MacMonagle remembers photographing the aftermath of one air disaster. He saw two of the dead, a mother with her child clasped to her bosom; both were like burned toast. In another crash, many survivors were rescued from the Shannon mudflats. MacMonagle photographed one man, who turned out to be a Dutch businessman. "Amazingly, he wanted me to send him a print. If I'd been sitting in the Shannon for four hours, I wouldn't have wanted a picture of myself. Anyway, I sent it and next Christmas, I had a fine present of a bottle of brandy and cigars from the man in Rotterdam," he remembers. Limerick and Shannon were also enlivened by the presence of Kevin Collins, the late husband of Pan Collins of RTE. He worked for *The Irish Times* for several periods (so much so that he uses the place like a revolving door, said Jack White), but at this time, he was correspondent in Limerick for the *Irish Independent*.

The Murphys were still smarting at Independent House over the arrival on the newspaper scene of the *Sunday Press,* just as the *Irish Press* had caused intense resentment at Middle Abbey Street in the early 1930s. In these circumstances, perhaps the greatest scoop ever achieved during Hector Legge's thirty year term as *Sunday Independent* editor must have been some consolation to set against the launch of the *Sunday Press.*

He had written a piece in 1949 predicting that the External Relations Act was going to be abolished and that the 26 Counties would be proclaimed a Republic. Costello, the Taoiseach, was in Canada; Legge had already held the copy for a fortnight, but decided to go ahead and publish. At first Costello would not answer questions arising from Legge's article, but the day after it appeared, Costello gave in and held a news conference. *The Irish Times* remarked that the Taoiseach had run away to Canada to declare the Republic.

1949 also saw the first issue of a new Northern paper: the *Mourne Observer,* launched on October 8, just after the *Sunday Press* in Dublin. D. J. Hawthorne, generally known as Jim, had served his time with the *Leader* in Dromore; in 1947, in the austere days just after the war, he bought the *Dromore Weekly Times.* He decided to expand into an area where there was less competition, so as soon as the more severe

Cork Evening Echo **newsboy with the craze of 1957 — the Yo-Yo.**

243

Malcolm Brodie, sports editor of the Belfast Telegraph. His soccer column in Ireland's Saturday Night started in 1953, making it the longest-running soccer column in Irish journalism.

David Capper, first editor of the Ulster Star, Lisburn.
–BBC

newsprint restrictions were lifted in 1949, he set about establishing the *Mourne Observer*. A room was rented in the "Home from Home" guest house in Newcastle and a reporter was engaged. Big news in the 1,500 print run first issue was the Transport Tribunal hearing the case for the closure of the Belfast and County Down railway line (it did close down the following January).

The closure of the rail line made production of the *Mourne Observer* more difficult, because the train was used to carry copy to the *Dromore Weekly Times* printing works. Late copy was 'phoned through. Jim Hawthorne travelled from Newcastle to Dromore twice a week either by train or on his two stroke Enfield motor cycle. The *Dromore Weekly Times* was closed in 1952 and all energies concentrated on the Newcastle paper, whose chief reporter and sports editor, Kenneth Purdy, joined in the first year and who was to become as much an institution in Newcastle as Jim Hawthorne himself. Purdy later recalled that one of the main conditions of his employment with the paper when he joined was his ability to ride a bicycle!

Eccentricities were noted among certain other provincial newspaper owners in the North of Ireland. A Co Tyrone newspaper owner had his name prefaced by the word "Tank" — before setting up in the newspaper business, he had used a tank on a cart pulled by a donkey to deliver oil and paraffin to rural homes in his area.

This same newpaper owner did not believe in appointing local correspondents: they cost too much. Instead, he sent his regular reporters out to specific villages, with half a crown in expenses and instructions to call on the local worthies, such as the parish priest and the RUC man in the barracks to find out who was doing what. Community relations were easier then and the only time a Catholic reporter from the South of Ireland working on a northern weekly found the local RUC man less than helpful was when he had to tell the reporter that his work permit was not being renewed. The policeman obviously regretted having to do his duty, but the young reporter had to leave the North.

Thirty years ago, work permits were used most rigorously in the North of Ireland to prevent people from the South taking up permanent residence north of the border and distorting voting patterns. Just as the Tyrone newspaper owner was mean with his local news coverage, so it was said that an Armagh newspaper proprietor of slightly earlier vintage was so illiterate that all he could write were his cheques. Yet another Northern newspaper owner was also a grocer, with a country shopkeeper's appreciation of news values. He weighed his reporters' copy every week, as Jasper Tully in Co Roscommon had done years before, but his staff were quick to work on poundage rather than linage and simply wrote less copy to the sheet.

Not all Northern newspaper stories of this austere time thirty years ago, when the war-time rationing was still in force, concerned

meanness of spirit. Ralph Bossence and James Kennedy, two noted Belfast journalists, walked from Dunmurry to Lurgan, having a drink in every pub along the way. Cecil Orr of the Belfast *New Letter* once showed great generosity to Tom Samways, who was in looking for a job at the time. In the old Duke of York pub almost next to the *News Letter* offices, everyone in the party (including the almost penniless Samways) was set to buy rounds of drinks, all large whiskies. Cecil Orr followed Samways into the lavatory and said to him: "Samways, you're broke. Here's a couple of quid for the drinks. At least I have a job and my bus fare home."

Austerity punctuated the news bulletins on Radio Eireann; they were pasted up from the *Dublin Evening Mail,* remembers John Ross, who had started his career on *The Irish Times* and then joined Radio Eireann after hearing a tip-off from Leslie Luke, public relations man at Guinness, that a job was going in Henry Street. Ross also remembers one lady announcer reading the news — and doing her knitting at the same time!

Life's pleasures then were far simpler, plainer, too. In the Royal Hibernian Hotel in Dawson Street, Dublin (now awaiting the demolition men), the National Union of Journalists held a Press Ball one winter's Saturday night. The ballroom was hot and the dancing energetic; the diminutive Tom Hennigan (then working at Burgh Quay; he later crossed the river to do the *Evening Herald* diary) was tired after a long week. He slipped out of the dance to sit down on the sofa that used to provide comfort in the entrance hall of the Hibernian. As he dozed, Phenie MacGabhann, wife of Liam, crept up to him and planted a big lipstick kiss on his bald head. Later, Hennigan awoke from his slumbers and eventually toddled home in the style of journalists the

Michael Rooney (extreme left), retired as editor of the Irish Independent **in 1968; the presentation was made by Hector Legge (centre) then editor of the** Sunday Independent. **Looking on is Aidan Pender, who retired in May, 1982, as editor of the** Irish Independent.
–Irish Independent

(Right): Photograph taken at Dublin Airport in 1961 when journalists were returning from covering the Congo war. From left: Cathal O'Shannon, who was working for The Irish Times, **Alan Montgomery,** Irish Times' **editor and John Ross, who was in the Congo for RTE. Ross later recalled landing at a remote airstrip in the Congo, to be greeted by an immaculately attired Raymond Smith of the** Irish Independent.

Biddie Brewster was a noted Dublin clairvoyant; she is seen here during her birthday party (about 1950) entertaining a group of friends from the press.

world over after an enjoyable night out. What Mrs Hennigan said when she saw the "I love Hennigan" message planted on his head during the course of his inebriation, is not recorded for posterity.

Down in Cork, John Healy on the *Cork Examiner* was also coming to the end of his career; he had been editor since early in the century. No-one, including himself, was quite sure how long he had occupied the editorial throne, but it was certainly a good fifty years. Ted Crosbie, a young man at the time, remembers being delegated to try and shift Healy into a new part of the building. Nothing would persuade him to move, not even the promise of numerous electric fires; later, Crosbie found that Healy *had* moved and having complained about the six electric fires plugged in a semi-circle round his new office, promptly unplugged them!

The same year that the Bairds killed off the *Irish Daily Telegraph,* 1951, Bill Sweetman left the editorship of the *Irish Press.* Donal MacMonagle, whom Sweetman had earlier suspended twice for refusing to take particular photographs on the instructions of his union, the NUJ, was the best of friends with the departing editor at his farewell party in Petronella O'Flanagan's flat in Leeson Street. The reasons for Sweetman's departure from the paper are as unclear as those surrounding the departure sixteen years previously of Frank Gallagher, but like Gallagher. Sweetman moved outwards and upwards, becoming a District Justice. Somehow, the show always went on as was the case with Jack Reardon, the racing editor of the *Cork Examiner,* sent to cover the races at Thurles. On the way back to Cork, the car crashed. Reardon's daughter was killed and the photographer suffered a broken collar bone. Reardon himself was uninjured, but severely shaken. He went straight to a nearby hotel and 'phoned his copy through to Cork.

The Irish News Agency was one of the most innovative features of the early 1950s, but it fell foul of various vested interests. Sean MacBride had broached the idea of an Irish news agency with de Valera as far back as 1939, but until he was leader of Clann na Poblachta and Minister for External Affairs in the first Inter-Party government, which came to power in 1948, he was unable to put his interest into practice. Conor Cruise O'Brien, in charge of the information section in MacBride's Ministry, was appointed managing director when the Agency came into being in 1950. MacBride had intended Noel Harnett, a radio announcer who had become a Senator in the Clann na Poblachta interest, to be managing director. Instead, Harnett joined the board, with fellow directors Robert Brennan and Peadar O'Curry. An independent chairman was appointed, Dublin solicitor Roger Greene.

Kevin Collins (Irish Independent) **at an Ennis hotel in 1947 with Frank Robbins (right,** Irish Press**) and an unnamed barmaid.**

(Below): Kevin Collins (left) and Cathal O'Shannon testing what was said to have been an anti-alcohol pill.

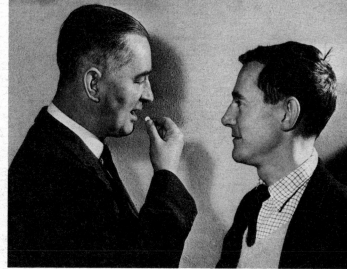

247

A thirty-three year old journalist with wide experience of news agency work, Joseph Gallagher, was appointed to manage the news agency. Gallagher, who had worked with United Press in London, developed the Irish News Agency along the lines well pioneered by the Press Association and Reuters. To the agency's offices in Fleet Street, Dublin, came a whole galaxy of journalistic talent. Dan O'Connell from Limerick was its first editor, followed by Douglas Gageby. Both were later to work for the *Evening Press*. John Healy was there with Matt Farrell, so too was Brendan Malin from the *Irish Press,* who worked for the INA for seven years, first as political correspondent, then as managing editor. He later went to work for the *Boston Globe.* Jim McGuinness, later *Irish Press* editor, was London editor for a while. The work was hard, remembers Seamus McConville, now editor of the *Kerryman,* who joined the agency in 1954. "You could not work there and be work shy." The sub-editors' desk was continually swamped with copy. The INA had a tremendous infusion of talent, but the basic conflicts of its existence were never resolved. Certain people in the higher echelons of the Dublin newspapers wanted to keep the agency weak because they thought that it might interfere with their second jobs as correspondents for newspapers outside the country.

A senior journalist on the *Irish Independent* was also the Irish correspondent for Reuters. Most other senior Dublin journalists also had secondary lines going; George Burrows of the *Times Pictorial* was also the Irish correspondent of the *Daily Telegraph* and Alan Montgomery performed the same function for *Time* magazine. Smyllie was correspondent for the London *Times.* According to Sean MacBride, both Reuters and Independent Newspapers campaigned strongly

Left to right: Tony Kelly, Cathal O'Shannon, Seamus Dignam (now in advertising) and the late Sam Edgar who worked for the old Empire News

(right) From left: Cathal O'Shannon, Tony Kelly and Alec Newman, former editor of The Irish Times.

against the agency, although Bertie Smyllie of *The Irish Times* was fairly neutral.

Admits MacBride: "I under-estimated the strength of the opposition both from the *Independent* and from journalists with vested interests. The National Union of Journalists feared that newspaper owners might make the agency the excuse for cutting down on staff. As the difficulties of setting up a news service to supply local newspapers multiplied, a deal was concluded with United Press International for it to market the agency's copy abroad and for the agency to sell UPI copy in Ireland. Most of the major newspapers, like the *Cork Examiner,* had an interest in the Press Association, so the number of papers able and willing to use UPI copy was small. Joseph Gallagher stayed with the agency until 1952, the year of the Baltinglass post office siege, which amply highlighted the problem the agency faced. With so many journalists and correspondents covering the events of Baltinglass, and protecting their own livelihoods, the agency could do little except supply feature material. When the agency did report matters truth fully, complaints flooded in about "letting the country down". Restrictions on covering home news, as well as on reporting parliamentary and court proceedings, meant that the news agency never broke even.

"I would not like to go through that mill again," confesses Dr Conor Cruise O'Brien. Neither would Seamus McConville, who was irritated

Cork made the headlines when its Opera House burned down on December 12, 1955.
Cork Examiner

John O'Donovan, who brought fresh air and fresh ideas to the new Evening Press in 1954.
–RTE

John Healy, who revolutionised Irish political reporting with his "backbencher" column in the Sunday Review.
–The Irish Times

at having to 'phone O'Brien at 7.30 every morning to give him the latest news developments. Sean MacBride, undeterred after all these years by the suspicions of most Irish newspaper owners and journalists towards the scheme, believes that there is still scope and need for an Irish news agency. When de Valera swept Fianna Fail into power in the 1957 General Election, a budget brought in drastic cuts in public spending. To save £30,000 a year, the Irish News Agency was closed down, seven years after it started. Nearly thirty years later, the main achievement of the Agency is regarded as the beneficial effect it had in raising salaries and improving working conditions for Dublin journalists.

Just as the Irish News Agency was getting under way, *The Irish Times* reaped the circulation rewards of a tremendous controversy in the Letters to the Editor column. The "Liberal Ethic" debate went on for weeks, so much so that on occasions, classified advertisements had to be left out of the paper to accommodate all the letters. The subject of the debate may now seem exceptionally abtruse, but says Bruce Williamson, with infinite wisdom, all subsequent public debates on matters of morality, starting with that on the "Mother and Child" medical care scheme, have stemmed from the "Liberal Ethic" controversy. Indeed the columns of Letters to the Editor of *The Irish Times* in 1983 about the recent Constitutional Amendment on abortion seem at times like a straight re-run of that far-off dispute of 1950.

The Irish Times reaped great public sympathy from its fire on September 16, 1951. Work was almost completed on the installation of the new press when the fire started (the exact cause was never found). The flames, which provided attraction for large crowds in the street, engulfed the new press, destroyed the Linotype setting facilities, the despatch department, the record department and other sections of the building then being reconstructed. Another casualty was the photographic library, so that today, *The Irish Times* has relatively few photographs pre-dating the fire. The commercial departments and reporters' room were saved. On the afternoon of the big blaze, with setting and printing facilities destroyed, *The Irish Times* made emergency arrangements to bring out the next day's paper. Jack Webb, the general manager, rang up J. C. Dann of the *Evening Mail*, who was also secretary of the Dublin Newspaper Managers. John Dunne of the *Irish Independent* was over within an hour offering to help, as was Jack Dempsey of the *Irish Press*.

The damage could have been even worse but for Sergeant Kelly, the head porter, who put corrugated sheets round the new press to try and stop the fire spreading. It took about six months to start getting over the effects of the fire; the new press was going within about a month and the paper bought Linotypes being disposed of by the *Belfast Telegraph*. There were many stories of devotion to duty, starting with the heroic deeds of Sergeant Kelly who badly burned his hands. Jack Webb, soaking wet from the fire hoses, sent a van to get a change of clothing from his house and stayed in the office for the next two days.

Patrick Campbell, a colourful character who was works manager and who was famous for spending an evening with the Knights of Columbanus before deciding against pursuing his enrolment, thus giving rise to dreadful jokes about a Knight for a night, worked like a trooper to get production restarted in *The Irish Times'* building. All the labels for the newsagents, together with all their records at the paper, were destroyed, so Dan O'Shea, the circulation manager, was kept going with cups of tea throughout the night while he wrote out all the labels from memory.

By 4 p.m., the sub-editors from *The Irish Times*, led by Smyllie's brother, Donald, who was to die tragically young in keeping with others in the Smyllie family, were seated around the table at the *Evening Mail* office in Parliament Street. One young sub there was Tony Kelly, now with Nissan, the car firm. Type was set in Burgh Quay and taken over to the *Mail*, where *The Irish Times* was printed, so that the following morning, the *Times* came out in a four page edition with the news of its own fire the main lead story. A *Dublin Opinion* cartoon showed Smyllie leaving the *Times'* building with a typewriter in one hand and a Union Jack in the other.

Some sources claim that in the turmoil after the fire, Frank A. Lowe, the chairman, decided to keep a prior appointment in Killarney. In those days, with a circulation of about 30,000, *The Irish Times* was making miniscule profits of about £400 a year, claims Jack Webb. The

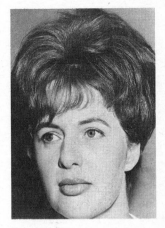

Patsy Dyke, one of the Sunday Review **"stars".** **Later, she moved to the** Sunday Press. –Film & Illustration Library RTE

Dr Conor Cruise O'Brien — wouldn't like to go through the mill of the Irish News Agency again. –The Irish Times

The last page of the Dublin Evening Mail printed at Parliament Street, on December 3, 1960, goes off the stone to the stereo department.
The Irish Times

Like so many other journalists, Jack White of The Irish Times moved into television after RTE came on the air in the early 1960s.
–The Irish Times

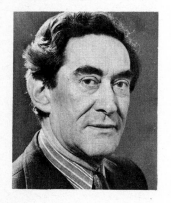

heady financial days of Sir John Arnott, the first baronet, were long gone; fortunately, the insurance claim resulting from the fire was settled in full, but that process took two years. The strain of the fire may have shortened Smyllie's life; he died three years later after a prolonged period of ill-health.

National tragedy struck on the evening of January 10, 1952. An Aer Lingus DC3, "St Kevin", flying from London to Dublin, crashed into a North Wales mountain. There were no survivors and no explanation was ever found for the 'plane being off course and crashing. By general consensus among newspapermen, the best report of the disaster was written for the *Irish Press* by its London editor, Terry Ward. He was said to have known every stationmaster along the line in North Wales, so that with a few judiciously placed 'phone calls, he was soon able to pinpoint the crash site.

Ward started his career with the *Derry Journal;* he was also a strongly convinced Republican. Somewhat paradoxically, he loved London. He also loved the newspaperman's curse, drink, and at one party of London-Irish journalists held not long after that fateful Aer Lingus crash, Terry Ward was to be seen sprawled out on the floor, twitching violently.

The hostess of the party, fearing that Terry Ward (whose son Sean is now editor of the *Evening Press*) was suffering from an epileptic fit, rang for an ambulance. Two days in hospital and several extensive tests later revealed Terry Ward as having suffered from an extreme overdose of alcohol. Seamus Kelly of *The Irish Times* also had an unusual experience in England at about the same time: he had travelled up to Hertfordshire to visit George Bernard Shaw, who showed him round the house most courteously. Then with a walking stick, he poked under the bed and fished out a chamber pot. "This", said Shaw with due ceremony, "is the most useful thing in the house."

There were two memorable, but short-lived newspapers in Dublin at this time. During 1952, Paddy Kavanagh published his *Kavanagh's Weekly*; it was printed by the young Hugh McLaughlin at his Fleet Printing Company in Eccles Place. April saw the querulous Paddy Kavanagh, poet and sage of McDaid's pub off Grafton Street (where Smyllie went once for a brief, uncomfortable evening) bring out the first issue of his *Kavanagh's Weekly*. He wrote in that first issue that he hoped that the rumoured return of Jack White from *The Irish Times'* London office would rescue the paper from the turgidity of the Book Pagers and the Quid Nuncs. For some years now, wrote Kavanagh in the second issue, the paper has pandered to the dullest and deadest elements in the country. He also remarked that de Valera's original intentions with the *Sunday Press* were to have a cross between the *Observer* and the *Universe*. There were other gems, such as: "The national radio station is financially independent and is not forced to be subservient to the opinions of illiterate journalists." If *The Irish Times*

Eoin Neeson, when he worked for the Irish Pictorial.

Off on an American Airlines flight to New York in 1947 are second left to right: Kevin Collins, Arthur Quinlan and Donal MacMonagle. Seeing them off is an unnamed American Airlines' executive.
–*Pan Collins*

Douglas Gageby, who joined the Irish Press in 1945. Assistant editor of the Sunday Press when it was launched in 1949, he then joined the Irish News Agency before returning to Burgh Quay to be founding editor of the Evening Press. He is now editor of The Irish Times.
–The Irish Times

was dull and dreary, it was only reflecting the ethos of the early 1950s. Kavanagh himself did not have much luck with his weekly publication, which he wrote almost entirely by himself; there were stories of him burning piles of returned copies in the grate of his flat in Pembroke Road. Finally, a libel action finished the paper after thirteen weeks in existence. Then during the Dublin newspaper printers' strike in the summer of 1952, a newspaper called the *News Record* came out, with the blessing of the unions involved in the strike, but then it carried just racing news.

Paddy Kavanagh and strikes were far from the minds of the seventy or so employees of the Wexford *People* that summer. They were taken on the firm's third annual staff outing, enjoying a day out in Bray, then an elegant seaside resort. Over dinner that night in the International Hotel, ribald stories and songs poured forth in alcoholic profusion. Eamonn Andrews, then a young radio critic for the *Irish Independent,* spotted a major flaw in a Radio Eireann recording of T. S. Eliot's play, *Murder in the Cathedral.* The play had been recorded on four discs, which were labelled incorrectly and in the wrong sequence. All the radio critics raved about the programme, except the young Andrews, who spotted the fatal error.

In 1952, George Hussey, for years a district reporter of the *Drogheda Independent* and later to spent twenty years as editor of *The Argus,* saw what was probably the first television picture in Ireland. A Co Meath man called Shane McNamee had built a TV set; Hussey saw flickering pictures of a cricket match in England, relayed from the Holme Moss transmitter in the North of England. In June of the following year, 1953, the television coverage of the London coronation of Queen Elizabeth II firmly established the new medium in the public eye. Reporters on the *Meath Chronicle* in Navan at this time used telephones very sparingly, in common with most other country newspapers. The 'phone in the *Chronicle* office was used mainly for advertising.

Telephones and television may have been rarities but 1952 produced another great news story, the Baltinglass post office siege. A change was made in the arrangements for running the office in this bleak Co Wicklow town; it resulted in fierce national controversy and family "splits" even. When the changeover was made, from one post office to the other, hordes of reporters descended on the place. Some rival newsmen even beat each other up, to the consternation of the local gardai, who said that Baltinglass wouldn't return to respectability until the reporters left.

The "Pope" O'Mahony arrived, dressed in a scruffy báinín jacket, to try and settle the differences of opinion. The car in which he was being driven to Baltinglass got lost; when the "Pope" knocked up the inhabitants of a cottage to ask the way, his white beard frightened one child, who announced that Father Christmas had come.

There were some great fights in town too; Jack Mooney, the public relations man, remembers having a terrific punch-up once with a journalist on the pavement in Fleet Street. He won't reveal the name of the other combatant, but says that afterwards, they shook hands and went for a meal. Then there was the case of the six bored comps from *The Irish Times,* who took to cycling round the base of Nelson's Pillar opposite the GPO. When they were needed for work that day, they had to be rescued from the cells at Pearse Street garda barracks.

George Leitch, the principal photographer at *The Irish Times,* had a reputation for getting people involved in arguments. On one occasion that he was going to Belfast to cover a women's branch meeting of the British Legion, he found himself in a corridor compartment of the train with six ladies. He got them entwined in fierce arguments among themselves before slipping unseen from the compartment. Leitch was not always infallible. He hired a 'plane one Saturday to cover an important race meeting at Aintree: his idea was to secure aerial photographs, innovation indeed. Off went Leitch to Aintree, at great expense. He rushed back to the darkroom, only to find that in the excitement, he had forgotten to load his camera with film.

Brian Inglis is also said to have encouraged a splendid punch-up once between the late Seamus Kelly, an able boxer, and Sydney Robbins of *The Irish Times'* sports department. Kelly, remembers Robbins ruefully, ruined his dress shirt. Equally memorable, although never made

Raymond Smith of the Irish Independent. *–Bobby Pyke*

In merry mood, Cathal O'Shannon (left) and Sam Edgar.

Enjoying a visit to New York in 1947, from left: Arthur Quinlan, Donal MacMonagle, Kevin Collins and Alec Newman.
–Pan Collins

Dick Wilkes of the Sunday Press: described by Douglas Gageby as "having a heart as big as a house".

public, was the panic at the *Irish Independent*. Churchill was still Prime Minister in Britain, although aged and addicted to drink. The paper had a well-placed Tory writing a political column from London; a typesetting error in one of his reports had Churchill being "addicted to the Parliamentary bottle". It may have been quite true, but it should have read "battle". The presses at the *Independent* were stopped after 8,000 copies had been run off and the mistake was corrected.

The Irish Times gradually recovered from the ravages of the 1951 fire. It brought in a new circulation expert, a North of England gentleman from a Manchester paper. He was said to have been a genius at raising circulation, but he knew little about Ireland. In his gruff North of England accent, he addressed more junior employees in *The Irish Times* with "Top of the morning". Thereafter, he became known as "Top of the morning" Myers. His briefcase was by popular repute believed to carry little more then the sandwiches for his lunch.

After helping out *The Irish Times* following its fire in 1951, the *Evening Mail* went from strength to strength. In 1952, it secured the contract to print the *Farmer's Journal;* Joe Anderson was doing good work as editor. He kept a benign eye on his staff. One summer, he was short of staff and offered a job to Tommy Cleary of the *Irish Independent*. Cleary gave a month's notice to the "Indo", but was due twenty-one days off for night work. He took the days off in lieu and at the start of his last week at the "Indo", he was told he could take the rest of that week off. Towards the end of the week, the *Sunday Press* rang up; it too was short of staff, so for the Saturday night, Cleary worked for them. He therefore claims that he is one of the very few newspapermen in Dublin to have worked for three newspapers at the same time! When he did get to the sub-editor's desk on the *Evening Mail*, he found Anderson a gracious person for whom to work and the atmosphere friendly. On one rare occasion, Anderson had to sack a reporter because a bottle of whiskey was found in his desk; whatever sins were permitted, *Evening Mail* staff could not drink on duty.

Then the story of the crippled ship, the "Flying Enterprise" and her heroic Captain Carlsen, who stayed abroad until just before the ship sank in the Atlantic, captured the imagination of newspaper readers the world over. The last section of the ship sank one afternoon at 4.11 p.m.; at the *Evening Herald*, various versions to the end of the story had been set, so when the news came through, the right line was set in and the edition was on sale in O'Connell Street at 4.22 p.m. It was a great scoop for the *Herald*, then edited by Leslie Nivison, the first (and last) Protestant editor at Independent newspapers.

Personal tragedy struck, too. Ernie O'Reilly had worked for the *Mail* before joining the *Irish Independent*. He hated motor cars, regarding them as dangerous inventions, so he travelled everywhere by taxi. In Dublin then, traffic in the city centre was light, but one evening, when O'Reilly was in a taxi crossing Capel Street bridge, the cab hit another vehicle and O'Reilly was thrown through the windscreen. A sliver of glass cut his jugular vein, killing him instantly. For years afterwards, the extraordinary chance by which the reporter met his death was talked about wherever journalists meet to yarn.

Personal tragedy also struck the Baird family, owners of the *Belfast Telegraph*. William Robert Baird, the last member of the family to control the paper, was killed practising for a car race at Snetterton in Norfolk in the east of England. By this tragedy, the way was left open for the take-over of the firm by Roy Thomson, the Canadian newspaper tycoon, eight years later. That year, 1953, must have seemed peculiarly fated in the North, for at the end of January, the ferry, the "Princess Victoria", had gone down off the Co Down coast with the loss of more than a hundred lives; many prominent Northern personalities died in the disaster.

There were professional tragedies too, in that narrow-minded time; journalists with even mildly left-wing sympathies were deeply suspect. It was the McCarthy era in the USA and the time of Maria Duce in Ireland; Liam MacGabhann fell foul of the moral censors when he went on a visit to the Soviet Union. He wrote a series of articles about that country for *The People*, for which he was Irish correspondent. All hell broke loose; the regular series of "Topical Talks" which he gave after the 1.30 p.m. news on Radio Eireann, in which he held much of the country spellbound with his deep, intoxicating Kerry accent, was dropped.

Anna Kelly of the *Irish Press* threw a party for him at her Rathgar

Tom Tobin when editor of the Limerick Chronicle.

257

house: "just to show those bastards that we all love Liam and we're all behind him, no matter what happens." The party attracted a tremendous gathering of Dublin newsmen and women (not that there were many women working in the Dublin newspapers in the early 1950s). As dawn was breaking, Tom Barrett strolled down Rathgar Road with his friend Liam MacGabhann; Liam remarked "Tom, boy, it did my old heart good." The *Standard* had been particularly vitriolic in attacking MacGabhann, so much so that twenty years later, in 1973, when the then Taoiseach, Liam Cosgrave, was presenting him with his Gallaher press award, he said to MacGabhann: "I hope the *Standard* has a photographer here."

Being a correspondent for the cross-channel papers was lucrative; Sam Edgar, that polished, suave, journalist from Newtownards, left *The Irish Times* to represent the *Empire News* in Ireland.

Cathal O'Shannon represented both the *News of the World* and the *Sunday Times*. Irish editions of the London and Manchester Sunday papers were very circumspect; in many cases, Sam Edgar (whose widow, Honor is the well-known cookery writer) and Liam MacGabhann had to do little more than write Irish copy to fill in the blanks left by the omission of bikini-clad girls from the Irish editions. Generally, the news editors of these papers had a derisive and derogatory approach to Ireland, seeing it as the source of amusing and odd copy. "Find us something funny" the North of England voice would bellow down the 'phone to Sammy Bestic, when he was Dublin representative of *The People*. Nothing serious, just funny. When the

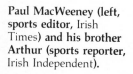

Paul MacWeeney (left, sports editor, Irish Times) and his brother Arthur (sports reporter, Irish Independent).

same paper ran a piece about Sir Roger Casement's homosexuality, copies were burned in the streets of Limerick, perhaps the last time newspapers were burned in Ireland. Sammy Bestic, after his stint on *The People* in Dublin, made the break for London in 1953 and has been there ever since. Today, few Irish journalists head for Fleet Street, which has lost much of its glitter. Instead like Henry Kelly, they head for London's electronic media.

1953 saw George Hodnett in action for Radio Eireann at the great Stan Kenton concert in Dublin. He still graces the review columns of *The Irish Times.* That year saw great excitement at *The Irish Times.* IRA threats were made against the *Times Pictorial* covering the coronation of Queen Elizabeth II in London. The staff defied the warnings; they were locked in for the night to produce the issue, while gardai were on duty outside the building. The newspapermen were fortified with beer and sandwiches; next morning, the "Pic" came out. Nothing happened. Regarding the whole proceedings with some amusement was an ex-RAF flyer, complete with walrus moustache, who was on the staff of the *Pictorial* and one of whose claims to fame was that he could stand on his hands and keep his hat on.

Gordon Clark, who worked for the Leinster Express for a period after the war.

Myles na gCopaleen continued to take himself very seriously; from time to time, he would write a letter of denunciation to the directors of *The Irish Times,* complaining that they considered him as just a funny man. He also sought a rise. Others at the paper had less pleasant dealings with the board. One senior editorial person told the directors that if they made any changes to his paper, he would resign. He was told to go ahead and do so. Next day, he was back on the subs' desk. For some time after, staff joked: "Who is in charge today?"

Foul language could often be heard at *The Irish Times.* A sub called George McAnnoy, who hailed from Belfast's Sandy Row, was said to have had the most vituperative language ever heard in a Dublin newspaper. One night, McAnnoy was shouting when other members of staff realised that a Church of Ireland dignitary was within earshot. "My apologies," said a journalist to the prelate, "that's our cultural correspondent."

Maurice Liston of the *Irish Press* claimed that he had heard similar language from a Reverend Mother. A fire at a convent was missed by one newspaper reporter; he rang Liston, who claimed that when he had telephoned the convent, the Reverend Mother told him: "There's fuck all in it."

Another foul temper was often in evidence in Kilkenny; Ned Keane, father of John Kerry Keane, the present owner and editor of the *Kilkenny People,* had a volcanic temperament that often impressed itself on the staff of the paper and anyone of the town's inhabitants who happened to be within earshot. He was described by Dan Nolan as being "truculent and mercurial, brilliant in his command of language and in his use of it to the discomfiture of those who were ungodly in his

In the Limerick Leader editorial department before the technological revolution (from left): Michael Barber, Bernard Carey (now News Editor), Gerard Ryan and chief reporter, Joe Mulqueen.

estimation." People who landed the wrong side of Keane could expect short shrift. One local dignitary who offended Keane was thereafter always referred to in the paper as "Mr--------, BA Pass." The lack of standing in the poor man's university degree became the means by which Keane continually berated him.

The *Limerick Leader* lifted copy from the *Limerick Chronicle* and had to apologise in print, but ended its piece by saying that the *Chronicle* was never a reliable source. The *Leader* took over the Protestant *Chronicle* in 1953. The *Limerick Chronicle* had been sold to three of its staff, including editor Paddy Fitzgibbon. After the take-over by the *Leader*, the two papers were run separately, although later, Fitzgibbon became editor of both, replacing Con Cregan, a remarkable but remote editor, who had kept the *Leader* going through the dark days of war. One of the *Chronicle's* staff took the emigrant ship soon afterwards, along with so many others from Ireland. Jack Cronin went to New York, where he is now a director of J. Walter Thompson, one of the world's largest advertising agencies.

In early 1954, Bertie Smyllie died; he had the appearance of a grossly overweight and very old man. He was sixty. For over a year before his death, his illness had been sufficiently serious to silence his violin and keep him from directing affairs at *The Irish Times*. His Presbyterian funeral attracted an enormous gathering of friends and admirers. For the last time, the funeral of a Dublin newspaper editor inspired the pulling down of blinds in the city centre. He was succeeded by his deputy, Alec Newman; the right of succession was sacrosanct and no-one questioned the right of Newman to succeed Smyllie, even though many staff on the paper had doubts about Newman's ability to be more than a very skilled Number Two. In Cork, Jack Healy, editor of the *Cork Examiner,* died after more than half a century in the editorial chair. He was eighty-five. He was succeeded by Paddy Dorgan, in turn succeeded by Tim Cramer.

In Mullingar, too, that year, another venerable newspaper figure died, J. P. Hayden, owner and editor of the *Westmeath Examiner,* who had founded the newspaper in 1882 at the age of eighteen. He was succeeded as editor and managing director by the young Nicholas Nally, who is still a shareholder, along with Hayden's son, John, who lives in North Wales. When Peadar O'Curry, the editor of the *Standard,* arrived back at Dublin airport one day in 1954, he too suffered a terrible fate. Met by Terry O'Sullivan, he was asked if he had heard anything untoward. No, said O'Curry. The rest of Dublin *did* know —

Sidney Buchanan of the Londonderry Sentinel. **As a young reporter, he wrote up the Soviet nuclear bomb "scoop" in 1946.**

In 1960, the Mourne Observer, **Newcastle,** published a special supplement to celebrate Down's victory in winning the Sam Maguire cup. Second from right (in boiler suit) is D. J. Hawthorne, with an unnamed member of staff and two members of Down GAA.
–*Mourne Observer*

Joe Sherwood by
Bobby Pyke.

J. J. McCann, founder
of the highly
successful Radio
Review and joint
managing director of
The Irish Times,
1957-1959.

that in his absence on a press trip abroad, he had been sacked by the directors of the paper.

Not long after Smyllie died, the man who later succeeded him as editor at *The Irish Times*, Douglas Gageby, was starting work on the greatest newspaper launch of the 1950s. Jack Dempsey and his team planned the *Evening Press* with meticulous care in 1954; it had to be successful, just as it was essential for the future of the *Irish Press* that the *Sunday Press* turned out to be successful. Gageby had moved from the *Sunday Press* a couple of years earlier to become editor-in-chief of the Irish News Agency.

In a London pub during 1953, he met up with Jack Dempsey and as the talk grew congenial, the pair started to talk about evening newspapers. The brief existence of the *Evening Telegraph* at Burgh Quay in 1932 came up; Dempsey had taken careful note of the lessons from that debacle. He now had something much more substantial in mind. Gageby returned to Burgh Quay in early 1954 with a put-up job as managing editor; he was scheduled to be the editor of the evening paper that Dempsey and Major Vivion de Valera were planning. His "cover" was helping the editors of the two existing newspapers, Matt Feehan on the *Sunday Press* and Jim McGuinness on the *Irish Press,* but in practice, he was planning the new paper as actively as Dempsey.

September was chosen as the launch month, but the news did not become official until the *Irish Press* annual general meeting in June, although it had been common pub gossip around town for months previously. The first editorial appointment under Gageby was John O'Donovan to be assistant editor and chief sub. O'Donovan was one of the fittest people ever to work at Burgh Quay; a non-smoker, a non-drinker and a vegetarian, he insisted on keeping the windows open. Tim Pat Coogan, who joined the new paper as a copy boy (having done a little schoolboy sports reporting for the *Irish Independent)* remembers that most people were too scared of O'Donovan to ask him to close the windows. O'Donovan certainly set a cracking pace, in at seven every morning.

In Gageby's words, O'Donovan was precise, voluble, scathing and a kindly uncle by turns. A theatrical figure himself, he decided to hire Gabriel Fallon as drama critic. Another man, a long-time friend of Gageby, applied for a job as Number Two to Fallon. At this stage, before the launch of the paper, Gageby and O'Donovan were the only two members of staff on the *Evening Press.* Gageby introduced his friend to O'Donovan and then heard his stentorian tones exclaiming: "Well, Mr So and So, you are interested in the drama, I hear. Suppose we take Coriolanus Act II and you will remember where in the second scene . . . perhaps you will give me your opinion on that and on another passage with which you are no doubt familiar."

Suddenly, a chair scraped back, a fist thumped on the table and the angry voice of Gageby's friend blurted out: "And I've a damn good

Sean MacBride, who was instrumental in setting up the Irish News Agency. In an earlier period of his life, he spent some six months working as a sub-editor on the ultra-Conservative Morning Post in London — under an assumed name, since he was on the run at the time.
–The Irish Times

mind to give you a puck on the jaw, too." The acerbic O'Donovan has been known to have that effect on the mildest of people.

Slowly, the team came together. On the advertising side, Jim Furlong had such volcanoes of energy as Tommy Mangan and Horace Denham (the latter now in the London office of *The Irish Times*). Liam Pedlar, the circulation manager and his Number Two, Padraig O Criogáin, were all set to repeat the thorough distribution achieved for the *Sunday Press*. Just as Denham ended up working for *The Irish Times*, so too did others on that new paper of thirty years ago. John Healy was there, writing about amateur drama and other matters and regarded as having an enormous capacity for copy production. Michael Finlan, now Galway correspondent of *The Irish Times*, was also there. A slim young fellow called Jim Downey also worked there, said to have joined the paper at the age of seventeen because a girl in Kilkenny had jilted him and to have left it two years later because a girl in Dublin did the same.

Downey, who worked in his youth on the *Nationalist and Leinster Times*, Carlow, under the able guidance of Liam D. Bergin, the editor and John Ellis, the works manager, and who is now deputy editor of *The Irish Times*, says that the story is not true. Another one is, about the time Jack Smyth, the news editor, had him dress up as a Russian general and walk up and down O'Connell Street for a couple of hours. Next day, Smyth wrote a story: "Yesterday, a Russian general walked down O'Connell Street — and nobody even noticed."

The first issue came out; making the front page was a photograph of Betty Whelan's marriage that morning. For later editions, an artist touched up her neckline. A young reporter in the early days of the paper was herself the cause of similar problems; Deirdre McSharry, now editor of *Cosmopolitan* magazine in London, is said to have gone to interview more than one bishop wearing a dress whose neckline did

not leave everything to the imagination.

The *Evening Press* hit the streets with a wallop, surviving a minor first morning strike by some print workers. David Luke, in charge of promotion (Paul Meehan, now publicity manager of Independent Newspapers was his assistant), hired a couple of elephants from the Zoo as well as the ITGWU band. This strange assorted medley of animals and musicians fired the public's imagination; the first day's print run of 100,000 was soon sold out. The great delivery innovation of the *Evening Press* was the fleet of scooters, which had the copies out to the suburbs before the other two evening newspapers, the *Herald* and the *Mail*. Classified advertisers in the other newspapers were telephoned by the *Evening Press* canvassers and given virtually free advertising. Every sales and promotional gimmick was tried, so much so that the day the *Evening Press* was launched, a leader in the *Evening Mail* remarked quite scornfully, "We've seen them come and we've seen them go."

The day the *Evening Press* was launched was the day the *Evening Mail* started to die by degrees. When the *News Chronicle,* London, folded in 1960, its demise was attributed to thrombosis: "circulation impeded by clots". A similar fate befell the *Dublin Evening Mail.*

The new *Evening Press* had an excitement and sparkle that had not been seen in Irish journalism since the launch of the *Irish Press* in 1931.

Staff and directors of the
Limerick Leader, **1959.**
–Limerick Leader

Joe Sherwood, one of the few survivors from that earlier launch, came back with a vengeance, his abrupt departure from the *Irish Press* sports editorship in the 1930s glossed over. Sherwood was always keen to come back to Ireland and over a glass of port in Mulligans, he told Paddy Flynn, the *Evening Press* sports editor, that he would like to write a series of reminiscences about famous sports personalities and games.

With smoke curling out of his hooked briar pipe, Sherwood said in his clipped Cumbrian accent: "I tell 'ee lad, there's nowt I haven't seen in sport. I remember stories you never 'eard of. I can do 'ee a favour." Joe Sherwood soon fell foul of his reading public; his enthusiasm often outran his accuracy. As sports editor of the *Irish Press*, he ran a column called " In hot water"; as sports writer for the *Evening Press*, he started a column called "In the soup".

Sherwood worked odd hours: he wrote his column after midnight and Paddy Flynn had the copy collected at 4 a.m. He was continually in the soup, even barred from his local pub at Stillorgan once because he started such disputation about sporting matters among the drinkers. The IRFU banned him from Lansdowne Road for a time, but his most famous encounter was at a press conference in the Gresham Hotel. He came to blows with an Australian coach called Percy Cerrutty; they ended up rolling round the carpet, struggling furiously before an astonished and delighted audience of Dublin sports journalists.

Seamus Kelly of *The Irish Times* had a "bit" part when the harbour scenes of "Moby Dick" were filmed at Youghal, Co Cork. When director John Huston heard Kelly's rasping Belfast accent, most of his part is said to have ended up on the cutting room floor.

The new *Evening Press* liked to boast that it was ahead of the times. So it was, but not in quite the way claimed by Dempsey and de Valera. One elderly reporter was so attached to morphine that he had to send out for his daily supply, which he then stirred into his tea. So addicted did he become that eventually, he could do little else except sub the fatstock prices, singing and humming to himself about bullocks and heifers. In its early days, the paper had two reporters who seemed to do little except gaze into each other's eyes. Suddenly, they disappeared. Days later, the distraught Mammy of one of them came into the office to find out what had happened. The two homosexuals had eloped to Amsterdam, dear, she was told. The *Evening Press* discovered drugs and homosexuality twenty years before society at large.

Jack Smyth, the news editor of the *Evening Press,* had one ultimate ambition, to file a story datelined the Moon. He survived his training on the *Connacht Tribune* and World War II as a correspondent for Reuters news agency. He survived the paratroop landing at Arnhem in

Photograph taken in April, 1959, during fifty years' service presentation to John J. Dunne, chief executive, Independent Newspapers (second from left, seated). He was succeeded shortly afterwards (December 1959) by Bartle Pitcher. Also in the photograph are Frank Geary, editor, Irish Independent (third from right, seated), Hector Legge (far right, seated), E. C. Maguire, advertisement manager (centre, seated) and Billy King, advertisement department (far right, standing).

The great Irish Times'
**fire of September 16,
1951. Subsequent issues
of the paper were
printed by the** Dublin
Evening Mail.

the Netherlands in 1944, writing a book about the experience called
Five Days in Hell. He died a pointless death in the River Liffey, but not
before he had organised some memorable news scoops for the *Evening
Press.*

His coverage of the Berrigan Baby case is said by many in the
newspaper business to have been the single news story that firmly
established the new *Evening Press.* All sorts of minor innovations did
help the paper, like the Bush system, which enabled local news (and
more importantly, local deaths) to be printed onto blank columns of
the paper at eight centres round the country, such as Waterford and
Cork. Even Newry had the Bush system for a while. The machine was
also used at major race meetings for printing special racing editions —
an improvement on Day One of the *Evening Press,* when the wires broke
down and the sports staff had to go to nearby bookmakers' shops to get
the racing results!

The Berrigan Baby saga provided the real push. On Saturday,
December 18, 1954 (thirty years to the day since the *Freeman's Journal*
closed down), shoppers in Dublin's Henry Street were startled by the
cries of twenty-one year old Teresa Berrigan. While she had been
shopping for a teddy bear for her son Patrick, the child was snatched
from his pram. Over the next few days, public interest in the case was
intense. All Garda leave was cancelled and the story filled column after
column in the *Evening Press,* as well as the other Dublin papers.

The following Tuesday, Mrs Louise Doherty from Belfast identified
a photograph of Patrick Berrigan as the baby who had travelled North
with a woman on the 6.25 p.m. train from Dublin the previous
Saturday evening. On the Wednesday, the baby was found in the
home of a Belfast couple. The *Evening Press* broke the news to the

From left, in a Cork bar, Louis MacMonagle (Cork Examiner), **Tommy Lavery** (Irish Press), **Roy Hammond (then a "stringer" in Cork for the** Irish Press, **now with RTE in Cork), an unidentified Cork lady and bus driver and Donal MacMonagle** (Irish Press). **The "commentary" mimics Hammond's pronounced Cockney accent.**

HAMMOND: I met a poor old lady with white hair, lines on her face and a shawl down the Dyke yesterday. Told me she was the Duchess of Kent at one time and now she was down and out — starved with the hunger — hadn't a cent.

CHORUS: What did you give her?

HAMMOND: Coo, blimey! I really shouldn't tell you, but I gave her 250th at f11 with a green filter on HP3. Cor! Wo' a lark!

Berrigans, who were rushed North in a car belonging to the newspaper. The RUC then discovered that the other child of the Belfast couple, Bernadette, was the same age as Elizabeth Browne, who had been taken as a three month old baby from a pram in Henry Street in November, 1950, four years earlier. The Belfast husband made a tearful plea to be allowed to keep Bernadette; it turned out that he did not know she was not his rightful child. His wife had feigned pregnancy before bringing Elizabeth Browne home and just before she had taken Patrick Berrigan, had given birth to a stillborn infant. The Belfast woman was sentenced to two years' imprisonment in Armagh women's prison, but was released thirteen months later.

That was not the end of the "missing babies" story, much to the delight of Jack Smyth and his team of reporters on the *Evening Press*. Pauline Ashmore had been snatched from her pram outside a furniture store in Camden Street, Dublin, on October 19, 1954. By the time the other two babies had been reunited with their respective parents, there was still no trace of the Ashmore child, but on January 25, 1955, this third story broke.

An anonymous 'phone caller told the *Evening Press* that a woman who had had a baby at the Coombe Hospital on October 19 had just given birth to another child — three months later. A reporter and a photographer went to the address supplied, in Oliver Bond Street, and managed to get a photograph of the October baby, subsequently identified by Mrs Ashmore as her daughter Pauline.

The Ashmore baby became Mrs Kevin Jenkinson, who is married to an electrician and lives in Ballymun. The Berrigan baby is now thirty, works as a printer and is married and living in Lucan; he prefers to forget about that kidnapping back in 1954. The way in which the *Evening Press* helped solve the cases of the three missing babies met with national approval. The *Irish Press* gave its infant evening sibling a pat on the back; its leader said: "There are many ways in which a newspaper can serve the public, and we can imagine no better service than that of being instrumental in restoring a baby to its mother."

Building on the confidence engendered by those three cases, the *Evening Press* went from strength to strength. The team was powerful and other public favourites in addition to such columnists as Terry O'Sullivan and Joe Sherwood were wildlife man J. Ashton Freeman, Cathal O'Shannon senior on books and the young Brendan Behan. Behind the scenes, such people as Dick Wilkes (father of *Evening Press* chief sub-editor and motoring correspondent Alan Wilkes) laboured on production of the paper. Dick Wilkes, on loan from the *Sunday Press* and described by Douglas Gageby as having a heart as big as a house, was helped by such people as Troy Kennedy Martin (later to achieve fame as a TV scripwriter in London) and Brian Cleeve (later to become a Messianic writer and novelist).

Success was tempered by tragedy, the death of Jack Smyth and his wife Eileen, who also came from Galway. On Saturday, December 1, 1956, they had been attending a function in the now-defunct Majestic Hotel at the corner of Upper Fitzwilliam Street and Lower Baggot Street. News came through of Ronnie Delaney's sensational gold medal win in the 1500 metres race in the Melbourne Olympics. Smyth decided to get back to Burgh Quay to oversee production of the news of this tremendous achievement. The night was bad as the Smyths drove across to Burgh Quay; turning on to the quays, near Butt Bridge, Smyth realised too late that in the fog, he was headed straight for the river. He braked, but the car skidded violently and plunged into the Liffey. A man on the quayside heard shouts from Jack Smyth as the

Maureen O'Hara and Pat O'Brien entertain the Irish press to lunch at the RKO studios, Hollywood, 1948. Left to right, Arthur Quinlan, Kevin Collins, Joseph Harty (American Airlines), Pat O'Brien, Donal MacMonagle, Alec Newman and Maureen O'Hara.

car went down, but the wash from a docking ship pushed it beneath the water. Jack Smyth had clambered out, but his body was never found, giving rise to much speculation at the time that he had just disappeared, rather than drowned. When the car was raised, the body of his wife Eileen, whom he had married in Galway in 1945, was found on the back seat.

The two young Smyth children left orphaned by the car crash were looked after by a man called Shannon who worked for the ESB, and who knew the family well. One winter's night, almost two years to the day after the accident that killed the Smyths, the children's guardian was returning from Finglas to the southside of the city. The night was very foggy and he ended up at Kingsbridge, where he took directions about getting to the southside by way of the quays. Driving along the quays, towards the Ringsend gasometer, his car veered off the roadway and into the Liffey, not more than fifty yards from where the Smyths' car had plunged in. Shannon, too, was drowned and when the news of the accident and the most extraordinary coincidence it involved, reached the *Evening Press* newsroom, the reporters were so stunned and disbelieving that at least one edition of the paper came and went without mention of the second accident, until the story had been checked and rechecked. Smyth's son, Peter, now works for the *Evening Press*.

Great newspapermen either die in harness, generally to widespread public sympathy, or they fade away in the oblivion of retirement, like actors from whom the magic of applause has been forcibly removed. Poor Terry Ward, of the *Irish Press,* that genial, much-loved and respected newspaperman, passed on long before his time. When he died in 1955, he looked like a man of ninety-three, rather than a man of fifty-three, in the words of Ben Kiely.

There were lighter moments on the *Evening Press* and the other Dublin papers. Joe Sherwood struck an extraordinary wager in the Silver Swan one night. He bet that no-one could drink twenty pints, one after the other. He put up a lot of money, safe in the knowledge that he was not risking his cash; when one of the newspaper sellers came in to the bar and took up the challenge, Sherwood scoffed. Addressing him as "Lad", Sherwood told he was wasting his money. The newspaper seller told him he would be back later; a couple of hours on, Joe Sherwood was convinced that he was safe. In came the

The Cork Examiner football team of 1949. Front row, left to right: Connie Carroll, Finbarr Herbert, Willie O'Leary, Billy Cotter, Frankie Linehan, Donal O'Hara. Back row, left to right: Seamus O'Leary, Dick Delanty, Chris Callaghan, Jack Lynch (goalie), John Crowley, Ray Riordan, John Tynan, Tom West and Charlie Duggan (referee).

When the Down Recorder celebrated its 125th anniversary in 1961, one of its photographs showed works foreman John McQuoid (left) and compositor George Wallace standing over the formes on the make-up "stone".

newspaper seller, apologising for the delay. He had been practising for the feat; Sherwood felt even safer. The other man promptly downed twenty pints, one after the other and won his money (about £5, equal to a week's wages for many people then).

An equally celebrated press occasion took place when Toddy O'Sullivan opened the penthouse suite in the Gresham Hotel. The Grsham was at the height of its fame and prestige; twelve representatives from the *Irish Press,* seven from *The Irish Times* and four from the *Independent* decided that they had better cover this important event and sample O'Sullivan's renowned hospitality.

After Dick Roche joined the *Irish Independent,* he asked Frank Geary, the editor, for a rise. Since he was on the union rate, Geary wanted to know what he was doing that merited the extra amount. Roche replied that his wife was expecting a baby and that the additional money would be useful for the forthcoming extra mouth in the Roche household. "The *Independent* cannot be held responsible for that," joked Geary. In Dick Roche's recollection, it was the only time Geary ever cracked a joke.

Myles na gCopaleen spent a night in custody at this period; he had been arrested outside Trinity College for being atrociously drunk and was locked up for his own protection. Later, Myles, together with Brendan Behan and the painter Sean O'Sullivan, could be heard outside Mitchell's Café in Grafton Street, berating the lack of characters on the Dublin scene!

Brendan Behan was starting to write for the Burgh Quay papers; once, when he was passing through London, he told Des Fisher, then *Irish Press* London editor, now with RTE, that he could have two articles if he was paid the £5 for them immediately. Another occasion in London, a very drunk Behan went to the *Irish Press* office, sat down at the editorial secretary's desk and got sick. To relieve himself, he simply opened a drawer of her desk, retched and shut it again, leaving it for the unfortunate woman to find next morning.

Before the *Evening Press* settled down to a quieter respectability, one character took everyone by surprise. Sean Cronin was a most diligent and able sub-editor. He had known Gageby when both were in the Regular Army during the Emergency; as Tim Pat Coogan points out with suitable irony in his book on the IRA, much of Gageby's work in military intelligence was devoted to keeping tabs on that organisation. Cronin was and still is, an exceptionally able newspaperman. In the *Evening Press,* he was renowned for arriving five minutes early every morning. His American accent earned him the title of the "Sheriff".

One day, Cronin handed in his notice, saying that he was going to take up a commission from an American newspaper chain. Shortly afterwards, he was picked up on the border. Later, he appeared in the columns of the *Evening Press* after he was in court, charged with being adjutant general of a certain illegal organisation. After these

Joe Anderson was editor of the Dublin Evening Mail from 1936 to 1958. He is seen here (extreme left, seated) with some of the Mail's staff just before his retirement from the paper.

The Irish Times

SATURDAY, JULY 28, 1945.

Cruiskeen Lawn

By Myles na gCopaleen

CIVIS Romanus *homme.* I am of course a visitor here (just when does a visitor become an inhabitant? The wife's 'brother' has been on a 'visit' in my house since 1924) but that is not to say that I am destitute of posed war plans for the land of May had option I beg pardon the land of my adoption. Readers will be aware of the constitutional position. We are in the Empire but not Ovid. Distinguished British statesmen resident in Co. Belfast have seen fit to make discourteous references to your republic, even suggesting that it would be no harm if you packed up and clear doubt! I . . . . . I wonder would Mister Churchill really like it that way? Take a look at Ireland:

Does it look to you like a timorous, depressed, decadent country? A land afraid of the future? A realm with no prospects? In reality it looks jaunty and gallant, very much as if it were going to go places. Suppose . . . . . suppose I were to tell you that I have devised a system of . . . . . land migration, a system based on liquefaction and pumping such as would enable the sovereign republican government of your Ireland to . . . . . literally to run the country, have it go and come as they please? Suppose you were, early one morning, to leave the so-called Empire in the most devastatingly literal sense, simply disappear bag and baggage? Wouldn't the British be just a little bit sorry? Know for the first time what you so patiently put up with from the Atlantic Ocean?

And where to go? Well, *there* is one idea. Set up house in the middle of the mild blue Mediterranean, become hot Latin persons.

Observe reader, the bare forsaken aspect of England and Scotland on that map. Do they want it that way? Do they *really* wish to traverse the Bay of Biscay and squeeze in through the tortuous portals of Gibraltar just to have a steak in Dublin? Do they seek a situation wherein a visit to Ireland even for the purpose of collecting debts involves an expensive ocean voyage? I doubt it very much. And let me add that if your somewhat severe governors think that there is much to be, said against the South of France as a latitude unsuitable for your Ireland, why——

——there are other places. What's wrong with being anchored off New York harbour? Would not that substantially reduce the expenses of emigration? *And* if that ultimately bores, there are, as I have shown on my map, other places. (And still others—I understand the climate is very temperate around Japan?)

Certain is this much: you are the worst in the world because you're here; and if you go away you'll be the worst in the world.

"Cruiskeen Lawn"
column from The Irish Times

adventures, Cronin went to work for the *Irish Independent.* Later, he returned to the USA, where his achievements in a distinguished career include the position (current) of Washington correspondent for *The Irish Times,* under editor Douglas Gageby. Historical irony has turned full circle.

The *Argus* which published editions in Drogheda, Dundalk and Monaghan, changed hands twice in the 1950s. In 1952, the directors of the *Standard* bought the paper. At the end of the decade, the *Argus* was bought by Seamus Rourke, a director of the *Drogheda Independent.* After its office moved to Dundalk, the *Argus* was notorious for its inefficient book-keeping; for years, its sole means of keeping track of its financial resources was a cash book. Everyone on the staff, including the reporters, made such entries as "£1 received today from Mrs-----", "Mrs So and So will pay £2 next week". Chaotic and all as the paper was, many of the best-known names in today's media passed through the *Argus,* like Ted Nealon (Minister in charge of Local Radio), John McDonnell (editor of *Ireland's Own),* Fintan Faulkner, Kevin Marron, Patsy McArdle, Michael Hand (editor, *Sunday Independent)* and Joe Kennedy, first editor of the *Sunday World.*

March, 1956, saw Ted Gallagher, the Belfast-born journalist, turn in his last issue of the *Kerryman,* where he had been editor since 1944. Dan Nolan had "rescued" him from the Defence Forces, where Gallagher was editor of *An Cosantoir* and acting as press officer for the First Division. In twelve years, the drive and determination of Nolan and Gallagher pushed the *Kerryman's* circulation up from 15,000 to double that figure. Gallagher went to be managing editor of the Mercier Press in Cork (Nolan recollects that he had given the then-young firm much help by means of extended credit) and from Cork, Gallagher returned to his native Belfast, when he was appointed editor of the *Irish News.* In 1955, that paper had celebrated the centenary of the founding of the *Belfast Morning News* with a comprehensive supplement, in which it referred quaintly to its lady correspondent, Anne Fitzpatrick. 1957 saw Ted Gallagher make his last contribution to his old paper, the *Kerryman.* He wrote a series of articles on Ireland's plight, remarkably similar to the present day, with talk of economic collapse, the decline in national morale and the problem of the border.

The Irish Times was soon to have its own set of problems. The paper was about to launch the *Sunday Review;* it was also about to take over the ailing *Dublin Evening Mail.* The first issue of the *Sunday Review,* on November 3, 1957, showed James Carroll, T.D., the Lord Mayor of Dublin, pressing the button to start the press, watched by J. J. McCann, the new joint managing director and Ralph Walker and Sir Lauriston Arnott, both directors. Frank Lowe, the chairman, was heard to remark that they had laboured for months to produce a mouse.

Economic conditions were depressed; the emigrant ships were

At the news desk of the Connacht Tribune, **Galway, in 1959 are from left: Sean Fahy (now editor), Joe Fahy and Sean Duignan.**
–Connacht Tribune

packed with talented people. Advertising for the new paper was hard to come by and the space buyer of one Dublin advertising agency claimed that since the *Sunday Independent* and the *Sunday Press* covered the market, there was no justification for using the *Sunday Review*. The paper, despite many good editorial features, turned out to be a premature publication.

With John Healy (its last editor) and Ted Nealon as news editor, the *Sunday Review* attracted good writers and a sound editorial reputation. Healy introduced the "Backbencher" column, which opened up politics and demonstrated that newspapers would no longer take the line of the moment from politicians. He was credited with breaking down the barriers that distanced politicians from the people who voted them into power. Until then, many reporters would have shied away from the idea of telephoning a Government Minister at home. After the *Sunday Review* folded, the column was transferred to *The Irish Times*, with equal success. Patsy Dyke, the English-born wife of Cathal O'Shannon (former *Irish Times* and BBC and RTE television reporter and now public relations man for the Alcan project near Limerick) brought in another innovation — a Saturday night column chronicling the doings around town. After the *Sunday Review* closed, Patsy Dyke took her column to the *Sunday Press*. Others to work for the paper included Donal Foley (London correspondent), Terence de Vere White, who wrote under a nom de plume, Nicholas Leonard (then the "Business and Finance" editor of *The Irish Times* and now London editor of Independent Newspapers), who was writing on tax matters, Bronwyn Conroy, whose fashion and beauty column also transferred to the

Terry Ward (front row, left), pictured in the mid-1950s at Joe May's pub in Skerries, Co. Dublin. Next to Terry is the late Joe Fox, who became a Fianna Fail TD for the area and who died in a car crash in north Co. Dublin in 1982. Back row, left is Sean Cryan, now assistant news editor, Irish Press. Centre is the unidentified taxi driver who brought the Irish Press group to Skerries to cover the rescue of a man from a boat. Right is Brendan Ryan, at the time an Irish Press reporter, now retired.

Sunday Press, Charlie Orr ("The Week As I Saw It"), who later went to the *News of the World* as its Irish correspondent, Dermot Mullane, now with RTE, Marion FitzGerald (who did a "Purely Personal" column) and Michael Hand (now editor of the *Sunday Independent*), who was a layout man.

So good was the *Sunday Review* that as soon as the first copies were off the presses on Saturday nights, correspondents of the British Sunday papers would scan through them to see if there were any good stories they had missed and which could be discreetly "lifted". There were even plans for a coloured comic section, but these did not materialise, because *The Irish Times'* press was an odd size and there were problems matching page sizes. The paper even had gravure printed colour sections, printed by Hely Thoms, but there were many technical problems with these pages, too.

The same year that the *Sunday Review* was launched, the North of Ireland also had a new paper, the *Ulster Star* in Lisburn, just outside Belfast. Jim Morton of Mortons in Lurgan had made take-over approaches to the two papers then published in the town, but neither was amenable. Morton went ahead and produced his own paper, the *Ulster Star*, edited by a young journalist called David Capper, who went on to a more public career as a reporter with the BBC in Belfast. The *Lisburn Standard* closed down in 1959, the *Lisburn Herald* in 1969. The *Ulster Star*, having survived various changes of editors in its early years, after Capper left, is still going strong.

At the time the *Sunday Review* was being launched, J. J. McCann (often compared with the Aga Khan, the great socialite of the time) was crowning a colourful career in publishing by joining *The Irish Times.*

He brought with him the paper he had launched, the *Radio Review.* He had prospered mightily with the publication; its crosswords and its listing of all the BBC programmes helped win it an enormous circulation, not only in Ireland, but in the North of England. It evaded several threats by the BBC for 'pirating' its copyright on the *Radio Times,* but nothing happened. The *Radio Review* managed to print all the week's BBC programmes by the simple expedient of paying a docker in Dublin port a pound or two for slipping out a copy of the *Radio Times* on its way to its Irish distributors.

The enormous prize money on the crosswords created great public interest. On one occasion at the Theatre Royal, David Luke, the man who masterminded the publicity for the new *Evening Press* in 1954, handed over a cheque for £4,500 — much money for over thirty years ago. McCann himself remembers driving down to Co Wicklow to tell the winner of one competition of his great good fortune. After unearthing the remote cottage, McCann knocked at the door, then told the startled occupant that he had won an all-expenses paid holiday to Rome. "Sure, what would we want with that? We're Protestants." *The Irish Times* was printing the *Radio Review* and some sources claim that McCann joined the paper under threat of withdrawing the printing contract from the firm.

For an unhappy two year period, McCann tried to impose his ideas on *The Irish Times.* He was made less than welcome. He says that he produced a dummy of how he would like the paper to look, including a preview of the next day's feature contents, in similar style to the previews done today. "Take it away, it makes me sick," is how McCann remembers Frank Lowe, the chairman, reacting. Despite his troubles, McCann was renowned for his impish sense of humour. Once, he was reported as saying that he had seen a sub-editor coming up the stairs to work-on his hands and knees. Short as McCann's stay was at *The Irish Times,* that of his assistant, Bartle Pitcher, was even briefer. Pitcher, an accountant by profession, joined *The Irish Times* in 1957 and stayed just nine months. John Dunne was retiring as general manager of Independent Newspapers and Pitcher promptly stepped into his shoes. At the time, McCann and Pitcher were inseparable, having both laboured for long on the *Radio Review.* Now McCann likes to retail the story of how Ossie Dowling, a great favourite among his journalistic colleagues until his untimely death from cancer, had gone to work for the *Evening Herald* after the demise of the *Sunday Review.* All of a sudden, in one of those quick, unexpected palace revolutions that characterise the Dublin papers, Dowling's TV column was dropped from the *Herald.* He is said to have gone to see Pitcher to beg transfer to some other editorial slot of equal status, only to be told by Pitcher, in McCann's words, that such decisions were not his responsibility.

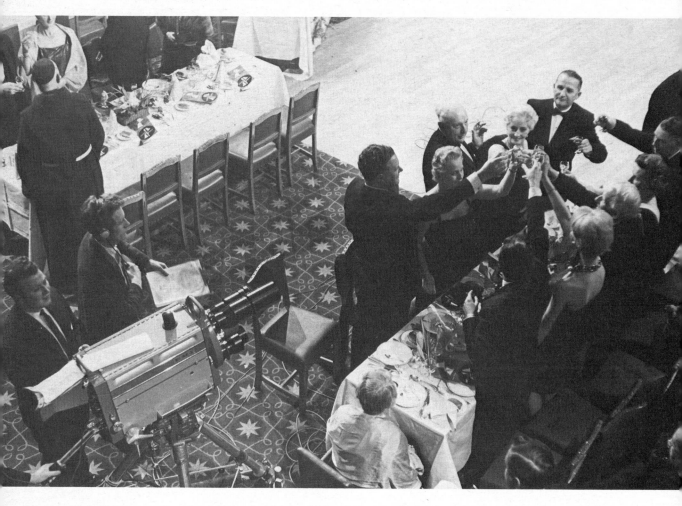

Toasting the infant RTE television in 1961.
–Lensmen

While these squabbles were surfacing in Dublin, trouble was in the air too at the *Connacht Tribune* in Galway. Jack Fitzgerald, the genial, slow-moving editor appointed in 1950, used to have some spectacular rows with his news editor, a man called Bill King. The two were said to have had incompatible personalities. The placid, easy impression given to the outside community by Fitzgerald was reverse imaged inside the *Connacht Tribune*.

A murder at Kilmallock, Co Limerick, provided a glimpse into the old-fashioned workings of the mind of Con Cregan, then editor of the *Limerick Leader*. When he heard about the murder, on a Friday, he is said to have instructed: "Tell our correspondent in Kilmallock to send in a paragraph for next week's country edition." Cregan also took great exception to the efforts of the paper's photographic staff to get a photograph of the murder scene. But towards the end of the 1950's some country newspapers still had a dual purpose — a good read and a good tablecloth.

1957 saw an old hand at Burgh Quay return to the fold. Francis Carty, who had been a sometimes permanent sub at the *Irish Press* during the war, went on to spend thirteen years with Fallons, the school book publishers, where J. J. O'Leary put him in as general manager. After the abrupt departure of Jim McGuinness from the *Irish Press* editorship, allegedly after a blazing row with Vivion de Valera (years later, after McGuinness retired from RTE, he ran a fruit and vegetable shop in Monkstown), Carty was the surprise and resented choice of editor, at a salary of £1,700 per annum.

In those days at the *Irish Press,* nearly thirty years ago, when little planning went into newspaper editorial production and where so many people were sacked that it became almost a badge of honour to leave Burgh Quay in a hurry, Carty's appointment was kept secret for a long time. McGuinness left in the Spring and Carty, who joined in May, was not allowed by Vivion de Valera to tell anyone for a number of weeks, not even O'Leary, who was naturally very curious to know the destination of his very able manager. No doubt Eamon de Valera himself thoroughly approved of the appointment; Carty worshipped de Valera and the day he died in 1972, de Valera spent the afternoon at his bedside.

Short in stature, Francis Carty was known by all at Burgh Quay as the "Little Man". Doing cartoons there at the time was Bobby Pyke, a handsome man in the 1950s; happily, he is still turning out his cartoons of newspaper characters. Once, Pyke crept into Carty's office and is said to have tapped him on the head while jokingly incanting the following: "Little man, Black and Tan".

Considering Carty's distinguished record in the Republican movement in Wexford during the War of Independence, the sentiments were incongruous to say the least!

Sunday Press infighting even extended to the Church of the Most Holy Trinity at Dublin Castle. A former member of the paper's editorial staff had been ordained a priest and was saying his first Mass, at the church. Burgh Quay staffers served at the altar and there was said to have been a considerable degree of jostling among the place seekers.

The year after the *Sunday Review* came out, the *Sunday Press* attempted to reply with technical innovation. By printing several colours on ordinary newsprint, it was hoped to provide a good approximation of a colour photograph. In keeping with the aims and aspirations of its readers, one Sunday in 1958, the *Sunday Press* went to great lengths to secure a suitably pietistic photographs of Dr McQuaid, the Archbishop of Dublin. The printing technique failed to work; one colour ran into another, producing a very smudged brown study, abstract in appearance, rather than a nicely tinted photograph taken in

Frank Geary, editor of the Irish Independent, **in Hollywood in 1949 with William Holden.**

the library of the Archbishop's Place, where brown was the predominant background colour. The Archbishop accepted the apologies of the *Sunday Press* with good grace. 1958 also saw Leslie Nivison leave the editorship of the *Evening Herald.* He was succeeded by Pearse Kelly. Two Dublin journalists of the period were reputed to have once been in a certain illegal organisation. There, they were said to have sentenced each other to death. Happily, that fate never overtook them.

In the late 1950s, Dr Noel Browne, the former Health Minister and TD, was active in promulgating Dail debates on the financing of the *Irish Press.* He was unsuccessful in having disclosed the ultimate secrets of the *Irish Press* financial structure. Only ten years before Browne's efforts, one of the Monument Creamery Ryans, a shareholder in the paper, became so exasperated with what she considered the lack of progress being made by the *Irish Press* that she had committed the ultimate heresy of putting an advertisement in the *Irish Independent.*

Gramophone records were still on the black market and she said that she was willing to swop her *Irish Press* shares for gramophone records!

Douglas Gageby joined *The Irish Times* in 1959, its centenary year, when the directors paid out a celebration bonus to the members of staff — "five pounds or one week's wages, whichever is the lower". Reporters used to jokingly subtract the number of deaths reported in the paper from the circulation figure, then standing at a lowly 33,000. In 1959, Gageby was approached by George Hetherington, managing director, and invited to become managing editor. At first Gageby refused, later changing his mind when a directorship was offered. He left the *Evening Press* to become joint managing editor with Hetherington.

The *Times Pictorial* suffered various changes of editor and titles as it struggled to keep alive. When it closed in 1958, it was known as the *Irish Pictorial*. Young members of staff, such as Jim Downey and Eoin Neeson, went on to greater prominence. After the closure, the next disaster to befall Westmoreland Street was the acquisition by *The Irish Times* of the *Dublin Evening Mail* in 1960. The purchase cost £200,000, but the rot was too far gone to be reversed; the *Evening Press* was making great inroads into the Dublin evening newspaper market. After Joe Anderson's retirement in 1958, several editors followed, including Norman Browne, but the competition posed by the brash new *Evening Press* was too stiff. Ironically, the man who did most to set the *Evening Press* on the right road, Douglas Gageby, was soon to become editor of *The Irish Times*. After the takeover, Alan Montgomery was appointed editor of the *Evening Mail* for a short time, before being transferred to the editorship of *The Irish Times* in succession to Newman.

A little bit of newspaper history died with the *Mail* takeover. The *Dublin Daily Express* had been founded in 1851 as a Tory paper, with the help of William Howard Russell, the famous Co Dublin-born correspondent of the London *Times*. The *Dublin Daily Express* folded as a newspaper in 1921, but every publication day thereafter, the *Evening Mail* printed just one copy of a special single sheet issue, containing the masthead of the *Express* and the date, for registration purposes, to keep the title alive. That practice ended at the close of 1960, following the takeover of the *Mail.*

Ted Keane died in 1960; he had only ruled the roost at the *Kilkenny People* for thirteen years, but he had made his presence felt in no uncertain fashion. His fiery words were widely read, yet when he mellowed, he often referred the old style cost of living as "thrippence a pint." After Ted Keane's death, his son, John Kerry Keane, took over as owner and editor of the paper, positions he holds to this day.

Shortly afterwards, Alex Newman fell from grace at *The Irish Times*. A classical scholar by inclination and temperament, he performed to perfection on radio programmes like "Information Please". He was regarded as an exceptionally able Number Two to Smyllie's Number

One, but when he was translated from his role of "Lord in Waiting", his lack of effectiveness as an editor became apparent. Widely regarded as having the very essence of politeness and gentility, he used to shock friends by telling them to "kiss his arse". When he was drunk, his language grew steadily more profane and his obscenities were said to have been audible over a wide area of *The Irish Times'* office. At home, he was troubled by a gravely handicapped son.

When the bombshell struck, a shaken Newman emerged from a meeting of the directors to tell fellow journalists that "the bastards have got me." He had been sacked, coldly and clinically, in the best newspaper style, with no "thank you" for thirty years of loyal service.

1. Alan Reeve, who drew this Palace Bar, Dublin, caricature.
2. Ewart Milne.
3. W. A. Newman.
4. J. P. Colbert.
5. G. H. Burrows.
6. Lynn Doyle.
7. G. J. C. T. O'Mahony.
8. L. H. Yodaiken.
9. A. J. Leventhal.
10. R. Farren.
11. F. McManus.
12. M. J. McManus.
13. E. Sheehy.
14. Maurice Walsh.
15. Tom.
16. P. Kavanagh.
17. P. O'Connor.
18. R. C. Ferguson.
19. Flann O'Brien.
20. Esmunde Little.
21. Liam Redmund.
22. R. M. Smylus.
23. William Conor.
24. Harry Kernoff.
25. Donagh MacDonagh.
26. Brinsley MacNamara.
27. I. M. Chichester.
28. Seumas O'Sullivan.
29. Sean O'Sullivan.
30. Jack.
31. G. P. Leitch.
32. Austin Clarke.
33. Cathal O'Shannon.
34. Padraic Fallon.
35. Arthur Duff.
36. Jerome Connor.
37. F. R. Higgins.
38. Desmond Rushton.
39. Sean.
40. David Sears.
41. Mick.

He spent the rest of the few years remaining to him writing for the *Irish Press.* Alan Montgomery took over as editor.

At the *Irish Independent* in 1960, the venerable Frank Geary retired as editor. He was succeeded by assistant editor, Michael Rooney. When the earthquake struck Agadir in Morocco in 1960, the *Evening Press* managed to get first-hand details from an Irish eye-witness. Dáithí P. Hanly, then Dublin city architect, was there on his honeymoon and a 'phone call from the *Evening Press* gave the paper a great "scoop".

An even greater "earthquake" was about to strike Ireland and its newspapers; on the very last night of 1961, the Irish television service opened with a gala programme at the Gresham Hotel, Dublin.

CHAPTER IX

Foley's inheritance
1962-1968

Today's cigarette is a Bristol. Only 2/7 for 20.
EVENING HERALD, 1962

Dublin-Isle of Man return £5 4s. Aer Lingus.
SUNDAY PRESS, 1966

If it's Saturday, it must be Lemon's. (Cartoon by Warner)
THE IRISH TIMES, 1966

At first, the threat from the new-fangled medium of television was laughed off by newspaper owners, while many journalists, such as Cathal O'Shannon of *The Irish Times,* Jim McGuinness and Des Fisher (both *Irish Press*) were tempted into TV. Revenue dipped for both national and provincial newspapers as scarce advertising money was channelled into TV.

John Kerry Keane, newly arrived in the editorial chair at the *Kilkenny People* and full of crusading zest, was determined that the paper now in his charge would continue to live up to its reputation set by Lennox Robinson, the Abbey playwright and habitué of the Number 15 tram, who regarded the *Kilkenny People* and the *Kerryman* as the two classic weeklies in Ireland. Keane took up the case of an eighty-year old Callan, Co Kilkenny, lady who was deprived of her old age pension because the local welfare office found she had been knitting and sewing for profit. Despite her protest that her earnings were minute, she was ordered to repay about £80 to the Department of Social Welfare. Keane found that the lady was suffering from malnutrition and was so destitute that she depended on the charity of a niece who had four children and an unemployed husband. Keane fired off a telegram to the Minister, ran the story on the front page, had the old lady's case investigated and her pension restored.

Recently deceased was the *Sligo Independent,* just at the start of the

decade. It was one of the last Protestant papers in the Republic. The *Sligo Independent and West of Ireland Telegraph* was founded in 1855; William David Peebles, father of Ivan Peebles, a past president of the NUJ and chief sub editor of the *Ballymena Observer* and *East Antrim Times,* bought the paper from Alexander Gillmor in 1921 and for the next forty years, ran it virtually single-handedly. With the departure of staff, it became impossible to run; Mr Peebles himself was in his seventies.

October, 1961, saw the passing of a great Belfast newspaper cartoon tradition. Since 1898, just four years after *Ulster Saturday Night* made its first appearance, "The Doings of Larry O'Hooligan" were published every week. The last artist to draw the cartoon was Billy Conn, who was also a noted contributor to *Dublin Opinion,* for which he did full page black and white drawings every week for many years. In more recent years, his Northern cartoon tradition has been ably maintained by Rowel Friers, who contributes weekly to such publications as the

Bertie Trimble of the Impartial Reporter, **Enniskillen, enjoying a chat with President de Valera at a function in the Gresham Hotel, Dublin, in the mid-1960s. They were exactly the same age.**

Wesley Boyd, head of news at RTE, via the Northern Whig **and** The Irish Times. *–RTE*

Belfast Telegraph and *The Irish Times.* Meanwhile, "Larry O'Hooligan' with his tall hat may have long faded into the North's folk memory, but the Malcolm Brodie soccer column still lives on; first written in 1953, it is claimed as Ireland's longest-running football column.

Just before Christmas, 1961, Frank Geary, once chief reporter of the *Kilkenny People,* died. He had retired as editor of the *Irish Independent* the previous year. One of his proudest moments had been the Pope's telegram on his silver jubilee as editor: "Holy Father sends Fraternal felicitations."

The first of the great shocks suffered by the newspaper industry after the advent of RTE television was the death of another Protestant paper, the Dublin *Evening Mail.* For years, newsboys had cried out: "Herald O' Mail". "Jiggs and Maggie" and "Mandrake" cartoons, An Oige notes, cycling notes, Letters to the Editor, Man about Town, and a host of other small, familiar features had built up the *Mail* into a great favourite of Dublin newspaper readers. With a circulation of around 100,000 copies a night, it brought out its first edition at the gentlemanly time of 3 p.m. A small crowd used to gather at the dispatch room door at the back of the Parliament Street buildings waiting for the first edition, with its jobs advertisements. Great characters worked for the *Evening Mail,* such as Jimmy Doran O'Reilly, who had a tremendous reputation for turning out features on the personalities of the day. Journalists who are well-known today, such as Frank Cairns, the property editor of the *Irish Independent,* worked on the *Mail.* So too did Michael Hand, now editor of the *Sunday Independent.* The young Hand is remembered arriving hotfoot from Drogheda and taking the most menial help-out job in the *Mail* editorial department; soon, he made himself so useful that his promotion was inevitable. After the launch of the *Evening Press* in 1954, the writing was on the wall for the *Mail.*

The scooters used for delivering the *Evening Press,* the Bush system for countrywide copy inserts, its brash editorial approach, its dynamic canvassing of small advertisements, all these and a host of other factors ensured the death, little by little, of the *Evening Mail.* Only the board of *The Irish Times* failed to realise that the much-loved *Mail* was beyond hope of redemption. One journalist who saw the take-over happen said that the *Times* had neither the financial resources nor the editorial manpower to revitalise the *Mail. The Irish Times* paid £200,000 for the *Mail* and the newspaper was said to have lost the same sum again in the two years it was printed and published in Westmoreland Street. After Alan Montgomery became editor of *The Irish Times,* John Healy was appointed editor of the *Dublin Evening Mail;* he was the last man to occupy the editorial chair there. The paper changed from broadsheet to tabloid and went after a country readership for the first time in its life. The measures were too little, too late; by the time the last issue was published on July 19, 1962, circulation was down to just

David Luke with the one that got away — the Sun series of newspapers published in Dublin and various provincial centres in early 1967.

over 50,000. Copies of the last issue were signed by such notables as Seán O Ceallachain (the sports journalist), Jack Mooney, Des Murphy (now PR man with Glaxo), Ken Gray, Charlie Orr, John Healy, Paddy Downey, Michael Hand, Peter Byrne and Jim Downey. The last issue advertised cream with fresh strawberries at the Monument and Liptons Golden Tips tea for 1/10 a quarter pound. Normally, when a newspaper suspends publication, it happens overnight, but in the case of the *Mail,* it was a lingering death. In order to facilitate the paper's workers, publication did not stop for three weeks after the fatal decision was taken by the board. When the *Evening Mail* closed, editor Healy was temporarily out of a job. He had transferred from the *Sunday Review* to the *Mail* and when the latter paper closed, Ted Nealon vacated the editor's chair he had held at the *Sunday Review* to go into RTE television and give Healy a job. "It was a nice, gentlemanly gesture and we are still the best of friends," Nealon comments now.

The start of 1962 had seen the *Larne Times,* founded by the *Belfast Telegraph* in 1891, change its name to the *East Antrim Times.* Under editor Emil Thompson, the readers of Larne, Carrickfergus and district were promised better and brighter coverage, all for 4d a copy. Perhaps the best-known "graduate" of the paper in recent times has been Diane

Jim Morton of Morton Newspapers, Lurgan: when the owners of the two existing newspapers in Lisburn, Co Antrim, refused to sell out to him, he started the Ulster Star in 1957. The two rival newspapers later closed down. He also installed Ireland's first web offset printing press in 1962.

Harron, who started her journalistic career there and who is now a reporter for BBC television. 1962 also saw a young Northern journalist "graduating" to Dublin, following the time-worn track of so many predecessors. Andrew Hamilton had learned his trade with the *Impartial Reporter* in Enniskillen for four years before moving to *the Irish Times,* where he is now motoring correspondent. He had shown signs of his future speciality at the Enniskillen paper, where he is remembered even today for his extraordinary ability to memorise car numbers.

Not long after the death of the *Dublin Evening Mail,* other newspaper owners were fighting valiant rearguard actions. Pat Dunne of the *Leitrim Observer* had fought to the death against changing the "tablecloth" format of his paper; the uncut paper was also extremely useful as a tablecloth for its readers and Dunne only started cutting the paper at about the time the *Mail* folded in Dublin. At this same time, he also pondered the ultimate technological change for his paper, the regular use of news photographs. Dunne was one of the last of the great traditionalists in country newspapers; he disliked bringing the concluding paragraph in the report of a court case to the top of the story. If a county councillor complained about being left out of the previous week's report of the county council, Dunne simply met the man in a Carrick-on-Shannon pub and made up a few soothing words to slip into next week's report. Bluff and blunt, often dressed in a "salt and pepper" tweed suit, he would first ask travellers looking for their money: "How many dogs are there in the well this month?" A sucker for children, he held a Children's Pay Day every Saturday, when he would solemnly hand out sixpence to each child present. He was a very cautious man, very wary of libel. His great belief was "if in doubt, leave out". As a result, he is said never to have caught for libel in his entire career.

Across the border, a genuine technical revolution was taking place, as significant in its way as the introduction of the rotary newspaper press and the Linotype composing machine in the nineteenth century. Web offset printing, pioneered in the USA, means far faster running speeds on the press, big improvements in reproductions of photographs and the easy use of colours, right up to full colour work. The Morton group in Lurgan, a fast-expanding newspaper firm that owned such papers as the *Londonderry Sentinel* and the *Ulster Star,* installed a four unit web offset press in 1962, the first of its type in Ireland. The following year, the Record Press in Bray, Co Wicklow, installed the first web offset press in the Republic. Soon afterwards, the new press was being used to print the *Farmer's Journal,* a printing contract that only thirteen years previously, had boosted the fortunes of the *Dublin Evening Mail.*

The North also pioneered in journalism; the *Belfast Telegraph* had had a woman's editor since 1920, probably the first in Ireland, a dour but able lady called Gertie Corscadden. She ruled the roost for nearly forty years, being succeeded eventually by Betty Lowry, who later remembered that even though she was woman's editor, under that unsmiling, straight-laced editor John Sayers, she often did not have a page to edit. Still, the principle of having women journalists was established at the *Belfast Telegraph* well in advance of most Dublin newspapers.

The *Belfast Telegraph* was all prepared to continue its time-honoured ways, until the shock announcement that Roy Thomson, the Canadian and UK press magnate, was making a bid for the firm. Thomson, by his own admission, was a failure in life until he was forty; then he started to build up his empire of Canadian newspaper and radio stations. At the age of sixty, he bought the *Scotsman* in Edinburgh and soon came up against the clannish aloofness of Scottish society. His red socks were reckoned to be a serious deterrent to social acceptance, but his trials and tribulations in Edinburgh, where taking the small advertisements off the front page of the *Scotsman* was equivalent to having the Pope bless the Presbyterian church, were nothing compared with his battle in Belfast.

Following the death of William Baird in a car crash in 1953, most of the *Telegraph* shares were in the hands of a trust, some held for a minor. Roy Thomson found himself locked in a court battle over the ownership of the minor's shares; the case was settled in Thomson's favour and he became the new owner of the *Belfast Telegraph*. He said later that he had found that W & G Baird had articles of association which, to his Canadian eyes, looked very peculiar. "I had no idea what formidable characters were opposed to me when I put my innocent toe tentatively into these dark waters."

He described the newspaper as a stout pillar of the Unionist establishment in Northern Ireland and went on: "It can be imagined that there was alarm in the bridge-playing echelons of the establishment when it was known that a bid was possible from someone like me, unpledged in Ulster politics and already notorious for giving editors complete freedom of editorial opinion."

After the case was over, he remarked: "Such imputations of my integrity and honour as were made in Belfast have never been made in any other court, or as far as I know, in any other place." Lord Thomson said that he would never return to that tragic city, even though he owned its main newspaper. He kept his word, although his son Kenneth, who runs what is now a world-wide organisation, has made occasional visits. Since the Thomson take-over of the *Belfast Telegraph* and its weekly newspapers, no other Irish newspaper or Irish newspaper group has been bought over from outside the country.

1962 saw the mild-mannered Francis Carty move from the *Irish Press* (where he was succeeded by Joe Walsh) to the *Sunday Press*, in succession

Judith Rosenfield, once woman's editor of the Northern Whig, **Belfast**. In a prolific career, she wrote several plays, worked for the BBC in Belfast and compiled several books. Three of the books, one on astrology, one a guide book and one on health care, were on subjects she had no interest in and no knowledge of, according to her sister, Ray, a Belfast critic for The Irish Times.
–Ray Rosenfield

Lord Thomson, who fought an acrimonious legal battle to win control of the Belfast Telegraph **just over twenty years ago.**
–Thomson Organisation

to its founding editor, Lt Col Matt Feehan. Carty maintained the successful editorial formula that ensured the *Sunday Press'* place as the top selling newspaper in Ireland, well over 400,000 copies a week, to a large extent outside church gates. Liam Pedlar's original decision in 1949 to rope in the parish priests had been sound. Just before Carty took over the paper, it acquired its first woman journalist: Brid Mahon. She had been working for the Folklore Commission and was asked by Feehan if she would take over the page he planned for women on a six weeks' temporary basis, until he found someone permanent. That permanent person was Brid Mahon herself. The six weeks turned out to be ten years. She remembers that Dick Wilkes, father of Alan Wilkes, was second in command; he was a thorough newspaper man and a thorough-going gentleman, in her recollection. The two idioms are far from compatible. Gerry Fox was news editor — he is still there, as Number Two on the *Sunday Press*. So too was Tom Hennigan.

Once, the chef in a top city centre hotel did a recipe for Christmas cake in the *Sunday Press;* when it was set, a teaspoon of salt came out as a tablespoon of salt. Some unknowing cooks followed the recipe to the very letter; the following week, an irate reader stormed into the front office at Burgh Quay and demanded profuse apologies. Hennigan was sent down to pacify the woman; he trotted down to the front office and talked briefly with the woman, who promptly thrust a piece of cake into his fist. He took a lingering bite and in the interests of the vast *Sunday Press* readership, pronounced it the best cake he had ever tasted.

Visits to Birr, Co Offaly in 1961 and 1962 by Princess Margaret and Lord Snowdon (her then husband's mother lived at Birr Castle) aroused the ire of Republicans in Ireland. The visits also provided Birr publicans with a substantial influx of funds. On one visit, remembers Tony Kelly, Cathal O' Shannon and himself covered the event for *The Irish Times.* About a hundred other journalists arrived in Birr with similar intentions. While the Princess was staying in Birr Castle, it was locked up to prevent the newsmen getting near, so with the help of a £5 note from every reporter, all enjoyed a rip-roaring party in Dooly's Hotel. The reporters were so drunk that when Princess Margaret strolled through the town at 11 a.m. next morning to attend Communion in the local Church of Ireland, everyone missed the story. 1963 saw Jimmy Fanning close down the once-Unionist *Midland Chronicle* (previously *Offaly Chronicle*) in Birr, in its 118th year of publication. By the time of its demise, it was down to four pages, with little or no advertising. The Roscrea to Birr branch railway line had just closed down and Fanning came back to Birr on the very last train.

Brid Mahon claims to have been the first person to give editorial coverage to the two young brothers, Peter and Mark Keaveney, when they started their first hairdressing salon in Grafton Street. They had borrowed £500 for the venture, recalls Brid, and their mother was terrified of them ending up in the bankruptcy court. Both are now extremely wealthy, from a business that has expanded and prospered mightily. During Brid Mahon's ten year stint at the *Sunday Press*, other women journalists came in, like Patsy Dyke, to do the Saturday night round-up that she had pioneered on the *Sunday Review*, and Angela McNamara, who started to give Christian advice to the lovelorn. Ironically, Brid's sister, Brenda, performed the same function for a while with the *Sunday Independent*.

Another senior figure at the *Sunday Press* featured largely and for weeks afterwards in the much-retailed story of his overnight drunkenness. Apparently, he had attended a function in Dublin on behalf of the paper and became so drunk that he was quite incapable of being brought home, let alone drive. So colleagues took him to another hotel, somewhere on the south side of Dublin, sneaked him into an empty room and left him sprawled on the bed. When he came to in the morning, he spent some time wondering exactly where he was: one version of the story, still retailed twenty years later, has him creeping down the fire escape to bypass the reception, while the other version has him having to pay a not inconsiderable sum for spending an unexpected night in the luxury hotel.

In 1963, a great newspaper tradition ended in the North of Ireland, with the closure of the *Northern Whig*, Belfast. Founded in 1824, it had long been the superfluous third morning newspaper in the city. The

William Peebles, forced to close down his Sligo Independent **newspaper over twenty years ago because of staff shortages. It was one of the very last Protestant papers in the Republic.**

William Peebles (left) together with his son Ivan, hands over copies of the Sligo Independent **(which closed down in 1961) to Sligo county library.**

Belfast *News Letter* was the Protestant market leader, while the *Irish News* served its Catholic readership faithfully. The latter paper did however have the odd Protestant reader, attracted by its excellent horse and greyhound racing coverage. For some years previously, the *Northern Whig* had run at a substantial loss; in 1962-63 alone, the paper lost over £30,000. Five journalists were dismissed as part of an economy drive; the remaining twenty went on strike in July, 1963.

All the other eighty workers remained at their posts, but the paper had severe difficulty in maintaining production. During the course of the strike, claims were made by the late Betty Sinclair, the Belfast trade unionist, that the paper's circulation had dropped to 19,000, a claim refuted by the management, which said that the paper's daily sales remained at 32,000. Towards the end of September came the announcement from the paper's management that it was closing forthwith. The *Northern Whig,* a paper in what was called the Liberal-Unionist tradition, had been a daily paper since 1858. Among its employees just before it closed in 1963 were Wesley Boyd (London editor), who went on to become *Irish Times'* diplomatic correspondent and who is now head of news at RTE and Judith Rosenfield, the Belfast journalist who died recently and who was woman's editor.

A new publication was born, thanks to Hugh McLaughlin, who surfaced once again, as he was to do many times during the ensuing twenty years. A popular story in newspaper circles at the time had

Front page of the Cork Examiner **detailing President Kennedy's assassination in November, 1963.**

McLaughlin's wife, Nuala, getting into conversation during a train journey with Nicholas Leonard, then business and finance editor of *The Irish Times.* By the end of the journey, the upshot was that Leonard decided to go along with the McLaughlins' idea for a business magazine, edited by himself. Twenty years ago, *Business and Finance* came into being; eventually, Leonard, through the association with his great friend Tony O'Reilly, became a director of Independent Newspapers and is now London editor for that group. At this time, another financial genius was making his mark in the pages of *The Irish Times.* A young economist called Garret FitzGerald, now An Taoiseach, wrote a series of brilliant economic articles that did much to prepare the way for Ireland's eventual inclusion in the EEC.

Tom Hennigan, who crossed the river from Burgh Quay to do the Evening Herald **diary.**

The summer of 1963 had seen the visit of President Kennedy to Ireland; he received an emotional welcome from vast crowds in Dublin, Co Wexford, Cork and Galway. All along his itinerary, tremendous throngs of people came out to greet the boyish looking Irish-American President of the United States of America. No visit to Ireland by a foreign dignitary had ever proved so successful and moving; just before his 'plane left Shannon, he was wished long life and an early return to Ireland. That was never to be; barely five months later, he was assassinated in Dallas, Texas. His shooting was the end of the great American dream; as the news came over the infant RTE television, given by Charles Mitchel, who looked pale-faced even in black and white, the Irish nation was plunged into grief and wailing. News of Kennedy's killing came through on the Friday night; like everyone else, Matt Farrell had an exact recollection of where he was at the time, with a group of Burgh Quay friends, having a quiet, pre-weekend drink in a nearby pub. They immediately went back to the office and produced a special late edition of the *Evening Press* (about 20,000 copies in all), which came out at 10 p.m. For the best part of a hundred years, Dublin newspapers produced special editions for particular disasters (the worse the news, the better they sold). This late edition of the *Evening Press* was probably the last such "late special" produced in Ireland. Staff at the *Sunday Review* had rather more time (twenty-four hours) to put together a twenty page special on the life and death of President John F. Kennedy; as they unfurled this great Greek tragedy, their own was also being played out. Under editor John Healy, this was the last issue of the *Sunday Review.* It never quite reached the magic circulation figure of 200,000, said to represent break-even point. RTE television was siphoning off much potential advertising.

Some sources say that if the *Sunday Review* had continued for another six months, it would have survived to this day, removing the necessity for the *Sunday World.* In the event, it was an accountants' decision to close the paper. 1963 saw the *Sunday Independent* make a premature and heavily loss-making excursion into a colour magazine, printed on the gravure presses of the Independent group in Dublin. The magazine

Front page of the last issue of the Sunday Review, **November 24, 1963.**

lasted from November, 1963 (just as the *Sunday Review* folded) until the following May and although the paper achieved a record circulation then of around 400,000 copies a week (it has since lost some 150,000 of that circulation), the magazine venture lost £4,000 a week because it couldn't attract sufficient advertising, remembers the then editor, Hector Legge. One innovation by Legge at that time has happily proved more durable; Legge brought in a journalist called Ciaran Carty, who was working for a newspaper in the north-east of England. He applied for a job as a sub-editor on the *Sunday Independent* and Legge says that he recommended him to the board, despite the fact that Ciaran Carty's father Francis was then editor of the rival *Sunday Press.* Ciaran Carty is still with the *Sunday Independent,* as arts editor.

With the loss of the *Radio Review* (when RTE started producing its own programme guide), the *Dublin Evening Mail* and the *Sunday Review, The Irish Times* went through a particularly troubled patch in its existence. Alan Montgomery left after two years as editor of *The Irish Times* to take over public relations at Guinness. Stories of the time say that Montgomery was called in to advise the brewery firm on selecting a new public relations head and that he ended up being appointed himself. He says that it didn't happen like that and that the main, immediate cause of him leaving the paper was the refusal the board to give him a car. When Montgomery (known to everyone in the newspaper business as "Monty") left for Guinness, Michael Rooney of the *Irish Independent* told him, in jest, that he had let the side down. "Editors are either fired or die on the job. They never retire."

Montgomery does however admit that too many of the people

working in the editorial department of the paper were personal friends to allow him to wield the axe that was needed at the end of the Newman era. The new infusion had to be left to Donal Foley, Douglas Gageby and Major McDowell. For four years, Douglas Gageby, by his own admission, had been "pottering around" as joint managing editor of *The Irish Times,* a largely administrative job. He took over as editor from Montgomery in October, 1963, and with his colleagues, set about revitalising the fortunes of *The Irish Times,* whose circulation stood at about 35,000. Gageby was to finish the task of turning the paper into a truly national publication (in every sense of the word), a job started before the war when Smyllie started slipping the paper away from the dying fortunes of Southern Unionism, unseen by most of his readers.

Just as important as Gageby's appointment as editor was that of Donal Foley as news editor. For many people on *The Irish Times,* the day in January, 1964, that Foley started with *The Irish Times* in Dublin was the day the real revolution started on the newspaper. Foley was born and brought up in Ring, Co Waterford; towards the end of the war, he left his humble porter's job at Waterford railway station and went to London. He started his newspaper work as a junior in the *Irish Press* office there; after a spell as London reporter for the Irish News Agency, he returned to the *Irish Press* London office. In Fleet Street, he was working among a gang of great Irish reporters and made the most of several notable "scoops", for he had an innate news sense. One night during the IRA border campaign, he was drinking in a pub in Fleet Street, London. Arthur Christiansen, the editor of the *Daily Express,* was there with a colleague and Donal was chiding him over the fact that it rarely carried a good Irish story and that when it did, it was usually petty. A big Irishman came in and whispered in Donal's ear; he shot out of the pub after 'phoning the *Irish Press* office in London; twenty minutes later, he came back with a wide grin on his face and told Christiansen and his colleague: "You'll have a big Irish story on page one of your London edition tomorrow."

Foley was quite right about the story. The British authorities had given permission for the London GAA Board to play two important matches on the sports ground attached to the British Army's Arsenal barracks. In turn, Sinn Fein had persuaded the London Board to give them permission to take up a collection at the matches. Eventually, Foley left the *Irish Press,* because Major de Valera refused to pay the small rise sought by the reporter. He crossed over to *The Irish Times'* London office making a most bizarre match with Sir John Arnott, of the Arnott family which had once owned the paper. On one occasion, Arnott, who had just broken off an engagement with a girl in England, is said to have pawned the very large ring with equally large stone in aid of *The Irish Times* fund, during one of the paper's financial crises. Arnott gave the impression of being an Empire Loyalist, very upper class, tapping out the "London Letter". When he answered the telephone and said "Arnott here," Foley used to be intensely annoyed, yet the pair of them, as dissimilar as one could imagine, got on well together. Foley loved London (his widow Pat is English), but it was not his ruination as it had been with Terry Ward. In London, Foley's social conscience was very much in evidence, ever since the days just after the war when he and the whole London-Irish "gang" were active supporters of the British Labour Party.

One London incident related by his close friend, Wesley Boyd, demonstrates Donal Foley's great hatred of injustice. On a summer's evening, some twenty-five years ago, Boyd and Foley were wandering their way from Fleet Street to the Irish Club by way of Ward's Irish House in Piccadilly when they saw a young drug addict being roughly arrested by the police. Foley was irate; he went over and waved his press card: "Watch it, we're journalists and we're observing all this." One of the young policemen glanced at Donal and said: "Oh, fuck off Paddy, can't you see we're busy." After all those years in London, Donal took the brave step of coming to the head office of *The Irish Times* in Dublin, a city he had never worked in. Too often, correspondents come back to Dublin and slip into an easy obscurity, just as Terry Ward seemed to lose some of his fire once he returned from London and Bill Sheedy, once London editor of *The Irish Times,* could often be found at the early morning pubs near the Dublin markets after he had returned to Ireland. Not so with Donal Foley; his best work was to come.

1964 saw the end of a once-great newspaper dream in Derry, the *Derry Standard,* run by its workers as a co-operative since 1932. Just as in Belfast, there was just room for one Protestant and one Catholic morning paper, so too in Derry, just one Protestant paper (the *Sentinel)* and one Catholic paper (the *Journal)* were able to survive. 1964 also saw the end of the *Belfast Weekly Telegraph;* weekly newspapers were fast becoming an anachronism. The *Weekly Irish Independent* had closed down four years previously and now that the man most associated with the *Belfast Weekly Telegraph,* John Caughey, gave up writing, that paper too closed down. Caughey had officially retired from the *Belfast Telegraph,* where he was highly regarded for his sports writings, as well as for being one of the city's few teetotal journalists, in 1960. However, the arrangement was made that as long as he was able to keep writing his "Calling All Exiles" column, the *Weekly Telegraph* would stay in existence. That column was so popular that hundreds of people used to queue at the *Telegraph* office on a Friday to buy copies early and mail them to their relatives overseas. Restyled into *Ulsterweek,* the paper only survived for eighteen months, before it was sold off to Morton Newspapers in Lurgan. For them, the new paper proved a poor investment, as did *Scene* magazine at this same period. Mortons promptly rechristened the paper *City Week* and turned it into a purely Belfast publication.

Caughey did not long survive the demise of his wife and the *Weekly Telegraph*. In 1913, he had fallen in love with Mary "Mollie" McMullan, a trainee bookbinder in the *Belfast Telegraph* jobbing department; they married two years later. They were a devoted couple for fifty-one years and when Mary died in 1966, at the age of seventy-five, he started to die also. It took him four months to go, but as he told his family — two sons and three daughters — with "Mollie" away, he did not wish to live any longer.

While Caughey's contributions to journalism finished, a well-known country newspaper editor found his services dispensed with overnight. After meeting a female of standing from his home city in a nearby seaside resort, he is said to have written a somewhat unflattering portrait of her in the next issue of his paper. The directors considered him unsatisfactory, but he continued to make a good living freelancing. On the *Cork Examiner*, a stoneman called Nelis O'Callaghan, who had been taken on in 1899 on three months' trial, asked Ted Crosbie of the owning family, "Am I satisfactory?"

"In my estimation, you are very satisfactory. Why do you ask?" replied Crosbie.

"Well", said Nelis, "your grandfather took me on a trial basis and I've never been told since whether I'm satisfactory."

A proof reader of the period at the *Cork Examiner* was said to have been the only man in Munster who could wear a collar without a shirt; he wore it above a gansey. Then there was the comp who carried a copy of a sheet marked "Thoughts and Trifles" in his back pocket. When he was setting the legendary *Holly Bough* at Christmas, this sheet was whipped out to fill any blank spaces. Then there was the case of the sack oozing blood in the machine room, for one of the printers who was on day shift, a sheep's head was brought in from the market once a week. Suddenly, the man was changed to night shift, but the man bringing the sheep's head didn't know this, so he just left the sack for the man to collect — and ooze blood over the floor.

Lemass and O'Neill had their historic but ultimately unproductive cross-border "Summit" meetings early in 1965. When Captain O'Neill came to Dublin, one young reporter with *The Irish Times*, Dermot Mullane, now with RTE television, spent an entire morning glued to the railings outside Iveagh House, home of the Department of Foreign Affairs, to discover the identity of the mystery guest, whose name was carefully concealed from virtually everyone in the Department itself. Mullane landed himself a minor "scoop".

Another historic breakthrough came at the *Drogheda Independent;* in common with many other provincial newspapers of the time, it started putting its lead stories on the front page. Advertisements, for the first time in its history, started inside on page two. The nineteenth century ways of one of its editors, Michael A. Casey, still lived on in the memory of its staff during the mid-1960s. One exploit in particular

Mary Kenny in her mini-skirted days.
–Film and Illustrations Library RTE

stood out as typifying life on country newspapers, even as late as twenty years ago. Under Casey's regime, the paper carried regular weekly religious articles with such headlines as "Christ the King" and "Catholic Calendar". One week, a lengthy report on the provision of a new sewerage scheme for Drogheda was set in type; all the pages had been locked in their formes for printing. The reporter who wrote the story was adamant that it was so important that the "Christ the King" story would have to be lifted out. The paper appeared with the sewerage story; when George Hussey took the first copies off the press to Casey's house in Newfoundwell, Casey roared: "Who put that shit there. Where is Christ the King?" He rushed to the printing works, stopped the press and had "Christ the King" put back in its rightful place. Old newspaper ways died hard, not only in Limerick, where staff still had keen memories of the recent furore over their plans for photographic coverage in the *Limerick Leader* of the Kilmallock murder case, but in Drogheda and all other provincial towns. Still, there were moments of light relief. During a Co Louth funeral, there was much rain. A mourner slipped in the mud and fell in on top of the coffin. "This", said the local paper, "added further gloom to the proceedings."

The year after Donal Foley came to *The Irish Times* in Dublin, Eileen O'Brien joined as a reporter. A most self-effacing and charming lady, she is widely regarded as one of the best reporters in the country, having served a thorough-going apprenticeship under Dan O'Connell on the *Connacht Tribune* in Galway. She also has one of the strongest social consciences, as seen in her "Candida" column on Mondays. Together with Foley, she started the "Tuarascáil" weekly news feature in Irish, which has continued to the present day. Foley, coming from Ring, Co Waterford, was a native Irish speaker and one of his many innovations at *The Irish Times* was to give full support to the Irish language, a far cry from the days when Irish words in the paper had to be set in italics because they were foreign.

As Eileen O'Brien was settling into *The Irish Times*, Maureen Browne was causing a great sensation at the *Limerick Leader*. Maureen, wife of Michael O'Toole, who used to do the "Dubliner's Diary" column in the *Evening Press*, is now a freelance medical journalist in Dublin. She remembers being the first woman reporter to join the *Limerick Leader*, in October, 1964; together with Micheline McCormack of the *Sunday World*, who had trained on the *Nationalist and Leinster Times*, Carlow, she was among the very first women journalists to work on a country newspaper.

After Eileen O'Brien, Mary Maher joined *The Irish Times*. Donal Foley decided to start recruiting women journalists and in so doing, he started a real revolution in Irish newspapers. Despite her name, Mary Maher comes from Chicago, where she had worked on a local newspaper. Other women writers came along, like Elgy Gillespie (English, like another noted *Irish Times'* writer, Michael Viney) and Maeve Binchy, who had been a school teacher. Donal Foley did his recruiting in the nearest pub, on the basis that he could get to know the people he was taking on much better that way. He detested the thought of a formal interview. When Caroline Walsh, a daughter of Mary Lavin, the novelist, joined the paper, he took her for a drink on her first night, to Bowes, the Fleet Street pub. She ordered an orange: "Oh God, we haven't hired a Holy Mary have we. Would you sit down and have a proper drink." Foley also steered away from recruits with orthodox newspaper backgrounds; people like Maeve Binchy, who turned out to be the most perceptive and successful writers, did not have a standard journalistic training. He was a bad man on the 'phone, all grunts and "yes" and "no". As often as not, he would hang up in the middle of a conversation. He was so appalling on the 'phone that as Maeve Binchy recalled, you would often end a conversation with him wondering whether you had been fired or dropped from his list of friends.

Mary Maher remembers that when she had newly arrived at *The Irish Times*, there were rows morning, noon and night, mostly inspired by Donal. The paper started to stir from the long lethargy with which it had been inflicted since the days of Smyllie. The stories, often concerning drink, told about Donal Foley would run into scores if not hundreds. A very persistent public relations consultant had persuaded at least four *Irish Times'* journalists to attend the launch of some minor product, lured with food, drink and a lift to the "do". En route, the public relations hustler announced her gratitude: I'm so glad you came, I was terrified that everyone would go to the Claddagh reception tonight. "Donal said from the back seat: "Jesus, let me out — I knew there was somewhere else I wanted to go." Tact was never his strongest point.

Yet, there was another side to Foley the lovable teddy bear, as Jim Downey, deputy editor, recalls. "Everyone will tell and retell the legion of Foley stories, but he had another side — the Foley of the intense social conscience, the passionate arguer for his vision of Ireland and for everything that was truly best in Ireland. "Under his guide, *The Irish Times* became a sharper and better paper; news coverage improved, the women journalists breathed life into the new style womens' pages — knitting patterns were out. He also did the "Man Bites Dog" column, a satirical look at the week's news that was often more realistic than the real news copy. The *Man Bites Dog* books went into ten editions; another of his innovations was the "Saturday Column" in *The Irish Times,* a miscellany of mainly political news and gossip. The column started in 1976 and is still going strong nearly ten years later, under Conor O'Clery. When Donal Foley died in the summer of 1981, a lamp went out in *The Irish Times* and as old timers and fans of his like Mary Maher, admit, the place has never quite been the same again. However, the Foley tradition continues; his son, Michael, is tourism correspondent.

1965 saw a paper being born and a paper dying. In Belfast, to widespread astonishment and some cynicism, Century Newspapers, publishers of the Protestant Unionist Belfast *News Letter,* brought out a new Sunday paper called the *Sunday News.* Cynics said that it aimed to attract the Catholic audience on Sundays, while the *News Letter* catered for its Protestant readership the remaining six days of the week. For the *Sunday News,* Pat Carville was recruited as editor from the *Irish News.* The new paper had a strange mixture of columnists and features; "Dear Abby" consoled readers on their personal problems, John D. Stewart wrote extensively on local political problems (he supported the burgeoning civil rights movement), Patrick Riddell wrote his own quirky column and Stephen Preston, a journalist with a colourful and mysterious background, made his own notable contributions. The editorial mixture was new and avant-garde for the very traditional Northern newspaper market; some sources believe that its circulation never really took off until the advent of the Troubles in 1969 provided man-made gore every Saturday night. Meanwhile, as the *Sunday News* struggled to achieve lift-off in Belfast, the Kenealy family in Kilkenny decided to kill off a venerable newspaper tradition. The *Kilkenny Journal,* dating from 1767, and once run by that astonishingly able woman owner/editor, Catherine Finn, folded just two years before its two hundredth birthday. For over ten years, John Kerry Keane of the *Kilkenny People* would have the local newspaper market almost to himself, without serious competition from other local sources.

In Galway, the city's third newspaper was squeezed out. The Scott family had run the *Galway Observer* for many years; it was so much a Galway city paper that even Oughterard represented foreign parts. In 1946, at the end of the war, John Robinson came to Galway from England (his mother was one of the Scott sisters) and worked on the *Observer*. The paper survived many vicissitudes, including the post-war strike by newsboys when the cover price went up from 1d to 2d; they wanted their share. But as the years wore on, profits were so thin that no money was put aside to replenish the machinery. Towards the end, when the press broke down, the paper had to be printed by the *Connacht Tribune*. Then on the first day of October, 1966, the last issue was produced. John Robinson still owns the title of the *Galway Observer*, but of the little house with the printing press and one of the Scott sisters, Roseanna, setting the type, there are now only memories. Until O'Gorman's, the Galway printing house where Nora Barnacle, James Joyce' wife, once worked in the finishing department, launched the *Galway Advertiser* four years after the closure of the *Observer*, the *Connacht Tribune* and *Sentinel* had the city to themselves. While the Scotts were winding down the *Galway Observer*, at least two journalists of note were working at the *Connacht Tribune* under Jack Fitzgerald, the editor. Joe Fahy, now information office in Dublin for the European Parliament and Sean Duignan, RTE's political correspondent, were working at the *Tribune*. Fahy's brother, Sean, chief reporter at the *Tribune* for many years, succeeded Fitzgerald when he retired.

In 1967 came the decision of Mirror Newspapers to print web-offset at a new plant at Suffolk, near Belfast. Irish editions of the *Daily* and *Sunday Mirrow* produced on the press, complete with full colour editorial photographs, made a big impact on the Northern newspaper market in particular. The Irish editions of the *Sun* and *The People* were also printed there. This step forward in newspaper technology was relatively short-lived: five years later, the plant was blown up. The man who made the ultimate decision to print in Ireland, Cecil King, then chairman of the Mirror group of newspapers in London, is himself of partly Irish extraction and now lives in retirement in Dublin.

That same year, Douglas Gageby took the prescient step of appointing Fergus Pyle as *The Irish Times'* first resident correspondent in Belfast. The cynics were out in force, including Captain Henderson of the Belfast *News Letter*. For years, Bertie Sibbett of that paper covered the North for *The Irish Times*, leisurely sending down his copy by telephone every night. Pyle developed many good contacts in the North and these he put to good use in providing sound, comprehensive news and feature coverage when the Troubles started in 1969. He also covered the Parliament proceedings at Stormont; when Bill Craig was sacked by O'Neill in 1968, Pyle sent down a 13,500 word report, which was used almost in its entirety.

During Pyle's period in Belfast, from 1967 until 1970, he gave *The Irish Times* a head start on all the other Dublin newspapers, although the *Irish Independent* had a veteran correspondent in the shape of James Kelly, so long at the reporting business that he was first Belfast correspondent of the *Irish Press* back in 1931. But before the Troubles blew up, when Kelly reported in his pungent way for the *Sunday Independent,* his copy would be used for its Northern edition, but not for those in the South.

Also in 1967, towards the end of his career with the *Sunday Press,* Francis Carty had a row with the Major over a leader. A committee was reviewing the Constitution that year and Carty took the very rare step for the *Sunday Press* of writing a leader on the subject. It was so inoffensive, in keeping with the gentle character of Carty, and recommended such mild constitutional change, that no-one could have taken offence. Major Vivion de Valera was greatly put out by the piece and two days after it was published, sent the clipping back to Carty with a five letter word scrawled across it. Shortly after this incident, Carty retired as editor of the *Sunday Press,* although he continued to write book reviews for it until very shortly before his death in 1972. He was succeeded in the job by Vincent Jennings, still editor today, a long tenure of office by Dublin newspaper standards.

When Mervyn Dane, the present editor of the *Impartial Reporter* arrived to see Bertie Trimble about a job, he had been warned that new reporters had to learn "the case" — setting by hand. All Trimble said was that the young Dane would have to do whatever he was asked: "If I want a pound of nails from Richardsons, you'll fetch them." Mervyn Dane never had to set type, but he watched Trimble the sub hacking all the unnecessary pieces out of his copy. "Get the meat of the subject. Cut out the trivia," Trimble used to say. One of his regular rounds was the annual grand tour of the creamery meetings, or the creamery tea, as he called them. On one such jaunt, Trimble and Dane were pressed to stay. As they drove home later that evening, Trimble looked at his watch and said: "Good heavens, we'll be killed." Trimble did everything on the paper, from reporting to subbing to standing in for the machine man; until a few weeks before his death in 1967, at the age of eighty-four, he was playing the organ in his customary fashion at the Presbyterian church in Enniskillen. After his death, his daughters Joan and Valerie took over the running of the paper.

1968 saw Tim Pat Coogan take over from Joe Walsh as editor of the *Irish Press.* Like Jennings, Coogan has enjoyed a long term of office. Tim Pat Coogan's father, Eamonn, was a Fine Gael TD for Kilkenny, a sign in itself that the old mould was being broken at Burgh Quay. Tim Pat Coogan's first taste of reporting, of schoolboy sports, was for the *Irish Independent,* but he joined the fledgling *Evening Press* as a copy boy and worked his way up to the editor's office in the *Irish Press.* In his nearly twenty years as *Irish Press* editor, he has moved the paper forward and

Pat Dunne (right) of the Leitrim Observer **pictured at a printing trade exhibition in Hannover, West Germany, in 1950. With him is Oscar Trankner of the Hayward Company.**

away from a slavish devotion to Fianna Fail policy. He has introduced many innovations, such as the "New Irish Writings" page and a growing emphasis on news coverage aimed at young people. Some sources say that his arrival in the editor's office, complete with its famous horsehair sofa, saved the *Irish Press* from a major decline in circulation. Tim Pat Coogan has also written a number of major books, including one volume on the IRA and another on the Maze hunger strikers in the North of Ireland.

The year that Tim Pat Coogan breathed new life into a quiescent *Irish Press,* the last of the old-style brigade in provincial newspapers died. Pat Dunne of the *Leitrim Observer* was laid to rest in 1968 with the usual country obituaries. "In our grief, a sense of numbness has gripped us and the necessary phrases to portray him just fail to come." He was laid to rest "where Shannon waters flow", an appropriate place, since he had helped Richard Hayward prepare an authoritative volume on the Shannon years before. Dunne was eighty-four when he died and had worked until shortly before his demise. He had seen off the ill-fated attempt by the *Longford Leader* to establish the *Leitrim Leader* in the county from 1950 to 1952; after he died, his nephew, Gregory Dunne, saw off an attempt to set up the *Leitrim News* by a photographer who had worked for the *Leitrim Observer*.

The late 1960s saw a flowering of talents in strange places in Dublin. *Nusight* was launched as a student publication in October, 1967. It started as a tabloid and soon changed into a news magazine, complete with full colour cover, a forerunner of the *Magill* format. The first editor proper of *Nusight* was Michael Keating, in 1968. He is now Lord Mayor of Dublin. A whole of other now-famous names worked on the

MONUMENT
cream with
fresh
strawberries
—delicious!
MONUMENT CREAMERIES LTD.

Evening Mail

Dublin, Thursday, July 19th, 1962   3d.   CITY FINAL

LIPTONS
GOLDEN
TIPS TEA
ONLY
1/10 Qr.
COUPON IN EVERY PKT.

Record 8,150 reach Dublin market...
SALMON GALORE—AT HIGH PRICES!

Congo chief blames natives

The MAIL suspends publication

WITH this issue, the "Evening Mail" suspends publication.

The decision to suspend, as already announced, was taken some time ago, but publication was maintained for the past three weeks after consultation with the trade unions concerned in a bid to facilitate their mem-

Still selling at 6/- per lb.

SUPPLIES of salmon reached an all-time record figure on the Dublin fish market this morning—8,150 fish—but the prices in Dublin shops went up from last week.

In the past eight days, more than 43,000 salmon have been sold through the markets, the biggest glut the city has ever experienced, but there has not been any drop in the prices in the shops.

In Clifden, Co. Galway, salmon was selling at 3s. per lb. In Dingle, it was 4s. But in Dublin, the retail price

UNITED Nation Congo chief, Mr. Robert Gardiner has blamed Katangan gendarmes for the deaths of three civilians in the Elizabethville riots two days ago, it was learned to-day.

Mr. Gardiner accused Katanga officials of destroying "human lives . . . for useless purposes" and of organising the riot for political ends.

Mr. Gardiner, in Elizabethville talks with President Tshombe, told Tshombe that the riot and two boys killed were more than an hour before U.N. troops opened fire to end the riot.

The charge was contained in a letter, which he gave to Mr. Tshombe, and which was released in Leopoldville.

Mr. Tshombe had called the three women, "patrons" of Katanga and martyrs to liberty," and has ordered a large crowd to attend their funeral to-day.

Mr. Gardiner said only the fact that U.N. troops used "cool heads before this intolerable provocation" prevented more deaths.

Front page of the last issue of the Dublin Evening Mail, **1962.**

magazine as well, although at least one, Brian Trevaskis, the great controversialist of that era, met a tragic end. Ciaran J. McKeown, who later worked for the *Irish Press* in Belfast and still later achieved worldwide fame with the Peace People, before disappearing from the limelight, wrote for the magazine. So too did a youthful John Bruton, on the subject of education. Like Keating, he went on to make his mark in the Fine Gael party and in Government. John Feeney was there, together with Kevin Myers, who now writes the Irishman's Diary in *The Irish Times*. Also with that paper now is Howard Kinlay, who was chairman of the *Nusight* company. John Kelleher, now managing director of the *Sunday Tribune,* was a contributor to the magazine. Cecily O'Toole worked on it; later she went to work with *Magill* when it was founded by Vincent Browne in 1977. Browne himself not only became editor of *Nusight,* but he achieved the distinction of being thrown out of the Young Fine Gael branch at UCD. A whole UCD/Young Fine Gael group had built up at *Nusight* and has since moved, in middle age, into many powerful positions in the present-day print media.

Just as many of the inhabitants of the *Nusight* offices later rose to positions of importance in the "settled" media, so too did the employees of a small, obscure publishing company in Ballsbridge constitute, in retrospect, a remarkable collection. Jim Gilbert was there, aided placidly by Kevin Collins, once described as looking like someone from the Quai d'Orsay (the French Foreign Ministry), Eugene McGee, the GAA writer and Brendáin MacLua, who went on to set up what many at the time regarded as a wild and improbable venture, the *Irish Post* in London. Michael Keating was there as a journalist; so too was June Levine. Frank Khan, later to be tourism correspondent for the *Irish Independent,* worked at the firm, too.

Early in the summer of 1968, cobblestones flew in Paris at the younger generation rioted. Some people believe that the 1960s was the last golden decade — the Beatles, Mary Quant, "Swinging London" — and if that belief is true, the myth started to die with those French riots. Student revolt was in the air in Dublin, too, and student activists, mainly from UCD, were to the forefront of housing and other demonstrations. Once, Feeney, when working as a sub-editor at the *Irish Press,* had the embarrassing experience of being confronted with photographs intended for publication and which included himself on a student demonstration.

When Tim Pat Coogan took on Mary Kenny as woman's editor of the *Irish Press,* little did he know what he was letting himself in for. She wouldn't start at the paper until she had been allocated a proper office; when she did get going, the *Irish Press* features on such previously avoided womens' topics as the Merrion Square prostitutes aroused a storm of protests not just from readers of the newspaper, but others who wouldn't actually read the *Irish Press,* but who had heard about Kenny's doings. Kenny habitually wore a mini-skirt (symbol of the "liberated" 1960s) into the *Irish Press* office and caused staid eyebrows to rise as she ascended the stairs from the front counter at Burgh Quay. Perhaps the ghost of Brendan Behan still inhabited the chair placed in the front office for his benefit years before and gazed lovingly on this new apparition. More episodes followed, such as that in one of Dublin's newspaper pubs, where Mary Kenny was said to have removed her bra and set fire to it before some startled male colleagues.

In another incident, a mini-skirted journalist decided to hit back at the many derisive comments made by her male tormentors. She was admired for her courage by Mary Kenny; this second lady sat up on the subs' table and invited all her male colleagues to take a good look; they were struck dumb. 1968 also saw another equally dramatic gesture in the newspaper world. At the beginning of the year, Independent Newspapers in Dublin made a foray into provincial newspapers, buying up the *Drogheda Independent.* Three months later, Seamus Rourke, a director of the *Drogheda Independent,* sold the *Argus* to them, giving the Dublin group a near-monopoly on the Co Louth weekly newspaper market, with the exception of the Dundalk *Democrat.* The Dundalk *Examiner* had closed down in 1960.

The revolution in women's journalism was gathering pace; so too was the Northern conflict. For some time, it had been simmering beneath a seemingly placid surface, but disquiet over housing allocations in Co Tyrone signalled a far deeper discontent. On Saturday, October 5, 1968, the famous Civil Rights march took place in Derry. Television, not newspapers, brought the Northern question to a world audience for the first time. Film of RUC men dispersing marchers and clubbing Gerry Fitt had a powerful visual impact, far surpassing any coverage newspapers could provide. The start of the decade was remarkably naive by present standards; (the Belfast *News Letter* talked of Ann Street being "Gay for Christmas".) The fleeting years of the 1960s, full of promise and liberation, ended nastily. The troubles to come were also to provide the makings of many of today's top names in journalism.

Ladies enjoy reading the Cork Examiner.

CHAPTER X

On the way to the Forum
1969-1983

Heinz beans 6p 15½oz. Jacobs cream crackers, 4½p pkt.
Lyons Premium Tea. 7½p qtr.
                            MOURNE OBSERVER, 1972

Keep up with the changing Times.
THE IRISH TIMES radio advertisement, 1983

The Northern troubles exploded in August, 1969; neither the North nor the newspapers of Ireland would ever be the same again. For many reporters from both parts of Ireland, the events of the Bogside in Derry and west Belfast that month proved not only startling, but helpful in their careers. Henry Kelly was working for *The Irish Times*; he was one of the UCD clique that included Vincent Browne, John Feeney and Kevin Myers. Kelly quickly had his first taste of the troubles in October of that year. At first, he went to Belfast on a part-time basis (three weeks a month) for *The Irish Times*. His first major news story there was the murder of Constable Arbuckle on the Shankill Road that same month. After he got married in 1970, Kelly went to Belfast as permanent Northern Ireland correspondent. He had his amusing incidents, such as when he was covering a riot on the Newtownards Road in east Belfast. One Protestant street in the Short Strand area had a ferocious little lady who waved Union Jacks in the style of "Orange Lil". When this riot was in progress, soldiers and policemen were going up the Newtownards Road followed by various assorted newsmen, including Henry Kelly. Taking up the rear was the Protestant lady, who laid about an unfortunate TV cameraman. He said that he wasn't Protestant or Catholic, he was merely doing his job. "You shouldn't be taking pictures of things that aren't happening," retorted the Protestant lady.

Henry Kelly — before he left The Irish Times **in 1976, he was embarrassed by the forged letter purporting to have come from Oliver J. Flanagan.**

Two of today's best-known journalistic "characters", **Maeve Binchy** (Irish Times) **and John Devine** (Sunday Independent).

On another occasion, Kelly's car was machine gunned. He escaped unhurt (the car didn't): very shortly afterwards, a telegram came from Douglas Gageby, on holiday in the south of France. It read: "The Lord looks after his own." To Henry Kelly, covering the 1973 Middle East war for *The Irish Times* was a "piece of cake" by comparison.

In 1969, John Feeney, too, got married, to Aoife Kearney, daughter of Stephen Kearney, secretary of the Department of Defence. Feeney's father, Professor Kevin Feeney, was a former Master of the Coombe hospital. The scourge of the Establishment, blacklisted by at least one major semi-State company, Feeney had a remarkably Establishment background himself. Soon, he too went North, to work out of the Belfast office of the *Irish Press.* At that stage, Vincent Browne (*Irish Press* Northern News Editor) and himself were great friends. There were humorous moments too; an American newsman paid a sociable call on the Belfast office of the *Irish Press.* "Say folks," he told all and sundry at the top of his voice, "I know Vivion de Valera well and she's a real nice person."

Feeney was staying with a Protestant clergyman and his family in the Ballygomartin district of west Belfast; under pressure of threats, Feeney had to leave his lodgings. The bitterness and the hatred built up, but to the visiting newspapermen, Belfast meant a big step on the road to promotion. Many journalists who were less well known before they went to Belfast, like Browne and Feeney, are now at the top of their profession. Some journalists had extraordinary escapes; when

Colin Brady, the Northern Irish correspondent of the *Daily Telegraph* was driving through the William Street area of Derry one day, a bullet from a sniper's gun entered the back of his car, tore through the wad of papers stuffed into his trouser pocket, setting fire to them and careered out through the radiator. Brady was unhurt, but badly shaken. Once when he was covering a riot, Brady did not realise he had been shot in the leg until he found his shoe full of blood.

During his three years in the North with the *Irish Press* (three formative and fascinating years), Vincent Browne's most famous escapade was undoubtedly that of the sub-machine gun. A member of the IRA showed Browne a machine gun which he said had been made in one of the city's loyalist engineering works. Browne arranged to collect the gun after he had been given certain assurances by a British Army press officer, but when he arrived at the Europa Hotel (now the Forum), complete with sub-machine gun, he was met by a posse of Army personnel. Someone from the army had rung the RUC to enquire if they were sending a representative to the Browne press conference. They sent forty-three. Vincent Browne was afraid that when he stood trial, he would be given the mandatory sentence of a jail term for carrying weapons, but the luck of this Co Limerick-born journalist held. He was fined £20. The story made excellent news copy.

Vincent Browne, founder of Magill **and editor,** Sunday Tribune.

Just as the Northern troubles were building up, the Women's Lib lobby became extremely vociferous. Mary Kenny led the way, with ample encouragement from Nell McCafferty, who came from Derry and who was just making her way in Dublin journalism. Soon, she became party of the famous women's "gang" on *The Irish Times*, where Nell's picturesque language made a startling impact on previously battle-hardened reporters. Her first day at *The Irish Times*, when she cursed the management in most unladylike language for not providing enough paper for the women's lavatory, is still remembered today. From a journalistic viewpoint, she is best remembered there for her memorable series of court reports.

One of the old-time brigade died, Leslie Nivison, editor of the *Evening Herald* from 1950 until 1958; he had joined the paper in 1928 as a sub-editor. He was also film critic on that paper for many years. When he left the *Herald*, he also left Dublin and at the time of his death, was working for a newspaper group in Kent, in south-east England.

The Troubles in the North were starting to have their impact on newspaper publication, closing some, spawning others. A new paper started in 1970, a propaganda sheet called *Voice of the North*, edited by that highly skilled Dublin journalist, Seamus Brady. It was printed by the *Anglo-Celt* in Cavan; who exactly financed the paper remains cloaked in mystery to this day. In Newry, once a great newspaper town, closures followed swiftly on the advance of the Troubles. First the *Newry Telegraph* closed down in 1970, then two years later, the

**Tomas Ó Duinn —
scholarly contributions
about the Enniscorthy/
Wexford area in** The
Irish Times.
–The Irish Times

appropriately named *Frontier Sentinel*, once one of the lynchpins of the *Omagh Herald* group, closed down. The *Telegraph* traced its antecedents back to 1812, the *Sentinel* to 1904. Today, Newry has only one newspaper left that is produced in the town: the *Newry Reporter*, owned by the Hodgett family, who also own the *Banbridge Chronicle*. Interestingly, the *Newry Reporter* was once run by James Burns, grandfather of Gordon Burns, who used to be a UTV presenter and who is now best known for presenting the "Krypton Factor" programme for Granada television.

One of Newry's most respected earlier newspapers, the *Newry Examiner*, had even crossed what is now the border, in 1880, to become transformed into the *Dundalk Examiner*. It finally closed in that town in 1960, for as Peadar O'Curry, once its editor, remarks: "Nothing could beat the *Dundalk Democrat*." Not even the linotype operator the *Examiner* once had, who could set a column and a half of type in an hour, in O'Curry's remembrance. Elsewhere in the North, progress was made. 1970 saw the *Northern Constitution* link up with the *Coleraine Chronicle* to form the Northern Newspaper group. Soon afterwards, the *Ballymena Guardian* was founded by that group.

In Belfast, the old *Weekly Telegraph*, which had closed in 1964, went through various changes of title in increasingly desperate attempts at survival. Restyled into *Ulsterweek*, the paper was soon sold off to Morton Newspapers, who rechristened it *Cityweek* and confined it to Belfast. Writing a pop music column for it in 1970 was Colin McClelland, now editor of the *Sunday World*. Jim Morton had already decided to close the paper. A nineteen year old Chris Moore (who now works for the BBC) was editor and he was given one last fling. The paper was changed into a pop paper aimed at the under-twenty market. It was rechristened *Thursday*, after its day of publication. After the overnight change of style, fifty letters came in from readers complaining about the missing births, marriages, deaths and bowling match results. The week following, 250 letters came in from teenage readers defending the changes, but *Thursday* went out in a blast of super-sound just five months later.

True to the casual form of the newspaper business, McClelland soon found himself another job. Walking across Donegall Square in Belfast one day, John Trew, features editor of the Belfast *News Letter*, spotted McClelland in the distance. "Psst, want a staff job?" Trew whispered out of the corner of his mouth. The out-of-work McClelland found himself on the *Sunday News*, published by Century Newspapers and aimed at a wide audience. The *Sunday News* remained a comparative failure until the start of the Troubles put atrocities on Sunday breakfast tables.

The 2 a.m. press deadline on Sunday mornings helped the paper provide an ample supply of bloody headlines. Listening to the police radios in the newsroom, the reporters kept track of every explosion

Major Vivion de Valera starting the press for the Golden Jubilee supplements of the Irish Press, **1981.**
–Irish Press

and shooting incident. They went trembling towards the sound of distant gunfire; Colin McClelland remembers going one Saturday night to cover a particularly vicious pub bombing in Short Strand, a small Catholic enclave in east Belfast. The pub had collapsed, pinning its occupants beneath tons of rubble. Human chains were formed to pull away the bricks and stones. Cars were parked so that their headlights shone on the wreckage. McClelland was next to one of these cars; its wheels were slipping. He wondered why, since it was a dry night — they were standing on the pavement in a sea of blood.

In the Duke of York pub, almost next door to the offices of the Belfast *News Letter* and *Sunday News,* an amiable and efficient barman served the orders of the newsmen (and women). Later, he rose to prominence as a leading member of Provisional Sinn Fein. As for the newsmen and their lady companions, some had a reputation of arriving at 9.30 in the morning, departing for a little light work before lunch, returning after lunch, slipping out at tea-time as editions were starting to go to press and then returning to the pub for a serious evening's drinking. Their drinking was far more time consuming than their work.

The alcoholic reputation of the reporting profession was ably upheld in Belfast in the early 1970s. McGlades bar was also a noted place of refreshment for a cosmopolitan crowd from the *Belfast Telegraph, Irish*

Vincent Jennings (left) editor of the Sunday Press **and Tim Pat Coogan, editor of the** Irish Press.
–Irish Press

News and international papers. When the crowd thinned out, remembers one journalist who was there, you knew you had missed out on a big story. The bar of what was then known as the Europa Hotel attracted the free-spending international journalists. Expense was no object, as Belfast taxi drivers soon found out, making fortunes out of taking foreign journalists on guided tours. Many stories about the Northern troubles were written at the bar in the Europa; the greater the consumption of alcohol, the more outlandish the copy. KGB and CIA agents were rumoured to have been among the throng of international journalists in Belfast, which added to the general air of excitement. The penthouse "pets" brought a touch of female glamour. Belfast had never been in the news like this before.

The Troubles of the early 1970s also produced many equally wild stories about absurd expense accounts enjoyed by London and Manchester-based journalists. One English journalist, on a visit to Dublin, put in the most original expenses claim ever, for hire of a boat to Usher's Island, £25.

The newspaper industry in the city had its own personal tragedy: Ralph "Bud" Bossence died, on November 3, 1971. Born in Belfast, but brought up in Detroit, where his father worked for the Ford Motor Company, he was educated at Detroit Central High. There, he developed a great taste for American literature, most notably the works of H. L. Menchen. He worked for the *Northern Whig* as a reporter from 1935 until 1947, when he joined the *News Letter*. Starting as a reporter there, he later became political correspondent and wrote a weekly column on the doings of the Stormont Parliament. Not until he started writing his humorous column, "As I See It", did Bossence really find himself. From 1964 until his death, this regular column in the *News*

Letter provided much fun for an avid following. Despite his strong Labour Party views (he was also a secretary and chairman of the Belfast branch of the NUJ), he rarely came into conflict with the *News Letter* management. Only once was his column "spiked". In many ways, he was the very essence of the Dickensian figure, with enormous belly, two large chins, curly hair, small spectacles and a great sense of humour.

But it was the social side of Bossence that drew the greatest applause. His collection of jazz records in his terraced house in Melrose Street off the Lisburn Road was one of the best in Ireland and he used to provide unforgettable experiences at NUJ dinners by singing his version of "Sugar". In his favourite pub, the Duke of York, where he was eventually honoured by a stained glass window (destroyed in the subsequent bomb explosion that wrecked the premises), his wit and witticisms in the style of Oscar Wilde kept the mostly male company, amused for hours on end. At Christmas, he was said to drink up to twenty-four bottles of stout at one go, perhaps in fond remembrance of that great pub crawl from Dunmurry to Lurgan. Sometimes, "Bud" Bossence would appear to be nodding off to sleep; the assembled company lived in hope of him spilling his drink, but he always "came to" just in time. He wa also a gourmet and while fellow workers at the *New Letter* brought in humble sandwiches, "Bud" would bring in a splendid

From left: **Vincent Doyle (editor,** Irish Independent), **Aidan Pender and Michael Hand (editor,** Sunday Independent**). The photograph was taken in May, 1982 on the occasion of Pender's retirement as editor of the** Irish Independent.

Ralph "Bud" Bossence of the News Letter, **Belfast.** Over a decade after his death, a host of stories still circulate about "Bud", including the time James Kennedy of the News Letter and himself walked from Dunmurry to Lurgan, stopping in every pub along the way.
–*News Letter*

Diane Harron, TV personality and "graduate" of the East Antrim Times.
–*BBC*

assortment of food for consumption during the long night shift.

Just before "Bud" Bossence died, Colin McClelland met him on the stairs at Century Newspapers. The rambling, Victorian building housing the firm in Lower Donegall Street also gave shelter to fifty old men, who seemed to spend all day shuffling up and down the rickety stairs. They were compilers of Century's Belfast street directory. One day, an old man stopped on the stairs to get his breath. McClelland did not recognise him. A gasping, plaintive voice cried out: "Do ye not know me, it's Bud."

Shortly afterwards, "Bud" Bossence died, and with him went a great tradition of Belfast newspaper characters. Bossence had much in common with that great nineteenth century columnist, Barney Maglone. In his will, Bossence had left enough money for his friends to "wake" him in style at the Duke of York, but instructions for no advance notice, so that only genuine friends would come. The pub was packed. The pub owner, Jimmy Keaveney ("Bud" was so close to him that popular rumour had him going on Keaveney's honeymoon), went round each table and asked the same question of each group: "Mr Bossence would like to know what you would like to drink."

After his death, the stories of "Bud" Bossence and the more outrageous of his newspaper colleagues who somehow managed to survive the rat race, provided flashes of light in the Stygian gloom. Cowan Watson, the avuncular editor of the *News Letter*, came and departed. Described in cordial personal terms by *Irish Press* editor, Tim Pat Coogan, who nevertheless once condemned the *News Letter* as a paper having obvious Northern attitudes, years before, Watson had aroused great wrath among certain members of the listening public by being appointed Northern correspondent of Radio Eireann. After Watson left the *News Letter* editorship, for health reasons, according to the official statement, the paper began to acquire the same reputation as the *Irish Press* had in the 1950s and 1960s: so many staff came and went that it became a badge of honour to have joined and left the *News Letter*. The directives of Ken Withers, the new editor after Watson, epitomised the growing dullness; out went pictures of dolly birds, in came pictures of trees, at least for a short while. Many people on the *News Letter* regarded it as a tragedy that John Trew, for long its features editor, had not been made editor in 1968. Trew came to the editor's job ten years too late, in many people's estimation, and he too had to retire from that post for reasons of ill-health.

Elsewhere in Ireland, there were beginnings and endings. In Dublin, Hugh McLaughlin set up *This Week* magazine, edited by Joseph O'Malley, brother of Desmond O'Malley, the Fianna Fail T.D. Working on the publication were Liam MacGabhann and John Feeney. After the demise of *This Week*, O'Malley left for the *Sunday Independent*, where he has been ever since, as political correspondent. McLaughlin also started the *Dublin Post*, which inaugurated the revolution in give-away newspapers in the Republic. One of its editors was Michael Keating, who has since moved upwards to become a Coalition junior Minister (briefly) and who is now ensconced in the comforts of the Mansion House, a far cry from the sweaty, tobacco-stained bowels of the former Player-Wills factory at Botanic Road that McLaughlin

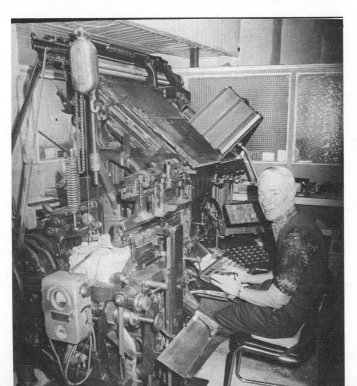

Jackie Slattery setting his retirement piece at the Nenagh Guardian **in 1982; he worked for the paper for fifty-four years, during which time, he set an estimated 5,000 miles of type. The paper recently installed a phototypesetting system, replacing the Linotypes, as seen in this photograph.**
–Nenagh Guardian

Michael Finlan, Galway correspondent of The Irish Times. **His first newspaper job was on the** Western People, **Ballina. The reporters' desk was a long wooden bench, complete with lone typewriter, placed in the caseroom so that editor Fred Devere could keep an eye on his editorial staff. Finlan's colleagues when he joined the paper included John Healy and Jim McGuire, but only one reporter (Tony Burke) could write shorthand.**
–The Irish Times

turned into an instant newspaper and magazine printing and publishing empire. In 1971, the *Wexford Free Press* succumbed to the opposition *People* (now part of Independent Newspapers) and closed down. The *Free Press* was always noted as a Fine Gael newspaper, but in a last desperate attempt at survival, the Republican card was played. Shortly afterwards, it folded.

1971 saw two former employees of the *Westmeath Examiner*, Dick Hogan, a reporter and Tom Kiernan, a printer, leave to set up their own paper, the *Midland Topic*. It later expanded to include the new *Offaly Topic*. Another ex-employee of the *Westmeath Examiner* also did well — Joe Dolan, the singer, who served his time there as a comp. In Athlone, Dublin printer John McManus, whose father had been a comp at the Athlone Printing Works, bought over the *Westmeath-Offaly Independent*.

1972 started off bloodily; in Derry on January 30, a march of civilians was fired on by British army paratroopers. Thirteen people were killed, among them Willie McKinney, a comp with the *Derry Journal*. Not since the War of Independence fifty years previously had a member of staff of an Irish newspaper been killed by British troops. Elsewhere in Derry, during this particularly anguished period of the city's history, other newsmen had amazing experiences.

Larry Doherty, a photographer with the *Derry Journal* since it started its own photographic department in 1945, remembers one incident, when a young Derry girl called Martha Doherty, who was going out with a British soldier, was tarred and feathered. At first, when Doherty saw the crowd outside the Bogside Inn, he thought that a young man was involved. He took his photographs, realising that the figure was a woman. He was the only photographer there, since the other photographers in the city were still in and around the City Hotel. He was half way through developing the film back at the *Derry Journal* when he heard frantic knocking on the window; it was the rest of the photographers, looking for prints. Being an obliging sort of man, Doherty handed them out. Soon, he was besieged with calls from Fleet Street photo editors. He was in exactly the same position as Cecil King had been in when Amelia Earhart landed in Derry forty years previously. Some incidents were more hair-raising; Willie Carson, another Derry area newspaper photographer, was standing near the Embassy Ballroom in the centre of Derry when a gunman used his shoulder as a resting place for his arm, so that he could start shooting at a British Army lookout on the roof of the ballroom.

By about 1975, the North suddenly became a source of boredom to the UK and international newspapers; what was happening was tragic, but repetitive, nevertheless. Many foreign correspondents left, never to return, except on rare occasions, such as the murder of eighteen British soldiers at Warrenpoint in the summer of 1979. Suddenly, the quiet, old-fashioned newspaper city of Belfast reverted to its former ways.

Vincent Gill of the *Longford News*, **enjoys a birthday celebration (cake and stout) with friends, including Derek Cobbe, second from left.**

The derelict remains of the cottage at Harbour Row, Longford that once housed both Vincent Gill and his *Longford News.*

1972 also saw two notable takeovers. Joe Moore's PMPA group, set up to provide motor insurance cover, bought out the *Leinster Express* from Fred Townsend, who had invested in new press facilities in a vain attempt to stabilise the operation of the newspaper. Moore was much impressed by a young journalist from the *Irish Press*, Dan Carmody, who interviewed him for the paper. It turned out the other way round: Moore was really interviewing Carmody and soon afterwards offered him a job as managing editor of the *Leinster Express* in Portlaoise. Independent Newspapers took over the *Kerryman* in Tralee. A 'phone call one day from Bartle Pitcher, chief executive of the Independent group in Dublin, to Dan Nolan started the ball rolling. Disagreements among the directors made Nolan receptive to the offer; eventually the

Three of the present generation of Crosbies at the Cork Examiner. **From left, Ted (chairman), Donal (editorial director) and George (advertising director).**
–Cork Examiner

other directors went along with the bid, just four years after the *Drogheda Independent* had been bought out. At Independent Newspapers in Dublin, trials and tribulations meant the sudden departure of Louis McRedmond as editor of the *Irish Independent,* just over ten years ago. He went to RTE to head up its information section.

The *Kerryman* in Tralee was one of the first provincial newspapers to go in for web offset printing, when it put in a new press in 1972. Another early provincial pioneer was the *Connacht Tribune.* In 1976, the *Connacht Tribune* expanded by taking over Donaldsons, the Celbridge, Co Kildare, legal printing firm. It was a disastrous decision and after heavy trading losses, Donaldsons had to be closed down in 1980.

During the 1970s, most of the provincial papers changed over to web-offset printing, a move that was not without its tragic and humorous moments. One weekly newspaper put in a new press and during its trials, a machine man decided to try and stop the machine by putting his arm in it. Large parts of the machinery had to be cut away to release the unfortunate printer. In another case, the female employee of a provincial paper was taken to Amsterdam by the manufacturers of the printing press for a pre-installation familiarisation course. Amid the various sights of that city, her behaviour was so wild that hardened male print workers found out things they never knew before about women in the industry.

In 1972, the RTE Authority was sacked, including long-time member Jim Fanning of the *Midland Tribune,* Birr. Fanning, a prominent and life-long member of Fianna Fail, found himself out in the cold, along with Micheál O'Callaghan of the *Roscommon Herald* and all the other members of the Authority after the famous Kevin O'Kelly interview with Sean MacStiophain of Provisional Sinn Fein. The interview was held to have been in contravention of Section 31 of the Broadcasting Act. Kevin

Myers, who had been working with RTE in Belfast, also left, to work for an American network in the North.

Des Morrow, the highly likeable motoring correspondent of the *Belfast Telegraph,* died in a car crash that year. He predeceased his famous father, Billy, by nearly ten years. Many stories were told about Des Morrow; one concerned a particularly boring meeting of the Belfast Chamber of Commerce he was covering. In the middle of the meeting, he asked to be excused. He left for half an hour in order to have a quick "canoodle" with a girl he had just met!

March, 1973, saw the most recent of the great newspaper launches in Ireland. There had been launches and flops since the last big one, the *Evening Press,* in 1954. *The Irish Times* had launched the *Sunday Review* in the late 1950s, but it sank to an inglorious and premature end in November, 1963. Hugh McLaughlin, the Donegal station master's son, had started work during the war for the "Indo" in Dublin and went into printing and publishing on his own account after the war, firstly with the Fleet Printing Company. His exploits and deeds were legendary; somehow, he always managed to survive. In the 1950s, he set up a publishing company called Creation and began turning out magazines. One of the first he launched, *Woman's Way,* is still going strong, as is *Business and Finance,* the weekly business paper whose founding editor was Nicholas Leonard. McLaughlin had such a reputation for starting and folding publications that when he and his advertisement director, Gerry McGuinness, who had started his career in a junior capacity at the Green Cinema, Dublin, launched the *Sunday World* in March, 1973, the "scoffers" were out in force. They were nearly proved right, because at the time, the new paper was said to have had just six weeks' money to pay the bills, particularly staff wages. Eight weeks is reckoned to be the period after which many new papers collapse; by then, the printers have to be paid.

McLaughlin and McGuinness commissioned a market research report which purported to show that there was a gap for the *Sunday World,* nipping in below and between the *Sunday Independent* and the *Sunday Press.* Joe Kennedy of the *Evening Herald* was invited to be the editor of the new paper; he joined a fortnight before the launch. In his turn, Kennedy brought in Kevin Marron, who was getting bored doing the television column on the *Sunday Press* under Vincent Jennings. When the *Sunday World* started, McLaughlin worked all out to ensure that the first issue took off; if it hadn't, the paper would have folded there and then. A dummy run was planned, but never happened, because the printers were not paid overtime to work on a Saturday night. Posters went up all round Dublin proclaiming the first issue.

Kennedy (who has now returned from journalistic retirement to write the *Evening Press* diary) and Marron hoped for a spot to themselves on RTE's "Late Late Show". The two journalists were furious when RTE insisted on keeping the balance by bringing on representatives of the other two Dublin Sunday papers, but the show helped sell out the first issue. Joe Kennedy made an apparently innocent remark about a million women not being satisfied on Sunday mornings — with their existing Sunday papers. This gave rise to a whole spate of innuendo about the *Sunday World*. In the primitive conditions of the former cigarette factory, in offices that were like horse boxes, Kennedy, Marron and company laboured to produce the instantly successful new Sunday paper.

One journalist who was present at the press conference that launched the *Sunday World* laughed when McLaughlin remarked, with his usual charming naivety, that he had been given a very attractive quotation by Creation to print the *Sunday World*. Since McLaughlin controlled Creation, the news came as little surprise.

The first issue became the dummy run, in archaic conditions. Headlines had to be hand set. It was like a Caesarian operation — the paper was dragged bleeding into the street, recalls Marron, who became the *Sunday World's* second editor, after Kennedy moved "upstairs" to become editor-in-chief. The first print run was 200,000. It sold out, fortunately, so financing the second and subsequent issues.

The new paper broke all the rules: full editorial and advertising colour became the norm, although the process had been pioneered in Ireland by the *Mirror* in Belfast, and Mortons in Lurgan, all journalists got by-lines (a practice said by older members of the profession to have been its ruination) and a business gossip page was started. All these innovations and more besides captured the public imagination, helped by writers like Tom Savage, who did the "agony" column in the early days, and by plentiful helpings of under-dressed models. The first "dolly bird" on the *Sunday World* was Jeananne Crowley, now better known for her TV work in London as a serious actress.

McLaughlin and McGuinness weren't the usual newspaper 'groupies'; there was tension between themselves and Kennedy and Marron. On one occasion, when Marron was standing in as editor in place of Kennedy, who was away, McLaughlin wanted some editorial taken out. Marron refused: "He fired me six times that night, I closed the place five times." Marron won his point and made it up later with his opponent, who nevertheless had a great ability to come back after making signed and sealed agreements, first at one shoulder, then at the other, with sly looks, remembers Marron.

McLaughlin started the paper under the aegis of the Creation group. Many suppliers found they had been supplying goods and services not to the *Sunday World*, but to Creation and when the group went into liquidation in 1975, many were left unpaid. The sprawling group, with a maze of interlocking companies, crashed with a total debt of about £1.5 million. The Revenue Commissioners alone were owed £½ million, which has never been recovered. Somehow, the *Sunday World* slithered out from beneath the wreckage of the Creation group and went on to ascend new heights.

Just before the crash of Creation, the *Sunday World* had slipped out of Botanic Road to the premises of the former Terenure Laundry. Even after the collapse of Creation, editorial and typesetting operations did not move out of Glasnevin immediately. The *Sunday World*, as a company, had been hived off from Creation, so that the day the Creation group was wound up by Court order, Gerry McGuinness, managing director of the Sunday newspaper, blithely carried on playing golf in the Canaries. Both he and McLaughlin, after the Independent group took over the paper, turned into millionaires.

McLaughlin himself survived his subsequent adventures, just as he had survived the debacle of Dr Paul Singer's Shanahan's Stamp Auctions thirteen years previously. McLaughlin had been printing the catalogues and the collapse of the stamp auctions idea, leaving hundreds of pensioners deprived of their savings, had also left McLaughlin's Fleet Printing Company in some difficulties.

Meanwhile, over in Middle Abbey Street, the Independent group had been taken over by Tony O'Reilly. T. V. Murphy was appointed a director by his uncle, William Lombard Murphy, in 1926; thirteen years later, he was appointed chairman and remained in that position until the O'Reilly takeover in 1973. T.V. Murphy was an active chairman; he often went round the premises at two in the morning to let the staff see that he was in control. He also admits that he often blue-pencilled copy, particularly at election times.

Tony O'Reilly bought the voting shares for £1.1 million; this gave him voting control of the company, but only rights to just over four per cent of profits. Further deals gave O'Reilly thirty-six per cent of the share capital. Today, O'Reilly's shareholding in Independent Newspapers is twenty-nine per cent. After O'Reilly's original bid, T. V. Murphy told him that he just wanted a "box of matches for nothing." After O'Reilly gained control, he wanted Murphy to stay on as chairman, but he refused: "It would have been an invidious position for me. I would have been subservient, when I once owned the group." Instead, his son Rodney became chairman; he died tragically young, of cancer, in February, 1980. The O'Reilly takeover made little practical difference to the running of Independent Newspapers, except that it is one more corporately owned newspaper group, like many others around the world, and accordingly colourless in characterisation.

1973 also saw John Feeney hit the national headlines. For some three years previously, he had managed to make rather than write the newspaper headlines. As a member of the left-wing Catholic group, Grille, he had attacked the then-Archbishop of Dublin, Dr McQuaid, over the Church's domination of hospital boards and other sundry topics. Then in February, 1973, came Feeney's surprise resignation from the RTE "Seven Days" programme; he complained about the mood in RTE and the threat of further Government control of the

Liam Robinson of the *Irish Press,* **by Bobby Pyke.**

Tony and Mary Mathews of Drogheda on their wedding day; Tony, who died some years ago, was a well-known journalist in Dublin.

station. Then he threw another great surprise, by joining the *Catholic Standard* as editor. He followed in the illustrious footsteps of such people as Peadar O'Curry, but like O'Curry, he too was to fall foul of the directors.

Vincent Browne had his rows at the *Independent.* He returned from Belfast to be political correspondent of the *Evening Herald,* only to find that the management had omitted to tell him that they already had a resident political correspondent for the paper. He was equally frustrated on the *Sunday Independent,* where he had proposed changes in the "Wigmore" column to Tony O'Reilly. These changes were stopped by Bartle Pitcher after an attack in print by Vincent Browne on the then Taoiseach, Liam Cosgrave, after Cearbhall O Dálaigh's resignation as President. Eventually, in 1977, Browne decided to set up his own magazine, *Magill.* This year he has been instrumental in reviving the *Sunday Tribune.*

1973 also saw the start of a disastrous venture at *The Irish Times* – the *Education Times,* started in April, 1973, just over ten years ago. Edited by John Horgan, who later went into Labour politics, it had such contributors as Noreen Erskine, who had been with the *Derry Journal,* and who is now with the BBC in Belfast. Eugene McEldowney contributed, so too did a young Michael Foley, son of Donal. During the paper's four year life span, circulation and advertising fell away. One issue of January, 1976, was entirely devoid of advertising — not even a single line of classifieds. When the *Education Times* sank, it joined those other honourable failures in Westmoreland Street, the *Dublin*

Evening Mail, the *Radio Review,* the *Times Pictorial* and the *Sunday Review.* Christine Murphy continues to uphold the standard of educational journalism on *The Irish Times.*

By 1974, Douglas Gageby had been editor of *The Irish Times* for eleven years. With Major McDowell as managing director, the paper had a remarkable duo guiding its fortunes. Gageby had brought up the circulation to around 70,000, double the figure for 1964. In a speech at University College, Galway, in 1971, Gageby remarked that about seventy per cent of the revenue of class papers, such as his own, was derived from advertising, with the remainder derived from sales of copies. Even a slight swing of ten per cent in advertising revenue, resulting from a slackening in consumer demand, can bring disaster. After the Arab-Israeli war of 1973 and the consequent soaring oil prices, economic disaster *did* hit the western world, including Ireland. When Gageby retired in mid-1974, it seemed that *The Irish Times* would turn in a profit for the year of about £400,000. It made a £100,000 loss. Cutbacks in advertising, particularly property advertising, hit the paper's revenue. In its 1975 financial year, *The Irish Times* lost nearly £300,000. Staff numbers had to be cut by about a hundred and the paper made another disastrous diversification move, into newsagents' shops, which were later sold off.

However, that year did provide a small bonanza for Irish newspapers; President de Valera died. Within two hours of his death, the *Evening Herald* rushed out a special edition with a full colour gravure printed photograph of him. Various newspapers, including *The Irish Times* and the *Kerryman,* produced special supplements. The *Drogheda Independent* published a supplement on Mother Mary Martin that had been prepared five years previously. The founder of the Medical Missionaries of Mary had been close to death, but she recovered, so the supplement was put into plastic bags until she did die in 1975.

1974 saw the *Belfast Telegraph's* new headquarters in Derry opened. Derry and North-West editions had up to four pages of local news and advertisement printed locally under the new arrangement, onto editions brought from Belfast, thus making the paper the only one in Ireland to be printed in two centres. 1974 also saw Brian Croley and Arthur Boucher from the Belfast *News Letter* take over Morton Newspapers in Lurgan. Jim Morton, son of its founder John, went into retirement on the Isle of Man. Last year, he came out of retirement and resumed control of the group, following severe trading difficulties. That same year also saw Roy Lilley take over the editorship of the *Belfast Telegraph* in succession to Eugene Wasson. Lilley had joined the group in 1957 and became political correspondent of the *Telegraph* in 1962. Another ex-political correspondent of the paper, John Cole, now works as BBC political editor in London. The *Limerick Weekly Echo* changed to web-offset printing in 1974, using the press of the *Connacht Tribune* in Galway. The paper had had an interesting career; after Ivan

Veteran of the Limerick Leader: **Earl Connolly, advertisement manager, who joined the paper before World War II and who is the only surviving serving member of staff from those pre-war days.**

Morris sold out in the mid-1960s, it was sold to local interests. Then in 1971, it was sold again to another consortium, including Tom Tobin, who had earlier been editor of the rival *Limerick Chronicle*. Tobin only stayed a year and in his place came another veteran Limerick journalist, Arthur Quinlan, who had been correspondent in the city for the *Cork Examiner*.

Fergus Pyle had gone from Belfast to be first Paris and then EEC correspondent in Brussels for *The Irish Times*. In the last week of June, 1974, in a 'phone call from Dublin, he was offered Gageby's job. At first, he was reluctant to accept, but nine days later, came into *The Irish Times* as editor. Jim Downey and Denis Kennedy (formerly of the *Belfast Telegraph*) were appointed assistant editors. Gageby had worked in a large room with other senior staff; Pyle moved into a smaller room previously occupied by Gageby's secretary.

At the same time that Gageby left, the provisions of the Trust were causing some disquiet among the staff. Three of the previous directors, George Hetherington, Philip and Ralph Walker, left the old board, while the two remaining directors, Douglas Gageby and Major McDowell, stayed. They were joined on the board of the new Trust by a representative liberal cross-section of Irish society, North and South. The terms of the Trust were specifically designed to prevent outside takeover and control; in recent years, Michael Smurfit is said to have been unable to "crack" the Trust in order to assume control. The terms of the Trust were generally welcomed; criticism was raised by the financial arrangements. The five directors of the old board sold their shares to the Trust for £1,625,000, which averaged out at £325,000 each. Later, Major McDowell insisted that the directors could have secured a much higher price for their shares on the open market. *The Irish Times* had to borrow £1.6 million from the Bank of Ireland to pay the five directors; this borrowing became a millstone that almost pulled the paper under.

Pyle began to work as editor against a background of deteriorating economic conditions and a degree of resentment among some members of staff about the monies paid to the directors on the conversion to the Trust. Many journalists felt that Donal Foley, who had contributed as much as Gageby, in different ways, to the success of the paper in the previous ten years, should have been made editor. Was it because he was a Catholic, wondered some sources darkly? *The Irish Times* remains to have its first Catholic editor, just as the *Irish Press* and *Irish Independent* remain to have their first Protestant editors.

The radicalism of the 1960s that had worked so much to Foley's benefit tapered off into the dull, repressive days of the mid-70's Coalition government. Fergus Pyle made *The Irish Times* appropriately duller. By 1976, sales were sliding. That year, management under-estimated the company's trading losses by £210,000 in negotiating their inability to pay the terms of the National Wage Agreement. By this time, the paper was indebted to the Bank of Ireland for £2.5 million.

While this high financial drama was being acted out, Maeve Binchy created her own kind of drama at *The Irish Times*. In reporting the wedding of Princess Anne in London in 1974, she used several mild enough phrases (in public and in private, Maeve is the kindest and most comforting of people, quite unlike the stereotyped image of some women journalists). Her words about the wedding were not unkind, but they unleashed hidden torrents from readers; hundreds of letters poured in to the paper. No report she produced before or since has had quite the same effect. Another devastating change was under way at the *Northern Constitution;* at about this time, it took the advertisements off its front page, replacing them with news. It was one of the last papers in Ireland to make the change.

Just minutes after Seamus McConville took over as editor of the *Kerryman* in Tralee in February, 1974, he had a telephone call to the effect that if he published an article about the Price sisters, then on hunger strike in an English jail, he should make his last confession. Con Houlihan, the ebullient Kerry journalist who now does a splendidly idiosyncratic sports column in the *Evening Press* and who is reported to wear his anorak on all occasions in all temperatures, was doing the weekly column in the *Kerryman* at the same time and he did not support the Price sisters' demand to be moved to Northern Ireland. McConville decided to face down the threat, so he went ahead and published. It was the first and last threat made against him.

Michael Nagle of the *Dungarvan Leader* made a criticism about modern journalists often echoed in the newspaper world. "The fact that journalists have university degrees after their name does not mean that they are good journalists. A good command of the English language and a flair for writing are all important," he said. Tom Samways of Belfast also bemoaned the passing of the old ways, when lunch could stretch into dinner and beyond over many pints. Now, journalists have to be back at their desks at 2.30 p.m. sharp.

Also in 1974, the new *Sunday World* created a furore by running a full colour photograph of a girl called Maeve Golden, who was wearing just a garland of flowers. The protests rolled in and sales went up. In 1974, President Erskine Childers collapsed at a Dublin function one Saturday night and was rushed to hospital where he died soon afterwards. The other Sunday papers were edged in black, but not the *Sunday World*. Its printers had gone on a late night strike, so the paper came out complete with four colour dolly birds and not a word about Childers' death. Sales were said to have increased that Sunday.

Henry Kelly managed to move out of Belfast before departure from that city became popular; he returned to the Dublin headquarters of *The Irish Times*. His most exciting moment there, before leaving Dublin in 1976 for London to pursue his broadcasting career, was the episode

Joan Tighe, Evening Herald **columnist.**

of the forged Letter to the Editor, purporting to come from Oliver J. Flanagan, the veteran T.D.

Someone (Kelly has no idea of his or her identity) stole some headed Dáil Eireann notepaper, wrote a letter urging support of abortion, contraception and several other modern "misdemeanours" and signed it with the Deputy's "signature". In Kelly's absence, someone let through the letter. Kelly says he knows the culprit's name, but that he will take the secret with him to his grave.

When it happened, Kelly rang up Flanagan and apologised profusely. The Deputy, in Kelly's words, behaved like a perfect gentleman and merely said "these things happen." The incident with the forged Flanagan letter highlighted a great source of potential abuse in the Dublin papers, all of which are now very stringent indeed in checking the authenticity of readers' letters. The Irish Times' letter page remains by far the most comprehensive and literate of any newspaper in Ireland.

John Healy left The Irish Times temporarily in February, 1976. The Irish Independent was said to have offered him £15,000 a year, but the move was blocked by the National Union of Journalists, because at the same time, the Independent was trying to make several journalists redundant. Healy never wrote a word for the Independent, but collected his fee and returned to the Times. A year later, he invested the money in the new Western Journal in Ballina. The Western People lost the battle to have "Western" excluded from the title of the new paper, but won the war. After recriminations at the Western Journal, Jim McGuire left to become managing director of the Drogheda Independent, where Geoffrey O'Donoghue had been manager and director; McGuire's salary was £11,000 a year. McGuire, who had few known connections with the Drogheda area, had worked for the Independent group before, as managing director of the Kerryman in Tralee. At the Western Journal, McGuire is said to have faced a seventeen page dossier of criticisms from his fellow directors. He moved to Drogheda in early 1979 and is still there, now facing strong competition from a paper set up in early 1983 by various ex-employees of the Drogheda Independent. The Western Journal closed down this year; among its debts was the printing bill at the Connacht Tribune, Galway, believed to have been for around £20,000.

1976 was the year that the great but eccentric Vincent Gill of Longford died. A couple of years previously, he had sold out the Longford News to local TD Albert Reynolds for around £12,000. Gill was long notorious for all his doings; when a local man emigrated, he ran the story under the headline "Town Improvements". When he was short of copy one issue, he got hold of a full page block used the previous week for an ESB advertisement, turned it round so that it printed solid black and ran the caption "Blackout at Drumlish".

He was the subject of a famous profile on the BBC television programme "Tonight" in the early 1960s; the week the film crew arrived in Longford, they were delighted to see the headline in the *Longford News:* "Groom punches best man." Disappointingly, Gill had made up the copy. Another journalist came to Longford in search of Gill; later, he said he was always two pubs behind. On this diet of rural eccentricity, Gill's paper patched up an existence. Gill was not bothered about money and modern accounting methods; people coming with planning applications to insert in the paper were invited to contribute to the coffers, i.e. silver in the bowl. When a large bill came up for payment, such as for the ESB, Gill simply went to his regular advertisers and asked them to give a suitable donation for their year's advertising. Gill toured the countryside in his famous van, full of his yapping dogs, distributing the copies of the paper. Sometimes, it was a day or two late, but Gill never fussed. Always, he feared that the rival *Longford Leader* would buy out the paper after his death, so on the strength of the connection by name (Vincent's grandfather was called Reynolds), he sold out to Albert Reynolds. Not that Vincent was ever precise about finances: during the 1940s, he wrote several articles for the *New Yorker* magazine, but never cashed the cheques. Vincent Gill was also a very charitable man; old people in Longford pubs would often be slipped a pound or two, while he often took parcels of groceries to pensioners living outside the town. Gill died in 1976; he was buried in Ardagh churchyard, near where he had lived out the last days of his life in a run-down caravan. As his coffin was being lowered into the ground, the heavens opened, drenching the mourners. Gill would surely have approved this final two-fingered gesture from the Almighty.

When Reynolds bought the *Longford News,* it was a mere pinprick compared to the *Longford Leader.* That latter paper employed a Protestant from Dublin's South Circular Road, Derek Cobbe, as its general

Joan Trimble, managing director, Impartial Reporter.
–Impartial Reporter

manager. Cobbe compiled the fine seventy-fifth anniversary supplement of the *Longford Leader* in 1972, but after Reynolds took over the tiny *Longford News,* Cobbe moved in to build the paper into a modern provincial weekly. The Farrell family, who ran the *Longford Leader* until it suspended publication earlier this year and who are now planning to resume publication, found Cobbe's move hard to forgive and subsequently, relations between the two papers became very frosty. When Gill was running the *News,* it was little more than a source of amusement; when Cobbe took, it became a serious challenge. The *Longford News,* with the infusion of modern printing techniques and editorial coverage, including full colour news photographs, is now selling around 20,000 copies a week. Albert Reynolds in turn sold the paper in 1979 to Jack Davis, who owns the *Meath Chronicle,* and Davis sold the *News* to Derek Cobbe last year. Cobbe is well able for the rough and tumble of provincial newspaper life; at the age of ten, he bought a job lot of prints of some obscure Italian saint and sold the entire bundle to the inmates of Grangegorman mental institution. His later career, before he became involved with newspapers, involved managing hundreds of variety artistes including jugglers and clowns. In time and in his own right, Derek Cobbe, a shrewd and able newspaper owner, will come to be seen as much a "character" as Vincent Gill, Pat Dunne of the *Leitrim Observer* and J. P. Hayden of the *Westmeath Examiner.*

A great tragedy overtook the *Kerryman* in 1976. Harry Hudson, a Londoner, had only been production manager at the paper for two years before being killed in a car crash. His death came as a major blow to the paper; also in the South at the same time, Joseph O'Regan of the *Southern Star,* Skibbereen, died. he became a director in 1919 and owner in 1946. He was succeeded in the business by his son, Liam.

A young *Westmeath Examiner* reporter covering a lunch in the Army barracks at Mullingar in 1976 had one of the greatest "scoops" of the decade. Don Lavery, who now works for the *Irish Press,* noted Defence Minister Donegan's remarks about the President, Cearbhall O Dálaigh. He called him a "thundering disgrace" because O Dálaigh's close scrutiny of a parliamentary bill was holding up its progress into legislation. Lavery took down what Donegan said; his words went round the country. Shortly afterwards, O Dálaigh resigned in protest at the slight on his high office.

In September, 1976, death and destruction came to the *Belfast Telegraph,* in scenes reminiscent of the blitz on Belfast in April, 1941. That year, the *Telegraph* printed its own editions and those of the other three Belfast papers put out of action by the German bombers. In 1976, local bombers struck; they left a van loaded with a bomb on board in the newspaper's loading bay. It exploded as hundreds of employees were leaving the building. Stereo operator Joe Patton had a leg severed; he was rushed to hospital, but died four days later. Thirteen other people were taken to hospital, including Stewart

McCann, a member of the composing room staff, who broke his shoulder trying to get out of the lavatory in which he was trapped when the bomb went off. Damage to the office was extensive: the building had no heating, light or water and the editorial and production departments were in chaos. Next morning began the work of getting out that day's paper.

The newly installed phototypesetting system at the *Belfast Telegraph* had been destroyed, so copy was set at the *Northern Whig* printing firm offices, the *Irish News,* Belfast College of Technology and at two Co Down centres. In the spirit of improvisation, chief court reporter Stanley Aiken, who had started work on the paper twenty years before as a copy taker, reverted to his original role. Chief librarian Walter Macauley acted as copy runner for the day. The four page emergency edition published that evening and dubbed the "Penny Marvel", was printed on the one press out of four still working at the *Telegraph* and at the Bangor *Spectator.*

Roy Lilley, the editor, wrote in the final paragraph of his leader: "One day we shall overcome." Lord Thomson, son of the Roy Thomson who had bought the *Telegraph* in 1962 and who had never revisited Belfast after the bitter court case involving his purchase of the shares, arrived in the city for a two day visit and told managing director Tim Willis: "You must be the proudest publisher in Britain (sic), Tim, and with good reason." Over the months that followed, the *Telegraph* slowly battled its way to production normality, although for a considerable time after the explosion, pagination was limited to twenty-four pages, compared with the previous thirty-two. Last copy time for reporters was moved forward from 4.10 p.m. to 2.15 p.m. That year went out in continued tragedy for the paper; two vanmen, John Maguire and Charles Corbett, were delivering copies of *Ireland's Saturday Night* on the Crumlin Road in Belfast when they were held up, robbed and shot dead, in front of John Maguire's ten year old son Michael.

In November, 1976, John Feeney's career as editor of the *Catholic Standard* came to an abrupt end. The directors took exception to Feeney's article for the first issue of the *Mongrel Fox* entitled "The Nepotist Bishops". Out went Feeney in haste; nowadays, he is well ensconced on the *Evening Herald* diary. In 1977, Century Newspapers, Belfast, bought the *Carrickfergus Advertiser,* founded in 1883. John Caughey was its editor at the time. Owner John Pollock said that there was no longer a place in the publishing world for the small independent operator.

In 1977, Fergus Pyle left the editorship of *The Irish Times.* So many grievances had arisen among both management and journalists that the time had come for Pyle to go. Three NUJ representatives, Paul Gillespie, Don Buckley and Dick Walsh went to Gageby's house to discuss the situation. Gageby let it be known that he was available to

Billy Flackes, formerly BBC Northern Ireland's political correspondent. A native of Donegal, he began his career with weekly newspapers in Derry, Enniskillen and Armagh before joining the Belfast News Letter in 1945. After a period with the Press Association Parliamentary staff at Westminster, he went to the Belfast Telgraph in 1957, moving on to the BBC in 1964.
–BBC

Hugh McLaughlin, **creator of** Business and Finance, Woman's Way, **the** Sunday World **and publisher of the first version of the** Sunday Tribune. **His most recent newspaper launch, the** Daily News, **collapsed ignominiously after a fortnight's publication.**

come back and Pyle stood down in order to let Gageby return. The day of Gageby's return to edit the paper, there was said to have been dancing between the desks in the newsroom. One memo in circulation is said to have read: "St Douglas is back. We can do no wrong". Andrew Whittaker, who now runs the *Southside* series of giveaway papers, was referred to in a similar memo and accorded a "Sainthood" also.

Fergus Pyle became information officer at Trinity College, Dublin. Earlier this year, he returned to *The Irish Times* as a senior journalist. When Douglas Gageby returned to the paper in 1977, initially he intended staying for about two years, to see the publication out of its then intense difficulties. Since Gageby returned to the editorship, the paper has once more been hit by depressing national economic difficulties. This time, however, it has been much better prepared. There are no costly subsidiary papers (just the weekly *Irish Field)* and over the last five years, the paper has changed over to modern production methods, using computerised phototypesetting. There are even girl compositors; the old bowler-hatted brigade would be mortally astonished if they could see the change. *The Irish Times* also plans to install a web-offset press. With its advanced production techniques and Douglas Gageby's steady hand on the tiller, *The Irish Times* is riding out the present economic storm in much better shape than it did the previous downturn in trade, ten years ago. Advertising revenue is difficult, but the circulation of *The Irish Times* has stayed remarkably buoyant at around ·86,000. It remains the only Irish newspaper with a truly international reputation. The other two Dublin newspapers groups of long-standing, the *Independent* and the *Press*, still have to make the change to new technology, which is as

330

revolutionary in its way as the first Linotype nearly a century ago. In another recent advance, the night town reporters on the three Dublin morning papers were all women. Twenty years ago, that would have been unthinkable.

1978 saw the *Drogheda Express* launched, with editions covering the Dundalk and Navan areas. Despite a good editor (Tony Meade from the *Kerryman*), it failed to last the pace. The *Express* was one of a number of new provincial papers set up in the late 1970s, including the *Western Journal* and the *Kilkenny Standard*, when the newspaper industry was still enjoying a modest "boom", but which did not survive.

In Waterford in 1979, a new paper claimed to "tell it straight". The *Waterford Weekly Post* created a good deal of controversy (Irish provincial and national papers are often far more interesting for what they leave out rather than for what they put in), but some six months after it started, an extensive blaze at its printing and publishing premises proved very disruptive. 1979 also saw Co Clare produce its own newspaper disaster, the *Clare News*. In theory, it should have been successful; the *Clare Champion* had the county largely to itself for many years and several members of staff were ex-employees of the *Clare Champion*, including Sean Moloney, who had worked for that paper for forty years. Lastly, the new paper, which was edited by John Howard, had impeccable Fianna Fail connections. Despite all these factors in its favour, the *Clare News* collapsed amid recriminations and debts said to have totalled up to £¼ million.

Liam Flynn, long-serving art editor at the Irish Press **group.**

The *Kilkenny Standard* was launched on literally a shoestring, a prayer and a coinbox telephone. From the start, it was printed by the PMPA-owned *Leinster Express* in Portlaoise; later, the latter paper took over the *Standard*, which was closed down early in 1983 after suffering severe losses. In the summer of 1979, the short-lived *Frontier Times* was printed in Monaghan and published in Newry. Edited by Fabian Boyle, who previously worked for the *Observer* group in Dungannon, it did not last.

1979 saw the deaths of some notable journalistic characters. In January, Liam MacGabhann died, wasted away by illness and disappointed that the *Sunday World* did not prove to be the socially aware paper he thought when he left *The Irish Times*. His great stories and great exploits, mainly concerning the under-privileged, were told and retold by his friends. Seamus Kelly, the often abrasive Quidnunc of *The Irish Times*, also died. At his funeral, embarrassment was caused when both his wife and his girl friend arived. Finally, came the death of Terry O'Sullivan, for long the doyen of the diary columns. 1980 was marred by the death of Michael McInerney, that much-loved political correspondent of *The Irish Times* for twenty-two years until his retirement in 1974. He had spent five years in Belfast as editor of the Communist Party newspaper, *Unity*, before joining *The Irish Times* in 1946 and was one of the key figures in the post-war drive to improve salaries and conditions for members of the NUJ on Dublin newspapers.

John Hickey, managing director, Connacht Tribune, **Galway.**

Also in 1979, the memoirs of John Healy were said to be due for publication within the next few months. Healy, whose recollections of life on the *Western People*, the *Evening Press* and *The Irish Times*, to mention but three papers he has worked on, should be exceptionally interesting when they are published.

The deaths in a car crash two years ago of Mary McSparran and her brother Dr Daniel McSparran, led the way to major changes in both ownership and editorial style at the *Irish News*, Belfast. Its present editor, Martin O'Brien, who joined from the *Belfast Telegraph*, is said to be the youngest newspaper editor in Ireland and one of the most energetic, having made many changes to the paper. That summer, 1981, also saw the sudden death of Donal Foley from *The Irish Times*. Hundreds of friends from the journalistic profession and elsewhere, turned up at the funeral, to give him one of the best "wakes" ever seen in Irish newspapers.

In 1981, Jim Hawthorne's family *(Mourne Observer)* took over *The Leader* in Dromore, Co Down, with Will Hawthorne as managing director. Not only was a declining circulation halted but, despite the recession which has meant a general drop in newspaper sales, *The Leader* circulation figures have been rising steadily. The paper was founded by Joseph Lindsay in 1916 as a rival to the *Dromore Weekly Times* which started in 1900 and was edited by Robert J. Hunter. The *Leader's* rather clumsy four-page format was produced on a quad-crown flatbed press, requiring two printings. During the 1939-45 war the paper flourished and despite newsprint shortages, which seemed to more seriously affect *The Leader's* rivals, the circulation reached almost 10,000. In those days the paper was hand-folded — a laborious task for a staff of about half a dozen. An unique feature of *The Leader* was its "tight" make-up, with headings seldom larger than 8 pt. black caps for even the most sensational news. Now, the format has been completely transformed. The paper is still a broadsheet, but has increased to fourteen pages and banner headlines and pictures have brought *The Leader* up to modern standards. Like its sister publication, the *Mourne Observer*, it is one of the few in Ireland still produced by the hot metal system, using Intertypes and Linotypes, and the paper is printed on a Cossar press. Another link with the early days was established last September when Harry McCandless, who served his apprenticeship with *The Leader* in the early forties, returned as editor. Any history of *The Leader* would be incomplete without mention of William McCarthy who spent his entire working life with the paper since it was founded. "Willie" was a Linotype operator and compositor and was one of the most skilled craftsmen in the printing industry. He retired in 1982. William Lindsay also assisted his brother in the running of the business until his death in 1965. Another "product" of *The Leader* is Andrew Doloughan, who was a reporter on the paper for many years. He is now editor of the *Banbridge Chronicle*, which is based seven miles south of Dromore.

Two years ago, the *Sunday Journal* was going through its death throes, despite fervent claims to the contrary by the PMPA, which had bought over the paper not long after it started and changed its profile from a rural Sunday to a *Sunday World*-type pubication without the pin-ups. Selling far less than the 100,000 copies it needed to be profitable, the *Sunday Journal* failed to survive even the brave rescue attempts made by Dan Carmody. The venture was said to have cost the PMPA about £1 million. Hugh McLaughlin was making simultaneously optimistic noises about the new *Sunday Tribune*, complete with colour magazine. The *Tribune* had emerged from the ashes of *Hibernia*, the weekly news publication; at first McLaughlin and John Mulcahy, the editor and owner of *Hibernia*, formed an uneasy alliance. Later Mulcahy, now the urbanely successful owner and editor of the aptly-named *Phoenix*, was succeeded in partnership by the Smurfit group. As McLaughlin brought out his first colour magazine with the *Sunday Tribune*, sales soared to 130,000. Under editor of the newspaper, Conor Brady, who had been tempted away from *The Irish Times*, to which he later returned, and editor of the magazine, tall, gangling Tom McGurk, the *Tribune*, first version, seemed set for permanent success. McGurk, who had gone to the *Tribune* from RTE, later went to work for a London television station at a salary reputed to have been around £40,000 a year. After McGurk gave up editing the *Tribune* magazine, it seemed to have a veritable procession of new editors.

Fred Gamble, who started writing the "John Pepper Column" in the Belfast Telegraph **in the 1950s, immortalising many North of Ireland catch phrases.**
–Belfast Telegraph

McLaughlin was not deterred by the imminent collapse of the *Tribune*, with many contributors left unpaid; he started the *Daily News* last October. Just as the *Sunday World* had to be successful from its first issue to generate sufficient cash flow, so too did the *Daily News*. It lasted for a grand total of fifteen issues; legions of stories abound about the disaster. McLaughlin wooed John Feeney, unsuccessfully, with an offer to quadruple the £50,000 salary Feeney allegedly receives for writing the *Evening Herald* diary pages five nights a week; wisely, he stayed at the *Herald*, improving his company car in the process. One English journalist had been at his desk on the *Daily News* for just an hour when he took a 'phone call from his wife in England to say that the sale of their house had been completed. Then he received the news that the *Daily News* was folding.

One compositor managed to clock up a wages cheque worth well over £1,000 by the end of that week, taking in pre-launch setting work. When he went to cash it on the following Tuesday, it bounced. Other workers were put in even worse predicaments. Noel Reid had been tempted to leave a good job at the "Indo" to become sports editor of the new paper. He had a large family to support, but was lucky to get alternative work in RTE. Myles MacWeeney spent an energetic time doing the diary; he went on to be founding editor of *The Local News* in Drogheda. Other people had lucky escapes, too, from the collapse of McLaughlin's latest venture. A man at *Business and Finance* magazine had given in his notice to go and work on the *Daily News*; he managed to get his notice withdrawn. The most lasting effect of the *Daily News* was to stimulate the *Evening Herald* into going tabloid. Just after the war, the paper changed from broadsheet to tabloid, but the move was so unpopular that it changed back again a fortnight later. This time, the tabloid move has been rather more successful.

At the end of 1982, Morton Newspapers closed the *Armagh Guardian*, which had been in existence for over 130 years. For most of that time, it had been owned by members of the Trimble family, closely related to the *Impartial Reporter* owners in Enniskillen.

The most recent newspaper launch, earlier this year, was of the *Sunday Tribune* under new ownership, management and editorship. Most of the financial backing for the new paper has come from aviation man Tony Ryan. Its chairman is Sean MacBride and managing director is John Kelleher. Editor is Vincent Browne. Under Browne's editorship, the second version of the *Tribune* seems to have far greater staying power than the original. Browne as an editor has come a long way from August, 1968, when by his own account, he sent "dreadful" copy on the Soviet bloc invasion of Czechoslovakia to *The Irish Times*.

Last year, William O'Connell, a comp with the *Derry Journal*, was elected Mayor of the city, a rare honour for the newspaper industry. This year, Michael Mills, for twenty years political correspondent of the *Irish Press*, has been appointed Ombudsman for the Republic. Newspapers and the craft of journalism are becoming most respectable.

Today's national newspapers, run by accountants and editors, with the afternoon editorial meetings to decide the running order of the next day's stories, the computerised phototypesetting, high grade wire photographs from all over the world, from space even, it's all far from the first Irish newspapers, put together and printed by those Dublin stationers of long ago. Soon, newspapers in Ireland will move into an era when journalists will direct input their copy for setting, web offset presses will run regularly in full colour and newspapers will find new means of competing with the electronic media. Changes in the newspaper world are happening faster than ever before, yet the personal feuds will not be changed by computerisation. One of this year's graduates from the School of Journalism in Rathmines was Tim Healy; he holds an illustrious name in Irish journalism.

Other problems for the industry remain the same as always, except that they change their guises. The crippling VAT rate on cover sales and advertising is but the old Stamp Duty and advertisement tax in new clothes. Somehow, something will happen to save the newspapers. When Reuters, the international news and financial information agency, goes public shortly, the cash benefits of the share flotation will directly benefit Irish daily and Sunday papers. The Press Association has a forty-one per cent share in Reuters and Irish daily and Sunday papers have, in turn, stakes in the PA. The *Cork Examiner* is

Tom Glennon of The Irish Times **enjoyed many hilarious experiences working for provincial newspapers. His father, John E. Glennon, was once editor of the** Westmeath Independent **in Athlone.**
–The Irish Times

likely to benefit to the tune of some £4 million, the Independent group by about £6 million, while the *Sunday World* will get around £½ million. Other beneficiaries should include the *Irish Press* group, the *Irish News* and Century Newspapers in Belfast and *The Irish Times.* Battles lie ahead, such as the competition to be set up next year for newspapers, particularly the provincial weeklies, by the advent of local radio. Yet, optimism surfaces through the gloom. The *Belfast Telegraph's* vast new web offset press should be operational by the end of next year, when that organisation may start its own Sunday paper.

When Samuel Dancer started his *Mercurius Hibernicus,* when George Faulkner began his *Dublin Journal* and when Major Knox founded the present *Irish Times,* could they have foreseen how the newspaper industry of Ireland would develop? The concluding paragraph of the history of Ireland's press hopefully remains very far into the future; in the meantime, for tomorrow's copy deadline . . .

THE NATIONALIST
AND
LEINSTER TIMES.

ENLARGED EDITION

With THE NATIONALIST and LEINSTER TIMES of
THIS DAY,
SATURDAY, JANUARY 24th, 1891,
and every Week afterwards will be issued a

FOUR-PAGE SUPPLEMENT
OF
TWENTY COLUMNS!

CONSISTING OF

A SERIAL STORY !

GENERAL NEWS, AGRICULTURAL AND
HOUSEHOLD NOTES,
Useful and Entertaining Miscellaneous Reading—
carefully selected.

This Addition to THE NATIONALIST AND LEINSTER
TIMES will make it
**THE LARGEST PROVINCIAL WEEKLY
IN IRELAND !**
AND FROM
THE EXTENT AND VARIETY OF ITS LOCAL NEWS
(Embracing the Counties of Carlow, Kildare, Queen's
County, and portions of Kilkenny and Wicklow),
Supplemented and enhanced by the Attractive
Features of the New and Enlarged Issue, the
Journal will be found to fulfil all the re-
quirements of
A FIRST CLASS LOCAL AND FAMILY
NEWSPAPER.

To be had from the Office :—
DUBLIN STREET, CARLOW ;
or from Newsagents in every Town in the District.

PRICE : 2d. per Week, or Free by Post, 10s.
per Annum.

**Nationalist and Leinster
Times 1891**

PARLOPHONE RECORDS
from

GRAMOPHONE STORES
6 JOHNSON'S COURT
Grafton St., Dublin

Open Sundays, 12 till 3
Week days, 9 till 9

LOOK FOR ELECTRIC SIGN

Dublin Opinion 1927

INFLUENZA.
Prevention is Better than Cure.
In warding off this enemy the great
thing is to avoid a chill.

Leinster Express 1892

PREPARED ONLY BY
BEWLEY, OWEN AND CO.
APOTHECARIES,
(Late Bewley, Fisher and Co.)
Chemists in Ordinary to the Queen and Prince Albert,
DAME STREET, DUBLIN.

THE ROYAL SHAVING CREAM,
UNSURPASSED for promoting Comfort in Shaving,
as used by Prince Albert, the King of the Belgians, the
Lord Lieutenant of Ireland, Field Marshal the Duke of Wellington, the Duke of Devonshire, the Lord Mayor of London,
the Marquis of Abercorn ; and a large number of the Nobility
of the United Kingdom.

The great and increasing popularity of this excellent preparation renders recommendation in this place needless. In
respect of it, Bewley, Owen, and Co. will content themselves
with making the announcement, that in consideration of the
present depressed condition of monetary affairs, and to render
the ROYAL SHAVING CREAM available to all classes of the
community, they have reduced the price of it to one-half. The
Shilling and the Two Shilling Jars contain twice as much as
those sold by their predecessors at the same prices respectively.

1850

THE LATEST :: :: ::
Electrical Discovery.

ANOTHER OSRAM SUCCESS !

A 16 Candle Power (20 watt) Lamp for 200 to 260 volts.

Made with one continuous jointless filament of
great tensile strength combined with pliability.
Almost unbreakable. Absolutely shockproof.
Stronger than any other Lamp. :: :: ::
Consumption, 1 unit in 50 hours. :: ::

—— Price, 3s. 3d. each. ——

Further Particulars
at the Stand of the **General Electric Co.,**
DUBLIN OFFICES:—13 TRINITY STREET.

Dublin Exhibition Catalogue 1911

CORCORAN & CO.'S
LEMONADE.

Only Prize Medal Awarded, Cork Exhibition, 1883.

LEMONADE,
SODA WATER,
GINGER BEER,
CHAMPAGNE CIDER,
AROMATIC GINGER BEER,
SELTZER WATER,
DOUBLE SODA WATER
(CARBONATED).
MANUFACTURED BY STEAM POWER.

PRIZE MEDAL AND CERTIFICATES
OF MERIT,
DUBLIN AND CORK EXHIBITIONS, 1882-1883.

WORKS:
24, Wellington Square, Carlow.
(ESTABLISHED A.D. 1827).

REPORT.
From CHARLES A. CAMERON, M.D., Fellow and Professor of
Chemistry, Royal College of Surgeons, Medical Officer of
Health for Dublin :—
" I have submitted to careful analysis specimens of the various aerated
beverages and Mineral Waters prepared by Messrs. Corcoran & Co.,
Carlow. I have found them of excellent flavour, and their chemical
composition shows that they have been manufactured from the best and
purest materials. The water used in the preparation of these articles is
of good quality, and free from sewage matter, which is not always the
case with water used in Mineral Water Manufactories"
CHARLES A. CAMERON.

Nationalist and Leinster Times 1888

By Royal
Warrant to   His Majesty
King George V.

VALUE
IN
IRELAND.

BEWLEY, SONS, AND CO., LTD.,
DUBLIN.

COUNTRY ORDERS CARRIAGE PAID.

The Irish Times 1916

FOR SUPERIOR & PAINLESS
DENTAL TREATMENT
VISIT
Mr J. J. MORRIS,
36 Henry Street Dublin,
Estd. 1903.
Hours : 10 to 7. Consultations Free
Fees Moderate.

Fortnightly Visits in Towns as under—
NAAS—Mondays at Cunningham's
Hotel.
DUNLAVIN—Wednesdays, Imper-
ial Hotel.
KILCULLEN—Saturdays, Mrs. Dil
lon, T' Square.

Leinster Express 1929

336

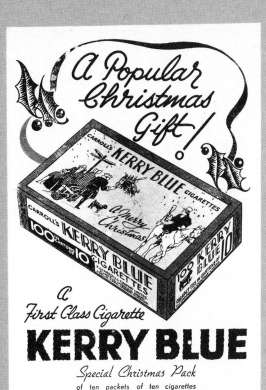

A Popular Christmas Gift!

A First Class Cigarette

KERRY BLUE

Special Christmas Pack
of ten packets of ten cigarettes

Nenagh Guardian 1938

GREAT NORTHERN RLY

DAY EXCURSION FROM

DUBLIN TO BELFAST

THURSDAY NEXT, 14th SEPT.
EXPRESS CORRIDOR TRAIN
FARE

| Amiens Street dep. 11.40 a.m. | **6/-** | Belfast dep. 8.15 p.m. |

Two-day Tickets will also be issued by this
Special, valid for Return by any train on
FRIDAY, 15th SEPTEMBER
THIRD CLASS FARE **13/8**

Children Under 14 Years Half Fare.

PASSENGERS DO NOT REQUIRE
PASSPORTS, OR OFFICIAL TRAVEL
PERMITS.

Please BOOK IN ADVANCE at City Office,
2 Lower O'Connell Street, or Amiens Street
Station.

GEO. B. HOWDEN, General Manager.
Dublin, Sept., 1939.

The Irish Times 1939

MORRIS CARS

1937 SEASON — 1937 SEASON

THIS IS THE CAR YOU HAVE BEEN
WAITING FOR

Prices from £175 to £375
ALL ASSEMBLED IN THE I.F.S.

SOLD AND SERVICED BY THE COUNTY
SLIGO AND LEITRIM MAIN AGENTS

HENDERSON'S
Motor and Engineering Works

WINE STREET, SLIGO.

PHONE: 10. 'GRAMS: "REPAIRS."

Sligo Champion 1937

Twilfit

The Choice of Well Dressed Women

MODEL 8300—
Front - lacing
Corset with dia-
gonal boning
over diaphragm
in lightweight
brochó material
fastening with a
lightning fast-
ener at side.
6 suspenders. In
tea-rose. Sizes
24-32 ins. Price,
18/11

MODEL 6366—
Wrap-round in
strong light
coutil suitable
for the average
or heavier fig-
ure. Elastic
panels over hips
are 14-ins. deep.
Two pairs sus-
penders fitted.
In tea-rose.
Sizes, 24-32 ins.
Price,
6/11

Model 6372. Twilfit light weight Girdle
in tea-rose lâstal brochó and "Lastex"
Yarn brochó. 14 ins.
deep over hips.
Sizes 24-36 ins.
12/11

All "TWILFIT" CORSETS are
fitted with "TWILGRIP"
Suspenders.

MADE IN THE IRISH FREE STATE AND FULLY GUARANTEED.

Sligo Champion 1936

RIALTO Londonderry's Bijou Cinema — TO-DAY

BOGART AS YOU'D NEVER SUSPECT HIM IN

CONFLICT ALEXIS SMITH—SYDNEY GREENSTREET

First Official Film of the BURMA CAMPAIGN
"BURMA VICTORY"

Londonderry Sentinel 1946

Of course I take a laxative

HOW DO YOU THINK I KEEP
SO FIT AND ENERGETIC!

To keep yourself fit—take Beecham's
Pills. For over ninety years Beecham's
Pills have been trusted as the safest,
purest, most effective laxative the
world has ever known. Make it your
Golden Rule to take Beecham's Pills
when you feel feverish, irritable or
tired. Begin a course of Beecham's
Pills to-day. Sold everywhere.

My laxative is

Beecham's Pills
WORTH A GUINEA A BOX

Irish Press 1939

UNITED STATES LINES
Operating the only fleet of passenger ships under the American flag between Ireland and America.

COBH to NEW YORK

S.S. "Republic"
(17,910 Tons).
Cabin and Third Class.
S.S. "President Harding"
and
"President Roosevelt"
(14,187 Tons).
Cabin and Third Class.
S.S. "America"
(21,144 Tons).
"The Largest Cabin Ship in
the World, now refitting.
S.S. "Leviathan"
(59,956 Tons).
The Largest Liner in the
World.
S.S. "George Washington"
(23,788 Tons).
A Great Favourite.

The best cuisine on the Atlantic, prompt attentive
service, comfort and enjoyment mark every hour of
the journey. No effort is spared by the whole
personnel in making every passenger feel thoroughly
at home. It is an unrivalled opportunity of meeting
Americans and experiencing American customs and
hospitality during the actual voyage. Music, Dancing, Deck Games, including Tennis and Golf, and
other entertainments make the trip a genuine
holiday.

It is our business to make TRAVEL
EASY, and a pleasure to lighten the
problems of transportation. In Dublin
we are in the heart of the city at
3-4 College Street, and in Cobh at 12
Westbourne Terrace, where you will find
a Cead Mile Failte when you call, write
or Te'ephone.

Send for Illustrated Booklet "D."

Any Travel Agents will tell you
about United States Lines Service.

14 REGENT STREET, LONDON, S.W.1.
And all Principal Cities.

Dublin Opinion 1927

337

Sources

Personal recollections and newspaper files in individual newspaper offices, at the National Library, Dublin and the Newspaper Library, Colindale, London, provided most of the source material for the book. The following books were consulted:

Advertisers' ABC. London, 1897.
After I was sixty. Lord Thomson of Fleet. London, 1975.
An Irishman's Diary. Patrick Campbell. London, 1950.
An Open Book. John Huston. USA, 1980.
As I was going down Sackville Street. Oliver St John Gogarty. London, 1937.
Samuel Beckett, a biography. Deirdre Bair. London, 1978.
Books, Newspapers and Pamphlets printed in Waterford, 1801-1820. Ernest Dix. Waterford, 1916.
As He Saw It. Ralph Bossence. Belfast, 1971.
By the Banks of the Dordogne. R. M. Smyllie. Dublin, n.d.
Carpathian Days – and Nights. R. M. Smyllie. Co Louth, 1942.
Carpathian Contrasts. R. M. Smyllie. Dublin, 1938.
Cavendish Family. F. L. Bickley. London, 1911.
A biography of Dracula – the story of Bram Stoker. Harry Ludlam. London, 1962
Dictionary of Irish Biography. Henry Boylan. Dublin, 1978.
Dublin Made Me. C. S. Andrews. Cork, 1979.
Charles Gavan Duffy: patriot and statesman. Leon O'Broin. Dublin, 1967.
Fifty Years of Irish Journalism. Andrew Dunlop. Dublin, 1911.
Flann O'Brien. Anne Clissmann. Dublin, 1975.
Freedom of the Press in Ireland, 1784-1841. Brian Inglis. London, 1954.
History of Advertising from the earliest times. Henry Sampson. London, 1874.
History of Clonmel. Rev. William P. Burke. Waterford, 1907.
History of the County of Longford. J. P. Farrell. Dublin, 1891.
History of the Irish Newspaper, 1685-1760. Robert Munter. Cambridge, 1967.
History of Irish periodical literature. R. R. Madden. London, 1867.
Ireland in the Age of Imperialism and Revolution, 1760-1801. R. B. McDowell. Oxford, 1979.
Ireland in the war years. Joseph T. Carroll. Newton Abbot, 1975.
Irish Booklover. Various issues, c.1909.
Letters of James Joyce. Ed: Stuart Gilbert (vol i), Richard Ellman (vols ii & iii). London, 1957-66.

Man of Wars. William Howard Russell of The Times. Alan Hankinson. London, 1982.

Memoirs of CGD. Charles Gavan Duffy. Dublin, 1849.

My Life and Easy Times. Patrick Campbell. London, 1967.

Newspaper Gazetteer. R. D'A Newton. London, 1860.

Newspaper Press Directory, 1884-1921. London.

C. S. Parnell. Paul Bew. Dublin, 1980.

C. S. Parnell, the man and his family. R. F. Foster. USA, 1976.

Paper Making in Ireland. Desmond J. Clarke and Patrick Madden. Dublin, 1954.

Printing in Ireland. Desmond J. Clarke and Patrick Madden. Dublin, 1954.

Printing in 19th century Limerick. Ernest Dix. Dublin, 1913.

Printing in Waterford, 1821-1900. Ernest Dix. Dublin, 1906. (Typescript).

Sheridan Le Fanu. Nelson Browne. London, 1951.

Tales relating to some Dublin newspapers of the 18th century. Ernest Dix. Dublin, 1910.

The Devil You Know. Jack White. Dublin, 1970.

The Emergency. Neutral Ireland, 1939-1945. Bernard Share. Dublin, 1978.

The Great Hunger. Cecil Woodham-Smith. USA, 1962.

The IRA. Tim Pat Coogan. London, 1970.

The Life and Death of the Press Barons. Piers Brendon. London, 1982.

The Newspaper, an International History. Anthony Smith. London, 1983.

The Sword of Light. Desmond Ryan. London, 1939.

Wilkie Collins, Le Fanu and other. Stewart M. Ellis. London, 1931.

Written on the Wind. Ed: Louis McRedmond. Dublin, 1976.

List of Newspapers

Major newspapers, together with major changes of title, are listed. The first date is the year of foundation and the second date where appropriate, is the year that publication ceased. In some cases, the date given is approximate, marked 'c'. Irish language newspapers, "Mosquito" press titles and minor titles and other details have had to be omitted for reasons of space; Dublin alone produced some 200 newspapers titles during the eighteenth century, but many were ephemeral and copies cannot be traced.

Achill Island	1837	1869
Achill Missionary Herald and Western Witness		
Arklow		
Arklow Reporter	1890	1893
(incorporated with Bray Herald)		
Weekly Gazette	1958	1959
Armagh		
Armagh Conservative	c1844	c1844
Armagh Guardian	1844	1982
Armagh Observer	1930	——
Armagh Standard	1879	1909
(incorporated in Ulster Gazette)		
Armagh Volunteer	c1821	c1824
Ulster Gazette	1844	——
Athlone		
Athlone Conservative Advocate	1837	1837
Athlone Independent	1833	1836
Athlone Mirror	1841	1842
Athlone Sentinel	1834	1861
Athlone Times	1889	1902
Westmeath Herald	1859	1860
Westmeath Independent	1846	1968
(merged with Offaly Independent in 1968 to form Westmeath-Offaly Independent)		
Westmeath-Offaly Independent	1968	——
Ballina		
Ballina Advertiser	1840	1843
Ballina Chronicle	1849	1851
Ballina Herald	c1866	1962
(incorporated with Western People)		
Ballina Impartial or Tyrawly Advertiser	1823	1835
Ballina Journal	1882	1895
Connaught Watchman	1851	1863
Tyrawly Herald	1844	1870
Western Gem	1843	1843

Western People	1883	——
Western Journal	1977	1983
Ballinasloe		
Connaught Leader	1904	1907
Connaught People	1882	1886
East Galway Democrat	1913	1949
Loughrea Nationalist	c1902	c1912
(breaks in publication)		
Western Argus	1828	1833
Western News	1877	1926
Western Star	1845	1902
Ballinrobe		
Ballinrobe Chronicle and Mayo Advertiser	1866	1903
Ballymena		
Ballymena Advertiser	c1866	1892
Ballymena Chronicle and Antrim Observer	1970	——
Ballymena Guardian and Antrim Standard	1970	——
Ballymena Mail	1882	1884
(incorporated with Larne Weekly Recorder)		
Ballymena Observer	1855	——
Ballymena Weekly Telegraph	1887	1966
(continued as Ballymena Times, 1966-1970; incorporated with Ballymena Observer, 1970)		
Ballymoney		
Ballymoney Free Press	1863	1934
(incorporated with Coleraine Chronicle)		
North Antrim Standard	1887	1922
Northern Herald	c1860	1862
Ballynahinch		
Ballynahinch Herald	c1920	c1920
Ballynahinch Star	1974	c1975

Ballyshannon Ballyshannon Herald — 1832 — 1873

	Start	End
Donegal Democrat	1919	——
Donegal Independent	1884	1921
Donegal Vindicator	1889	1956

Banbridge

	Start	End
Banbridge Chronicle	1870	——

Bangor

	Start	End
County Down Spectator	1904	——
North Down Herald	c1880	1957

Belfast

	Start	End
Banner of Belfast	1842	1869
Belfast Advertiser	1879	1886
Belfast Advertiser	1933	1934
Belfast Citizen	1886	1887
Belfast Commercial Chronicle	1805	1855
Belfast Courant	1745	1746
Belfast Daily Mail (prospectus issued 1870, never published)		
Belfast Daily Post	1882	1882
Belfast Evening Star	1890	1890
Belfast Evening Telegraph (continued as Belfast Telegraph from 1918)	1870	——
Belfast Mercantile Register	1882	1894
Belfast Mercury	1783	1786
Belfast Mercury	1851	1861
Belfast Daily Mercury	1851	1861
Belfast Morning News (incorporated into Irish News, 1892)	1855	1892
Belfast News Letter (continued as News Letter from 1962)	1737	——
Belfast Times	1872	1872
Belfast Times	1979	1979
Belfast Weekly Mail	1852	1854
Belfast Weekly News (merged with Belfast News Letter)	1855	1942
Belfast Weekly Telegraph (continued as Cityweek, 1964-1970; Thursday, 1970-1971)	1873	1964
Castlereagh Courier	1980	——
Evening Press	1870	1874
Irish News	1891	
Irish Weekly News	1891	1981
Morning Post	1855	1858
Northern Herald	1833	1836
Northern Star	1792	1797
Northern Star	1868	1872
Northern Star	1897	1908
Northern Whig	1824	1963
Sunday News	1965	——

	Start	End
Ulster Echo	1874	1916
Ulster Examiner (incorporated with Morning News)	1868	1882
Ulster Guardian	c1907	c1920
Ulster Observer	1862	1868
Ulster Saturday Night (continued as Ireland's Saturday Night from 1896)	1894	——
Ulster Times	1836	1843
Ulster Weekly News (incorporated with Weekly Examiner)	1873	1882
Vindicator	1839	1848
Weekly Examiner (incorporated with Irish Weekly News)	1870	1892
Weekly Northern Whig	1858	1940
Weekly Observer	1868	1872
Weekly Press	1858	1875
Weekly Vindicator	1847	1852
Witness	1874	1941

Birr

	Start	End
Galway Free Press	c1910	1912
King's County Chronicle (continued as Offaly Chronicle, then Midland Chronicle)	1845	1922
	1922	1963
Midland Tribune	1881	——

Boyle

	Start	End
Boyle Gazette	1891	1891
Roscommon and Leitrim Gazette	1822	1882
Roscommon Constitutionalist	1889	c1891
Roscommon Herald	1859	——
Western Nationalist	1907	1920

Bray

	Start	End
Bray Gazette	1861	1873
Bray Herald	1876	1927
Bray People	1979	——
Bray Tribune and East Coast Express (continued in Dublin under various titles until 1952)	1936	1946

Carlow

	Start	End
Carlow Independent	1875	1882
Carlow Morning Post	1817	1835
Carlow Nationalist and Leinster Times (Nationalist and Leinster Times from 1885)	1883	——
Carlow Post	1853	1878
Carlow Sentinel	1832	1920
Carlow Standard	1832	1832
Carlow Vindicator	1892	c1898
Carlow Weekly News	1858	1863
Leinster Reformer	1839	1841

Carrickfergus

Carrickfergus Advertiser	1883	——

Carrick-on-Shannon

Leitrim Journal	1850	1872
Leitrim Leader	1950	1952
Leitrim News	c1972	1972
Leitrim Observer	c1889	——

Castlebar

Connaught Telegraph	1828	——
Mayo Constitution	1812	1872
Mayo Examiner	1868	1903
Mayoman	1919	1921
Telegraph	1830	1870

Cavan

Anglo-Celt	1846	——
(breaks in publication between 1847 and 1864)		
Cavan Herald	1818	c1818
Cavan Observer	1857	1864
Cavan Weekly News	1864	1907
Irish Post	1910	1920

Clonmel

Clonmel Advertiser	c1811	1838
Clonmel Advertiser	1843	c1843
Clonmel Advertiser	1884	1884
Clonmel Chronicle	1848	1935
Clonmel Gazette	c1792	c1792
Clonmel Herald	1813	1841
Clonmel Free Press	1826	1880
Munster Tribune	1955	1967
Sporting Press	1951	——
Tipperary Champion	c1898	1910
Tipperary Constitution	1835	1848
Tipperary Free Press	1826	1881
Tipperary Nationalist	1886	——
(previously published in Thurles, 1881-1883)		
Tipperary People	1865	1866

Coalisland

Democrat	c1966	——

Coleraine

Coleraine Chronicle	1844	——
Coleraine Constitution	1875	——
(Northern Constitution from 1908)		
Coleraine Herald	1897	1902
Coleraine Weekly News	c1865	c1865

Cookstown

Cookstown News	1896	1916
Mid-Ulster Mail	1891	——

Cork

Constitution	1823	1924
Cork Advertiser	1810	1824
Cork County Chronicle	1934	1936
Cork Examiner	1841	——
Cork Free Press	1910	1916
Cork Herald	1858	1901
Cork Idler	1715	1715
Cork Sun	1903	1905
Cork Weekly Examiner	1896	1981
Cork Weekly News	1883	1923
Evening Echo	1894	——
Freeholder	1716	1716
Harp of Erin	1797	1797
Irish Monthly Mercury	1649	1650
Munster Advertiser	1839	1841
North Cork Herald	1904	1908
Southern Reporter	1813	1871
continued as Irish Daily Telegraph and Southern Reporter	1871	1873
Weekly Herald	1867	1901
Weekly Star and General Advertiser	1864	1869

Curragh

Curragh News	1891	1891

Derry

Derry Journal	1772	——
(Londonderry Journal until 1880)		
Derry Weekly News	1892	1956
Irish Daily Telegraph	1904	1952
Londonderry Chronicle	1829	1872
Londonderry Guardian	1857	1871
Londonderry Reporter	1810	1811
Londonderry Sentinel	1829	——
Londonderry Standard	1836	1964
(Derry Standard from 1888)		

Donegal

Donegal People's Press	1931	——
(now published Sligo)		

Downpatrick

Down Recorder	1836	——
(Downpatrick Recorder until 1878)		
Downshire Chronicle	1839	1840
Downshire Protestant	1855	1862

Drogheda

Advertiser	1896	1924
The Conservative	1849	1908
Drogheda Argus	1835	——
(continued as the Argus from 1951; also published Dundalk & Monaghan)		

Drogheda Conservative Journal	1837	1848
Drogheda Express	1978	1980
Drogheda Independent	1884	——
Drogheda Journal	1788	1843
Drogheda Reporter	1861	1865
The Local News	1983	——

Dromore

Dromore Weekly Times	1900	1952
Leader	1916	——

Dublin

An Account of the Chief	1659	1659
Occurrences of Ireland	(old calendar)	
Constitution or		
Anti-Union Evening Post	1799	1800
Constitution	1854	1855
Constitution and Church Sentinel	1849	1853
Correspondent	1807	1826
Daily News	1982	1982
Dublin Chronicle	1787	1793
Dublin Chronicle	1815	1817
Dublin Courant	1702	1725
Dublin Courier	1759	1766
Dublin Daily Express	1851	1921
(registration issues, 1921-1960)		
Dublin Evening Herald	1804	1814
Dublin Evening Herald	1821	1822
Dublin Evening Herald	1846	1853
Dublin Evening Mail	1823	1962
Dublin Evening Post	1732	1734
(revived)	1737	1741
Dublin Evening Post	1778	1875
Dublin Gazette (Weekly Courant)	1703	1728
Dublin Gazette (now Iris Oifigiúil)	1705	——
Dublin Intelligence	1690	1694
Dublin Journal	1726	1824
Dublin Local Advertiser	1858	1861
Dublin Mercury	1704	1760
Dublin Morning Post	c1804	1832
Dublin News-Letter	1685	1685
Dublin Post (Freesheet)	1968	c1971
Dublin & Provincial Sun Series	1967	1967
Dublin Weekly Programme	1893	1896
of Events		
Esdall's News-Letter	1746	1752
Evening Freeman	1831	1871
Evening Herald	1804	1814
Evening Herald	1891	——
Evening Irish Times	c1860	1921
Evening News	1859	1864
Evening News	1887	1888
Evening Packet	1828	1862
(incorporated with		
Dublin Evening Mail)		
Evening Press	1932	1932
Evening Press	1954	——
Evening Telegraph	1871	1924
Evening Telegraph	1932	1932
Faulkner's Dublin Journal	1725	1825
Flying Post (Post Master)	c1699	1710
Freeman's Journal	1763	1924
General Advertiser	1837	1923
Hamilton's Advertiser	1736	1736
Impartial Occurrences	1704	1780
Irish Daily Independent	1891	1904
(continued as Irish Independent		
from 1905)		
Irish Field	1894	——
Irish Peasant	1905	1910
Irish Press	1931	——
Irish Weekly Independent	1893	1960
Lady's Herald	1895	1908
Magee's Weekly Packet	1777	1793
Mercurius Hibernicus	1663	1663
(Irish Intelligencer)		
Morning Mail	1870	1912
Morning Register	1824	1843
Nation	1842	1900
National Press	1891	1892
Patriot	c1811	1828
People's Weekly (see Bray Tribune)	1946	1952
The Press	1797	1798
Protestant Post Boy	1712	c1724
Radio Review	1949	1961
Rathmines News and	1895	1907
Dublin Lantern		
Reilly's Weekly Oracle	1736	1736
Saunder's Newsletter	1755	1879
Southside Series (Freesheets)	1979	——
Sport	1880	1931
Sport	1946	1950
Sunday Freeman	1913	1916
Sunday Herald	1898	1898
Sunday Independent	1905	——
Sunday Journal	1979	1982
Sunday Observer	1831	1836
Sunday Press	1949	——
Sunday Review	1957	1963
Sunday Tribune (break in publication)	1980	——
Sunday World	1895	1897
Sunday World	1973	——
The Irish Times	1823	1825
The Irish Times	1859	——
Times Pictorial	1941	1958
(various changes of title)		
Tribune	1834	1835
Tribune	1855	1856
Volunteer Journal	1783	1784
The Warder	1822	1919

(continued as Sports Mail and		
Irish Weekly Mail until 1939)		
Weekly Freeman's Journal	c1817	1924
Weekly Irish Times	1875	1941
(continued as Times Pictorial)		

Dundalk

Argus (see under Drogheda)		
Dundalk and County Louth	1908	1909
Independent		
Dundalk and Newry Express	1860	1870
Dundalk Democrat	1849	——
Dundalk Examiner	1881	1960
Dundalk Herald	1868	1921
Dundalk Patriot	1847	1848

Dungannon

Armagh-Down Observer	c1966	——
Dungannon Democrat	1913	c1924
Dungannon News	1893	1916
Dungannon Observer	1930	——
Mid-Ulster Observer	1952	——
Tyrone Courier	1880	——
Ulster Chronicle	1807	c1824

Dungarvan

Dungarvan Leader	1938	——
Dungarvan Observer	1912	——

Dun Laoghaire

Dun Laoghaire Borough Times	1948	1949
East Coast Express (see Bray)	1936	1939
East Coast	1974	1974
Kingstown Gazette	1868	1869
Kingstown Standard	1885	1886

Ennis

Clare Champion	1903	——
Clare Examiner	1879	1887
Clare Freeman	1853	1884
Clare Independent	1876	1885
Clare Journal	1828	1917
Clareman	1897	1903
Clare News	1979	1980
Clare Weekly News	1878	1880
Ennis Chronicle	c1803	1831
Ennis Gazette	c1813	c1813
Man in the Moon	1878	1878
Saturday Record	1898	1936
(continued as Saturday Record and		
Clare Journal from 1917)		

Enniscorthy

Echo	1902	——
Enniscorthy Guardian	1889	——
Enniscorthy News	1860	1912
Enniscorthy Recorder	1893	1902
The Watchman	1869	1886

Enniskillen

Enniskillen Advertiser	1864	1876
Enniskillen Chronicle	1808	1893
(incorporated with Impartial		
Reporter)		
Enniskillen Gazette	c1854	c1854
Enniskillen Press	1895	1907
Enniskillen Sentinel	c1877	c1877
Enniskillen Watchman	1848	1848
Fermanagh Herald	1904	——
Fermanagh News	1894	1920
Fermanagh News	1967	——
Fermanagh Sentinel	1854	1855
Fermanagh Times	1880	1949
Impartial Reporter	1825	——

Galway

Connacht Sentinel	1925	——
Connacht Tribune	1909	——
Connaught Champion	1904	1911
Connaught Journal	1813	1840
Galway Advertiser	1970	——
Galway American	1862	1863
Galway Express	1853	1920
Galway Free Press	1832	1835
Galway Independent Paper	c1825	1832
Galway Mercury	1844	1860
Galway Observer	1881	1966
Galway Packet	1852	1854
Galway Patriot	1835	1839
Galway Pilot	1905	1918
Galway Press	1860	c1861
Galway Standard	1842	1843
Galway Vindicator	1841	1899
Galway Weekly Advertiser	1823	1843
The Irishman	1835	1835
Warden of Galway	1853	1853

Kilkeel

Kilkeel Gazette	1888	1889

Kilkenny

Finn's Leinster Journal	1767	1965
Kilkenny People	1892	——
Kilkenny Standard	1980	1983
Kilkenny and Wexford Express	1878	1907
Kilkenny Moderator	c1775	1924
The Post	1925	1960

Kinsale

Bee	c1832	c1832

Kilrush		
Clare Advertiser	1868	1888
Kilrush Herald	1879	1922

Larne		
Larne Observer	1906	1906
Larne Times	1891	——
(East Antrim Times since 1962)		
Larne Weekly Recorder	1881	1883
Larne Weekly Reporter	1881	1904

Letterkenny		
Derry People and Donegal News	1902	——

Limerick		
General Advertiser	1804	1820
Limerick and Clare Examiner	1846	1855
Limerick Chronicle	1766	——
Limerick Echo	1899	1947
Limerick Evening Echo	1899	1899
(incorporated with Limerick Echo)		
Limerick Evening Herald	1833	1835
Limerick Evening Post	1828	1833
Limerick Herald and	1788	1789
Munster Advertiser		
Limerick Herald	1831	1835
(incorporated with Limerick Times;		
closed 1837)		
Limerick Journal	1739	1744
(changed title to Munster Journal)	1744	c1777
Limerick Journal	1779	1819
Limerick Leader	1889	——
Limerick Newsletter	1716	1716
Limerick Observer	1856	1857
Limerick Reporter	1839	1849
(continued as Limerick Reporter and		
Tipperary Vindicator)	1850	1896
Limerick Standard	1837	1841
Limerick Star	1893	1894
Limerick Weekly Echo	1897	——
Munster Journal	c1737	1777
Munster News	1851	1935
Southern Advertiser	c1889	1893
Southern Chronicle	1863	1885

Lisburn		
Lisburn Herald	1891	1969
Lisburn Standard	1876	1959
Lisburn Weekly Mail	1903	1920
Ulster Star	1957	——

Longford		
Longford Independent	1868	1918
Longford Journal	1839	1914
Longford Leader	1897	——
(break in publication 1983)		

Longford Messenger	1837	c1837
Longford News	1936	——
Midland Counties Gazette	1853	1863

Lurgan		
Lurgan and Portadown Examiner	1930	——
Lurgan Chronicle	1850	1851
Lurgan Gazette	1861	1874
Lurgan Herald	1960	1961
Lurgan Mail	1890	——
Lurgan Times	1877	1915
Lurgan Weekly News	1873	1877

Mohill, Co Leitrim		
Leitrim Advertiser	1870	1916

Monaghan		
Argus	1875	1881
Argus, 1950s (see under Drogheda)		
Monaghan People	1906	1908
Northern Standard	1839	——
People's Advocate	1876	1906

Mullingar		
Midland Chronicle	1827	1827
Midland Topic	1971	——
Westmeath Examiner	1882	——
Westmeath Guardian and	1835	1928
Longford News-Letter		
Westmeath Journal	1823	1834
Westmeath Nationalist	1891	1939

Naas		
Kildare Observer	1879	1935
Leinster Express		
(published at Naas, 1868-1873;		
1874-1947)		
Leinster Leader	1880	——

Navan		
Meath Chronicle	1897	——
Meath People	1857	1863

Nenagh		
Nenagh Gazette	1841	1842
Nenagh Guardian	1838	——
Nenagh News	1898	1924
Nenagh Tribune	1980	1982
Tipperary Advocate	1858	1889
Tipperary Vindicator	1844	1871

Newcastle		
Mourne Observer	1949	——

New Ross		
New Ross Reporter	1871	1910
New Ross Standard	1889	——

Newry

Frontier Sentinel	1904	1972
Frontier Times	1979	1979
Newry Commercial Telegraph	1812	1970
(Newry Telegraph from 1877)		
Newry Examiner	1830	1880
(continued as Dundalk Examiner)		
Newry Herald	1858	1864
Newry Journal (Jones)	c1770	c1776
Newry Journal (Stevenson)	c1774	1788
Newry Reporter	1867	——
Newry Standard	1879	1899

Newtownards

Newtownards Chronicle	1873	——
Newtownards Spectator	1904	——

Omagh

Tyrone Constitution	1844	——
Ulster Evening Herald	1914	1915
Ulster Herald	1901	——

Portadown

Portadown Express	1906	1920
Portadown Times	1922	——
Portadown (Weekly) News	1859	——

Portlaoise

Leinster Express	1831	——
(see Naas entry)		
Leinster Independent	1834	1840

Rathfriland

Outlook	1940	——

Roscommon

Roscommon Champion	1927	——
Roscommon Journal	1828	1927
Roscommon Reporter	1850	1860
Roscommon Weekly Messenger	1848	1935

Skibbereen

Skibbereen and West Carbery Eagle	1857	1929
(various title changes; popularly		
known as Skibbereen Eagle. Break in		
publication, 1920-1926)		
Southern Star	1889	——

Sligo

Sligo Champion	1836	——
Sligo Chronicle	1850	1893
Sligo Guardian	1849	1850
Sligo Independent	1855	1961
Sligo Journal	c1807	1866
Sligo Journal	1980	1983
Sligo Nationalist	1913	1920
Sligo Observer	1828	1831
Sligo Star	1899	1902
Sligo Times	1909	c1914

Strabane

Strabane Chronicle	1896	——
Strabane Weekly Post	1812	1837
Strabane Weekly News	1908	——

Strokestown

Strokestown Democrat	1913	1945

Thurles

Tipperary Leader	1855	1856
Tipperary Leader	1882	1885
Tipperary Star	1909	——

Tralee

Chute's Western Herald	c1802	1835
Western Herald	1828	1835
Kerry Advocate	1914	1916
Kerry Champion	1928	1958
Kerry Evening Post	1813	1917
Kerry Evening Star	1902	1914
Kerry Examiner	1840	1856
Kerry's Eye	1974	——
Kerry Independent	1880	1884
Kerry News	1894	1939
Kerry People	1902	1922
Kerry Press	1914	1916
Kerry Sentinel	1878	1918
Kerry Star	1861	1863
Kerry Weekly Reporter	1883	1936
Kerryman	1904	——
The Liberator	1915	1939
Tralee Chronicle	1843	1881
Tralee Mercury	1829	1839

Tuam

Connaught Patriot	1859	1869
Tuam Herald	1837	——
Tuam News	1871	1896

Tullamore

Central Weekly Times	1859	1859
Leinster Reporter	1859	1929
(included Central Times)		
Tullamore and King's County	1894	1968
Independent (Break in publication,		
1920-1922; Offaly Independent		
from 1922, merged with		
Westmeath Independent in 1968 to		
form Westmeath-Offaly		
Independent)		
Tullamore Tribune	1977	——

Waterford

Chronicle	1844	1910
Citizen	1859	1906
Evening News	1899	1957
The Mail	1823	1908
Mail and Waterford Daily Express	1855	1860
Munster Express	1860	——
(included various subsidiary titles; Munster Express only from 1930)		
News and Star	1959	——
(Waterford News & Star, 1959-1966)		
Ramsey's Waterford Chronicle	1765	1844
Waterford Evening Star	1917	1940
Waterford Flying Post	1729	1729
Waterford Freeman	1845	1847
Waterford Herald	c1789	1796
Waterford Journal	1765	1771
Waterford Mirror	c1798	1843
Waterford Mirror and Tramore Visitor	1860	1910
Waterford News	1848	1958
(merged with Waterford Star)		(Dec.)
Waterford Standard	1863	1953
Waterford Star	1892	1959
(incorporated with Waterford News)		
Weekly Waterford Chronicle	1827	1844

Warrenpoint

Warrenpoint Weekly	1953	1953

Westport

Mayo News	1893	——

Wexford

County of Wexford Express	1875	1907
County Wexford Independent	1906	1908
Free Press	c1890	1971
Guardian	1847	1856
Ireland's Own	1902	——
The People	1853	——
Sporting	1892	1893
Wexford and Kilkenny Express	1878	1907
(continued with County of Wexford Express from 1878)		
Wexford Conservative	1832	1846
Wexford Constitution	1858	1887
Wexford Evening Post	1826	1830
Wexford Freeman	1832	1837
Wexford Herald	c1806	1865
Wexford Independent	1830	1906

Wicklow

Wicklow News-Letter and County Advertiser	1857	1926
Wicklow People	1886	——
Wicklow Press	1905	1916
Wicklow Star	1895	1900

Index

McGuinness, Gerry, 319, 321
McGuinness, Jim, 238, 248
McGuire, Jim, 82
McInerney, Michael, 228, 331
McIntyre, Patrick, 128
McKinney, Willie, 316
McLaughlin, Hugh, 253, 292, 293, 319
McManus, M. J., 172, 221
McNamara, Brinsley, 226
McRedmond, Louis, 318
McSharry, Deirdre, 263
McSparran, Dr Daniel, 194, 333
Meath Chronicle, Navan, founding, 90; suppression, 1918, 133
Medley, Cork, 31
Meehan, Paul, 264
Mercurius Hibernicus, 23
"Messiah", first performance, 30
Midland Chronicle, 290
Midland Topic, 316
Midland Tribune, Birr, founding, 78; Dáil Bonds advertisement, 1919, 140
Milligan, Cecil, 179
Mills, Michael, 334
Moles, Thomas, 120
Montford, Paddy, 156, 235
Montgomery, Alan, 185, 188, 281
Montgomery, Leslie, 185
Mooney, Jack, 254
Mooney, Joe, 133
Mooney, Leo (father), 133
Mooney, Leo (son), 133
Morning Chronicle, London, 64
Morning Post, London, 168
Morning Register, Dublin, 46
Morrow, Billy, 212, 218
Morrow, Des, 319
Morton, Jim, 288, 323
Morton, John, 19
Mourne Observer, Newcastle, founding, 243
Movita, 202
Mrs Synnott's Agency, 233
"Muirchu" sinking, 228
Mulhern, Jim, 122
Mullane, Dermot, 297
Muller, Aga, 238
Mullock, Charles, 220
Mulvey, Anthony, 196
Mulvey, Gerry, 227
Munster Express, Waterford, during Civil War, 152; World War II, 7, 8, 202
Munster Journal, Limerick, 32
Murphy, Pat, 147
Murphy, T.V., 321

Murphy, William Martin, career, 100, 118; founds *Irish Independent,* 20, 100, 118
Murphy, Dr William Lombard, 157
Murray, Ernie, 18

Nagle, John B., 9
Nagle, Michael, 325
Nation, Dublin, 58, 59
National Union of Journalists, 17, 192, 227, 249
Nationalist and Leinster Times, Carlow, censored, 122; founding, 80, 81
Nealon, Ted, T.D., 275
Neeson, Eoin, 253
Nenagh Guardian, founding, 54; taken over, 1916, 55
Newman, Alec, editor, *The Irish Times,* 281, 282; joins *The Irish Times,* 163; sacked, 282; whiskey supply, 185
Newry Telegraph, 311
Newtownards Spectator, 112
Nivison, Leslie, 257, 309
Noble Art O'Leary, 41
Nolan, Dan, 19, 202
North Antrim Standard, Ballymoney, 149
North Down Herald, 110
North Strand bombings, Dublin, 1941, 210
Northern Constitution, Coleraine, 16-17, 113
Northern newspapers owners' eccentricities, 244
Northern Standard, Monaghan, fire, 1930, 162; founding, 55; New editor, 1920s, 158
Northern Star, Belfast, 40
Northern Whig, Belfast, closes, 1963, 291, 292
NUJ agreement, Dublin, 1947, 227
Nusight, 303

O'Brennan, Kathleen, 178
O'Brien, Dr Conor Cruise, 247, 249, 251
O'Brien, Eileen, "Candida" column, 299; joins *The Irish Times,* 298; Tuarascáil column, 299
O'Brien, Tommy, 192
O'Callaghan, Micheál, 216
O Conaire, Padraic, 159
O'Connor, Frank, 218-219
O Criogáin, Padraig, 176, 238
O'Curry, Peadar, 189, 261-262
O Dalaigh, Aonghus, 173
O Dalaigh, Cearbhall, 173
O'Dea, Jimmy, 6
O'Donovan, John, 250, 262-263
O'Donoghue, "Bolger", 130
O'Donoghue, Con, 130
Offaly Chronicle, 192
Offaly Topic, 316
O'Farrell, E. French, 71
O'Hanlon, Edward, 71